Against Repression

Art and Thought: Histories of the Avant-Garde
Art et pensée : histoires des avant-gardes

Edited by
Dawn Ades and Timothy Mathews

PETER LANG
Oxford • Bern • Berlin • Bruxelles • New York • Wien

Against Repression

Surrealism, Sublimation and the Recuperation of Desire

Klem James

PETER LANG
Oxford • Bern • Berlin • Bruxelles • New York • Wien

Bibliographic information published by Die Deutsche Nationalbibliothek.
Die Deutsche Nationalbibliothek lists this publication in the Deutsche Nationalbibliografie; detailed bibliographic data is available on the Internet at http://dnb.d-nb.de.

Library of Congress Cataloging-in-Publication Data

Names: James, Klem, 1978- author.
Title: Against repression : Surrealism, sublimation and the recuperation of desire / Klem James.
Description: New York : Peter Lang, 2019. | Series: Art and thought = Art et pensée | Includes bibliographical references and index.
Identifiers: LCCN 2018008714 | ISBN 9781787077690 (alk. paper)
Subjects: LCSH: Surrealism--France. | Surrealism (Literature)--France. | Sublimation (Psychology) | Avant-garde (Aesthetics)--France--History--20th century. | Arts and society--France--History--20th century.
Classification: LCC NX456.5.S8 J35 2018 | DDC 700/.41163--dc23 LC record available at https://lccn.loc.gov/2018008714

ISSN 2296-1151
ISBN 978-1-78707-769-0 (print) • ISBN 978-1-78707-770-6 (ePDF)
ISBN 978-1-78707-771-3 (ePub) • ISBN 978-1-78707-772-03 (mobi)

Published by Peter Lang Ltd, International Academic Publishers,
52 St Giles, Oxford, OX1 3LU, United Kingdom
oxford@peterlang.com, www.peterlang.com

This publication has been peer reviewed.

Printed in Germany

Contents

List of Figures vii

A Note on the Translations xiii

INTRODUCTION
Sublimation/Desublimation: A Question of Definition 1

CHAPTER 1
Tel Quel Critiques of Surrealism: Idealist, Sublimatory and Repressive 21

CHAPTER 2
The Breton-Bataille Polemic Revisited 49

CHAPTER 3
Breton's Non-Repressive View of Sublimation and Art 105

CHAPTER 4
Surrealism's Inner Alchemy: Perturbing the Senses, Awakening the Spirit 153

CHAPTER 5
The Surrealist Cult of Love: Extolling the Forbidden Fruit 213

Conclusion 263

Bibliography 273

Index 289

Figures

Figure 0.1: Selection of Surrealist artwork (l. to r.): René Magritte, *The Titanic Days* (1930) © René Magritte/ADAGP Magritte, Miro, Chagall. Copyright Agency, 2018. Hans Bellmer, *Untitled*, from *La Poupée* (*The Doll*) (1936) © Hans Bellmer/ADAGP. Copyright Agency, 2018. Salvador Dalí, *Scatalogical* OR *Surrealist Object Functioning Symbolically* (*The Surrealist Shoe – Gala's shoe*) – photo of object (1931) © Salvador Dali, Fundació Gala-Salvador Dali/VEGAP. Copyright Agency, 2018. Meret Oppenheim, *Luncheon in Fur* (Also known as: *Breakfast in Fur*) – photo of object (1936) © Meret Oppenheim/Pro Litteris. Copyright Agency, 2018. Salvador Dalí, *Young Virgin Auto-Sodomized by the Horns of Her Own Chastity* (1954) © Salvador Dali, Fundació Gala-Salvador Dali/VEGAP. Copyright Agency, 2018. 1

Figure 2.1: Taxonomy of 'Perversions' or Sexual Paresthesias as reproduced in Maurice Heine's 'Note sur un Classement Psycho-Biologique des Paresthésies sexuelles'. 72

Figure 2.2: Alberto Giacometti, *Boule Suspendue* (*Suspended Ball*) (1930–1931) – photo of sculpture © Fondation Alberto et Annette Giacometti/Copyright Agency, 2018. 78

Figure 2.3: Hans Bellmer, 'Variations sur le montagne d'une mineure articulée', Minotaure (1934–1935) © Hans Bellmer/ADAGP. Copyright Agency, 2018. 82

Figure 2.4: Pablo Picasso, 'Le Plumeau et la Corne' (*The Feather Duster and the Bull's Horn*) in *Minotaure 1* (1933) – photo of sculpture © Succession Picasso/ Succession Picasso. Copyright Agency, 2018. 86

Figure 3.1: Marcuse's model of sublimation and desublimation as applied to the interrelationship between art and society in *The Aesthetic Dimension* (1979). 125

Figure 3.2: Roberto-Sebastian Matta Echaurren, *L'Octrui* (1947) © Roberto-Sebastian Matta Echaurren/ ADAGP. Copyright Agency, 2018. 141

Figure 3.3: Roberto-Sebastian Matta Echaurren, *Science, conscience et patience du Vitreur* (*Science, Conscience and Patience of the Glazier*) (1944) © Roberto-Sebastian Matta Echaurren/ADAGP. Copyright Agency, 2018. 145

Figure 3.4: André Masson, *La Métamorphose des Amants* (*The Metamorphosis of Lovers*) (1938) © Andre Masson/ADAGP. Copyright Agency, 2018. 146

Figure 3.5: Vincent Van Gogh, *The Starry Night* (1889). 150

Figure 4.1: Hieronymus Bosch, *The Garden of Earthly Delights*, 1503 and 1515. 174

Figure 4.2: Symbols of birth and transformation (two aspects of Phanes, the hermaphroditic deity). (Left) Phanes,

the hermaphroditic deity entwined with a serpent and (Right) the Orphic (or Cosmic) egg from whence Phanes hatched (Jacob Bryant, 1774). 176

Figure 4.3: Hieronymus Bosch, *The Temptation of Saint Anthony*, triptych, 1505. 182

Figure 4.4: Hieronymus Bosch, *The Temptation of Saint Anthony*, panel. 184

Figure 4.5: Max Ernst, 'Chaque émeute sanglante la fera vivre pleine de grâce et de vérité' ('Each bloody riot will help her to live in grace and truth'). Illustration from collage novel *La Femme 100 Têtes* (1929) © Max Ernst/ADAGP. Copyright Agency, 2018. 188

Figure 4.6: Max Ernst, 'Rome'. Illustration from collage novel *La Femme 100 Têtes* (1929) © Max Ernst/ADAGP. Copyright Agency, 2018. 188

Figure 4.7: Max Ernst, 'images (untitled)'. Illustrations from Chapter 1 (Sunday – Mud) of collage novel *Une Semaine de Bonté* (1934) © Max Ernst/ADAGP. Copyright Agency, 2018. 190

Figure 4.8: Max Ernst, 'image (untitled)'. Illustration from Chapter 7 (Saturday – Desire or the great one times one) of collage novel *Une Semaine de Bonté* (1934) © Max Ernst/ADAGP. Copyright Agency, 2018. 190

Figure 4.9: Max Ernst, 'image (untitled)'. Illustration from Chapter 3 (Tuesday – Fire) of *Une Semaine de Bonté* (1934) © Max Ernst/ADAGP. Copyright Agency, 2018. 191

Figure 4.10: Max Ernst, 'image (untitled)'. Illustration from Chapter 4 (Wednesday – Blood) of *Une Semaine de Bonté* (1934) © Max Ernst/ADAGP. Copyright Agency, 2018. 192

Figure 4.11: Max Ernst, 'image (untitled)'. Illustration from Chapter 5 (Thursday – Blackness) of *Une Semaine de Bonté* (1934) © Max Ernst/ADAGP. Copyright Agency, 2018. 192

Figure 4.12: Max Ernst, *Les Hommes N'en Sauront Rien* (*Men Shall Know Nothing of This*) (1923) © Max Ernst/ADAGP. Copyright Agency, 2018. 195

Figure 4.13: Juan de Valdés Leal, *Finis Gloriae Mundi* (*End of the World's Glory*) (1660). 196

Figure 4.14: Illustrations of Flamel's *Exposition of the Hieroglyphical Figures*, reproduced in Robert Desnos' article 'Le Mystère d'Abraham Juif' (*Documents*, 1925). 201

Figure 4.15: Robert Fludd, *The Day and Night of the Microcosm* (1617–1619), reproduced in Grillot de Givry's *Le Musée des Sorciers, Mages et Alchimistes* (1929). 204

Figure 4.16: Images from Gichtel's *Theosophia Practica* (1736), reproduced in *Documents*, no. 2 (1929). 206

Figure 4.17: Max Ernst, *The Robing of the Bride* (1940) © Max Ernst/ADAGP. Copyright Agency, 2018 and, right, an illustration with a similar motif, Max Ernst 'Loplop et la Belle Jardinière' ('Loplop and the Beautiful Gardener'). Illustration from collage

novel *La Femme 100 Têtes* (1929) © Max Ernst/ ADAGP. Copyright Agency, 2018. 210

Figure 5.1: Man Ray, Photo of wooden spoon in the novel *Nadja* by André Breton (1928) © MAN RAY TRUST/ADAGP. Copyright Agency, 2018. 224

Figure 5.2: Allegory of the 'Sublime Point': Mount Teide, Tenerife. 225

Figure 5.3: Illustration of an anamorphoscope. 226

Figure 6.1: Table of binaries occurring in Bataillean thought (from Marie-Christine Lala's article 'Bataille et Breton : le malentendu considérable' ['Bataille and Breton: considerable misunderstandings']). 266

A Note on the Translations

Wherever an official English-language translation of a work exists, this will usually be quoted. In some cases, where I believe the translation has not rendered an important word or concept from the original into English, I have modified the translation and acknowledged this in a footnote. All foreign-language texts which do not have official translations have been translated by me, and for the purposes of economy, I have left these translations unreferenced. Occasionally, I have acknowledged a translation as my own in order to avoid confusion.

INTRODUCTION

Sublimation/Desublimation: A Question of Definition

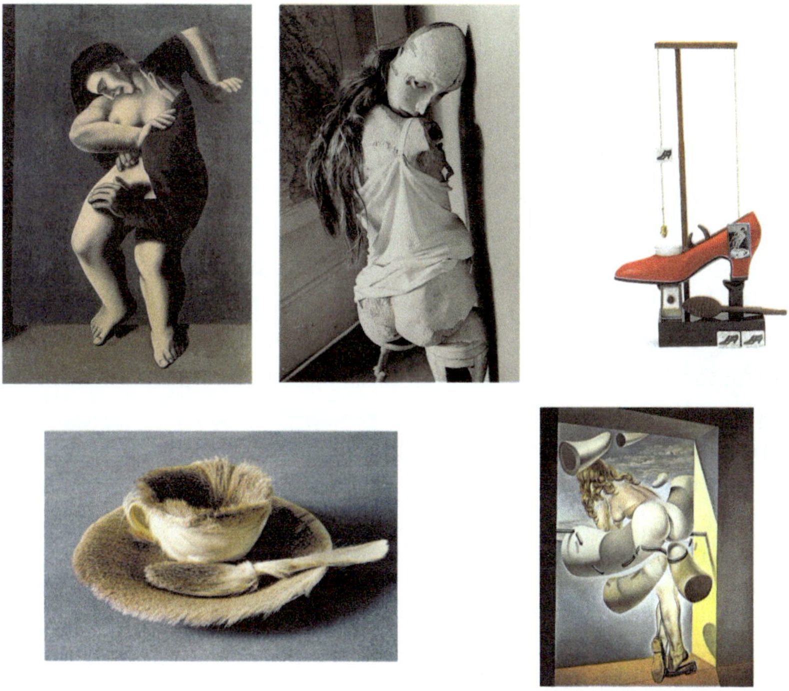

Figure 0.1: Selection of Surrealist artwork (l. to r.): René Magritte, *The Titanic Days* (1930) © René Magritte/ADAGP Magritte, Miro, Chagall. Copyright Agency, 2018. Hans Bellmer, *Untitled*, from *La Poupée* (*The Doll*) (1936) © Hans Bellmer/ADAGP. Copyright Agency, 2018. Salvador Dalí, *Scatalogical* OR *Surrealist Object Functioning Symbolically* (*The Surrealist Shoe – Gala's shoe*) – photo of object (1931) © Salvador Dali, Fundació Gala-Salvador Dali/VEGAP. Copyright Agency, 2018. Meret Oppenheim, *Luncheon in Fur* (Also known as: *Breakfast in Fur*) – photo of object (1936) © Meret Oppenheim/Pro Litteris. Copyright Agency, 2018. Salvador Dalí, *Young Virgin Auto-Sodomized by the Horns of Her Own Chastity* (1954) © Salvador Dali, Fundació Gala-Salvador Dali/VEGAP. Copyright Agency, 2018.

Although the connection between Surrealism and the erotic, instinctive-laden iconography seen in Figure 0.1 must seem obvious to many people, the movement has not ceased to draw criticism for representing a nefarious sublimation, repressive and idealist in nature. Denis Hollier affirmed that: 'Being Surrealist is learning to die. The idea, thanks to which the world cannot be world, transposes (transfigures) failure into victory, the fall into salvation. It permits revenge on the "bestiality" (animality) of those who would have the earth be low and the world be world'.[1] Here the word 'transposition' or 'transfiguration' is to be equated with the sublimation of all that is base and perverse in the world into a form of artistic symbolisation which masks or represses the desiring drive and the materiality of existence. The lineage of Surrealism's critics who share Hollier's view extends from the contributors published in the French journal *Tel Quel* in the 1970s to the October group of art historians whose writings are considered just as influential, and indeed authoritative, within the English-speaking world. The question remains, then, as to how such a reception of Surrealism has become entrenched within critical appraisals of the movement despite the very salient sexual symbolism running through its creative works.

Part of the answer can undoubtedly be found within the statements of the Surrealists themselves, some of whom like André Breton, the movement's chief spokesperson, explicitly advocated sublimation. He and many other Surrealists became interested in the concept through exposure to French translations of Freud's works.[2] In one of these texts,

1 Denis Hollier, *Against Architecture: The Writings of Georges Bataille*, trans. by Betsy Wing (London: MIT Press, 1989), p. 104.

2 The following works all contain references to sublimation and were contemporaneous to Surrealism's heyday in the interwar years: *Introductory Lectures on Psychoanalysis* (1917), trans. into French as *Introduction à la Psychanalyse* (1922); *Three Essays on the Theory of Sexuality* (1905), trans. into French as *Trois Essais sur la Théorie de la Sexualité* (1923); *Group Psychology and the Analysis of the Ego* (1921), trans. as *Psychologie Collective et Analyse du Moi* (1924); *Five Lectures on Psycho-Analysis* (1910), trans. as *Cinq Leçons sur la Psychanalyse* (1924); *Leonardo Da Vinci and a Memory of his Childhood* (1910), trans. as *Un Souvenir d' Enfance de Léonard de Vinci* (1927); *An Autobiographical Study*

Cinq Leçons sur la Psychanalyse (1924), Freud defines sublimation as the capacity of instincts 'for exchanging their sexual aim for another one which is comparatively remote and socially valuable. It is probable that we owe our highest cultural successes to the contributions of energy made in this way to our mental functions'.[3] In the 'Second Manifeste du Surréalisme' (1930), Breton paid tribute to 'cette donnée freudienne sous le coup de laquelle tombe la plus grande partie de leur agitation en tant qu'hommes'[4] ['the Freudian concept which affects the greater part of their deep concerns as men'[5]], 'their' referring to the Surrealists whom he enjoined to embrace the concept, above all as a means of giving visual expression to the uncharted spaces of the artist's psychic interior.

We are faced then with an apparent contradiction between Surrealist thought, which advocated sublimation, and Surrealist practice, which resulted in works in which images of sexual desire were often amplified rather than refined or transmuted. In art historical terms the latter process might rather be considered to be a process of 'desublimation', in other words of art's re-eroticisation and the inscription of the artist's instinctual life into his or her œuvre rather than its attempted concealment or transposition into non-sexual motifs. The term desublimation was not coined by Freud but was first defined in 1922 by the Swiss psychoanalyst Oskar Pfister who stated that 'in the conflict of the moral with the

---

(1925), trans. as *Ma Vie et la Psychanalyse* (1928); *The Ego and The Id* (1923) and *On the History of the Psycho-Analytic Movement* (1914), trans. as *Essais de la Psychanalyse* (1929).

3 Sigmund Freud, 'Five Lectures on Psycho-Analysis – Psychogenic Disturbance of Vision' (1909) in *Standard Edition of the Complete Psychological Works of Sigmund Freud – Five Lectures on Psycho-analysis, Leonardo da Vinci, and Other Works*, trans. by James Strachey in collaboration with Anna Freud (London: Hogarth Press, 1957), vol. XI, p. 54.

4 André Breton, 'Second Manifeste du Surréalisme' in *Manifestes du Surréalisme* (Paris: Gallimard, 1979), p. 109.

5 André Breton, 'Second Manifesto of Surrealism' in *Manifestoes of Surrealism*, trans. by Richard Seaver and Helen R. Lane (Michigan: The University of Michigan Press, 1969), p. 160.

primitive, the latter comes off victorious, the result may be a checking of the sublimated functions. I call this *desublimation*'.[6] The term was subsequently popularised by Herbert Marcuse in the work *One Dimensional Man* (1964)[7] and is widely used by art historians today in a general sense referring to highly eroticised, perverse or fetishistic art which renounces formal or aesthetic considerations. Much of the Surrealist scholarship of the last twenty years relies on this understanding of the term, as reflected in the writings of the October group, who have frequently analysed the ideas of Surrealism and Georges Bataille in terms of sublimation and desublimation.

Reflecting upon the reasons for Surrealism's puzzling and self-contradictory approach to sublimation is fundamental to establishing the focus of this book. I believe that one of the major reasons for this incongruity relates to the difference in the respective outlooks of Freud and the Surrealists toward sublimation. For although the latter were initially inspired by Freud's conception of sublimation, their view of the process nonetheless differed substantially from his later re-evaluations of the notion. In the same year that Breton had put into print his 'Second Manifeste', Freud had published the German edition of *Civilisation and Its Discontents*, which included a major new development in the theory of sublimation, though this work was only published in French four years later as *Le Malaise dans la Culture*. This is significant, as it was perhaps singularly responsible for promoting a view of sublimation which was entirely aim-inhibited (affording only limited instinctual satisfaction) and complicit in maintaining a repressive and unhappy civilisation. When Breton had set about writing

6 Oskar Pfister, *Psychoanalysis in the Service of Education*, trans. by Dr Charles Rockwell Payne and Dr F. Gschwind (London: H. Kimpton, 1922), p. 92.

7 Marcuse's definition is rooted in a Marxist-inspired critique of late capitalism and refers primarily to the flattening out of cultural production through the removal of transcendental elements of high culture and their adaptation to the processes of mass production. See Herbert Marcuse, *One Dimensional Man – Studies in the Ideology of Advanced Industrial Society* (London: Routledge & Kegan Paul Ltd., 1964), p. 57.

his second manifesto, it seems highly implausible that he envisaged sublimation as a renunciation of the instinctual life which was mostly subordinated to the demands of a collective civility. This seems further corroborated by the earlier works of Freud which Breton had kept in his possession and in which the assertion was made that the libidinal energy of the subject could be distributed more flexibly.[8] In these works, Freud had emphasised the plasticity of the instincts, their capacity to be divided into components, some of which would find satisfaction in reaching their proper ends whereas others would be sublimated or deflected into other processes:

> [Sublimation] enables excessively strong excitations arising from particular sources of sexuality to find an outlet and use it in other fields, so that a not inconsiderable increase in psychical efficiency results from a disposition which in itself is perilous. Here we have one of the origins of artistic activity; and, according to the completeness or incompleteness of the sublimation, a characterological analysis of a highly gifted individual, and in particular of one with an artistic disposition, may reveal a mixture in every proportion, of efficiency, perversion and neurosis.[9]

We may note that Freud speaks about the completeness or incompleteness of sublimation – as a relative attribute therefore – allowing for the possibility of libidinal efficiency (the putting to use of the instincts to their proper ends), even as the instincts are stymied in neurosis or diverted into other channels.

8 See those French translations of Freud's works already cited in the footnote above, all of which formed part of Breton's personal library.

9 Sigmund Freud, 'Three Essays on Sexuality – Summary' (1905) in *The Standard Edition of the Complete Psychological Works of Sigmund Freud – A Case of Hysteria, Three Essays on Sexuality, and other Works*, trans. by James Strachey in collaboration with Anna Freud (London: Hogarth Press, 1953), vol. VII, 238. For an explanation of component instincts see Sigmund Freud, '"Civilised" Sexual Morality' (1908) in *Standard Edition of the Complete Psychological Works of Sigmund Freud – Jensen's 'Gradiva', and Other Works*, trans. by James Strachey in collaboration with Anna Freud (London: Hogarth Press, 1959), vol. IX, 187 and 'Five Lectures on Psycho-Analysis – Psychogenic Disturbance of Vision' (1909) in *Complete Psychological Works* XI, p. 215.

In his early writings Freud had seemed more positive about the possibility of sublimation promoting the subject's psychic health, stating for example that it possessed an 'especially marked characteristic of being able to displace its aim [of libidinal satisfaction] without materially diminishing in intensity'[10] and qualifying it as 'a way out, a way by which those demands [the demands of the ego] can be met *without* involving repression'.[11] By the time he wrote *Civilisation and Its Discontents*, however, Freud's faith in the ability of sublimation to sustain the subject seemed to have withered, with the accent now firmly being placed on its life-denying qualities. As the keystone of a particularly bleak exposition of civilisation, sublimation was contextualised as:

> a vicissitude which has been forced upon the instincts entirely by civilization [...] it is impossible to overlook the extent to which civilization is built up upon a renunciation of instinct, how much it presupposes precisely the non-satisfaction (by suppression, repression or some other means?) of powerful instincts. This 'cultural frustration' dominates the large field of social relationships between human beings.[12]

According to Peter Gay, the book was Freud's most sombre, a veritable treatise on human misery.[13] Freud's final word on sublimation appeared then to qualify it as a symptom of mankind's unease and dissatisfaction with living.

On the basis of Breton's theoretical writings, it is evident that he did not advocate sublimation for its complicity in maintaining a repressive civilisation. In *Les Vases Communicants*, he metaphorised bourgeois civilisation as a 'frightful evildoing beast'[14] ('l'effroyable bête

10 Freud, *Complete Psychological Works* IX, p. 187.

11 Sigmund Freud, 'On Narcissism: An Introduction' (1914) in *Standard Edition of the Complete Psychological Works of Sigmund Freud – On the History of the Psycho-analytic Movement – Papers on Meta-psychology, and Other Works*, trans. by James Strachey in collaboration with Anna Freud, vol. XIV, p. 95.

12 Freud, *Complete Psychological Works* XXI, p. 97.

13 Peter Gay, *Freud – A Life for our Time* (London: Norton, 1988), pp. 534–544.

14 André Breton, *Communicating Vessels*, trans. by Mary Ann Caws & Geoffrey T. Harris (Lincoln & London: University of Nebraska Press, 1997), p. 126.

malfaisante'[15]) and 'monstrous oppressive organism'[16] ('le monstrueux organisme oppresseur'[17]), which threatened (wo)man's chances of happiness and self-expression throughout the world. He called upon readers to find the lucidity and courage to rise up against this entity and the 'increasingly bloody repression' for which it was responsible.[18]

Breton's denunciation of civilisation was inspired in part by an early belief in Marxism and in part by a general determination to dismantle those barriers within it that hindered all reasonable enquiry into the unconscious and the instinctual life (and their canalisation into art and poetry): 'Sous couleur de civilisation, sous prétexte de progrès, on est parvenu à bannir de l'esprit tout ce qui se peut taxer à tort ou à raison de superstition, de chimère; à proscire tout mode de recherche de la vérité qui n'est pas conforme à l'usage'[19] ['Under the pretence of civilisation and progress, we have managed to banish from the mind everything that may rightly or wrongly be termed superstition or fancy; forbidden is any kind of search for truth which is not in conformance with accepted practices'[20]]. Breton maintained that bourgeois civilisation was all the more damned for lacking 'poetic justification', a remark which once again underlined its dehumanising, unimaginative basis[21] and put it at odds with Surrealism, which valued the free, poetic (and artistic) expression of the human psyche, especially when in rupture with conformist thinking.

Unlike the repressive civilisation delineated by Freud, Surrealism was intrinsically life-affirming in its outlook: not only did it seek to free the imagination and unconscious through art and poetry, it also sought to create a socially just society in which the individual could find happiness

15 André Breton, *Les Vases Communicants* (Paris: Gallimard, 1955), p. 147.
16 Breton, *Communicating Vessels*, p. 126.
17 Breton, *Les Vases Communicants*, p. 146.
18 Breton, *Les Vases Communicants*, p. 146; Breton, *Communicating Vessels*, p. 126.
19 Breton, 'Manifeste du Surréalisme' in *Manifestes du Surréalisme*, p. 20.
20 Breton, 'Manifesto of Surrealism' in *Manifestoes of Surrealism*, p. 10.
21 André Breton, 'Position poétique de l'art d'aujourd'hui' (1935) in *Œuvres Complètes*, ed. by Marguerite Bonnet (Paris: Gallimard, 1992), vol. II, p. 431: André Breton, 'Political position of today's art' (1935) in *Manifestoes of Surrealism*, p. 226.

at work and in his/her personal life (with love being unshackled from religious imperatives). The essence of this outlook and the audacious will which sought to translate it into reality was represented in *Arcane 17* (1945) in the image of the Luciferian morning star. Lucifer was, however, evoked less in his Satanic aspect but rather in his capacity as liberator and bringer of light (and therefore knowledge) with his nickname 'the morning star' also referring to the planet Venus (and therefore love): '[c'est] la révolte seule qui est créatrice de lumière. Et cette lumière ne peut se connaître que trois voies: la poésie, la liberté et l'amour qui doivent inspirer le même zèle et converger, à en faire la coupe même de la jeunesse éternelle'[22] ['rebellion alone is the creator of light. And this light can only be known by way of three paths: poetry, liberty and love, which should inspire the same zeal and converge to form the very cup of eternal youth'[23]].

The question of how Breton and other prominent Surrealists might have re-conceived sublimation according to this more affirmative yet non-conformist world view is one which will be given careful consideration. This book begins by arguing that the Surrealists' conceptualisation of the term was, on account of their agenda for personal and social liberation, necessarily non-repressive in nature. In support of this argument, I outline the commonalities between the Surrealist understanding of sublimation and Marcuse's theory of non-repressive sublimation, which he situates within a society free from exploitative labour: 'Reactivation of polymorphous and narcissistic sexuality ceases to be a threat to culture and can itself lead to culture-building if the organism exists not as an instrument of alienated labour but as a subject of self-realisation [...]. The culture-building power of Eros *is* non-repressive sublimation'.[24] In other words, the instinctual self need not be regarded as hostile to the feats of culture or negated under the necessity of toil, if these can be transformed into sites of libidinal gratification and play.

22 André Breton, *Arcane 17* (Paris: Sagittaire, 1947), p. 174.

23 André Breton, *Arcanum 17* (Los Angeles: Green Integer Books, 2004), p. 132.

24 Herbert Marcuse, *Eros and Civilization* (Boston: Beacon Press, 1955), pp. 210–211. Marcuse's italics.

Both for Marcuse as for Bretonian Surrealism, this more optimistic view of the sublimatory process allows not only for a greater degree of libidinal gratification in the sphere of work and personal relationships but also for a greater exploration of art's sensual qualities and, as a consequence, a greater eroticisation of art: 'the affirmative character of art has yet another source: it is in the commitment of art to Eros, the deep affirmation of the Life Instincts in their fight against instinctual and social oppression'.[25] The term of non-repressive sublimation, as will be employed throughout, thus postulates an overcoming or balancing of sublimation and desublimation as antonymic states (and the self-actualisation of the sexual or instinctual, primarily through elective relationships, though also in art and work).

Breton's preference for sublimation has often been taken as evidence that he was an aloof and misguided romantic who fought to reclaim the rights of the imagination though lost himself in poetry's forest of symbols (a view whose genesis will be considered in depth in the opening chapter). In so doing, he is said to have decried sexual excess and base desire. This is an interpretation which has perhaps been somewhat overstated, focussing unduly on the polemical spirit of his youth. His utterances as an older man often paint a different picture. In response to a questionnaire on desire, a mature and more reflective Breton considered himself 'incapable d'établir une hiérarchie de mes propres désirs, naturellement je ne puis non plus me connaître de désirs "élevés"'[26] ['incapable of establishing a hierarchy of my own desires, naturally I am no expert either on "elevated" desires'[27]] and stated: 'Moniste matérialiste, je n'aperçois

25 Herbert Marcuse, *The Aesthetic Dimension – Toward a Critique of Marxist Aesthetics* (London: Macmillan Press, 1978), pp. 10–11 – Marcuse's capitalisations.

26 Breton, *Œuvres Complètes* II, p. 505.

27 My translation. Where an official English-language translation of a work exists, this will usually be quoted. In some cases I have modified an official translation and acknowledged this in the footnote. All foreign language texts which do not have official translations have been translated by myself (and henceforth these translations will no longer be referenced, except for a small number of cases where I have attempted to avoid confusion).

pas de différence essentielle entre les besoins sensoriels, matériels et les besoins spirituels'[28] ['As a materialist monist, I do not see an essential difference between the sensory and material needs and spiritual needs']. In an interview in 1952, Breton would again underline that sublimated love could not be regarded as distinct from the baser instincts of the subject; for if love were confined to the elevated spheres of poetry it would in its incandescence become too 'rarefied' and hence too subtle or slight to be recognised and appreciated:

> L'admirable, l'éblouissante lumière de la flamme ne doit pas nous cacher de quoi elle est faite, nous dérober les profondes galeries de mines, souvent parcourues de souffles méphitiques, qui n'en ont pas moins permis l'extraction de sa substance, une substance qui doit continuer à l'entretenir si l'on ne veut pas qu'elle s'éteigne.[29]
>
> [Such a flame's admirable, blinding light must not be allowed to conceal what it feeds on, the deep mine shafts criss-crossed by hellish currents, which nonetheless permit us to extract its substance – a substance that must continue to fuel this flame if we don't want it to go out.[30]]

In the same interview Breton remarked on the anxiety with which Surrealism approached the 'low' nadir of base desire. Rather than expressing any reluctance in engaging with the desublimatory, I believe that he was instead tacitly acknowledging the dangers of an unimpeded release of the instinctual. For the Surrealists, sexual liberation did not imply a permanent and full-scale regression to animalism and lawlessness but was rather to be equated with a free and natural expression of libidinal impulses. Breton affirms that in a society which had been freed from financial and social inequalities as well as moral strictures, the conditions would be right for elective monogamous relationships to flourish. In support of this claim, he cited Engels: 'La propriété privée une fois abolie, "on peut affirmer avec raison déclare Engels, que *loin de disparaître, la monogamie sera pour*

28 Breton, *Œuvres Complètes* II, p. 505.

29 André Breton, 'Entretiens' (1952) in *Œuvres Complètes*, ed. by Marguerite Bonnet (Paris: Gallimard, 1992), vol. III, p. 519.

30 André Breton, *Conversations: The Autobiography of Surrealism – With André Parinaud*, trans. by Mark Polizzotti (New York: Marlowe & Company, 1993), p. 111.

la première fois réalisée."'[31] ['Once private property has been abolished, "we can reasonably affirm," declares Engels, "that *far from disappearing, monogamy will be realised for the first time.*"'[32]]. This, Breton hoped, would avert any recourse to wanton dissipation or regression, which was, rather, the result of pent-up impulses exacerbating the subject's pathology. In an echo of these sentiments, Marcuse would delineate the fate of the libido in an egalitarian society in similar terms: 'sexuality is neither deflected from nor blocked in its objective; rather in attaining its objective, it transcends it to others, searching for fuller gratification'.[33]

I would contend, then, that the Surrealists sought an enrichment of life based on the complementarity of the low and the high rather than suppressing one term in favour of the other; and, in doing so, hoped to stave off any threat of the low becoming regressive (a premise which is fundamental to the remainder of the book). It is clear that, as the arbiter of Surrealism, Breton himself attempted to maintain the precarious balance between desublimatory and sublimatory tendencies of the movement, as defined by the theoretical positionings of its various members. His difficulties in doing so, and in being seen to pursue a form of sublimation which was censorial and homogenising,[34] formed the crux of his polemics with Georges Bataille and the subsequent polarisation of Surrealists between loyalists true to the idea of sublimation and those deserting the movement in favour of Bataille's alternative world view of base materialism (wherein brute instinct always remained *as is* and was never re-coded in art or literature).

This book reconsiders the theoretical viewpoints of Breton and Bataille, so often considered as antagonistic and irreconcilable and so often cited in establishing Bataille as the sole purveyor of the desublimatory on the margins of Surrealism. Whereas Bataille is more usually characterised as the martyr who rescued materialism from a repressive oblivion, Breton is made

31 André Breton, *L'Amour Fou* (Paris: Gallimard, 1937), p. 112 – Breton's italics.

32 André Breton, *Mad Love* (London: University of Nebraska Press, 1987), p. 77 – Breton's italics.

33 Marcuse, *Eros and Civilization*, p. 211.

34 We turn our attention to these criticisms in Chapters 1 and 2 as these are fundamental in the contemporary reception of the movement.

to assume the role of his nemesis, the 'dogmatic idealist', who, as Hollier claimed, was unable to accept the baseness of the world for what it was. This is a binarism which will be challenged in favour of a more nuanced view of both men, a view that recognises certain points of convergence in the development of their mutual standpoints both in the 1930s and in the aftermath of World War II.

Other than Breton and Bataille, the choice of artists and poets whose works will be subjected to analysis has been largely determined by the extent and depth of their opinions with respect to (a non-repressive view of) sublimation or because their poetic or artistic works seem to embody this alternate view of the concept. For this reason, whilst recognising that selectivity may well result in some unfortunate exclusions, the focus of this enquiry will be mainly on individuals from Breton's inner cabal (Benjamin Péret, Paul Éluard, Max Ernst); the artists who through their association with Surrealism rose to fame in the 1930s (Roberto Matta, Hans Bellmer, Alberto Giacometti, Salvador Dalí); those dissident Surrealists who defected to the rival avant-garde group centred around Georges Bataille and his journal *Documents* (Michel Leiris, André Masson, Robert Desnos); and those working relatively independently of the organisational machine of Surrealism or its dissident factions (such as Maurice Heine and Picasso).

In psychoanalysis and art history sublimation remains an abstract and philosophical notion rather than a concept derived from empirical enquiry. Consequently the term has tended to be apprehended and elaborated subjectively, having been variously defined by a large number of thinkers and psychoanalysts (from Goethe and Nietzsche to Freud, Jung, Melanie Klein, Lacan and Kristeva). In setting out Surrealism's alternative conceptualisation of sublimation, my approach is therefore largely theoretical, drawing mostly on psychoanalysis and psychological discourse. I elucidate the divergences between Freudian psychoanalysis and Surrealism, highlighting instead the latter's affinities with Marcuse's inverted Freudian reading of society but also with Lacanian psychoanalysis. Whereas these two theoretical frameworks originate from entirely different schools, they do highlight the ways in which sublimation can be achieved without a complete renunciation of libidinal satisfaction or detriment to the wellbeing of the ego. Lacan reworks Freudian theory to show that in sublimation desire need not be inhibited in its aims, but can be endlessly deferred and deflected from one love object to the next. He characterises the process as the temporary overvaluation of a desirable Other, a corrective to the emotional void which would otherwise govern our lives and is fundamental to human experience. This void results in endless endeavours to recuperate a person or thing with which one hopes to complete one's existence – and which I believe typify much of Surrealist poetry and literature. Indeed, Lacan refers directly to Surrealist authors and their works when providing examples of his theories (a fact which has been largely overlooked by previous scholars of Surrealism). He shows us the unforeseen consequences of the non-repressive sublimation first proposed by Marcuse from a perspective which, with its emphasis on flux and circularity in the realm of relationships, identifies a key paradigm underlying the lives and practices of the Surrealists, a paradigm which has only come to take on an even greater significance in contemporary postmodernity.

Lacan demonstrates that sublimation can result in endless detours unconsciously undertaken to reunite the subject with the love object (as in the Parisian *flâneries* of the Surrealists), a preoccupation with collecting (symbolic objects reminiscent of the sexes) and filling (empty spaces, canvases, human orifices) and (somewhat one-sidedly from a male perspective) the quest to find an ultimate signifier of vaginal emptiness. Sublimation thus exposes what we do when confronted by absence and lack. Significantly, Lacan stresses that the detours around this lack can lead the subject onto the path of transgressive desire, which is only exacerbated in the face of harsh moral imperatives. This assertion in particular is one that interests us since it applies also to the transgressive aspect of the Surrealists' lives and works in the realm of desire and eroticism. The critical apparatus that Lacanian theory affords again helps to demonstrate that the Surrealists were not puritanical idealists but were frequently inveigled into behaviours and projects which sought a release from their repression.

Intermittently this book considers peripheral psychological discourses of the type that may be considered esoteric. In defining Surrealism's relationship to idealism, it is necessary to consider whether it had any sympathies with a number of psychologists and writers known for their interest in psychical phenomena (Frederic W.H. Myers, William James, Charles

Richet and Carl Jung) and with which the movement has occasionally been associated. Surrealist criticism (particularly in the journal *Tel Quel*) has sometimes sought to stress the affinities between Surrealism and the psychism of a certain lineage of psychologists in order to underline its idealist basis. In the opening chapter of this book, however, it will be demonstrated that while Breton and the Surrealists shared some preoccupations with these men, there existed insuperable differences in their respective outlooks (with Surrealism declaring itself to be rooted in materialism rather than a belief system that posited the otherworldly).

I also examine the Surrealists' preoccupation with alchemy and alchemical sublimation, when these terms are understood in their psychological aspect rather than their metallurgical one. I highlight again that in drawing inspiration from this arcane discipline Surrealists were not seeking to lose themselves in esoteric or mystical practices. Alchemy after all concerns not only the transformation of base metals into gold but also the enrichment and ennoblement of the inner life. With their interest in opening up and mining the imagination and the unconscious, it is clear to see why they would have become enthralled with this latter (psychological) aspect of the discipline. They considered the site of the unconscious to be the *prima materia* – that is to say, the raw material – of alchemical sublimation with the words and symbols of automatic processes liberating instincts and affects which had hitherto been left unexplored or stagnant within the human psyche. The concept of alchemical sublimation served not as some abstract and spurious pseudo-scientific operation but was envisaged as a trope for the self-actualisation of the inner life (in defiance of the repressive barriers that stood in its way). The second and third generation of Surrealists of the 1950s and 1960s also understood the concept of alchemical sublimation in this way, having identified it as one of the defining notions of Surrealism in contemporary appraisals of the movement (many of them went on to become Surrealist scholars and commentators).[35] This shows us that far from being a moribund debate, the question of sublimation's meaning and centrality within Surrealism is still being widely discussed.

35 This includes names such as Vincent Bounoure, Michel Carrouges, Guy DuCornet, Michael Löwy and José Pierre.

In examining more incisively Surrealism's various forays into psychology, it is hoped that the arguments of this book will be enriched rather than diluted, and that they will shed light on a number of constants which help to re-establish the basic aim of this enquiry – the challenging of unilinear views of Surrealism as sublimatory and repressive. My work builds on a number of scholarly publications which have appeared since the new millennium and have already started to consider the desublimatory strand of Surrealism's œuvre.

Surrealism: Desire Unbound (2001), edited by Jennifer Mundy, is a collection of essays which demonstrate the many ways in which the Surrealists gave expression to desire both in art and literature, covering themes as diverse as Sadism, hysteria, historical attitudes to desire and pornography, gender fluidity, the staging of desire in exhibitions, objects of desire and male-female relationships. Together these contributions present a picture of the movement which shows how its members' treatment of desire accentuated the materiality, omnipotence and transgressiveness of desire in its myriad guises. They show how Surrealism did not recoil from overtly sexual or perverse impulses or attempt to repress them in any way. For this reason, this collection provides a solid basis for my own study, which considers the implications of this permissive stance for the Surrealist notion of sublimation.

Jennifer Mundy affirms in her overview of Surrealist desire that: 'The word desire runs like a silver thread through the poetry and writings of the Surrealist group in all its phases.'[36] Her essay highlights many of the questions which have already been broached in this introduction: the impact of Freudian theory upon the Surrealist view of desire, the interconnectedness of sexual desire and romantic love and the desire of Breton to propound a non-repressive view of reality in works such as *Arcane 17*. In the opening paragraph of her essay, Mundy even refers to love as 'sublimated' desire and underlines its centrality within Surrealist works. However, she passes over the term sublimation as being unproblematic and does not account for the discrepancy which arises between

36 Jennifer Mundy, 'Letters of Desire' in *Surrealism: Desire Unbound*, ed. by Jennifer Mundy and Dawn Ades (London: Tate Publishing, 2001), p. 11.

the centrality of sublimated love within Surrealism and the desublimatory themes covered in the rest of the collection. This book can, on the other hand, be seen as an attempt to explain and rationalise this discrepancy, to show how in Surrealism sublimated Eros could co-exist side by side with desublimatory iconography.

In his volume *Surrealist Art and Thought in the 1930s* (2004), Stephen Harris examines the desublimatory vein of the movement, specifically the collective activity of making Surreal objects with sexual or perverse symbolism. As such, his study considers the interrelationship between Surrealism's political ambitions and aesthetic output (or, more broadly speaking, Surrealism's attempt at merging art with life). This, he claims, aimed at a supersession of art, whereby art was no longer to be conceived as 'the production of rarefied commodities for connoisseurs'[37] but, in line with the movement's revolutionary ambitions, subordinated it to the principle of 'poetry made by all, not by one' to bring about 'a less repressive, happier social structure'.[38] For Harris, it was the Surrealist object which best embodied all of these aspirations to transcend traditional art forms:

> If the Surrealist object is located [...] between art and politics, the supersession of modern art, made possible by revolution, will be achieved through a radical regression to what Breton called in the first *Manifesto of Surrealism* "the sources of poetic imagination." Art making will be desublimated in this return to what was understood to be the substratum of human creativity and indeed of human existence, sexual desire.[39]

Significantly, he comments that desublimation was central to Surrealism's artistic project and was reflected in a return to 'the sources of poetic imagination'. With reference to Freud, he qualifies this process as the breaking down of complex ideas from the conscious mind to the raw sensory images from which they are derived (one of the functions of the subconscious mind). This was accompanied by a corresponding mistrust of sublimation,

37 Stephen Harris, *Surrealist Art and Thought in the 1930s: Art, Politics, and the Psyche* (Cambridge: Cambridge University Press, 2004), p. 3.

38 *Ibid.*, p. 4.

39 *Ibid.*, p. 5.

when this meant conformity 'à l'ordre de choses existant'[40] ['to the established order of things'] (a term that nonetheless comes to be viewed in a more positive light after Surrealism turns away from Marxism and becomes more orthodox in the 1930s). He also claims that by the late 1930s, when Surrealism's attempts at coupling artistic desublimation with political revolution had failed, the suspicion of sublimation had yielded to a position of acceptance, with Surrealist art having established its place as an orthodox art movement.

Although my own study owes a substantial debt to Harris' work, which hinges on the specificity of the interrelation of art and politics as expressed through the Surrealist object in the 1930s, I aim to be broader in scope, examining a variety of media in the interwar years as well as in late Surrealism. Late Surrealism offers us new insights into those areas of the movement which reflect a non-repressive and non-idealist view of sublimation (as reflected by the warming of relations between Breton and Bataille, Breton's increasing engagement with eroticism and transgression, and the growing interest in alchemical sublimation as a metaphor for inner change).

Although I believe Harris to be wholly justified in re-examining the desublimatory strand of Surrealist art, I have chosen to work with the dualism of sublimation and desublimation to better problematise both terms and to consider their interdependency throughout the entire spectrum of the movement. Moreover, to assert that the Surrealists denied the value of sublimation until the late 1930s seems to run counter to Breton's advocacy of the term in the 'Second Manifeste du Surréalisme' in 1930 and various other tracts published in the decade (a stance which he does not eschew even after 1945).

The other work which has greatly assisted in orienting my own project is Alyce Mahon's *Surrealism and the Politics of Eros, 1939–1968* (2005). In some senses, her work complements that of Harris by focussing principally on the late Surrealism of post-war France rather than its earlier incarnation of the 1930s.[41] Her grounds for concentrating on this period are to show

40 André Breton, 'L'Âge d'Or' (1930–1931) in *Œuvres Complètes*, ed. by Marguerite Bonnet (Paris: Gallimard, 1988), vol. I, p. 1025.

41 She does not, however, refer explicitly to Harris' work.

how the movement's post-1945 renaissance 'fortified pre-war interests and embraced myth, occultism and Sadean transgression in new ways'[42] as well as re-engaging with sexual politics. Like my own study, Mahon shows how the Surrealists were inspired by Freud, though departed from his thinking in terms of how they applied his theory:

> Surrealist art must not only be viewed in terms of Freud's concept of Eros, as the Surrealists rejected society's need to 'civilise' Eros, and that their radical "politics of Eros," which embraced the power of the id, is the best route to understanding post-war Surrealism, its subversive intent and vital role in the culture of that period [...] the Surrealists recognised the potential of Eros as one of man's primary means of unsettling and interrogating the reality of recovering collective psychic forces and of launching socio-political revolt.[43]

Mahon, like Harris, refers to the potential of Surrealist art to overcome repressiveness, recognising that it could 'make the unconscious conscious, it could liberate repressed instincts and, in the process, it could challenge reason and repression – the pillars of civilisation'.[44] In fact, both writers make mention of this phenomenon in their introduction, but without pursuing the idea in a more explicit and systematic way. This, then, is one of the principal reasons why the present treatise will pursue a detailed discussion of the non-repressive nature of Surrealist thought and works, and the implications this has for any conception of sublimation (as embodied in either).

In the first chapter, I attempt to trace the genealogy of the view of Surrealism as idealist, sublimatory and repressive; a view which has been so influential in much of Surrealism's contemporary reception and is in no small part responsible for the polarisation of critical debates over the movement in terms of two 'enemy camps', the Bretonian and Bataillean, and the subsequent exorcism of desublimatory discourse with respect to the former. I reconsider the underlying assumption that underpinning

42 Alyce Mahon, *Surrealism and the Politics of Eros, 1938–1968* (London: Thames & Hudson, 2005), p. 11.

43 *Ibid.*, pp. 14–15.

44 *Ibid.*, p. 14.

Surrealism's putative repressiveness is a coherent philosophy (in particular that of absolute idealism/Hegelianism) which can be seen as the driving force behind all of its activities; as I hope to show, Surrealism by its very definition consisted in the production of philosophical as well as artistic bricolage, thus rendering all such claims problematic.

In the second chapter, I question the view of Breton as 'Icarian idealist' and 'super-eagle', both terms of derogation originally used against him by Bataille, though still employed by Surrealism's detractors today to highlight its repressive idealism and insulation from the world. It will be argued that Breton's ideological struggles of the 1930s, his growing interest in scabrous themes and his writings on black humour, transgression and erotic art reflect an increasing engagement with the material and sexual aspects of reality. This contrasts with Bataille's sporadic interest in politics and increasing retreat from the world culminating in the formation of the mysterious cult-like grouping, Acéphale, which the Surrealists critiqued as idealist. Acéphale was organised as a cultish secret society, which allowed Bataille to indulge his interests in meditation, mysticism and fanaticism (hence the Surrealist criticism) and whose members were expected to bond via bizarre or extreme rituals.

In the third chapter, I elaborate what I understand as the Surrealist notion of non-repressive sublimation with reference to Marcuse, who adopted many of Surrealism's aims as his own and frequently referred to the movement in his writings. I argue that the overcoming of repressiveness is inherent within Breton's articulation of convulsive beauty (which channelled both erotic and destructive instincts) and affected artist and spectator alike, providing a salutary psychical release for the former and destabilising the latter (who, by means of arresting imagery, was led to question his or her role in a hostile social reality).

In the fourth chapter, I demonstrate how this process of inner transformation was conceived by the Surrealists as an alchemical trope, and specifically as a process of alchemical sublimation, which finds its correlates in the 'alchemy of the word' (as exemplified by their poetry) and various forms of visual alchemy. I then inscribe this view of alchemical sublimation into a vitalist view of the cosmos, whose uninhibited, energetic movements support the unobstructed flow of libidinal energy and like the

Surrealist movement itself are in a process of constant transformation and renewal. I also show that this preoccupation with alchemical sublimation pervaded all sections of the Surrealist movement, from Surrealist 'loyalists' to Surrealist 'dissidents'.

In the fifth chapter, I begin to consider the implications of a non-repressive view of sublimation for the postmodern, turning to Lacan's model of sublimation to demonstrate how Surrealism's vital approach to desire and love become translated into a never-ending quest for the love object. He thus shows us how desire is endlessly deferred and deflected from one love object to the next, becoming a metonymic representation of (wo)man's innate feeling of vacuity. This metonymic substitution can lead, on the one hand, to the idealisation of the Other and to works of courtly love poetry and, on the other, to the intensification of illicit desires experienced through the gates of deprivation (the transgressive nature of which is exacerbated by moral imperatives). I argue that these oscillations between sublimation and transgression are a prominent feature of Surrealist works.

As can be seen, this book attempts to qualify the view of Surrealism as repressive and idealist. However, much of the criticism of the movement from over the last forty years has perpetuated this view, believing it to foreclose the sexual and the material. It is to the origins of this criticism within the journal *Tel Quel* to which we now turn our attention in order to reconsider its premises.

CHAPTER 1

Tel Quel Critiques of Surrealism: Idealist, Sublimatory and Repressive

> Tout porte à croire qu'il existe un certain point de l'esprit d'où la vie et la mort, le réel et l'imaginaire, le passé et le futur, le communicable et l'incommunicable, le haut et le bas cessent d'être perçus contradictoirement. Or, c'est en vain qu'on chercherait à l'activité surréaliste un autre mobile que l'espoir de détermination de ce point.[1]
>
> [Everything tends to make us believe that there exists a certain point of the mind [/spirit] at which life and death, the real and the imagined, past and future, the communicable and the uncommunicable, high and low, cease to be perceived as contradictions. Now, search as one may one will never find any other motivating force in the activities of the Surrealists than the hope of finding and fixing this point.[2]]

This oft-quoted statement taken from Breton's 'Second Manifesto of Surrealism' frequently serves the exegete of Surrealism with a critical reference point with respect to the movement's philosophical or conceptual orientation. It is moreover frequently taken as evidence of Breton's underlying Hegelianism, with the proposed reconciliation of contrary states being read as a telos of the spirit in which all dialectical oppositions have been resolved. Whereas it is true (by Breton's own admission) that he was strongly influenced by Hegel, the question remains open as to whether he appropriated the latter's ideas wholesale and the quotation above therefore reflects an underlying belief in absolute idealism, Hegel's theory of history when conceived as an unfolding of interacting opposites.

Within Surrealist criticism the argument has certainly put forward that Breton's belief in Hegelian idealism was unqualified and that the movement was thus founded upon outdated philosophical and ideological premises,

1 Breton, *Manifestes du Surréalisme*, pp. 72–73.
2 Breton, *Manifestoes of Surrealism*, p. 123.

accounting for its ostensible 'inefficacy' in the real world. This stance was articulated in the 1960s and early seventies by the journal *Tel Quel*, whose account of Surrealism suggested that its idealism – which was bound up with its avowed preference for Freudian sublimation – was entirely repressive in nature, proscribing the material and the sexual dimensions of life.

In *Tel Quel* 46 (summer 1971), the journal's contributors brought together their already existing reservations about Surrealism in a series of articles which aimed at undermining the movement's intellectual credibility. Their intention was to counter the resurgence of neo-Surrealism (a movement of the 1970s which combined Surrealist practice with elements of Pop Art) within French intellectual life. This they considered an unwanted 'repetition' and regression to an ideological impurity which was at odds with their own Maoist stance, a stance which they nonetheless repudiated three years later. One could not claim to be a Marxist while espousing Hegelian idealism (which after all Marxism had sought to supercede), as well as the subjectivity of human psychology and art. Surrealism, they considered, was impure on account of its theoretical hybridisations, which became problematic in three areas: the psychoanalytical, the ideological-political and the philosophical. All three areas were critically reviewed by the *Tel Quelists* to highlight Surrealism's (repressive) sublimatory and idealist basis at the expense of a more authentic Marxist-Leninist stance. The wide-ranging impact these arguments have had on Surrealism's contemporary reception and, above all, on art historical criticism, make it necessary to examine in greater detail the foundations of their arguments.

In *Tel Quel* 46, 1971, in an article entitled 'Méconnaissance de la Psychanalyse dans le Discours Surréaliste' ['Misunderstandings of Psychoanalysis in Surrealist Discourse'], Jean-Louis Houdebine called into question Surrealism's psychoanalytic basis in the first of the three critiques. Above all, he questioned Breton's reliance on pre-Freudian non-materialist sources, specifically psychologists and writers with a known penchant for psychism (F.W.H. Myers, W. James and C. Richet) and whose thought was therefore at variance with the purely materialist lineage of *Tel Quel* – that of Freud, Lacan, Marx and Engels.

Although Breton was interested in the writings of the pre-Freudian authors, Houdebine uses this point to draw a number of hard-and-fast conclusions which I will now re-examine: firstly, that because of Breton's interest in their works, he was a spiritualist, that he believed in the world of spirits and the ability to communicate with the latter mediumistically. More importantly, Houdebine held that his belief in spiritualist-inspired psychology was irreconcilable with a belief in Freudian psychoanalysis:

> Ces configurations idéologiques pré-freudiennes, à l'intérieur desquelles Breton continue de se situer, tiennent entres autres à une série de discours qui se sont particulièrement développés en Europe (surtout en Angleterre) et aux États-Unis durant la seconde moitié du XIXe siècle et jusque dans les années 1920–1930; ces discours relèvent d'une pseudo-science [...]: 'la métapsychique' dont les références à Myers, Flournoy, à Richet, à W. James, marquent l'intervention massive dans le discours de Breton, intervention qui prend en écharpe la relation que celui-ci établit par rapport à Freud et en surdétermine les contenus selon une problématique de part en part spiritualiste.[3]

> [These pre-Freudian ideological configurations, in the midst of which Breton continues to situate himself, stem from, amongst other sources, a series of discourses which developed especially in Europe (particularly in Great Britain) and in the United States during the second half of the 20th century and right up to the years 1920–1930; these discourses are the product of a pseudo-science [...]: 'the psychism' which harks back to Myers, Flournoy, Richet and W. James and mark a massive intervention in the discourse of Breton, an intervention which throws the relationship between himself and Freud out of kilter and over-determines its basis with arguments and discussions which are in all respects spiritualist.]

It is true Breton had adopted some of the practices of mediumship in his early collections of texts *Les Champs Magnétiques* ['*The Magnetic* Fields'] (1920), for which he had entered into a passive-receptive state to produce automatic writings. Similarly, he had participated in experiments with hypnotic states and sleeping fits which had been undertaken by his Surrealist friends (during the infamous *époque des sommeils*) again with a view to obtaining written messages automatically. But did this make him a spiritualist?

3 Jean-Louis Houdebine, 'Méconnaissance de la Psychanalyse dans le Discours Surréaliste' in *Tel Quel* 46 (Summer, 1971), p. 69.

To determine the answer to this, it is worth re-examining what he states in an article on the subject entitled 'Le Message Automatique'. Here, he had paid tribute to the 'gothic psychology' of Myers while underlining the fundamental differences between the automatic writings of the Surrealists and the mediumistic practices of spiritualists: 'Il y a lieu d'établir une distinction précise entre l'écriture et le dessin "automatiques", au sens où ce mot est entendu dans le surréalisme, et l'écriture et le dessin automatiques tels qu'ils sont pratiqués couramment par les médiums'[4] ['A precise distinction must be established between "automatic" writing and drawing, in the sense that the term is used in Surrealism, and the automatic writing and drawing as they are commonly practised by mediums'[5]]. In making this distinction, Breton showed his disdain for the claims of spiritualists, dismissing their 'terminologie nauséabonde'[6] ['nauseating terminology'[7]] and bewailing the contamination of mediumistic writings by 'la navrante littérature spirite'[8] ['regrettable spiritualist texts'[9]], a process which he qualified as 'lamentable plaisanterie'[10] ['a deplorable joke'[11]] following 'un cours dégradant'[12] ['a degrading course'[13]].

Even so, Houdebine considered the spiritualist discourse which had made its mark on Breton's writings as 'forclusion du sexuel, forclusion du signifiant, et donc forclusion du corps et de la matière comme hétérogénéité radicale'[14] ['foreclosure of the sexual, foreclosure of the signifier, and therefore foreclosure of the body and of matter as radical heterogeneity'].

4 Breton, 'Le Message Automatique' (1933) in *Œuvres Complètes* II, p. 381.
5 Breton 'The Automatic Message' (1933) in *Break of Day* (London: University of Nebraska Press, 1999), p. 132.
6 Breton, *Œuvres Complètes* II, p. 385.
7 Breton, *Break of Day*, p. 136.
8 Breton, *Œuvres Complètes* II, p. 385.
9 Breton, *Break of Day*, p. 135.
10 Breton, *Œuvres Complètes* II, p. 385.
11 Breton, *Break of Day*, p. 136.
12 Breton, *Œuvres Complètes* II, p. 385.
13 Breton, *Break of Day*, p. 136.
14 Houdebine, *Tel Quel* 46, p. 79.

Houdebine was mistrustful of Myers' notion of the 'subliminal self', a potent agency within the unconscious which was able, he claimed, to receive messages from spirits and represented 'une idéalité de sens ayant trait à l'être spirituel des êtres et du monde'[15] ['an ideality of the senses which is related to the spiritual being of organisms and the world']. Furthermore, Myers had conceived the subliminal self as a wellspring of mainly latent yet extremely potent psychical capacities including all those phenomena associated with mysticism or esotericism which were in his eyes antagonistic to a materialist outlook (telepathy, automatic writing, mediumship, telesthesia, cryptaesthesia, hallucinatory experience). According to Houdebine, Breton had clearly been influenced by these notions, as Jean Starobinski had already argued (in his article 'Freud, Breton, Myers', 1968) and which for him was proven by statements in the *Second Manifeste.* Here, Breton had called for the reconsideration of discredited esoteric sciences such as cryptaesthesia.[16]

While it is evident that Breton was interested in these esoteric thought systems, does this necessarily qualify him as a stalwart of idealism who foreclosed the material? If, like Houdebine, we are to take the influence of Myers 'spiritualist' psychology upon Breton as one of the primary arguments for his idealism, then on the basis of the latter's comments this assumption becomes problematic. Breton was keen to stress that his interest in Myers related to the psychological (rather than the 'spiritualist') aspect of his writings. In 'Le Message Automatique', he refers to the need to address 'le problème de Myers (strictement psychologique): il s'agissait, il s'agit encore de déterminer la constitution précise du subliminal'[17] ['the (strictly psychological) *Myers problem.* This problem was, and still is, to determine the precise constitution of the subliminal'[18]]. According to Marguerite Bonnet the problem was considered as 'strictly psychological' for Breton because he was aware of the 'spectre psychique'[19] ['spectre of the psychical']

15 *Ibid.*
16 Breton, *Manifestes du Surréalisme*, p. 128; Breton, *Manifestoes of Surrealism*, p. 178.
17 Breton, *Œuvres Complètes* II, p. 379.
18 Breton, *Break of Day,* p. 129 – translator's italics.
19 Breton, *Œuvres Complètes* II, p. 1534.

which hung over the term 'subliminal self'. Moreover, in an interview he referred to his interest in Myer's major work *Human Personality and Its Survival of Bodily Death* as keen but 'sceptical'.[20] These comments along with the statements already cited which reflect Breton's dismissive attitude toward spiritualism suggest that he was not an uncritical reader of Myers.

In attempting to trace the influence of Myers upon Breton, Houdebine discusses the former's analysis of Freud and Breuer's *Studies on Hysteria* (1895)[21] and specifically a section which relates the case study of a woman whose preoccupation with an unrequited love and guilt about the ensuing negligence of her duties manifested themselves as olfactory symptoms.[22] Here Myers speaks of the convertibility of moral and physical sensations, specifically when an emotional idea or *idée fixe* is symbolised for the sufferer by a disturbance in one of the senses.[23] Houdebine believes that for Myers the potential for the neurotic individual to channel his/her impulses to their proper ends is greatly restricted (as illustrated by the woman in the

20 Breton, *Conversations*, p. 60; *Œuvres Complètes* III, p. 474.

21 Houdebine refers specifically to 'le passage où Myers cite en les commentant brièvement les *Études sur l'Hystérie*, parues à Leipzig en 1895' ['the passage in which Myers cites and briefly comments upon *Studies upon Hysteria*, which appeared 1895 in Leipzig'] as representing the most striking manifestation of this foreclosure – see Houdebine, *Tel Quel* 46, p. 78.

22 Myers relates the case of Miss Lucy R., a patient treated by Freud for hysteria but also for the external symbolisation of a sense perception – the persistent hallucinatory smell of burning. She had been employed as nanny in the home of a widower for whom she felt an extreme fondness. Her psychotherapy with Freud revealed the true cause of the olfactory hallucinations: during a moment's negligence, she had allowed the widower's children to burn a dessert while she, on the basis of an unconscious and unacknowledged love for their father, had attempted to insinuate herself into his favour. In recreating an apparent smell of burning, Miss Lucy R. had unconsciously been responding to her own sense of self-reproach for momentarily abandoning the care of these children (which was something she had promised their dying mother) and pursuing an attachment which had no hope of blossoming into a relationship. According to Houdebine, this was for Myers a victory of the 'subliminal self' over material reality; in which significantly, the sexual had been renounced in favour of self-abnegating, sublimated love and service for others.

23 Frederic W. H. Myers, *Human Personality and Its Survival of Bodily Death* (New York: Longmans, Green & Co, 1904), p. 51.

case study), favouring instead the sublimation and foreclosure of sexuality, 'forclusion qui a son corrélat obligé dans une sublimation de l'*amour*, et d'une manière générale de la "haute valeur morale", de la pureté'[24] ['a foreclosure which has its necessary correlate in a sublimation of *love*, and more generally, of "high moral values," of purity'].

For Houdebine, these are again ideas which have significant repercussions for Bretonian discourse.[25] Given his familiarity with the *Second Manifeste*, he nonetheless passes over Breton's statement that 'c'est l'idée de l'amour, seule capable de réconcilier tout homme, momentanément ou non, avec l'idée de *vie*'[26] ['the idea of love alone is capable of reconciling any man, momentarily or not, with the idea of *life*'[27]] and that the truth of love and our own truth are to be found in 'l'âme et le *corps* de cet être'[28] ['the soul and *body* of that person'[29]] who inspires us. These quotations suggest that Breton wants neither to deny the validity of physical love, nor the importance of physical reality itself. As will be shown in Chapters 2 and 5, he will valorise the sexual and transgressive aspect of love, dismissing the notion of '*pudeur*' (chastity, sexual purity) associated with sexual conduct. For this reason, Houdebine's assumptions may be in need of some qualification, for a closer examination of Breton's theoretical assertions (as will be cited throughout this book) reveal that an interest in sublimation, the inner self and the esoteric did not entail an abandonment of material life; indeed, the fruits of terrestrial life were to be cherished, especially in the consummation of love.

Again in *Tel Quel* 46, Guy Scarpetta in 'Limite-frontière du Surréalisme' ('Limits and Borders of Surrealism') set about critiquing the ideological-political stance of Surrealism in much the same terms. This was the second of the three areas subjected to a critical analysis by the *Tel Quelists*. Scarpetta found fault with the ideas expressed in the tract co-written by Breton and

24 Houdebine, *Tel Quel* 46, p. 78.
25 *Ibid.*
26 Breton, *Manifestes du Surréalismes*, p. 130 – my italics.
27 Breton, *Manifestoes of Surrealism*, p. 181 – my italics.
28 Breton, *Manifestes du Surréalismes*, p. 130 – my italics.
29 Breton, *Manifestoes of Surrealism*, p. 181 – my italics.

Trotsky entitled 'Manifeste pour un art révolutionnaire indépendant' ('For an independent revolutionary art') (1938), above all with its divergence from dialectical materialism, for ostensibly they did not view the oppressiveness of capitalism or the mounting threat of fascism as a result of a class struggle, but as a conflict between 'all of civilisation' and 'the eternal':

> [en citant Breton-Trotsky] '… Actuellement, c'est toute la civilisation mondiale dans l'unité de son destin historique qui chancelle sous la menace de forces réactionnaires armées de toute la technique moderne '. La lutte des classes est donc dès le départ évincé, la contradiction entre deux modes de production radicalement antagonistes est effacée, sublimée dans l''unité' mythique d'un 'destin historique' situé de façon imaginaire au-dessus de la lutte des classes.[30]

> [quoting Breton-Trotsky] '…. Currently, it is the entire global civilisation in the unity of its historical destiny which is reeling under the blows of reactionary forces armed with the entire arsenal of modern technology.' From the beginning the class struggle is thus supplanted, the contradiction between two highly antagonistic modes of production is effaced, sublimated into the mythical 'unity' of a 'historical destiny' situated by the power of the imagination beyond the class struggle.

Scarpetta hereby claims it is profoundly misguided to speak of civilisation as a unified whole as this would result in an impossible assimilation not only of antagonistic social classes but also of extremist political tendencies such as fascism and militant communism/Stalinism. 'Sublimating' these divergent and antipathetic groups into a historic totality is an ill-conceived sociological reduction which sanitises civilisation of its all too obvious antagonisms.

He continues that the 'mythic unity' of civilisation is rather reminiscent of the telos of Hegelian idealism and that this is further reflected in the authors' preoccupation with the eternal as expressed through art: 'l'important est que cette critique […] ne s'opère pas, dans le *Manifeste*, sur la *base* du marxisme-léninisme, mais au nom d'une idéologie de l'art "éternel" dont le moins qu'on puisse dire est qu'elle n'a rien à voir avec le matérialisme dialectique'[31] ['the important thing is that this critique […]

30 Scarpetta, *Tel Quel* 46, p. 62 – Scarpetta's italics.
31 *Ibid.*, p. 63.

in the *Manifesto* does not operate on a Marxist-Leninist basis, but in the name of an ideology of "eternal" art, of which the most one can say is that it has nothing to do with dialectical materialism']. Although Breton and Trotsky do not specifically refer to the ahistorical or eternal nature of art in their manifesto, Scarpetta takes their foregrounding of art as a symptom of a belief in the metaphysical and the religious, which exalts the artist to the level of a '"sujet-artiste," tout-puissant, démiurge'[32] ['"subject-artist," all powerful, demiurge'].

Scarpetta correctly establishes that the concern of Breton and Trotsky is not to present a defence of dialectical materialism per se, though he is unwilling to concede the function of their tract, which is to plead for autonomous art-making *contra* the increasing bureaucratisation of artistic and intellectual life in the Stalinist USSR (as well as fascist countries). This may have lifted art out of the sphere of social and political concerns, though it may be overstating the case to assert that they also elevated it to the status of a religious or transcendental phenomenon. Moreover, the plea was made not at the expense of an explicit revolutionary stance or the fundamental need for class struggle, for throughout the tract art's autonomy is anchored to the need for revolution in defiance of the 'usurpateurs de la révolution'[33] ['usurpers of the revolution'[34]]. The tract is peppered with statements such as: 'l'art véritable [...] ne peut pas ne pas être révolutionnaire, c'est-à-dire celui ne peut pas aspirer à une reconstruction complète et radicale de la société'[35] ['true art [...] is unable not to be revolutionary, not to aspire to a complete and radical reconstruction of society'[36]] and concludes with the injunctions 'L'indépendance de l'art – pour la révolution. La révolution – pour la libération de l'art!'[37] ['The independence of

32 *Ibid.*, p. 63.

33 Breton, 'Pour un art révolutionnaire indépendant' (1938) in *Œuvres Complètes* III, p. 690.

34 Breton, 'Manifesto for an independent revolutionary art' (1938) in *What is Surrealism?*, 2, p. 186.

35 Breton, *Œuvres Complètes* III, p. 685.

36 Breton, *What is Surrealism?*, 2, p. 184.

37 Breton, *Œuvres Complètes* III, p. 695.

art – for the revolution. The revolution – for the complete liberation of art!'[38]]. The purported ahistoricism of the tract appears to be somewhat overstated,[39] and it is perhaps ironic that the text's co-author, Trotsky, believed that in the wake of a new socialist world order, art would be superseded.[40] Breton, on the other hand, believed that revolution would result in a merging of art and life.[41]

Perhaps most significant about Scarpetta's critique is how he addresses Breton's/Trotsky's use of the term 'sublimation', whose function is set out as restoring 'l'équilibre rompu entre le moi cohérent et les éléments refoulés'[42] ['the broken equilibrium between the integral ego and the outside elements it rejects [/represses]'[43]]. He affirms that 'on peut noter comment la "sublimation" est ici privilégiée à l'exclusion de sa *condition négative* (le travail de la pulsion de mort à partir de sa limite: la castration)'[44] ['one is able to note how "sublimation" is here privileged to the exclusion of its *negative (pre-)condition* (the work of the death drive on the basis of its

38 Breton, *What is Surrealism?*, 2, p. 187.

39 Scarpetta himself concedes that of the tract's assertions, apparently indicative of the sempiternal transcendence of art, some are ambiguous ('toute licence en art' ['every liberty in art'] – 'il importe [...] que l'imagination échappe à toute contrainte' ['it is important [...] that the imagination escapes all constraints'] – 'pas la moindre trace de commandement' ['not the slightest trace of external commands'] – 'indépendance de l'art' ['independence of art']). These are in his view 'formules "justes", d'une certaine façon, si elles marquent le refus d'une attitude bureaucratique dirigée contre l'avant-garde, mais radicalement fausses dès lors qu'elles placent en quelque sorte l'art "hors d'atteinte" du matérialisme historique' ['"fair" statements in a certain way, if they signify the refusal of a bureaucratic attitude directed toward the avant-garde, but radically false as soon as they place art "out of reach" of historical materialism, so to speak']. It behoves the reader to decide whether the quotations above are loaded with metaphysical significance or not.

40 See Mark Polizzotti, *Revolution of the Mind: The Life of André Breton* (London: Bloomsbury, 1995), p. 463.

41 Breton would refer to the breaking down of the 'distinction, long held as necessary, between art and life' – see Arturo Schwarz, *Die Surrealististen* (Frankfurt am Main: Kulturgesellschaft Frankfurt mbH & Nuove edizioni Gabriele Mazzotta, 1989), p. 22.

42 Breton, *Œuvres Complètes* III, p. 686.

43 Breton, *What is Surrealism?*, 2, p. 185.

44 Scarpetta, *Tel Quel* 46, p. 65.

absolute limit: castration)']. Scarpetta's conception of sublimation dwells only upon the concept's negative and repressive aspects, harking back to Freud's statement about sublimation colluding with the mute unproductivity of the death drive:

> By thus getting hold of the libido from the object-cathexis, setting itself up as sole love-object, and desexualising or sublimating the libido of the id, the ego is working in opposition to the purposes of Eros and placing itself at the service of the opposing instinctual impulses.[45]

By characterising sublimation as resting entirely upon its negative precondition, Scarpetta in fact underlines the divergence of Surrealist thought from Freudian theory; for it is clear from the quotations above that Breton and Trotsky assign a salutary and non-repressive value to sublimation whereas it is Freud who speculates about its complicity with the death drive.

The *Tel Quelists'* third critique, that of the Surrealists' philosophical stance, berated Surrealism's confusion and conflation of 'idealist' Hegelian dialectics with dialectical materialism. In the same edition of *Tel Quel*, in an article entitled 'Esquisse Cartographique du Mouvement: Surréalisme' ('Cartographic sketch of a movement: Surrealism'), Pierre Rottenberg begins by setting apart the philosophies of Marx, Engels and Mao Tse-Tung from those of Hegel, Neo-Hegelianism and German idealism (to which he claims Breton is sympathetic). He maintains that the former advance the individual's liberty by considering his/her fate a product of historical and material circumstance, whereas the latter espouse a phallic totalisation (his words) in which individual will is eclipsed by a subjectless metanarrative of history dominated by spirit:

> Hegel avance, sans arrêt, à l'intérieur d'une histoire, sans sujet, sinon Hegel *même*. C'est toute la différence avec Marx [...]. Marx donne à chacun sa 'chance' historique. *Preuve* : 'Ce qui tout de suite se présente à nous dans l'évolution, c'est qu'il doit exister

45 Sigmund Freud, 'The ego and the id' (1923) in *Standard Edition of the Complete Psychological Works of Sigmund Freud – The Ego and the Id, and Other Works,* trans. by James Strachey in collaboration with Anna Freud (London: Hogarth Press, 1961), vol. IXX, p. 46.

> quelque chose qui se développe, donc quelque chose d'enveloppé, – le germe, la disposition, le pouvoir...', *Hegel*, mais, justement, Hegel a-t-il, à son tour, c'est-à-dire dans son 'tout' historique, *permis*, dans le réel historique, le développement ? Étant une totalisation de pensée, il *n'est pas* un libérateur populaire.[46]
>
> [Hegel continues without pause within a history without a subject, unless that subject is Hegel *himself*. This is entirely different from Marx [...]. Marx gives each person his historical 'opportunity'. *The proof*: 'In evolution, what immediately occurs to us, is that there must exist something which develops, something veiled therefore – the germ, the tendency, the power...' did *Hegel*, and this is precisely my point, did he in his turn, that is to say in his historic 'totality', ever *allow* for such development in historical reality? Representing a totalisation of thought, he *is not* a popular liberator.]

Rottenberg notes that, according to Marx in *The German Ideology*, the intellectual climate of Germany in the mid-nineteenth century was still being pervaded by Hegel's 'philosophic charlatanry'[47] – a trend which he regards as comparable with the resurgence of Hegelian idealism in Surrealism. In *The German Ideology*, Marx had critiqued the 'Young Hegelians', Feuerbach, Bauer and Stirner, for failing to engage with political problems as products of historical reality. The latter had incurred Marx's derision for promoting not only a notion of 'spirit', but of 'spirits', of human life as a struggle of apparitions rather than of corporeal entities in conflict over the Earth's resources:

> Without realising it, Saint Max [i.e. Max Stirner] has so far done no more than give instruction in the art of spirit-seeing, by regarding the ancient and modern world only as the 'pseudo-body of a spirit', as a spectral phenomenon, and seeing in it only struggles of spirits.[48]

46 Pierre Rottenberg, 'Esquisse Cartographique du Mouvement: Surréalisme', in *Tel Quel* 46, p. 42 – Rottenburg's italics.

47 Karl Marx and Friedrich Engels, 'The German Ideology – Extract' (1845–1846) in *Beyond the Body Proper: Reading the Anthropology of Material Life*, ed. by Margaret M. Lock and Judith Farquhar (Durham and London: Duke University Press, 2007), p. 114 (pp. 113–129).

48 Karl Marx and Friedrich Engels, 'The German Ideology' (1845–1846) in *The Collected Works of Marx and Engels* (New York: International Publishers, 1976), vol. 5, p. 152.

It is this tendency to treat the material word as a world of apparitions for which Rottenberg similarly reproaches Breton. In quoting various passages of *L'Arcane 17*, Rottenberg attempts to show how Breton's writing is influenced by this spectral view of reality, which he terms 'porosité[49] ('porosity'). Proof of this porosity is, however, only mediated in the nebulous and oneiric quality of *Arcane 17*'s narrative: Rottenberg cites the dream of an elderly gypsy with which the story opens and the journey to the Percé rock taking place under an overcast sky as examples. He concludes that Breton is '"ouvert," dilaté, poreux'[50] ['"open," dilated, porous']. Peculiarly though, these purely literary qualities are taken as reflecting a fundamental belief system which is similar to that of Hegel and his followers. Without any further substantiation, we are bound to wonder whether this assumption is entirely plausible, for, as oneiric and poeticised as the work may be, the 'porosity' of Breton's writings is part of a narrative which is literary rather than philosophical. Moreover, when Breton does address questions of political struggle, his approach appears sympathetic to Marxist concerns and is by no means in contradiction to them. The work begins with the slogan 'ni dieu ni maître'[51] ['neither god nor master'[52]] and ends with a condemnation of nationalism (at times making use of Marxist terminology[53]) as well as a discussion of the importance of resistance (the importance of conducting it effectively and its political significance in wartime France). The title of the book itself *Arcane 17* pertains to the seventeenth card of the major arcana, known as 'the star', which Breton interprets as the morning star

49 Rottenberg, *Tel Quel* 46, p. 46.

50 Rottenberg, *Tel Quel* 46, p. 45.

51 Breton, *Arcane 17*, p. 23.

52 Breton, *Arcanum 17*, p. 40.

53 'Les divergences d'idéal qui animent une nation contre une autre, un groupe de nations contre un groupe d'autres, si elles sont assez puissantes pour provoquer ou alléguer le sacrifice de million d'êtres, en motivant théoriquement les guerres, n'en appartiennent pas moins à la *superstructure*' – Breton, *Arcane 17*, pp. 190–191 ['Differences in ideals that set one nation against another, one group of nations against another group, may be strong enough to provoke or lighten the sacrifice of millions of beings, and while they theoretically motivate wars, belong nonetheless to the *superstructure*', Breton, *Arcanum 17*, p. 145] – Breton's italics.

of Lucifer, with all the implications this has of rebellion against authority and the exaltation of material or terrestrial life.

Even so, Rottenberg – who allows his criticisms to become increasingly personal – insists that the spectral view of reality shared by Breton and Hegel amounts to a repression of the material and the sexual: 'Hegel pousse chacun à avoir une sorte de phallus honteux [...]. Position refoulante, détestable, exécrable'[54] ['Hegel presses everyone to have a sort of shameful phallus [...]. A position which is repressive, detestable, execrable']. Referring to Breton, he contemptuously remarks that '*Presque* tout s'est passé dans la "tête" bourrée, occidentale, écumante, "presque" tous, mais l'homme castré, jeté aux chiens, c'est aussi la réalité de *deux* testicules translucides, vivants'[55] ['*Almost* everything has taken place in a brimming, Western, foaming "head," "almost" everything, but the castrated man thrown to the dogs is also the reality of *two* translucent, living testicles']. The notion of 'castration' plays a central role in Rottenberg's article since he believes it to be synonymous with the sexual repression which arises when men are regarded as mere apparitions or ideas – the products of an idealist viewpoint – rather than corporeal beings.

His claims continued a line of argumentation which began in *Tel Quel* 45. In this edition of the journal, Jean-Louis Baudry had first made the association between sublimation and a 'repressive' idealism:

> L'idéalisme a toujours cherché [...] à exercer une coupure entre la base matérielle du sexe et ses 'effets'. Il apparaît comme l'instrument philosophique cohérent par lequel le sexe, avec le travail, avec l'ensemble des mécanismes de production, est refoulé [...]. L'idéalisme convie à une 'sublimation' qui doit s'insérer dans le système de la production et à des investissements affectifs sur de pures notions idéologiques devant servir de toute façon au renforcement de l'exploitation de classe.[56]
>
> [Idealism has always sought.... to establish a split between the material basis of sex and its "effects." It appears as the coherent philosophical instrument by which sex is repressed by means of work, and the whole set of mechanisms of production [...]. Idealism evokes a "sublimation" which must be inserted into the system of production

54 Rottenberg, *Tel Quel* 46, p. 46.

55 *Ibid.* – Rottenburg's italics.

56 Jean-Louis Baudry, 'Pour une matériologie (fin)' in *Tel Quel* 45 (Spring, 1971), pp. 68–69.

and its emotional investments in purely ideological notions which are to serve in all instances as the reinforcements of class exploitation.]

Baudry's understanding of sublimation was merely that of a mechanism serving to reinforce the exploitative nature of class relations in capitalist society, whereby the working classes forgo sexual gratification afforded by the pleasure principle in favour of enhanced economic and industrial productivity.[57] Rottenberg imputes this repressive view of reality to Surrealism, a view which, as I will continue to argue, the Surrealists opposed with their antagonism towards Christian and bourgeois mores, their sedition toward the state and non-repressive counter-model of sublimation.

Rottenberg attempts to further substantiate his claims by citing Breton's endorsements of Hegel (such as 'Où la dialectique hégélienne ne fonctionne pas, il n'y a pour moi pas de pensée, pas d'espoir de vérité'[58] ['When Hegelian dialectic ceases to function, for me there is no thought, no hope of truth'[59]]). From this he infers that: 'Breton est attaché à Hegel'[60] ['Breton is attached to Hegel']. Like other critics, Rottenberg interprets Breton's call for the reconciliation of antinomies as an appropriation of Hegelian dialectics.[61] By Breton's own admission, Hegel's influence was decisive in the elaboration of the concept[62] though Rottenberg omits to

57 The discussion of class and its relationship to sublimation or the renunciation of pleasure is one, which, within the scope of this book, it will not be possible to cover in depth. Rather, the idea of class is of interest mainly in how it ties in with those general notions, such as 'bourgeoisie', 'civilisation ', 'repression', 'church' and 'state', against which Breton formulates his own view of reality. These terms are at least relevant to class in so far as they are associated with the exploitative nature of the bourgeoisie in Marxist theory.

58 André Breton, *Entretiens 1913–1952* (with André Parinaud) (Paris: Gallimard, 1952), p. 152.

59 Breton, *Conversations*, p. 118.

60 Rottenberg, *Tel Quel* 46, p. 43.

61 Baugh states for example that 'The Surrealists were drawn to Hegel's dialectical negations as a means of erasing the divisions between reality and dreams' – Bruce Baugh, *French Hegel: From Surrealism to Postmodernism* (London: Routledge, 2003), p. 1.

62 'C'est incontestablement Hegel – et nul autre – qui m'a mis dans les conditions voulues pour apercevoir ce point' – Breton, *Entretiens*, pp. 151–152 ['It was undeniably

mention that his quest for a dialectical resolution was similarly inspired by a large number of other sources including Freud, Marx, Heraclitus, Meister Eckhardt, 'occultism', the pan-Chinese philosophy of yin and yang as well as the works of logician Stéphane Lupasco and hermetic writer and exponent of Eastern philosophy René Guénon.[63] Surrealism's hybridisations did as much to undermine the movement's philosophical purity as they did to undermine the consistency and credibility of the *Tel Quelists*' critiques against them, which failed to take into account the movement's complexity. Breton, who had personally listed the latter influences in his works,[64] affirmed that 'la démarche surréaliste n'a trouvé là qu'à s'assurer. Elle ne s'est jamais départie de son indépendance'[65] ['surrealist reasoning has only found in these ideas certain means of self-assurance. It has never abandoned its independence'].

In my view this statement is crucial in understanding the movement's stance towards the philosophical thought systems it encountered, never assimilating them fully or unconditionally, but preferring instead to cull the most congenial elements from within them and thus engaging in a process of philosophical bricolage.

This approach could also be seen in the Surrealists' reading of Hegel, which never resulted in their borrowings from the philosopher – and, in particular, their view of dialectics – becoming inscribed into a system of absolute idealism. Although Surrealism was clearly future-oriented, Breton did not for example explicitly align his reconciliation of antinomies with a telos (when understood in a quasi-theological sense). This would have posited a notion of absolute spirit or consciousness as the ultimate reality of the universe, with matter being conceived merely as thought's

---

Hegel – and no one else – who put me in the condition necessary to perceive this point' – Breton, *Conversations*, p. 118].

63 See André Breton, 'Entretiens' (1952) and 'Situation du Surréalisme entre les deux Guerres' (1942) in *Œuvres Complètes* III, 626; 723–724; and the English translations of the latter, André Breton, *Conversations*, p. 240 and 'The Situation of Surrealism between the two Wars' in *Yale French Studies*, No. 2, Modern Poets (New Haven, CT: Yale University Press, 1948), pp. 67–78.

64 *Ibid.*

65 Breton, *Œuvres Complètes* III, p. 626.

objectification as it moves towards self-understanding. It is this notion that matter is 'derivative' of thought that Breton ultimately rejected; a viewpoint which he re-affirmed throughout his career. He first critiqued idealism in the early 1930s when he attempted to align Surrealism with dialectical materialism and identified 'un sentiment dominant que je regarde aujourd'hui comme très fâcheux, qui est le sentiment de *la primauté de la pensée sur la matière*'[66] ['a prevailing view that I look upon today as being extremely mistaken, the view that *thought is supreme over matter*'[67]]. While expressing admiration for Hegel and his reading of dialectics in the 'Second Manifeste', Breton also called for 'l' "avortement colossal" du système hégélien'[68] ['the "colossal abortion" of the Hegelian system'[69]] a stance which, he avowed, underlined Surrealism's affinities with materialism. Even after Surrealism's more esoteric turn in the 1940s and 1950s, he would in two interviews insist on the futility of pitting idealism and materialism against one another, by which he again referred to the privileging of thought over matter or vice-versa; in the most memorable of the two, he evaluated the importance of his work *Les Vases Communicants* (1932) as having presented to the world the notion of a capillary tissue between the inner life and the exterior world, dream and waking reality. 'A ce *niveau*' concluded Breton, 'la vieille opposition entre matérialisme et idéalisme se vide de tout sens'[70] ['In this *sense* [...] the outmoded opposition between materialism and idealism loses all meaning'[71]].

As Anna Balakian explains: 'The failing discovered in the case of Hegel was "the idealist error," that is, Hegel had considered real things to be a degree of realisation of the absolute idea; whereas in Breton's understanding of the word and in the poetic and artistic interpretation given to it by the Surrealists, the ideal is not an independent concept but the result of man's

66 Breton, *Œuvres Complètes* II, pp. 232–233. Breton's italics.
67 Breton, *What is Surrealism?*, 2, pp. 116–117. Breton's italics.
68 Breton, *Manifestes du Surréalisme*, p. 89.
69 Breton, *Manifestoes of Surrealism*, p. 140.
70 Breton, *Œuvres Complètes* III, p. 539; see also p. 623 where Breton makes a similar assertion.
71 Breton, *Conversations*, p. 134; see also p. 236 where Breton makes a similar assertion.

mental transposition and translation of the material universe'.[72] Balakian's comment is also interesting in what it implies about transposition,[73] for it is not – as in the writings of the *Tel Quelists* – presented as a corollary to an idealist viewpoint, whereby material forms and impulses are suppressed in favour of the ideal; rather, it is seen as the mind's translation of and engagement with material reality, and the latter's recreation on a visual or poetic plane.

To return to Surrealism's relationship to Hegel and dialectics, however, Breton's statement 'Freud est hegelien en moi' ['Freud is Hegelian in me'][74] indicates that he had expropriated the Hegelian dialectic from the great edifice of idealism to serve a purpose of his own making (after all, Freud and Hegel hadn't previously been considered to be natural bedfellows). In *Les Vases Communicants*, Breton advances a view of dialectics which consists not in a Hegelian 'negation of spirit', or even of the subject-object model posited by the master-slave dialectic, but in the interplay of external reality and the inner life (and thus the interiority of the self as understood psychoanalytically). As the title of the work 'communicating vessels' suggests, Breton's intention was to highlight the parity and interdependency of the inner life and exterior reality in (wo)man's everyday experience,[75] rather

72 Anna Elizabeth Balakian, *Surrealism* (Chicago, IL: University of Chicago Press, 1986), p. 138.

73 The term 'transposition' can be defined as 'transformation', 'transference' or 'transportation' as its etymology clearly implies; whether the term implies movement upward or downward is irrelevant. The term is, however, frequently used in Surrealist criticism (and by the October group in particular) to refer to the surmounting of the sexual and the material through an idealising sublimation (and in art through the abstracting process of symbolisation). These are, however, points which are contested by this book.

74 According to Roudinesco this was quoted by Pierre Macherey in his unpublished seminar (1980–1982), "Introduction of Hegelianism in France: From Victor Cousin to Alexandre Kojève" – see Elisabeth Roudinesco, *La Bataille de Cent Ans – Histoire de la Psychanalyse en France 2, 1925–1985* (Paris: Seuil, 1986), Part 1, p. 47; in English translation, see Elisabeth Roudinesco, *Jacques Lacan & Co: A History of Psychoanalysis in France,* 1925–1985, trans. Jeffrey Mehlman (Chicago: Chicago University Press, 1990), Part 1, p. 32.

75 According to Breton's biographer, the work was named after a scientific experiment in which gases and liquids pass back and forth between two joined recipients 'until

than to assert the primacy of thought or spirit over creation. Moreover, on reading the book, it seems clear that the routes to this point of reconciliation are varied: whether by the external manifestation of the unconscious in automatic works; whether through the meeting of 'inner desire' and 'external necessity'[76] (which brings about the Surrealist chance encounter or an experience of the marvellous), whether through the elaboration of the dream (itself inspired from reality) in Surrealist works or the realisation of an improved if not utopian social order. The manifold instances of dialectical resolution seem thus to estrange him from Hegelian philosophy: for they are not rooted in one of the great Hegelian meta-narratives of reality (pertaining to spirit, religion, reason or art), still less in the account of the Absolute Spirit's path to self-understanding, being based instead upon the osmosis between the inner life and external reality, especially when considered under the aspect of unconscious dream life and waking reality.

Another important consideration which Rottenberg passes over is Breton's reception of Hegel via a series of seminars led by Alexandre Kojève,[77] which first introduced the thinker to a French audience and was widely attended by the country's intelligentsia. Kojève interpreted Hegel's move to idealism as an attempt to show how the human mind could overcome the material world of nature, by creating its own world through the power of speech, language and thought, an ideological realm in which we feel at home and free. Thus Kojève arrives at a 'non-metaphysical, secularised conception of Hegel's philosophical history, and reads the end of his system in anthropological, not theological terms'.[78]

---

they reach equilibrium' (see Polizzotti, *Revolution of the Mind,* p. 367). This appears a novel appropriation of entropy in a movement nonetheless qualified by Breton as 'dialectical'! Breton also postulates the existence of a 'capillary tissue' or 'tissu capillaire' which regulates the permeation of the one in the other (see Breton, *Les Vases Communicants*, p. 161; Breton, *Communicating Vessels*, p. 139).

76 Breton, *L'Amour Fou*, p. 35.

77 By Breton's admission, though, he was first introduced to the philosopher by his philosophy teacher, a positivist, André Cresson in 1912 – see Breton, *Entretiens*, pp. 151–152.

78 'Hegelianism' in *Routledge Encyclopaedia of Philosophy* vol. 1.0 (London: Routledge, 1998), CD-ROM.

On account of Breton's explicit rejection of the ideal, it seems likely that Surrealism's dialectical resolution of antinomies was not envisaged as a termination of material reality in an eternal beyond, but was, rather, inscribed within the material itself. Moreover, if conceived in anthropological, socio-political or psychological terms, the finality of the dialectical resolution would perforce be uncertain since it was bound to give rise to cycles in which new forms of opposition would require resolution. In his manifestoes, Breton explicitly stated that it was not his intention to linger at a point of absolute synthesis – only to make it his inspiration for action in the world. In the 'Premier Manifeste' he declared, 'c'est à sa conquête que je vais, *certain de n'y pas parvenir* mais trop insoucieux de ma mort pour ne pas supporter un peu les joies d'une telle possession'[79] ['It is in quest of this surreality that I am going, *certain not to find it* but too unmindful of my death not to calculate to some slight degree the joys of its possession'[80]]; and in the 'Second Manifeste' he likewise affirmed, 'Il s'agit, non d'en rester là, mais de ne *pouvoir faire moins que de tendre désespérément à cette limite*'[81] ['It is a matter not of remaining at that point, but *of not being able to do less than to strain desperately toward the limit*'[82]].

In my view Surrealist activity was defined less by the determination to find resolution or perfection in an abstract, transcendental realm than by the desire to achieve a sense of harmonic (though transient) unity in various arenas pertaining to human experience and the material world: the social, the political, the artistic, the psychological and the sexual. As will be shown throughout this book, Surrealism's maxim of perpetual revolt, as well as its unerring defence of love and the imagination, mediated a sense of never arriving, of continuously looking to new stimuli and new challenges in the quest to liberate humanity from its serfdom. This, too, was fundamental in its mission to counter a view of civilisation which was predicated on a repressive form of sublimation.

79 Breton, *Manifestes du Surréalisme*, p. 24 – my italics.
80 Breton, *Manifestoes of Surrealism*, p. 14 – my italics.
81 Breton, *Manifestes du Surréalisme*, p. 137 – Breton's italics.
82 Breton, *Manifestoes of Surrealism*, p. 187 – Breton's italics.

Despite the obvious problems in approaching the question of Surrealism and philosophy, it is the view of an 'idealist' Surrealism that the theorist Denis Hollier (who had collaborated with the *Tel Quelists*) assimilated from the journal. When he later came to write for the American art journal *October*, the *Tel Quel* view of Surrealism was expressed in it and – although adapted to a deconstructive, rather than a Maoist stance – became doxa.

In his exegesis of Bataillean thought, *Against Architecture* (1989), Hollier allied art and literature with repressive sublimation on the one hand, and psychoanalysis with the overcoming of the need for artistic self-expression on the other:

> Artists, therefore, today are no more than the providers of "applied" psychoanalysis, they sell complexes [...]. Whereas the logic implied in the Freudian discovery would lead, Bataille thinks, to the total and irreversible demystification of the artistic realism, artists (*Surrealists*), on the contrary, find there one last resource, the material of one last burst of energy. Fearing to expose themselves "in person" to analysis, they offer their works to it – an intermediary protecting them against the effects of direct analysis [...]. The effect of psychoanalysis is a "reduction of repression" (a phrase that could describe perversion) as well as a "relative elimination of symbolism." Both of these elements are fatal to the mechanisms of sublimation, which they deprive of energy sources. Literature also (neurotic) is able to exist only through the exploitation of symbolic transpositions occasioned by repression.[83]

We may note with some interest that the Surrealists are once again identified as the proponents of a repressive sublimation, producing art as a means of symbolic escape from psychoanalytical treatment and thus evading the therapy by which their repression might be diminished.

Hollier is also explicit in highlighting the connection between art and the ideal. With reference to Bataille's work, he shows that architecture in its extended sense (such as painting and other art forms) reflects a misguided and overbearing elevation of the spirit, an impulse to an authoritarian idealism:

83 Hollier, *Against Architecture*, p. 111 – my italics.

> Each time that *architectural composition* turns up somewhere other than in monuments, whether it is in physiognomy, costume, music, or painting, one may infer a prevailing taste for divine or human *authority*. The great compositions of certain painters express the desire to force the spirit into an official ideal.[84]

His use of this quotation from Bataille, with its reference to painters who impose notions of the ideal on material form, also reflects what he thinks of Surrealism. Hollier believes that as an idealist movement it strove not only to reach a higher agency (either in metaphysical or in conceptual-theoretical terms) but, within its works, also elevated the materiality of existence in all its crudity to a level of poetic abstraction. Hollier's view of Surrealism is reminiscent of Guy Scarpetta's argument in *Tel Quel* that the movement was concerned with 'art' as an embodiment of the eternal. It is, however, a view which I believe can be qualified on the basis of the vast lexicon of Surrealist imagery, which straddles both the sublimatory and the desublimatory.

In 1990, Denis Hollier was to join Hal Foster and Rosalind Krauss on the editorial board of *October*, one of the foremost journals on contemporary art and culture in the Western world. The intellectual ferment created by these individuals was such as to reinforce the critiques of Surrealism as imported by Denis Hollier from *Tel Quel*; this was reflected in the works of Foster and Krauss. In Foster's *Compulsive Beauty* (1993) there is a critical link between sublimation, repression and Surrealist art. Surrealist iconography is considered through the optics of the uncanny, that sensation of dread or unease which sets in when 'repressed infantile complexes have been revived by some impression, or when the primitive beliefs we have surmounted seem once more to be confirmed'.[85] He approaches the relationship of Surrealism and repression principally via a psychoanalytical account of the behaviours and artistic practices of the movement's members. The title of his work itself is a play on 'convulsive beauty' and points not

84 Georges Bataille, 'Architecture' (1929) in in *Œuvres Complètes – Écrits posthumes 1922–1940*, ed. by Denis Hollier (Paris: Éditions Gallimard, 1970), vol. I, p. 171.

85 Sigmund Freud, 'The Uncanny' (1919), in *The Standard Edition of the Complete Psychological Works of Sigmund Freud*, trans. under editorship of James Strachey in collaboration with Anna Freud (London: Hogarth Press, 1955), vol. XVII, p. 249.

only to the uncontrollable irruption of repressed instincts and complexes[86] from the unconscious but also to their immanence in Surrealist art: '[in Surrealism] representation becomes other, fantasmatic – as if repressed in high modernism, it returns there uncannily, its distortion the mark of its repression'.[87]

Foster also asserts that as Breton uncovers repressed material (frequently linked to the sexual instincts or the death drive), he resists the consequences of what is revealed to him. For this reason, he presents Breton in opposition to desublimation (and its expression in art), upholding 'sublimated form and idealist Eros'[88] (a point to which we return in the following chapter). Thus, Foster characterises Surrealism and Breton in terms similar to those of the *Tel Quelists*.

In Rosalind Krauss' major exposition of Bataillean thought, *Formless* (1997), Breton is similarly characterised as an idealist. Commenting on the pamphlet *Un Cadavre* (1930), in which Breton had been represented by Bataille and the dissident Surrealists as a deceased messiah, she writes that:

> The Christ with whom Bataille is now identifying Breton is the very embodiment of what Bataille had contemptuously called "the simple (paternal) sign of universal homogeneity," which is to say, a cadaver that has passed beyond a state of rot into dust, having thus lost the lesson in doubleness and hence heterogeneity... And it is this same trafficking in the homogeneous that Bataille would accuse Breton of in "The Play of Transpositions," his text on Surrealism's play with psychoanalytical ideas of the unconscious, oneiric force shackled by Breton to the service of poetry, which itself serves the religious cause of idealism that seeks to elevate and sublimate...[89]

The homogeneity mentioned referred not only to the striving for Hegelian resolution in the ideal but to the exclusion of what was not ideal, of what was fundamentally heterogeneous to it. This encompassed not only material

86 According to Foster these include primal scenes, castration complexes, repressed traumas and the memory of death.

87 Hal Foster, *Compulsive Beauty*, Series: October Books (London: MIT Press, 1993), p. 96.

88 *Ibid.*, p. 111.

89 Rosalind E. Krauss, 'Cadaver' in Rosalind E. Krauss and Yve-Alain Bois, *Formless: A User's Guide* (New York: Zone, 1997), p. 66.

existence, but, in a general sense, all of the latter's undesirable imperfections and vices. Krauss suggested that this rejection of the 'heterogeneous' compromised Surrealism's claims of being an emancipatory movement and risked perpetuating the sort of intolerance to otherness it purported to overcome[90] (as reflected in Breton's early rejection of Bataille's base materialism, a philosophy which in Breton's eyes made of him a mere 'philosophe-excrément'[91] ['excrement philosopher'] who lacked intellectual credibility).

The view of Breton being a homogenising idealist again has clear links to the opinions expressed within the journal *Tel Quel*. Jean-Louis Houdebine had, as we have seen, critiqued the idealist transcendentalism of Breton's psychoanalytical sources. In addition to this, he took issue with what he considered to be Breton's attempt to subsume dialectical materialism into a covert teleological idealism since this was in his eyes a way of introducing formal logic into the universe and thus homogenising everything. He considered this a violation of the logic of dialectical materialism which for him resided in heterogeneity, in the irreducible nature of its components. Houdebine cited Breton's desired reconciliation of antinomies – especially of dream and reality as presented in *Les Vases Communicants* – as an example of his homogenising tendencies and concluded that:

> Cette 'grande clé,' dont rêve Breton, nous savons mieux aujourd'hui qu'elle forclôt, dans son fantasme de 'réconciliation', toute forme d'instance matérielle, et qu'elle n'ouvre sur rien d'autre que sur l'idéalisme positiviste, avec son envers obligé, l'idéalisme spiritualiste, dont les quatre dernières pages des *Vases Communicants*, justement, nous offrent des exemples flagrants.[92]

90 Although Breton's own attitude toward certain individuals (such as the Surrealist dissidents Bataille, Masson, Leiris and Giacometti), certain sexual practices (libertinism, homosexuality, perversion) is often taken as evidence of his homogenising tendencies, the diachronic account of Breton's statements and ideas presented in this book go some way in mitigating this view and showing above all that the late Breton evinced a much greater acceptance of alterity, perversion and transgression than he is generally remembered for. Above all, this is reflected in his growing respect for the ideas of Georges Bataille as is outlined in Chapter 2.

91 Breton, *Manifestes*, p. 135; Breton, *Manifestoes*, p. 185.

92 Houdebine, *Tel Quel* 46, p. 82.

[This 'great key' of which Breton dreams, we know more precisely today that, in its fantasy of 'reconciliation,' it forecloses all forms of materiality and that it opens out onto nothing other than positivist idealism, with its necessary complement, spiritual idealism, of which by way of illustration, the last four pages of *Vases Communicants* offer us flagrant examples.]

* * * * * * * * *

The *Tel Quelists'* critiques, which were later to be inherited by the October group, pre-suppose an explicit and categorical idealist or Hegelian stance on the part of Breton and the Surrealists. Yet, as we have seen, Breton's appropriation of Hegel was at best ambivalent and equivocal. Moreover, the question of whether Surrealism embodied any form of systematised philosophy is one on which there is no consensus, having been discussed only cursorily within critical accounts of the movement. It is clear that given the multiplicity of philosophers cited by Breton (and the Surrealists more generally) – ranging from Hegel, Pascal, Heraclitus, Hermes, to Marx, Engels, Fourier, Berkeley and Bataille – the task of extrapolating a coherent 'Surrealist' philosophy meets with obvious hazards. Indeed, such an operation is apt to result in an overdetermination of one strand of Surrealist thinking at the expense of another (idealist or materialist, Hegelian or Marxian, hermetic or anticlerical); whereas I believe that Surrealism's truth lay precisely in its sense of contradiction and desire to interweave diverse theoretical viewpoints.

In one of the few scholarly works which treats the question of Surrealism's philosophical standpoint(s) in depth – a collection of essays entitled *Surréalisme et Philosophie* (1992) – we read in the opening chapter that 'il n'y pas de "philosophie du surréalisme"'[93] ['there is no such thing as a "philosophy of Surrealism"']. The author, Gérard Legrand, is nonetheless willing to concede that the young Breton may have been attracted to a certain form of subjective idealism deployed at the service of poetry; though he then asks 'est-ce assez pour tirer le surréalisme vers la métaphysique? Nous n'en croyons rien [...] le refus opposé par Breton à toute espèce de

93 Gérard Legrand, 'Breton et l'inauguration philosophique du surréalisme' in *Surréalisme et Philosophie* (Paris: Éditions du Centre Pompidou, 1992), p. 14.

transcendance montre assez qu'il est exempt de toute "nostalgie" de l'Être'[94] ['is it enough to steer Surrealism towards metaphysics? Nothing could persuade us of this being so [...] Breton's refusal of all forms of transcendence shows well enough that he is exempt from all types of "nostalgia" for Being'].

Another contributor, Daniel Lindenberg, argues that 'le véritable métaphysique de la surréalité était plutôt chercher du côté des pensées qui soulignaient l'inanité des "illusions du Progrès" et prêchaient le "retour aux sources" et la rupture avec l'idéologie "occidentale"'[95] ['the real metaphysics of surreality consisted, rather, in looking amongst those thoughts which underlined the inanity of "illusions of Progress" and preached the "return to sources" and the rupture with "Western" ideology']. Lindenberg also disputes the argument that Surrealism could be considered a reworking of Hegel's absolute idealism: 'Les références de Breton à Hegel ne doivent donc pas faire illusion. Rien n'est plus éloigné de sa pensée que le fatalisme historiosophique du philosophe souabe'[96] ['We should not be under any illusion about the references of Breton to Hegel. Nothing could be more remote from his thinking than the historiosophical fatalism of the Swabian philosopher'].

His justification for this is Surrealism's initiatory basis, which by definition occludes the path to an essence of Surrealist philosophy. In the most general terms, it is the constants of revolt and gnosis which, Lindenberg affirms, underlie Surrealist thought.

According to the author of *French Hegel: From Surrealism to Postmodernism*, Bruce Baugh, Marxist and Surrealists agreed that 'Hegel had dissolved genuine social problems in the ether of pure thought, instead of seeking a concrete dialectic in social relations and upheavals and the psychic conflicts within individuals. Like so many others they wanted Hegel's method, but not his metaphysics'.[97] Baugh also claims that Surrealism did not aim at synthesis in the Hegelian sense. Although Breton talked about

94 *Ibid.*, pp. 16–17.

95 Daniel Lindenberg, '"Hypermatérialisme" et gnose' (1992) in *Surréalisme et Philosophie*, p. 22.

96 *Ibid.*, p. 22.

97 Baugh, *French Hegel*, p. 55.

undoing oppositions, Surrealist negation was not regulated by 'a totality that governs negations as component "moments" of a progressively developing whole'.[98] Surrealism consisted rather in a concatenation of negations and surpassings *ad infinitum*, which never reached resolution and thus reaffirmed the idea of the movement being in perpetual revolt.

Even so, it is in the *Tel Quelists'* terms that Hollier and others from the October group (Krauss, Foster, Bois) set about consolidating the view of Breton as repressive, idealist and homogenising and thereby underline his antagonism to Bataille. The ideological differences which beset Surrealism circa 1929, when a number of dissidents joined Bataille in his criticism of Breton, are usually portrayed as definitive in respect to both men's relationship to one another and the irreconcilability of their respective philosophical standpoints. At times this interpretation of events has, however, come at the expense of a more differentiated view of a complex and ambivalent relationship, which extended well beyond the two to three-year period usually dwelt upon by critics and which yielded to an attempt at mutual comprehension in their later life. Given that this point is as important as it is involved, I resume my discussion of both men's tortuous association in the second chapter, where I will argue that their mutual standpoints were by no means incompatible with one another.

98 *Ibid.*, p. 56.

CHAPTER 2

The Breton-Bataille Polemic Revisited

Je me persuade, en laissant reparaître aujourd'hui le *Second Manifeste du Surréalisme*, que le temps s'est chargé pour moi d'émousser ses angles polémiques. Je souhaite que de soi-même il ait corrigé, fût-ce jusqu'à un certain point à mes dépens, les jugements parfois hâtifs que j'y ai portés...[1]

[In allowing the *Second Manifesto of Surrealism* to be republished, I have talked myself into believing that time has accomplished for me the task of blunting its polemical angles. I only hope that it has corrected on its own – even though it were to a certain extent at my expense – the sometimes hasty judgements I made...[2]]

– ANDRÉ BRETON (1946)

... il y a bien d'autres choses dans ma vie avec lesquelles je ne suis pas d'accord, mais *Un Cadavre* en est. Je hais ce pamphlet [...] Ces accusations immédiates, sans recul, relèvent de la facilité et de l'agitation prématurée : comme le silence de part et d'autre eût été préférable.[3]

[... there are many other things in my life with which I do not agree, but 'Un Cadavre' is among them. I hate this pamphlet [...]. These immediate accusations, with no possibility of recall, came from facility and premature annoyance: how much better silence on both sides would have been[4]]

– GEORGES BATAILLE (c. 1954)

1 André Breton, 'Avertissement pour la Réédition du Second Manifeste' (1946) in *Manifestes du Surréalisme*, p. 63.

2 André Breton, 'Preface for the New Edition of the Second Manifesto' (1946) in *Manifestoes of Surrealism*, p. 113.

3 Georges Bataille, 'La Publication d' «Un Cadavre»' (c. 1954) in *Georges Bataille, Michel Leiris – Échanges et Correspondances* (Paris: Gallimard, 2004), p. 76 (pp. 73–80).

4 Georges Bataille, 'Notes on the Publication of "Un Cadavre"' (c. 1954) in *The Absence of Myth – Writings on Surrealism*, trans. by Michael Richardson (London: Verso, 1994), p. 32.

The binarisation of Surrealism into two antagonistic camps has, as we have already seen, resulted in the perpetuation of the view of Bretonian Surrealism as sublimatory and idealist as compared to the dissident camp of Surrealists which formed around Georges Bataille and the journal *Documents*, who advocated desublimation and base materialism. In Foster's *Compulsive Beauty* (1993), for example, 'Bataille, the base materialist' is portrayed as antipodal to Breton, 'the sublimator and idealist' as well as to the Surrealist movement as a whole, despite claiming himself to be the 'enemy from within':[5]

> it is at this point where sublimation confronts desublimation that Surrealism breaks down, and I mean this literally: such is the stake between official Bretonian and dissident Bataillean factions circa 1929 [...][6]

Whereas the polemics of 1929 are a well-documented instalment in Surrealism's history, in this chapter I re-examine the assumption that Surrealism 'breaks down' when confronted with desublimation by revisiting both men's exchanges in the aftermath of this wrangling. It will be shown that there are significant points of convergence in their ideas in the 1930s and after 1945, centring around the areas of transgression, eroticism and black humour. By tracing Breton's political struggles and re-examining his later writings (*L'Anthologie de l'Humoir Noir*, *L'Amour Fou* as well as his 'Introduction' to the international Surrealist exhibition of 1959), it becomes evident that his engagement with the material and the sexual was considerable, and was even on some occasions in consonance with the thinking of Bataille.

I view the 1930s as the turning point at which Breton and the Surrealists began to express a growing interest in eroticism and transgression as reflected in the journal *Minotaure* and the art forms of this period, above all the symbolic objects of Dalí, Giacometti, Bellmer and Picasso. My focus on these art forms reveals that they frequently consisted in overt sexual or perverse imagery and were not always predicated upon an enforced negation of the instincts.

5 Georges Bataille, 'A propos d'assoupissements' (1946) in *Œuvres Complètes – Articles 1 1944–1949* (Paris: Gallimard, 1988), vol. XI, p. 31; Georges Bataille, 'On the Subject of Slumbers' (1946) in *Absence of Myth*, p. 49

6 Foster, *Compulsive Beauty*, p. 110.

The Super-eagle and the Old Mole

> [on ne peut] nous reprocher de vivre retirés en notre pensée comme en une tour autour de laquelle les autres se fusillent. De notre plein gré, nous n'avons jamais voulu entrer dans cette tour et nous ne permettons pas qu'on nous y enferme[7]
>
> [no one can accuse us of living enclosed in our thoughts, as if in some tower while others are trading gunfire down below. With all our hearts, we have always refused to enter that tower, and we will not allow others to shut us up in it[8]]
>
> (André Breton, 1926)

In Bataille's text 'La "Vieille Taupe" et le Préfixe *Sur* dans les Mots *Surhomme* et *Surréaliste*' ('The "Old Mole" and the Prefix *Sur* in the Words *Surhomme* [Superman] and *Surrealist*') (1931), Bataille famously metaphorised Surrealism's revolutionary pretensions as the ascent of a *suraigle* or 'super-eagle', which in political terms symbolised the lofty might of imperial power, such as one might associate with the Napoleonic empire or military fascism; and which, in conceptual terms, represented the abstraction of 'the idea' not yet made concrete.[9] In Bataille's opinion, Surrealism was also a super-eagle for searching for an authority from above[10] in the ideal realm of 'esprit, surréel, absolu'[11] ['spirit, surreal, absolute'[12]], for remaining too aloof from the revolt of the working class and failing to eschew more explicitly its bourgeois inheritance. More importantly still, this striving for 'the ideal' and interest in all things sublimatory was premised upon a certain hubris which could only possibly lead to Surrealism's self-undoing: 'ainsi l'aigle a contracté alliance avec le soleil qui châtre tout ce qui entre en conflit avec lui (Icare,

7 Breton, 'Légitime Défense' (1926) in *Œuvres Complètes* II, p. 295.

8 Breton, 'In self defence' (1926) in *Break of Day*, pp. 37–38.

9 Bataille, *Œuvres Complètes* II, 96; Bataille, *Visions of Excess*, p. 34.

10 Bataille would say Surrealism was 'en quête d'une autorité *supérieure*', *Œuvres Complètes* II, p, 94 ['searching for an authority *from above*', Bataille, *Visions of Excess*, p. 33] – Bataille's italics.

11 Bataille, *Œuvres Complètes* II, p. 94.

12 Bataille, *Visions of Excess*, p. 33.

Prométhée, le taureau mithraïque)'[13] ['the eagle has thus formed an alliance with the sun, which castrates all that enters into conflict with it (Icarus, Prometheus, the Mithraic bull)'[14]]. It was this reasoning that furnished the crux of his critique of Surrealism: the latter, he explained, was an Icarian movement whose demise was, on account of its attempts to overreach itself, a pre-established fact:

> La voûte du ciel, encore l'illumination icarienne et la même fuite vers des hauteurs d'où il semble qu'il sera facile de maudire ce bas monde (mais d'où nous savons surtout avec quelle facilité dérisoire un homme est précipité), c'est dans l'immensité brillante du ciel, non dans le vide de l'être néant hégélien, qu'un élan verbal projette constamment M. Breton.[15]
>
> [Heaven's vault, still the Icarian illumination and the same flight toward the heavens from which it will be easy to curse this base world (but from which we know above all with what derisive ease a man is cast); it is into the brilliant immensity of the sky, not into the void of Hegelian being-nothingness that M. Breton is constantly thrown by verbal momentum.][16]

As a counter-model to the super-eagle, Bataille posited 'la vieille taupe' or old mole whose agitations stemmed from the bowels of the earth and took place amid the people rather than soaring superciliously above them. He

13 Bataille, *Œuvres Complètes* II, p. 96.

14 Bataille, *Visions of Excess*, p. 34. Translation slightly modified by me.

15 Bataille, *Œuvres Complètes* II, p. 107 – Interpreted in psychical terms, Bataille's warnings about Icarian flight seem to have some resonances with Freud's warnings about the risks of forced sublimation: 'The plasticity of the components of sexuality, shown by their capacity for sublimation, may indeed offer a great temptation to strive for still greater cultural achievements by still further sublimation. But just as we do not count on our machines converting more than a certain heat consumed into useful mechanical work, we ought not to seek to alienate the whole amount of the energy of sexual instinct from its proper ends. We cannot succeed in doing so; and if the restriction upon sexuality were to be carried too far it would inevitably bring with it all the evils of soil- exhaustion' – Sigmund Freud, 'Five Lectures on Psycho-Analysis' (1909) in *Complete Psychological Works* XI, p. 54.

16 Bataille, *Visions of Excess*, p. 42.

believed that Breton could never be an old mole since his lofty idealisms rendered him detached from the people whom he ostensibly represented.

This view of Surrealism as remaining vertically aloof and opposed to the subterranean dissension of the old mole has undoubtedly coloured the popular perceptions of Breton and Bataille in modern criticism. John Lechte, for example, states that 'Breton assumes a position on what we shall come to describe as the vertical axis, while, for his part, Bataille is located on what we shall describe as the horizontal axis'.[17] The linguistic component Lechte attributes to these axes further reinforces the clichéd view of both men, with verticality being equated with the 'metaphor' of Surrealist poetry, and horizontality being expressed in 'metonymy' or the direct, quasi-fetishistic chains of self-substitution of Bataille's writing. As examples of the latter, Lechte cites the interchangeability of eyes, eggs, testicles or of urine, tears, sperm and sweat in Bataille's fictional work *Histoire de l'Œil*.[18] Surrealist metaphor, on the other hand, attempts to objectify or reify those syntheses of images which, according to Lechte, reflects a broader concern with the idealist (Hegelian) resolution of contrary states.[19]

In Krauss and Bois's *Formless* (1997), the vertical is associated with the canvases of high art and the upright position of (wo)man, taken by Freud to be the mark of culture and civilisation. Surrealism is characterised as exalting culture and civilisation on the vertical axis; as such it indulges an overweening ambition to reach the lofty yet treacherous heights of

17 John Lechte, 'Surrealism and the Practice of Writing, or The "Case" of Bataille' in *Bataille – Writing the Sacred*, ed. by Carolyn Bailey Gill (London: Routledge, 1995), pp. 117–132.

18 Whilst Lechte underlines the horizontal self-substituting nature of these items (by virtue of a similarity in form or character), he concedes that these are initially inscribed 'within a structure of metaphor' – Lechte, *Writing the Sacred*, p. 125. He then explains, however, that these are the beginnings of metonymic chains which proliferate endlessly 'both anagrammatically and by homophony' – Lechte, *Writing the Sacred*, p. 126.

19 As Balakian states 'Hegel's imprint can also be noted in the philosophical significance attributed by the Surrealists to the creation of the metaphor. For them it is not a mere form of speech but the crystallisation of concept' – Balakian, *Surrealism*, p. 137.

love, poetry and the ideal. The horizontal is associated with new forms of deconstructive, anti-cultural operations, both in art (as in Jackson Pollock's 'drip paintings') and writing (as in Bataille's article on the big toe, which he considers the most human part of the body).

While Lechte, Krauss and Bois make some cogent points about the differences in outlook between both men, I want to suggest that it may be fruitful also to consider some of the shifting fault lines within both camps, and in particular the serious attempts at social and political engagement which mark out Surrealism's trajectory throughout the 1930s when its members became much more like old moles. In comparing the content of the two manifestoes of Surrealism, it seems evident that the Surrealism of 1924, of the *Manifeste du Surréalisme*, was more turned in on itself, being preoccupied mostly with the interpretation of dreams, reclaiming the rights of the imagination, defending the mentally ill and promoting automatism; the *Second Manifeste*, on the other hand, made an explicit statement of revolutionary intent: 'nous nous montrerions capables de faire, au point de vue révolutionnaire, tout notre devoir'[20] ['we shall prove ourselves fully capable of doing our duties as revolutionaries']. In fact, the 1930s saw Surrealism reorient itself several times in an attempt to find its own revolutionary voice: firstly in its failed attempts at reconciliation with the French Communist Party, then in its move away from mainstream politics in the formation of *Contre-Attaque* in the mid-thirties and, by the end of the thirties, in its campaign for an independent revolutionary art. This reorientation corresponds to Breton's assertion that the movement had from the late 1920s abandoned its neo-Romantic 'intuitive' phase, only to be superseded by its 'reasoning' phase.[21] The decade that followed, the thirties, seemed for Surrealism a time of reasonings and counter-reasonings with respect to its own revolutionary stance, an arduous journey of thwarted political negotiations and tactical repositionings.

It seems significant that Breton's language in his theoretical writings of this period marked a greater preoccupation with the rootedness of revolutionary struggle within terrestrial life and, one could say, with attempts

20 Breton, *Manifestes du Surréalisme*, p. 91.
21 Breton, *Œuvres Complètes* III, p. 231.

at changing life as an 'old mole'. In the *Second Manifeste* Breton asserted that Surrealism 'plonge ses racines dans la vie'[22] ['plunges its roots into life'[23]], speculating that 'il est trop tard pour que la graine n'en germe pas à l'infini dans le champs humain'[24] ['it is too late for the seed not to sprout and grow in infinite abundance in the human field'[25]]. Adopting a similar style in *Les Vases Communicants*, Breton set out his vision of a Surrealist movement in the service of Marxist revolution, affirming that action was the most fundamental resource on earth.[26] At a lecture given in Brussels to the movement's Belgian members two years later, he explicitly dismissed any apparent ties between Surrealism and the transcendental, re-affirming its objective of deepening out the foundations of the real:

> Une certaine ambiguïté immédiate contenue dans ce mot (sur-réalisme) peut en effet conduire à penser qu'il désigne je ne sais quelle attitude transcendantale (consistant à se placer au-dessus du réel) alors qu'au contraire il exprime – et d'emblée a exprimé pour nous – une volonté d'approfondissement du réel, de prise de conscience toujours plus nette en même temps que toujours plus passionnée du monde sensible.[27]
>
> [A certain immediate ambiguity contained in the word Surrealism is capable, in fact, of leading one to suppose that it designates I know not what transcendental attitude (which consists in placing itself above the real), when on the contrary it expresses – and always has expressed for us – a desire to deepen the foundations of the real, to bring about an even clearer and at the same time ever more passionate consciousness of the world perceived by the senses.[28]]

These comments had also played their role in appeasing the *Parti Communiste Français* (PCF) (with whom the Surrealists had been seeking active

22 Breton, *Manifestes du Surréalisme*, p. 74.
23 Breton, *Manifestoes of Surrealism*, p. 124.
24 Breton, *Manifestes du Surréalisme*, p. 78.
25 Breton, *Manifestoes of Surrealism*, p. 129.
26 Breton, *Vases Communicants*, p. 59 – Breton's italics; Breton, *Communicating Vessels*, p. 46 – Breton's italics.
27 Breton, *Œuvres Complètes* II, pp. 230–231.
28 André Breton, 'What is Surrealism?' (1934) in *What is Surrealism?*, 2, p. 115 – 'which consists in placing itself above the real' was omitted in the published translation and has been added by me.

collaboration in the early 1930s) and their artistic wing, the Association of Revolutionary Writers and Artists.

By 1935, Breton had, however, severed ties with both groups. As has been well-documented, his attempts at establishing a *rapprochement* with the PCF seemed problematic from the start. On more than one occasion, he was viewed with suspicion simply for being 'Surrealist' and not merely 'communist', for daring to discuss issues which appeared personal or aesthetic rather than ideological. *Les Vases Communicants*, which sought a more than partial alignment of dialectical materialism with Surrealism, was received coldly by Communist Party ideologues, who felt its contents to be an implicit criticism of PCF policy. Despite their reservations, Breton had spent ten months lobbying to gain entry into the Communist Association of Revolutionary Writers and Artists, only to be ultimately rejected by them. The Surrealist journal *Surréalisme au service de la Révolution* had in its first issue promised that if imperialist nations ever declared war on the Soviets they would willingly follow the directives of the third international position of the French Communist Party;[29] yet the journal itself became the reason for most of the Surrealists' disagreements with the communists. When, for example, the journal published Dalí's exhibitionistic reverie 'Daydream', those Surrealists who were PCF members were called to account for what the communists saw as bourgeois degeneracy and a wilful indulgence in Freudian perversion. In coming to Dalí's defence (which he still felt able to do throughout the early thirties), Breton alienated Aragon, who, unhappy with the artist's provocative and wholly apolitical art works and other 'renegade' Surrealist publications, felt his own position as a Communist Party member compromised. Breton consequently endured two great losses: that of Aragon, who deserted Surrealism in favour of the communists and, somewhat later, that of René Crevel, who committed suicide after failing to see a reconciliation of Surrealism with the PCF. Characterised by struggle and loss, the early thirties were later described by Breton as a particularly 'convulsive' time in Surrealism's history. Despite these setbacks, his revolutionary outlook remained as steadfast as ever, as did his desire to confront social reality and change it for the better.

29 *Le Surréalisme au Service de la Révolution*, 1 (July, 1930), p. 1.

Perhaps Breton had not been enough of an 'old mole' to be accepted by the communists. He remained, after all, committed to art forms which foregrounded the personal and psychological. On the other hand, his actions had by no means constituted an 'inner immigration' from the world or a retreat into a self-contained aestheticism. Rather, they had highlighted the concerted efforts on his part to engage with the political avant-garde of France's radical left (for the PCF represented the biggest party devoted to revolutionary Marxism) and, most importantly, to engage with the re-ordering and subversion of the material world itself. Bataille himself later described Breton's stance during this time as 'irreproachable'[30] affirming that the former's position at that time was the only one he could have reasonably taken.[31]

In 1935 Breton joined Bataille in a revolutionary offensive against fascism which banded together under the name of Contre-Attaque. In this new Surrealist-dominated movement, which had set itself apart from the official Communist Party of France, any past differences between both men were put to one side in favour of addressing the immediate threat of fascism (*as well as* the excesses of communism and capitalism). Appealing to a sense of what was 'real', the second resolution of Contre-Attaque's manifesto read that its members were:

> 2. Décidés à réussir et non à discuter, nous considérons comme éliminé quiconque est incapable, oubliant une phraséologie politique sans issue, de passer à des considérations réalistes.[32]
>
> [2. Determined to succeed and not just to deliberate, we will, discarding the phraseology of political stalemate, consider anyone who is incapable of taking to realistic considerations as lost.]

30 Georges Bataille, 'La Religion Surréaliste' (1948) in *Œuvres Complètes* (Paris: Gallimard, 1976), vol. VII, p. 389; Georges Bataille, 'The Surrealist Religion' (1948) in *Absence of Myth*, p. 77.

31 Bataille, *Œuvres Complètes* VII, 389; Bataille, *Absence of Myth*, p. 77.

32 André Breton, 'Contre-Attaque – Union de lutte des intellectuels révolutionnaires' (1935) in *Œuvres Complètes* II, p. 496.

The manifesto was signed by Breton and Bataille who both went on to become members of the dominant sub-grouping of the movement named 'Sade'. In fact, the historical Sade along with Charles Fourier and Nietzsche were designated as the patron saints of the movement: 'Sade for perversity, Fourier for passion and Nietzsche for the abundance of forces and consent to the world'.[33] Under the aegis of Sade's biographer, Maurice Heine, a programme was to be drawn up which would also make the intended revolution a revolution in morality. A number of 'low' or desublimatory themes became the basis of this programme and, according to Surya, 'drew André Breton and his friends further than Surrealism was perhaps prepared to go'.[34] The policies proposed were to allow the free expression of sexual urges, including those considered 'neurotic', a full sanctioning of the free play of passions and the freed citizen to be made a candidate for all pleasures due to him or her. In fact, Contre-Attaque's tracts were full of appeals to violence and Sadean desire; figuratively speaking, the group sought the creation of its own monster, similar to the bull-headed creature who emblematised the Surrealists' concurrent project of *Minotaure* (a journal published 1933–1939) and powerful enough to slay its enemies, the miscreations of nationalism, Stalinism and capitalism. In effect, the group had combined the strategies of both Breton and Bataille in forging a collective revolutionary effort on the one hand (à la Breton) while appealing to the rage and chaos of revolutionary protest (as advocated by Bataille).

If Breton and his friends reconciled themselves to a more liberal stance on sexual mores, it was at this time also that Bataille – although stopping short of ever promoting sublimation and transposition – came to realise the benefits of Surrealism's creative potentiality. In addition to lending his hand to the project which would see a revolution in moral norms, Bataille joined Breton in promoting a form of fanaticism which would be incited through 'plans of exaltation' and thereby make use of the creative currents within the movement's membership. The aim of these plans was specifically to create inspiring works of art and poetry and forge new mythologies

33 Michel Surya, *Georges Bataille: An Intellectual Biography*, trans. by Krzysztof Fijalkowski and Michael Richardson (London: Verso, 2002), p. 222.

34 *Ibid.*, p. 221.

in order to rouse the public to revolution (and active participation in the movement).

In the same way that he had called upon all artists to embrace sublimation and unleash the powers of the conscious mind in the *Second Manifeste*, Breton had, with Bataille's blessing, employed the same persuasive rhetoric to encourage artists and poets to produce stirring works which would incite the masses to social revolt:

> Pour […] répondre […] à l'objection qui nous a été faite, à savoir que pour inculquer aux hommes une foi fanatique en ce que nous voulons, il fallait être d'emblée en possession des moyens de les fanatiser, je dirai que la détermination de ces moyens est en notre pouvoir, à condition qu'aucune aide ne nous manque précisément dans le cercle de ceux qui se sont montrés les plus aptes, sur le plan poétique ou artistique, à ce genre de détermination. C'est essentiellement à eux qu'il appartient, même en commission très fermé, d'élaborer un plan d'exaltation générale.[35]
>
> [….to respond […] to the objection which has been made that in order to inculcate into men a fanatical faith in what we want, it is essential to possess from the outset the means of rendering them fanatical, I will say that the establishment of these means lies within our capabilities provided that we are not wanting of the help specifically from the circle of those who have, on the poetic or artistic level, proven themselves to be the most skilled at this type of activity. Even with such a narrow mandate it is essentially for them to elaborate a general plan of exaltation.]

Interestingly, Bataille himself was no stranger to the sorts of 'projects of exaltation' to which Breton alluded. In 1922, he had, on the basis of academic merit, been sent to the School of Advanced Spanish Studies in Madrid, where he had suffered from a sense of despairing isolation. To overcome this, he had devised different formulae for 'provoked dreaming' to 'imaginer des baisers brûlants ou des crépuscules parfumés en regardant des figures pas plus expressives qu'un pot allemand de bière ou une cravate à dix-neuf sous'[36] ['imagine burning kisses or fragrant dusks while looking

35 André Breton, 'Trois interventions d'André Breton à Contre-Attaque' in *Œuvres Complètes* II, p. 593.

36 One of three undated letters written to Marie-Louise Bataille between February to July 1922 in Georges Bataille, *Choix de Lettres* 1917–1962, ed. by Michel Surya (Paris: Gallimard, 1997), pp. 26–27.

at statuettes that are no more expressive than a German beer glass or a tuppenny neck tie'[37]]. The methods that he developed were recorded in his correspondence and show that he was, in the final stage, aiming at 'elation'. As his biographer states:

> The instruction to become elated is strangely reminiscent of Nietzsche; Bataille, alone in Madrid and still a Christian [...] was himself experimenting with techniques and thinking which relate in different ways both to Surrealism and to Nietzsche.[38]

Three years later Bataille was sent a photograph of a form of torture practised in China and known as the Torture of a Hundred Pieces. The photo depicted the ecstatic gaze of a man who was being cut into a hundred pieces for committing murder. By highlighting the inexpressible blend of joy and pain in death, the photo had an immediate and decisive impact upon Bataille, who felt a great kinship and love for the victim: 'This was a role equal, one can assume, to that of the discovery of laughter, and to that of Nietzsche: a role that shook his world to the core'.[39]

A similar capacity to elate and inspire to a backdrop of brutality and horror almost certainly nourished Bataille's fascination with Nazism in the 1930s at the time that he had joined Contre-Attaque (indeed, he had seen first-hand evidence of such awe-inspiring campaigns while convalescing in Italy in 1934). In fact, Bataille had maintained a longstanding interest in the perversity of fascism and taught the Surrealists much of what they knew about it. He also believed that the method of propagandistically elevating culture and myth to garner support could be adapted by Contre-Attaque in its rallying cry for revolution: 'Nous entendons à notre tour nous servir des armes créés par le fascisme qui a su utiliser l'aspiration fondamentale des hommes à l'exaltation affective et au fanatisme'[40] ['We intend in our turn to use for our benefit the weapons created by fascism, which has been able to use humanity's fundamental aspirations for effective exaltation and fanaticism'].

37 Surya, *An Intellectual Biography*, p. 40.

38 *Ibid.*, pp. 40–41.

39 *Ibid.*, p. 94.

40 Bataille, *Œuvres Complètes* I, p. 384.

Bataille proposed a co-option of the methods of Nazism with a view to developing a 'high' culture to rival that of fascist Germany and which consisted precisely of all those art forms he had previously rejected such as poetry and painting. He believed Surrealism would have a valid role to play in the establishment of this high culture. The creative talents of Contre-Attaque's Surrealist contingent, if harnessed correctly, could serve to exalt the populace and incite it to direct action against enemy ideologies.

Thus, Bataille rather paradoxically used his membership of Contre-Attaque not only to agitate for a moral revolution based on the twin monstrosities of violence and Sadean desire, but also to promote its ideological and cultural wing in the manner of the *suraigles* of imperialism – an action which only some years ago he had derided: 'he was where no one expected him to be, exhorting the servile person to violence, to be finally raised up and impassioned all the more for being destined to failure'.[41] Under his influence, Contre-Attaque sought to ascend to similar heights to the imperialist-nationalist *suraigles* against which its campaign was directed and whose Icarian downfall it wanted, rather hazardously, to orchestrate from there. Bataille thus found himself borrowing the ideas and practices from the two most homogenising political movements of the early twentieth century: communism, with its emphasis on overthrowing the bourgeoisie and establishing a collectivity of equals; and National Socialism, with its promotion of high culture and neo-pagan mythologies aimed at reinforcing the common origins of the Germanic Aryans.

It must be said that while Bataille was greatly intrigued by fascism, he did not sympathise with its basic beliefs.[42] A fellow member of Contre-Attaque characterised the dark appeal of totalitarianism which had held sway over Bataille and his associates:

41 Surya, *An Intellectual Biography*, p. 225.

42 See 'Everything calls for death which ravages us' in Surya, *An Intellectual Biography*, pp. 235–247. Surya makes the case that *Acéphale* actively opposed anti-Semitism and contested the fascists' false appropriation of Nietzsche (who was more anti-German than anything else). Bataille could not in his view have been a fascist therefore.

> this human ocean that Bataille had consigned to the storm produced waves of revolutionary romanticism which carried him along with his friends and so many others [...]. There is an inevitable movement from anguish to intoxication over fascist experience among Bataille and his friends. Later, the influence of Hitler's neopaganism was patent in the case of Acéphale.[43]

At this time Bataille would begin to see Surrealism not as the enemy camp but as the movement best equipped for creating the mythologies of a new age. In this regard, he would concur with Breton, who in 1935 had underlined the importance of Surrealism creating collective rather than personal myths.[44] In an interview in 1946, the latter likewise affirmed that Bataille was, on account of his breadth of knowledge and the untamed nature of his ideas, well qualified to help Surrealism in the creation of such myths.[45]

In the aftermath of the war, Bataille stated that the one prevailing myth which constituted a 'wretched void' and 'ruin of the universe'[46] was the absence of myth itself. Society had denied the validity of ancient myth founded on a mediation between humans and the natural world through which its cohesion and purpose was established. As a result, the sacred structures of society had been lost, in particular those of communication and community. It was in this vacuum that Surrealism had a role to play:

> il est évident que lorsque le surréalisme a mis en avant l'idée de mythe, il répondit à une nostalgie vivante dans l'esprit des hommes actuels, vivante non seulement depuis Nietzsche mais même depuis le romantisme allemand. De plus, ce qui constitue la religion est la liaison au mythe des rites. Or, personne n'ignore actuellement que la tendance nettement assurée du surréalisme est d'arriver à retrouver les attitudes qui ont permis aux hommes primitifs de se réunir dans des rites et plus exactement de retrouver dans des rites les formes les plus aiguës, les plus tangibles de la vie poétique.

43 Henri Dubief, 'Témoignage sur Contre-Attaque' in *Textures*, no. 6 (Brussels: Jan, 1970), pp. 56–57.

44 André Breton, 'Position politique de l'art aujourd'hui' (1935) in *Œuvres Complètes* II, p. 439; André Breton, 'Political Position of Surrealism' (1935) in *Manifestoes of Surrealism*, p. 232. Breton does not however elaborate on the value of Surrealism perpetuating such a collective myth.

45 Breton, *Œuvres Complètes* III, p. 599.

46 Georges Bataille, 'L'Absence de Mythe' (1947) in *Œuvres Complètes* XI, p. 236; Breton, *Absence of Myth*, p. 48.

> Tout ce que Breton met en avant, qu'il s'agisse de cette recherche du sacré, du souci des mythes, de retrouver les rites semblables à ceux des primitifs, représente cette exploration de la possibilité [...] d'explorer tout ce qui peut être exploré par l'homme, il s'agit de reconstituer tout ce qui était dans le fond de l'homme avant que cette nature humaine n'ait été asservie par la nécessité du travail technique.[47]
>
> [it is evident that when Surrealism put forward the idea of myth, it was in response to a vibrant nostalgia in the mind of contemporary peoples, which has been alive not only since Nietzsche but even since German Romanticism. Moreover, religion is constituted by the connection to the myth of rituals. No one, then, can fail to know that the clearest certainty of Surrealism is to manage to rediscover attitudes of the mind that allowed primitive man to unite in ritual and, more precisely, to find in ritual the most incisive and tangible forms of poetic life. Everything that Breton has put forward – whether it contains the quest for the sacred, the concern with myths, or rediscovering rituals similar to those of primitives – represents the exploration of the possibility [...] of exploring all that can be explored by man, it is a question of reconstituting all that was fundamental to man before human nature had been enslaved by the necessity for technical work.[48]]

However, before these words were written, Contre-Attaque experienced fissures which resulted in the breaking away of the Bretonian Surrealists. Bataille's dalliance with what they termed 'surfascism'[49] was ultimately

47 Bataille, *Œuvres Complètes* VII, p. 386.

48 Bataille, *Absence of Myth*, p. 75. The words 'combine in ritual' in the original translation have been changed by me to 'unite in ritual'.

49 'Les adhérents surréalistes du groupe "Contre-Attaque" enregistrent avec satisfaction la dissolution dudit groupe au sein duquel s'étaient manifestées des tendances dites "surfascistes", dont le caractère purement fasciste s'est montré de plus en plus flagrant. Ils désavouent par avance toute publication qui pourrait être faite au nom de "Contre-Attaque"' ['The surrealist adherents of the group "Contre-Attaque" note with satisfaction the dissolution of the aforementioned group at the heart of which so-called "surfascist" tendencies have presented themselves, whose purely fascist character has become increasingly obvious. They hereby disavow any future publication which could be made in the name of "Contre-Attaque"'] – André Breton, Adolphe Acker, Claude Cahun, Marcel Jean, Suzanne Malherbe, Georges Mouton, Henri Pastoureau, Benjamin Péret, 'La Rupture avec "Contre-Attaque"' in *Tracts Surréalistes et Déclarations Collectives 1922–1939*, ed. by José Pierre (Paris: Le terrain vague, 1980), vol. 1.

unacceptable to them and, as a consequence, they repudiated any involvement with the movement. Although Bataille had tried to appropriate only the methods of fascist propaganda in order to transcend it, many of Contre-Attaque's members were concerned that his fascination with the movement had become unhealthy, reflecting an enthralment with fascism proper.

If Breton had become known as the Pope of Surrealism in the late 1920s, Bataille now became infamous for appointing himself the chief minister of a new secret society entitled *Acéphale* – the mystical, neopagan grouping that he might have liked Surrealism to be.[50] The sect-like society afforded him the opportunity of indulging his interest in mythology and exalted fanaticism, which he had been unable to do unchecked in *Contre-Attaque* and, from its inception, he expounded beliefs that seemed mystical in nature. Although it was clear that any traditional notions of transcendence such as the God of Christianity or the *telos* of Hegelianism were rejected in this credo, a notion of secular transcendence did exist in the sense that Bataille sought to overcome the emptiness of the world by losing himself in Dionysian ecstasy and similar oceanic states.

In response to the inner retreat occasioned by *Acéphale*, the Surrealists published an article on Bataille entitled 'Nom de Dieu' ('Name of God') which was redolent of his attack on Breton in 1930 and critiqued his growing fascination with transcendence and idealism:

> M. Bataille avait disparu. Que faisait-il ? […] M. Bataille faisait des enfants. Et des enfants spirituels […] une marmaille qui vient de prononcer ses premiers mots. Dieu, Poésie, Esprit, Religion, Mystique. Les mots suivants seront sans doute : Pape, Eglise, Christ, Première Communion, Carême […]. Le Surréalisme – qui a changé, change et changera – est dorénavant lié à l'aventure humaine, à l'entreprise humaine. D'ailleurs à voir *Messages*, le Surréalisme ne nous semble remplaçable que par des vieilles lunes, la vieille lune idéaliste par exemple.[51]

50 Following the Second World War, Bataille would frequently refer to Surrealism as a religion, hence recasting it in his own image. Breton, however, generally avoided the term 'religion' to describe the movement.

51 Noël Arnaud, Maurice Blanchard, Charles Bocquet, Jacques Bureau, J.-F. Chabrun, Paul Chancel, Christian Dotremont, Pierre Dumayet, Aline Gagnaire, Jean Hoyaux, Laurence Iche, Rene Magritte, et al. 'Nom de Dieu' (1943) in *Tracts Surréalistes*

> [Mr Bataille disappeared. What was he doing? [...] Mr Bataille was having children. Spiritual children in fact [...] a horde of brats who have just uttered their first words. God, Poetry, Spirit, Religion, Mysticism. Its next words will undoubtedly be: Pope, Church, Christ, First Communion, Lent [...]. Surrealism – which has changed, continues to change and will change again – is henceforth linked to the human adventure. What is more, from seeing *Messages*, Surrealism would seem to us only to have been succeeded only by old moons, the old idealist moon, for example.]

Messages was the name of the journal Bataille was working on at that time and which, according to the Surrealists, had ambitions of replacing Surrealism. What was significant about this was that Bataille and Breton were now cast in exactly the reverse roles to those they had assumed ten years previously: while the Surrealists vaunted themselves as the 'old moles' who were closest to human life, Bataille was sardonically dismissed as 'the old moon' of sublimatory idealism.

Although many Surrealists signed the denunciation of Bataille, Breton's name was not amongst them; nor did Bataille, in his turn, allow himself to be provoked by the article or engage in the sort of lampooning of Breton which had characterised his writings in the early 1930s. Bataille did not, however, forget Surrealism; indeed, its haunting presence would ensure that for many years after these divisions, it would remain the subject of his writings.

In principle *Acéphale*'s programme underlined its function as a socially subversive movement. It announced for example that it strove to overcome the curse which 'sends men to wars they do not want, forcing them to a labour whose fruits escape them'.[52] In practice, however, the movement remained self-enclosed and secretive, its philosophical orientation geared towards the experience or exploration of extreme or liminal states, centring around eroticism, pain, death and emptiness. Bataille had consciously constructed the group on a heterological basis, attempting to bind its members together emotionally through a collective participation in extreme acts,

---

et Déclarations Collectives 1940–1969, ed. José Pierre (Paris: Terrain Vague, 1982), vol. 2, p. 9.

52 Georges Bataille, 'Programme (Relative to Acéphale)' in *The Bataille Reader*, ed. by Fred Botting and Scott Wilson (Oxford: Blackwell, 1997), p. 121.

a cohesiveness which was the stronger for distinguishing itself from the social ties of the outside world, governed as they were by more mundane concerns (such as family, work, political affiliation).

Acéphale's programme was in many ways a response to Nietzsche's proclamation that God was dead, embodying 'the irresolvable contradiction of ipse caught between divine absence and a return to undifferentiated, continuous being (death)'.[53] *Ipse* was a term Bataille had taken from Latin to refer to the discontinuous, atomic self alienated from the rest of the world and fundamentally distinct from those states which he considered as continuous (such as eroticism, death and mystical self-transcendence). *Acéphale* was thus a kind of religion created out of the wound left by the absence of God. For the individual to find his/her moorings within this wound, it was necessary to live out the most extreme experiences in order to reach to the limits of existence itself. This could equally be the pursuit of an ecstatic Dionysian eroticism, or, the drawing into oneself of the terror and decomposition of death from the macrocosm 'comme achèvement et non comme négation de l'être'[54] ['as the attainment not as the negation of being'[55]]. In other words, one would seek to internalise the very essence of Eros and Thanatos.

Bataille provided his initiates with instructions on to how to reach such a state (through an invocation of Thanatos) in a meditation entitled 'La Pratique de la Joie devant la Mort' (1939) ('The Practice of Joy before Death'). Here he provided the formula for an ecstatic contemplation not dissimilar to the type that he had devised as a student in Madrid and comparable to those he would devise in later works (*L'Expérience Intérieure*, 1943 and *Méthode de Méditation*, 1947). Although the meditation purportedly ended in a blowing out or a self-annihilation of the type which we would associate with Buddhism, it did engage the imagination to accomplish this – and again, we detect the influence of Surrealism here. One of the

53 Andrew Hussey, *The Inner Scar: The Mysticism of Georges Bataille* (Amsterdam: Rodopi, 2000), p. 68.

54 Georges Bataille, 'En Marge d'"Acéphale" – Programme' in *Œuvres Complètes* II, p. 273.

55 Bataille, *Bataille Reader*, p. 121 – translation modified by me.

images that Bataille recommended the reader to concentrate on was his/her own dissolution in the depths of the sky:

> 'La profondeur du ciel, l'espace perdu est joie devant la mort: tout est profondément fêlé.'
> 'Je me représente que la terre tourne vertigineusement dans le ciel.'
> 'Je me représente le ciel lui-même glissant, tournant et se perdant.'
> 'Le soleil, comparable à un alcool, tournant et éclatant à perdre la respiration.'
> [.....]
>
> 'Si je me représente dans une vision et dans un halo qui transfigure le visage extasié et épuisé d'un être mourant, ce qui irradie de ce visage éclaire de sa nécessité le nuage du ciel, dont la lueur grise devient alors plus pénétrante que celle du soleil lui-même. Dans cette représentation, la mort apparaît de la même nature que la lumière qui éclaire, dans la mesure où celle-ci se perd à partir de son foyer.'[56]
>
> ['The depth of the sky, lost space is joy before death: everything is profoundly cracked.' 'I imagine the earth turning vertiginously in the sky.' 'I imagine the sky itself slipping, turning, and lost.' 'The sun, comparable to alcohol, turning and bursting breathlessly.'
> [.....]
>
> 'If I imagine myself in a vision and in a halo that transfigures the ecstatic and exhausted face of a dying being, what radiates from that face illuminates with its necessity the clouds in the sky, whose grey glow then becomes more penetrating than the light of the sun itself. In this vision, death appears to be of the same nature as the illuminating light, to the extent that light is lost once it leaves its source.'[57]]

The man who once pictured an Icarian Breton bringing about his annihilation in the vault of the heavens now actively exhorted others to do precisely this, albeit only by way of a meditation. Moreover, he would return to this motif of celestial self-annihilation many times over in his writings. While Bataille may not have become the idealist the Surrealists claimed him to be, he would for some time continue to employ the forms and terminology of mystical and esoteric movements. Furthermore, Acéphale remained

56 Georges Bataille, 'La Pratique de la Joie devant la Mort' (1939) in *Œuvres Complètes* I, pp. 553–554.

57 Georges Bataille, 'The Practice of Joy before Death' (1939) in *Visions of Excess*, pp. 238–239.

inaccessible for the uninitiated, reflecting an insulation from the world which has more often been imputed to Surrealism.

From the time of his involvement in *Acéphale* to the publication of his major treatise on eroticism (*L'Érotisme*, 1957) Bataille came increasingly to relate the erotic to the extremities of (wo)man's 'inner experience' and their sacred basis. He developed a theory of sexuality which distinguished the 'eroticism' of humanity from the brute, unthinking sexuality of animals. This led him to consider also the precise relationship between sublimating civilisation and the erotic and which, paradoxically, helped him to formulate conclusions which both he and Breton could agree upon. As will be demonstrated later in the chapter, Breton, who rejected any repressive model of civilisation, openly expressed his approval of Bataille's theory of erotic transgression and its capacity to subvert civilised mores.

Some of the commonalities between Breton and Bataille concerning eroticism and transgression were prefigured in the journal *Minotaure*, a predominantly Surrealist publication, which nonetheless coopted some of the conceptual territory of *Documents*. Within its pages was evidence that Bretonian Surrealism was engaging with some of the morbid themes so typical of Bataillean thought, without, however, compromising the movement's values or marking a point of regression in its intellectual orientation.

Minotaure, Untamed Desire and Desublimatory Art

As a journal which was originally conceived as a successor to Bataille's *Documents*[58] by its publishers but fell largely under the control of the Bretonian Surrealists, and whose title betrayed a confluence with the ideas of Bataille yet operated almost entirely without him, *Minotaure* was certainly anomalous within the history of Surrealist journal publication. Even though Bataille

58 *Documents* had folded in January 1931.

declined a senior position on the publication's editorial board, his spectre hung over it in a subtle yet persistent way. The journal's name 'Minotaure' was probably chosen by Roger Vitrac, another 'Surrealist dissident'; though according to Bataille's biographer the name encapsulated the interests of Bataille and Masson who had nurtured a fascination for Greek myth since 1924. As José Pierre remarks: 'It was [...] easy to see the influence of Bataille and *Documents* in *Minotaure*, particularly in a marked bent for the horrible and also in a semblance of scientific analysis applied in pursuit of a kind of "frenzied" style'.[59] This nominally Surrealist journal warrants attention precisely on account of its articles on scabrous or desublimatory themes which were more redolent of *Documents* and sometimes provided by its former contributors.

In the eighth edition of the journal, Bataille's name joined Breton's amongst the list of its correspondents, though by this time both men had already collaborated on the activities of *Contre-Attaque*. Bataille's article was a short meditation entitled 'Le Bleu du Ciel' ('The Blue of Noon' – later to be incorporated into *L'Expérience Intérieure* and not to be confused with the novel of the same name). Like the later *Acéphale* text 'La Pratique de la joie devant la mort', this article provided the reader with instructions on how to bring about the dissolution of the self by contemplating the ego's destruction in the sky:

> C'est seulement par le moyen d'une représentation maladive – un œil s'ouvrant au sommet de ma propre tête [...] que l'être humain, oublié sur la Terre – tel qu'aujourd'hui je me révèle à moi-même, tombé, sans espoir, dans l'oubli – accède tout à coup à la chute déchirante dans le vide du ciel.[60]
>
> [It is only by means of a sickly representation – an eye opening at the summit of my own head [...] that human nature, forgotten here on earth – such as I am today revealed to myself, fallen, without hope, in oblivion – gain access suddenly to the heart-rending fall into the void of the sky.[61]]

59 José Pierre, 'André Breton and/or "Minotaure."' trans. by André Marling, in *Focus on Minotaure: The Animal-Headed Review*, ed. by Charles Goerg (Geneva: Musée d'Art et d'Histoire, 1987), p. 99.

60 Georges Bataille, 'Le Bleu du Ciel' in *Minotaure*, no. 8 (1938), p. 51.

61 Georges Bataille, 'The Blue of Noon' in *Inner Experience* (Albany, NY: State University of New York, 1988), p. 78.

Rather than arraign the Surrealists for annihilating themselves by an excess of Icarian idealism, Bataille again advocated the process himself, albeit to different ends (again, as a means of experiencing the fundamental emptiness of the universe in a quasi-mystical yet secular fashion).

By the time of the eighth edition, Breton had, for his part, admitted the presence of an increasing number of themes which would previously have been associated with Bataille. Given the *leitmotif* of the journal, one senses that his confrontation with more tenebrous issues was ineluctable. Though had the figure of the Minotaur ever been so remote from Surrealist thinking? In many ways not, for the Minotaur as half-man, half-beast seemed precisely the sort of hybrid creation which was favoured in Surrealist iconography and according to Gérard Fabre even represented something of Surrealism's aspiration to reconcile all antinomies.[62] The monstrous associations of the journal's title evoked the social upheaval needed for a more progressive society and were therefore conceived as 'à rebours de toutes les conceptions rétrogrades'[63] ['contrary to all retrograde conceptions']. This endowed the violence of the journal's bestiary with a degree of social utility which precluded the descent into barbarism.

In addition to its social utility, the animalistic rawness of the Minotaur evoked the nature of the *id*, the seat of the instincts, which as a concept so fascinated the Surrealists in their readings of Freud. Breton was himself preoccupied with baser themes at the time, a fact which was reflected in his literary output. Concurrent with his stewardship of *Minotaure*, he wrote *L'Anthologie de l'Humour Noir* and *L'Amour Fou*, which offered explicit concessions to the more scabrous aspects of human existence. Breton created the latter work out of a series of articles he had published in *Minotaure*.[64] In the section of the novel entitled 'Le Château Étoilé' ('The Starry Castle') he highlighted not only the transgressive nature of love but also eulogised

62 Georges Bataille, 'The Blue of Noon' in *Inner Experience* (Albany, NY: State University of New York, 1988), p. 78.

63 'Eternité de Minotaure' ['Eternity of Minotaure'] in *Minotaure*, nos. 12–13 (1939), p. 1.

64 'La Beauté sera Convulsive' ['Beauty will be Convulsive'], no. 5; 'La Nuit du Tournesol' ['The Night of the Sunflower'], no. 7; 'Le Château Étoilé' ['The Starry Castle'], no. 8.

carnal love and its more perverse manifestations.[65] In the same article he also paid tribute to the 'sublime imagination' of Sade, and presented an earnest attempt to gain insights into the nature of evil more generally:

> Le problème du mal ne vaut d'être soulevé que tant qu'on n'en sera pas quitte avec l'idée de la transcendance d'un bien quelconque qui pourrait dicter à l'homme des devoirs. Jusque-là la représentation exaltée du 'mal' inné gardera la plus grande valeur révolutionnaire.[66]
>
> [The problem of evil is worth discussing only for as long as we have finished with the idea of the transcendency of some good or other which could dictate to man his duty. Until that time, the exalted representation of an innate 'evil' will retain the greatest revolutionary value.]

Interestingly, Breton had again dismissed the notion of the transcendental as well as highlighting the revolutionary potential of evil. Surya remarks that 'as if yielding to the Greek night and its chthonian monsters, Breton [...] approved the reading of Sade that Bataille had made against him'.[67] To further promote his contemporaries' understanding of Sade, Breton now ensured that the latter's biographer, Maurice Heine (a former *Documents* collaborator), was on the editorial board of Minotaure and that his name appeared on the contents page of every edition. A regular contributor to the journal, he sought to expound the nature of perversion and present an honest account of the life of the Marquis to a wider audience in the most disinterested and amoral way.

Significantly, Breton's keenness to give him a prominent role in Minotaure, in addition to his statements in 'Le Château Étoilé', seem to contradict the image of a man entirely concerned with the romantic or exclusive aspects of love, bespeaking instead a willingness on his part to give a forum to perverse discourse.[68] Breton's readiness to have Heine preside

65 André Breton, 'Le Château Étoilé' in *Minotaure*, 8, 29 – full quotation given in Chapter 5.

66 André Breton, 'Le Château Étoilé' in *Minotaure*, 8, p. 39.

67 Surya, *An Intellectual Biography*, p. 194.

68 This again defies the common view of Breton as being hostile to perversion and censorial, a view which can be attributed to his statements in *Recherches sur la Sexualité*.

over the moral agenda of *Contre-Attaque* (as mentioned in the previous section of this book) also showed that his support of such discourse was not limited to the theoretical but extended into the programmatic. Heine's findings were of use to the extent that they could be adapted to the aims and ambitions of Surrealism's liberatory campaigns in the socio-political sphere, and thus be translated into reality.

In a double edition of the journal (covering editions 3 and 4), Heine discussed the merits and drawbacks of a schema of 'perversions' inspired by the studies of psychiatrist Krafft-Ebing (see Figure 2.1).

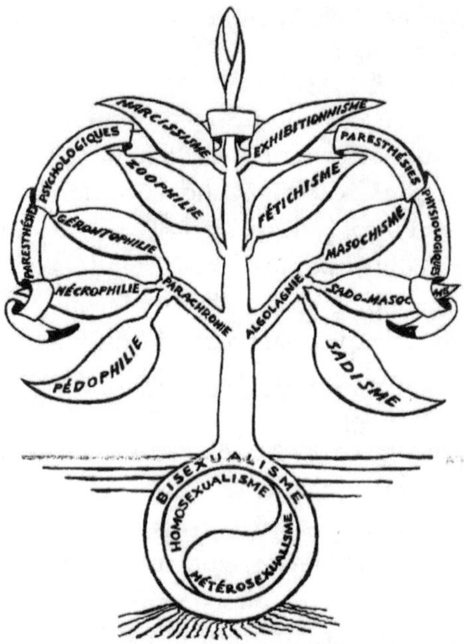

Figure 2.1: Taxonomy of 'Perversions' or Sexual Paresthesias as reproduced in Maurice Heine's 'Note sur un Classement Psycho-Biologique des Paresthésies sexuelles'.

Here, he approves of perversion generally while inveighing against homosexuality (except in women, Jean Lorrain and Sade); condemning libertinism (except when it is at the service of a higher goal such as the pursuit of love); and expressing a relative indifference to the practice of Sado-masochism (while defending the historical figure of Sade).

He underlined the objectivity with which Krafft-Ebing approached his field, for even the term 'perversion' could be displaced 'en adoptant une fois pour toutes le terme de *paresthésie* qui libère avantageusement le psychobiologiste de tout préjugé éthico-religieux'[69] ['in adopting once and for all the term *paresthesia* which, much to his advantage, frees the psychobiologist from all ethical and religious prejudice'].

Heine praised the schema for bringing together apparently distinct perversions or dispositions which would appear to exclude one another – like homo- and heterosexuality, sadism and masochism. Yet he also affirmed that in certain respects it did not go far enough in unifying the various forms of paresthesia, for the experiences of real people corresponded rather to 'cas intermédiaires', in other words, to cases in which two or more perversions have been combined. Heine suggested that Sade's writings would have an invaluable role to play in laying bare the compound perversions of actual people and thereby providing the sorts of case histories missing from contemporaneous scholarship on the subject.

It would have been interesting to know Breton's opinion on this very different approach to reconciling contrary states (which was, after all, substantially different from the dialectical resolution of antinomies he had proposed in the *Second Manifeste*). He did not address this question directly in his writings; yet he did praise the systematic nature of Heine's Sadean studies, which, in *Anthologie de l'Humour Noir*, he described as:

> une suite ininterrompue de conquêtes. Grâce à M. Maurice Heine l'immense portée de l'œuvre sadiste est aujourd'hui hors de cause : psychologiquement elle peut passer pour la plus authentique devancière de celle de Freud et de toute la psychopathologie moderne ; socialement elle ne tend à rien moins qu'à l'établissement, différé de révolution en révolution, d'une véritable science de mœurs.[70]
>
> [an unbroken string of triumphs. Thanks to Maurice Heine, the immense significance of Sade's writing is now beyond question: psychologically speaking, it can be

69 Maurice Heine, 'Note sur un Classement Psycho-Biologique des Paresthésies sexuelles' ['Note on the Psycho-Biological Classification of Sexual Paresthesias'] in *Minotaure*, 3–4 (1933), p. 36.

70 André Breton, 'D.-A.-F. de Sade', 'Anthologie de l'Humour Noir' in *Œuvres Complètes* II, pp. 890–891.

> considered the most authentic precursor of Freud's work and of modern psychopathology in general; socially, it aims at nothing less than the establishment of a true science of mores, which has been deferred from revolution to revolution.][71]

Here again, Breton relied on Heine's exposition of Sade to call specifically for a science of mores, again showing the practical value of the biographer's writings; for what previous revolutions had overlooked, Surrealism would mend with the help of the scholar's findings.

Two of Heine's other articles within *Minotaure* are similarly of great interest, especially in how they related both to Bretonian and Bataillean thinking. In Minotaure no. 6, Heine dedicated an article to the fetishism of women's footwear in the work of French libertine author and Sade contemporary Rétif de la Bretonne[72] (from whom the term for shoe fetishism or 'retifism' is derived). The article outlined the significance of this fetishism to the author, in particular the significance of props and clothing in the appreciation of the female form as compared to exposure to the naked body alone. While the object of fetish was always the foot's container rather than the foot itself, Rétif's work had a scandalous impact and contained numerous pornographic elements (alluded to in the article). The piece seems an ideal complement to Bataille's 'Le Gros Orteil' ('The Big Toe') in *Documents*, no. 6 (1929), in which he presented the big toe as emblematic of humanity's low, animalistic nature, being the most '*human* part of the human body'.[73] In his view the toe belonged to the repressed axis of (wo)man, the horizontal; its exposure was generally unwelcome for recalling (wo)man's fundamental rootedness in the grime of the earth and also for the base seduction it represented. The article is considered pivotal in expounding Bataille's philosophy of base materialism by members of the October group[74] whereas its counterpart

71 André Breton, 'D.-A.-F. de Sade' in *Anthology of Black Humour*, trans. by Mark Polizzotti (San Francisco, CA: City Light Books, 1997), p. 18.

72 Maurice Heine, 'Rétif de la Bretonne et la Femme Féique' ['Rétif de la Bretonne and the Fairy Woman'] in *Minotaure*, 6 (1935), pp. 53–56.

73 Georges Bataille, 'Le Gros Orteil' in *Documents*, ed. by Bernard Noël (Paris: Mercure de France / Gallimard, 1968), p. 75. Bataille's italics.

74 In *Formless* Krauss and Bois frequently cite the text as an example of Bataille's defiance of sublimation. For example, 'The rotation implied by this lowering is one of

in *Minotaure* (and its relation to Surrealism proper) has more usually been passed over. While the focus of the article on Rétif was admittedly literary (rather than underpinning a philosophy of life), it is apparent that Breton, who held great sway over editorial matters, approved the article's publication and would undoubtedly have sabotaged it if he had found the subject matter too unseemly or at variance with the objectives of Surrealism.

Heine's other article, entitled 'Eritis sicut Dii' in *Minotaure*, no. 11, examined a number of Tibetan sculptures embodying the erotic union of the Gods Shakti and Shiva, which in the eyes of Tibetan Buddhists attests not to some base profanity but to the innocence of physical love and the naturalness of procreation. Referring to a photograph taken by Raoul Ubac, in which we are confronted by a scene of divine mating, Heine wrote 'Chaque partenaire contribue à exalter jusqu'à son expression suprême l'inégalable sadisme du couple'[75] ['Each partner helped to raise to supreme heights the expression of the couple's insuperable Sadism'].

Clearly, the sculptures of Heine's article embodied both a ferocity and an innocence which would have captured the imagination of Breton and Bataille. We may be reminded of Breton's description of an individual's state of mind during the act of love described in *Le Château Étoilé* as 'l'incapacité où sont le plus grand nombre des hommes de se libérer dans l'amour de toute préoccupation étrangère à l'amour, de toute crainte comme de tout doute, de s'exposer sans défense au regard foudroyant du dieu'[76] ['the incapacity of most people, even in love, to free themselves from any preoccupation foreign to it, from every fear as from every doubt, exposing themselves without defence to the furious gaze of god'[77]]. In discussing the commonalities of mystical ecstasy and eroticism Bataille also wondered

---

the strategies put to work in the most insistent way by Bataille (it governs many texts in *Documents*, such as the entries "Bouche" [Mouth] and "Le Gros Orteil" [The Big Toe]): man is proud of being erect (and of having thus emerged from the animal state, the biological mouth-anus axis of which is horizontal), but this pride is founded on a repression' (Bois, *Formless*, p. 26). See also Bois, *Formless*, pp. 50–51.

75 Maurice Heine, 'Eritis sicut Dii' in *Minotaure*, 11 (1938), p. 33.

76 André Breton, 'Le Château Étoilé' in *Minotaure*, 8, p. 37.

77 Breton, *Mad Love*, p. 93. Translation slightly modified by me (the word 'foudroyant' has been translated as 'furious' rather than 'overwhelming').

whether 'la peur, justement, ne fonde pas le "sexuel"; et si la relation du "mystique" et du "sexuel" ne tient pas à ce caractère abyssal, à cette obscurité angoissante, qui appartiennent également à l'un et à l'autre domaine'[78] ['fear is not precisely what does underlie "sex"; and whether the connection between "mystic" and "sexual" has not something to do with the gulfs of terrifying darkness that belong equally to both domains'[79]].

Heine's interest in the omnipotence of physical desire was shared by a number of Surrealist artists who attempted to give expression to the instinctual life in works of art which also featured in *Minotaure*. These works are especially significant in establishing a Surrealist view of non-repressive sublimation for they demonstrate again that Surrealist art didn't necessarily foreclose the material or the base. Indeed, for many of the artists showcased in *Minotaure* – including Dalí, Giacometti, Masson, Ernst, Picasso and Bellmer – art became a conduit to the desublimatory or perverse instincts of the psyche. This is significant for, although they were all involved themselves in the activities of the Bretonian Surrealists (even after periods of estrangement), they are frequently regarded as distant or marginal to the latter or as covert sympathisers of Bataille.

Until his departure from the movement in the late 1930s, Salvador Dalí was one of Surrealism's foremost exponents of a more sexualised (and indeed perverse) form of art. In an article entitled 'De la beauté terrifiante et comestible de l'architecture Modern Style' ('On the terrifying and edible beauty of Modern Style architecture'), he theorised upon the role of perversion within aesthetics, stating that 'la beauté n'est que la somme de conscience de nos perversions'[80] ['beauty is only the conscious survey of our perversions']. He claimed that erotic desire supplanted all traditional notions of the aesthetic rooted in an intellectualised Kantian appreciation of beauty (which he referred to as 'the Venus of logic') and replaced these with perverse and anti-aesthetic gestures ('the Venus of bad taste').

78 Bataille, *Œuvres Complètes* X, p. 219.

79 Bataille, *Erotism*, p. 222.

80 Salvador Dalí, 'De la beauté terrifiante et comestible, de l'architecture Modern Style' ['On the terrifying and edible beauty of Art Nouveau architecture'] in *Minotaure*, 3–4, p. 76 (pp. 69–76).

One presumes that Breton, with his control over editorial matters and his claims on the artist himself (who then was still a member of Surrealism's inner cabal), must have sanctioned, albeit tacitly, the contents of the article.

This tacit approval may have come from an awareness of Dalí's keen interest in Freudian theory and the prospect that he may even have been guided by a notion of sublimation (since the immediacy of indulging in actual perversion is substituted by a visual elaboration of such an indulgence). Then again, if Dalí's more sexualised works could be considered sublimatory, they nonetheless presupposed the full flight of the instincts rather their masking, elevation or recoding.

Dalí's focus on perversion – particularly in the context of the 'the Venus of bad taste' – even began to evoke Bataillean thinking. This convergence was also apparent in Dalí's most successful Surrealist project: the manufacture of symbolic objects (*objets à fonctionnement symbolique*), which frequently assumed an overt sexual meaning. Constructing these suggestive assemblages of arbitrary bric-a-brac became something of a craze for the Surrealists in the early 1930s, and not least for Breton, 'one of the most assiduous makers of Surrealist objects'[81] since he had, for a long time, wanted to put objects into circulation which were both 'intriguing' and 'problematic'.[82]

Dalí not only provided the impetus behind this new form of Surrealist art-making but also expounded its theoretical basis. In a text entitled 'Objets Surréalistes', he identified Giacometti's sculpture as a prime example of a 'symbolically functioning object' which he defined as:

> actes [qui] correspondent à des fantaisies et désirs érotiques nettement caractérisés. L'incarnation de ces désirs, leur manière de s'objectiver par substitution et métaphore, leur réalisation symbolique, constituent le processus type de la *perversion sexuelle*, lequel ressemble, en tout point, au processus du fait poétique.[83]

81 Polizzotti, *Revolution of the Mind*, p. 383.

82 Breton, 'Introduction to the discourse on the paucity of reality' (1924–1925) in *Break of Day*, p. 18; 'Introduction au discours sur le peu de réalité' (1924–1925) in *Œuvres Complètes* II, p. 277.

83 Salvador Dalí, 'Objets Surréalistes' (1931) in *Oui 1* (Paris: Denoël/Gonthier, 1971), p. 178. Dalí's italics.

> [acts [which] correspond to clear and blatant erotic fantasies and desires. The incarnation of these desires, the way they objectify themselves through substitution and metaphor and are enacted symbolically, constitute the process typical of *sexual perversion*, which resembles, in every aspect, the process the of the poetic phenomenon.[84]]

Giacometti's infamous *Boule Suspendue* (*Suspended Ball*) sculpture (Figure 2.2) had been showcased in the precursory publication *Surréalisme au service de la Révolution*. The sculpture is undoubtedly one of the artist's most memorable exhibits on account of its striking symbolism – a ball with a groove suspended over a phallic crescent – and its capacity for polysemic interpretation.

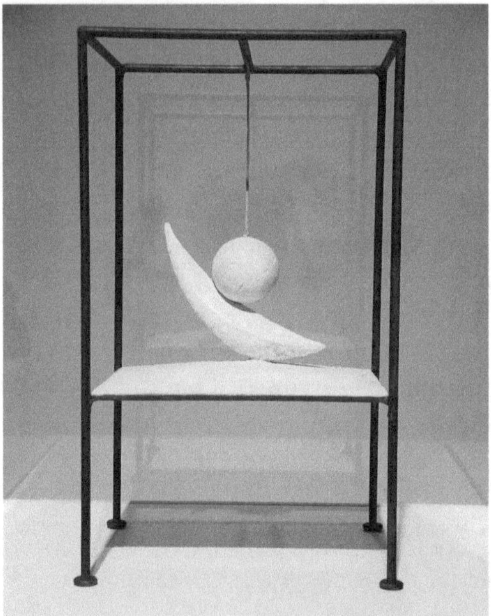

Figure 2.2: Alberto Giacometti, *Boule Suspendue* (*Suspended Ball*) (1930–1931) – photo of sculpture © Fondation Alberto et Annette Giacometti/Copyright Agency, 2018.

84 Salvador Dalí, 'Surrealist Objects' (1931) in *Oui 1*, trans. by Yvonne Shafir (Boston, MA: Exact Change, 1998), p. 136. Dalí's italics.

With reference to Dalí's equivalence between perversion and poetry, Harris reads Giacometti's sculpture as representative of a natural and unconscious poetry, whereby the poetic 'to the extent that "poetic" is identified with "perverse,"' is 'a return to the sources of imagination in unconscious desire. It is extra-aesthetic insofar as it is desublimated'.[85] Suggestive or desublimated works such as this were not, moreover, isolated cases but manufactured by a wide spectrum of artists from the loyalist to the dissident wings of Surrealism.

Giacometti's subsequent presence in *Minotaure* can in itself be considered in relation to the journal's positioning between Bataillean and Bretonian influences. For Giacometti himself first befriended the dissident Surrealists such as Leiris and Masson in 1928–1929, before coming under the direct influence of Bataille and the *Documents* group, where he undoubtedly became exposed to their interest in primitive art and which, according to Harris, 'may partially explain Giacometti's reorientation to the base in so many of the gameboard sculptures of his Surrealist period'.[86] Having shaken the art world with his exhibit *Boule Suspendue*, a prime example of this re-orientation, he was nevertheless asked by Breton to join the Surrealist movement, a request to which he acceded whilst choosing not to participate in all of its activities.

In her reading of the artist's sculpture, however, Rosalind Krauss considers the overt sexual symbolism of *Boule Suspendue* as proof of the artist's exclusive propinquity to Bataille; which, according to her, was further reinforced by the ambiguity and tension of the display (for the two objects are not assigned specific roles or genders). For her, *Boule Suspendue* reflected Giacometti's desire to challenge distinct meanings and forms in the manner of Bataille's *informe* and his work, therefore, 'has little to do with the notions of convulsive beauty authorised by Surrealism',[87] the transgressiveness of

85 Harris, *Surrealist Art and Thought*, p. 30.

86 *Ibid.*, p. 241.

87 Rosalind Krauss, 'No more play' in *The Originality of the Avant-Garde and other Modernist Myths* (London: MIT Press, 1987), p. 61.

Boule Suspendue setting itself apart from 'Breton's adamant rejection of the sexually perverse'.[88]

Whilst Krauss is correct in stressing the obvious affinities between the installation's perverse form and Bataille's valorisation of the base, it is worth reconsidering whether Giacometti was quite so antagonistic to the Surrealist visual. After all, Breton specifically courted Giacometti on account of the subversiveness and polysemy of the *Boule Suspendue* (which were rooted in the sexual) and ensured he was showcased first in *Surréalisme au service de la Révolution* and then in *Minotaure*. The artist also occupied a prominent position at the start of Breton's novel *L'Amour Fou* as one of convulsive beauty's major exponents. Here he described the enchanting effects of Giacometti's work upon him, specifically a female figure seemingly holding an invisible object[89] (which Breton associated with the lost love object). He also spoke of the objects he and the artist had found at a flea market: a warrior's mask, reminiscent of death, and a highly concave wooden spoon, evoking both phallus and vagina. Breton's appreciation of symbolically significant objects (whether manufactured or found) was self-evident with their recuperation playing a central role in his artistic agenda.

After 1945, Giacometti, who now worked independently of the artistic avant-garde and Surrealism, began to produce sculptures of elongated nudes, both otherworldly and sensuous (with a markedly primitivist appearance). Breton, clearly impressed by this turn in the artist's work, praised him for representing the summa of all of Surrealism's anterior concerns and thus preparing the ground for the style of a new era.[90]

Evidently, it can be problematic to characterise artists such as Giacometti purely as exponents of Bataille's base materialism, since a case can equally be made that they represent a strand of Surrealist iconography which deserves to be examined on its own merits. For this reason Harris

88 *Ibid.*, p. 62.

89 The statuette was later to be known as *L'Objet Invisible* [*The Invisible Object*] (1934).

90 Breton, *Œuvres Complètes* III, p. 592.

appears to take issue with Hal Foster, claiming that he downplays the desublimatory strand of Surrealist art in *Compulsive Beauty* and allows the question of sublimation and desublimation to become too closely associated with questions of personality (that is to say, alignments with Breton or Bataille):[91]

> Whereas for Theodor Adorno, Surrealism is a movement in which 'art batters its own foundations', for Foster, who reads Surrealism through Bataille, it is as sublimated as any other form of art. This is in spite of the fact that he acknowledges the desublimating strategies of Ernst and Hans Bellmer, who were both part of the 'Bretonian' Surrealist group rather than of any dissident faction.[92]

Harris' statement is one which warrants closer attention. If, for example, we examine Foster's discussion of Bellmer,[93] it is significant to note his underlying assumption that the artist is peripheral to Surrealism purely on account of his desublimatory artworks.

Foster begins by qualifying Bellmer's works as products of the uncanny; specifically, they represent 'uncanny confusions of animate and inanimate figures, ambivalent conjunctions of castrative and fetishistic forms, compulsive repetitions of erotic and traumatic scenes, difficult intricacies of Sadism and Masochism, of desire, defusion, and death'.[94] To make his case, he refers to a number of (written and visual) works, in particular to the *poupées* of 'Variations sur le montage d'une mineure articulée' ('Variations on the Montage of an Articulated Minor'; Figure 2.3) published in *Minotaure*, no. 6 (1934–1935).

91 In a letter to Roger Caillois in the mid-thirties, Bataille admitted that the question of personalities had to be put to one side – 'it seems impossible to me to continue to raise narrow questions of personalities' – Bataille, 'Letter of 26 September 1935' in *Lettres à Roger Caillois 4 août 1935 – février 1959*, ed. by Jean-Pierre Le Bouler (Paris: Folle Avoine, 1987), p. 41.

92 Harris, *Surrealist Art and Thought*, p. 11.

93 The desublimating strategies of Ernst are covered in the fourth chapter.

94 Foster, *Compulsive Beauty*, p. 101.

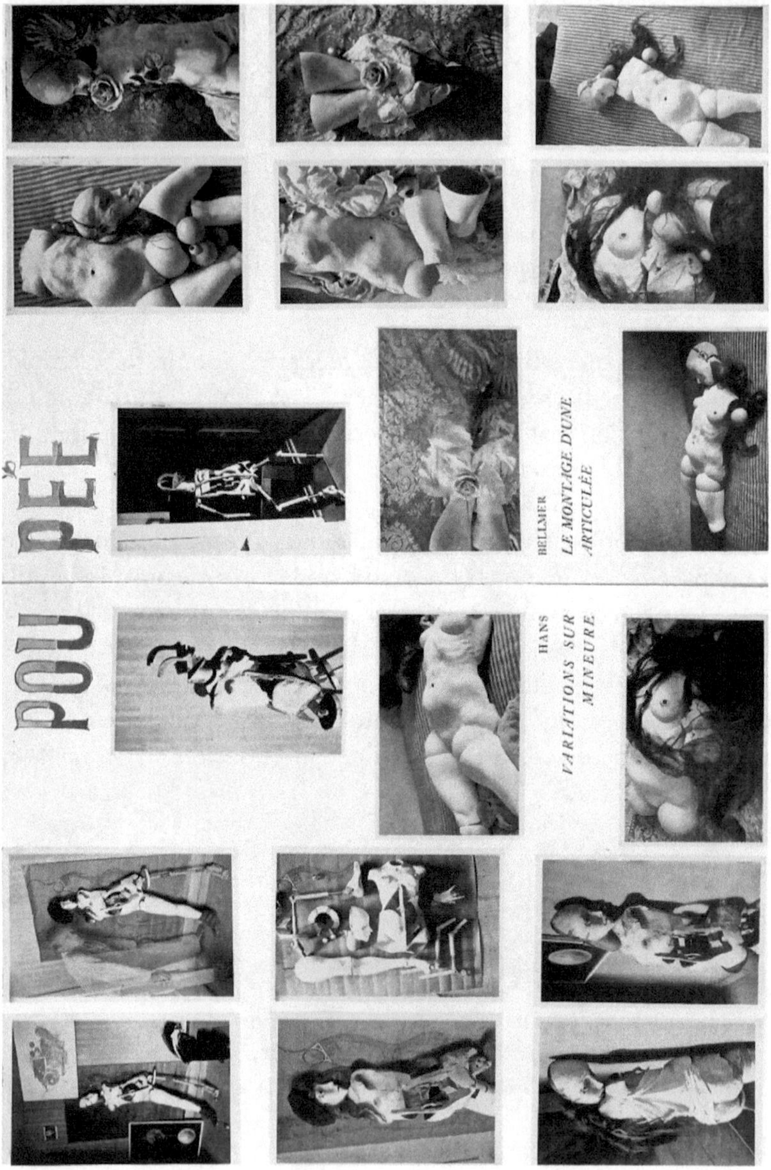

Figure 2.3: Hans Bellmer, 'Variations sur le montagne d'une mineure articulée', Minotaure (1934–1935) © Hans Bellmer/ADAGP. Copyright Agency, 2018.

He focusses on the Sado-masochistic qualities of these *poupées*, which reside in the staged oscillation between erotic fusion and sexual diffusion, a shattering of the self through Masochism and a subjugation of the other through Sadism. For him, such impulses reflect a notion of transgressive eroticism which suggest a kinship with Bataille rather than Breton: the latter prefers the sublimation of Sado-Masochistic impulses in a revised notion of beauty and art, whereas Bataille reads art through the concept of *altération*, suggesting a defacement and deformation of the artist's model similar to the Sadistic operations to which Bellmer's dolls are subjected. 'Altération' – a keystone of Bataille's thinking signifying 'distortion', 'deterioration', 'vitiation' in English – designates the artistic process by which a subject is imperfectly rendered or reproduced onto a surface which is in itself defaced in the process: 'l'art [...] procède dans ce sens par destructions successives. Alors qu'il libère des instincts libidineux, ces instincts sont sadiques'[95] ['art [...] proceeds in this way by successive destructions. To the extent that it liberates libidinal instincts, these instincts are sadistic'].

Whereas Foster's interpretation of Bellmer seems valid to a point, it seems apposite to consider whether the Bellmer-Bataille connection might not have been somewhat overstated and how we might therefore qualify the idea of Breton (and his brand of Surrealism) as being solely representative of a sublimating idealism. Commenting on Breton's apparent fears over the anti-civilisational forces (such as transgression and perversion) embodied by the *poupées*, he states:

> Breton is wracked by the ramifications of such transgression, by the defusion, even the death at its core. This is why he ultimately values sublimated form and idealist Eros, and upholds the traditional notion of the aesthetic: the normative reconciliation of contrary modes of experience (in Kant nature and reason, judgements of fact and value, and so on).[96]

It is here where I believe we might be able to engage with Foster's contention. Whereas there is within Breton's work a striving to understand better the

95 Georges Bataille, 'L'art primitif' ['Primitive Art'] in *Documents 7* (1930), p. 396.
96 Foster, *Compulsive Beauty*, p. 111.

reciprocal relationship between 'contrary modes of experience', he does not specifically address the Kantian categories mentioned, nor enlist them in an elaboration of beauty or art, whether in an idealist or an aesthetic discourse. Further, one might ask if there can be a neat transcendental synthesis in Breton's view of art, when conscious painterly craftsmanship is (at least in principle) replaced by the automatised expression of the subject's unconscious psychical impulses. Breton had, after all, rejected any discussion of Surrealism as a fixed aesthetic or style: 'le surréalisme n'est pas intéressé à tenir grand compte de ce qui se produit à côté de lui sous prétexte d'art, voire d'anti-art'[97] ['Surrealism is not interested in giving very serious consideration to anything that happens at its sides, under the guise of art, or even anti-art']. Moreover, the disinterestedness of Kantian aesthetics would seem to be abandoned in Surrealism precisely because the subject gives expression to feelings and sensations deeply rooted in the psyche, including any sexual and aggressive impulses as well as critical responses to social reality.[98] The 'convulsive' aspect of Breton's conception of art was perhaps not as 'normative' as Foster has claimed. 'Convulsiveness' denoted those paroxysmal experiences such as orgasm or hysteria which were far-removed from the banality of life; it was therefore far more radical than the castrated hedonism of Kant, with its emphasis on the disinterested intellectual appreciation of regular forms. Breton's interest in Bellmer's dolls shows how he deviated from conventional modes of aesthetic appreciation, though Foster observes that:

> with the dolls, the surreal and the uncanny intersect in the most difficult desublimatory way – which is one reason why Bellmer is marginal to the literature on Surrealism, devoted as it mostly is to the sublimatory idealisms of Breton.[99]

Foster correctly establishes that Bellmer has frequently been confined to the margins of literature on Surrealism, though I want to suggest that this need not be the case given that Breton did not proscribe Bellmer for

97 Breton, *Manifestes du Surréalisme*, p. 73.
98 Breton, *Manifestoes of Surrealism*, p. 125 – translation modified by me.
99 Foster, *Compulsive Beauty*, p. 101.

the restaging of violently Sado-Masochistic fantasies but rather expressed admiration for them:

> c'est aussi, mais adolescente, la femme éternelle, pivot du vertige humain, qui a retenu Bellmer dans les affres de la création et de la vie imprévisible des golems dont participe sa Poupée.[100]
>
> [it is also eternal woman, pivot of man's vertigo, but in adolescence now, that has obsessed Bellmer in the anguish of the creation and the unpredictable life of the golems in which his Doll plays a role.[101]]

The term 'golem', which refers to an animated being created entirely out of inanimate matter,[102] is ambiguous, suggesting both a biddable servant and a Frankenstein's monster. It is Hebrew for 'shapeless form' and is used in the Bible to refer to an embryonic or incomplete substance. With its associations of monstrosity and formlessness, Breton's description of the dolls as golems does not seem so remote from Bataille's belief in the formlessness of matter.

The early thirties also saw Surrealists' working practices converge with those of Picasso. After being temporarily co-opted by Bataille in the years 1929–1930, he now joined his friend Leiris in actively collaborating with *Minotaure* and started to make assemblages and objects of a Surrealist nature.

In the October group's re-reading of modern art through Bataille's concept of the formless, Yve-Alain Bois expresses surprise at the latter's silence over a number of Picasso's assemblages of this period, including *Le Plumeau et la Corne* (*The Feather Duster and the Bull's Horn*, 1933; Figure 2.4): 'one might expect Bataille to have celebrated it [...], so much does it seem to illustrate his "impossible and fantastic vision of roots swarming under the surface of the soil, nauseating and naked like vermin."'

100 André Breton, 'Genèse et Perspective Artistiques du Surréalisme' (1941) in *Œuvres Complètes*, ed. by Marguerite Bonnet (Paris: Gallimard, 2008), vol. IV, p. 446.

101 André Breton, 'Artistic Genesis and Perspective of Surrealism' (1941) in *Surrealism and Painting*, trans. by Simon Watson Taylor (London: Macdonald and Co., 1972), pp. 80–81 – translation modified by me.

102 Bois, *Formless*, p. 83.

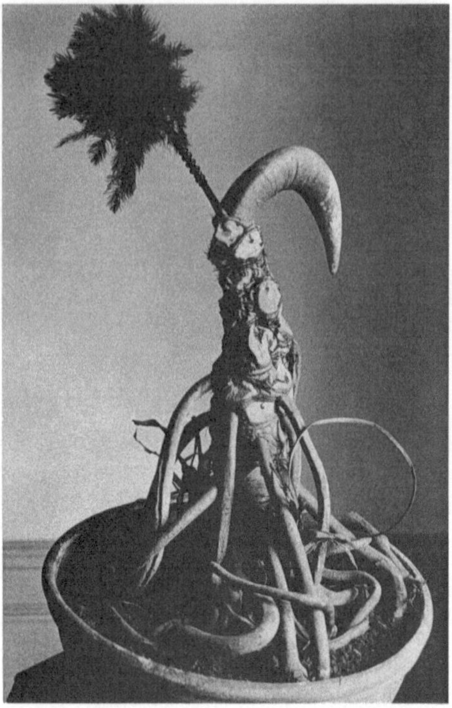

Figure 2.4: Pablo Picasso, 'Le Plumeau et la Corne'
(*The Feather Duster and the Bull's Horn*) in *Minotaure 1* (1933) –
photo of sculpture © Succession Picasso/Succession Picasso. Copyright Agency, 2018.

He continues by expressing even greater incredulity over Breton's interest in these objects – a fact which seemingly put him at odds with his own 'idealising' and 'sublimating' tendencies: 'Now – extraordinary cat's cradle – it is the very high priest of "transposition" [....], it is André Breton who became the great advocate of these objects'.[103] However, there was nothing unusual about Breton's fascination with polysemic objects of desire. He had acknowledged the erotic nature of such objects in a talk which he gave in 1935 entitled 'Situation Surréaliste de l'Objet'[104] and, even as early as 1924, had affirmed that:

103 *Ibid.*
104 Breton, *Œuvres Complètes II*, p. 494; Breton, *Manifestoes of Surrealism*, p. 276.

> Le fétichisme humain, qui a besoin d'essayer le casque blanc, de caresser le bonnet de fourrure, écoute d'une oreille tout autre le récit de nos expéditions. Il lui faut absolument croire que c'est arrivé. C'est pour répondre à ce désir de vérification perpétuelle que je proposais récemment de fabriquer, dans la mesure du possible, certains de ces objets qu'on n'approche qu'en rêve et qui paraissent aussi peu défendables sous le rapport de l'utilité que sous celui de l'agrément.[105]
>
> [Human fetishism, which needs to try on the white helmet, to caress the fur bonnet, listens to the tale of our expeditions with an entirely different ear. It must absolutely believe that this happened. It was to respond to this desire for perpetual verification that I recently suggested manufacturing, if possible, some of the objects that one approaches only in dreams – objects that seem wholly unjustified from the viewpoint of both usefulness and enjoyment.[106]]

For a moment, Bois draws attention to the existence of a more desublimatory strand of Breton's thinking and even concedes that he 'was even more enslaved to a figurative aesthetic of "deformation" than Bataille';[107] yet he is unable to account for the discrepancy between Breton's preoccupation with deformation and symbolic objects and his ostensible role as the 'high priest of transposition'.

'To pervert' means to turn an object away from its proper ends. In their manufacture of symbolic objects the Surrealists were doing just that – turning objects away from their conventional usage to desire-inducing or fetishistic ends. This activity along with their enquiries into Sadism and other sexual behaviours reflected a growing interest in sexuality and perversity on the part of the Surrealists in the 1930s. *Minotaure* provided ample evidence of this interest, developing the darker hues of Surrealism, and perhaps even pre-empting any further criticism of Breton as an over-zealous idealist who denied the value of the base and the perverse. This had after all formed the crux of a polemic against him in *Documents*.[108]

105 Breton, *Œuvres Complètes* II, p. 277. Breton's italics.

106 Breton, *Break of Day*, p. 18. Breton's italics.

107 Bois, *Formless*, p. 83

108 Also in *Documents*, there had been criticism of him for his attempted appropriation of Picasso: 'Or, parmi les grossières, mais pernicieuses erreurs qui, dans le courant de ces dernières années, ont été propagées sur le compte de Picasso, celle qui vient au

In an article Breton wrote about Picasso in the first edition of *Minotaure*, he succeeded in encroaching on some of the ground previously occupied by Bataille though without antagonising the latter or abandoning all of his former beliefs (such as dialectics and automatism, which he also referred to in the article). He ended the piece by explaining how Picasso had inspired him to think of art as a form of 'excretion' and describing how excrement could be used in making art:

> Tout en s'assurant de sa sécheresse, il m'expliqua que le sujet de cette toile devait être un excrément, comme cela apparaîtrait du reste lorsqu' il aurait disposé les mouches. Il déplorait seulement d'avoir dû suppléer par la couleur au manque d'un véritable excrément séché et très précisément d'un de ceux, inimitables, qu'il arrive de remarquer dans la campagne à l'époque où les enfants croquent les cerises sans prendre la peine de rejeter les noyaux. Le goût électif pour ces noyaux à cette place me parut, je dois dire, témoigner le plus objectivement du monde de l'intérêt très spécial qui mérite d'être porté à ce rapport de l'inassimilé et de l'assimilé, dont la variation dans le sens du profit de l'homme peut passer pour le mobile essentiel de la création artistique.[109]
>
> [Picasso explained to me that this painting was intended to represent a piece of excrement, as, indeed, would become quite evident once he placed the flies in position. He only deplored the necessity of using colour for want of a suitably durable genuine dried excrement, and regretted especially the impossibility of reproducing one of those particularly inimitable excrements that he sometimes noticed in the country at that time of the year when children eat cherries without bothering to spit out the stones. The deliberate taste for cherry-stones in this situation seems to me, I must say, to provide the most objective proof possible of the very particular interest which the relationship between the unassimilated and the assimilated should arouse:

---

premier plan est celle qui tendait à le confondre plus ou moins avec les surréalistes, somme toute à faire de lui une sorte d'homme en révolte ou bien plutôt en fuite [...] devant la réalité' ['Now, amongst the crude, yet pernicious errors, which during the course of these last years have been propagated on account of Picasso, the error which comes most visibly to the fore, is that of tending to confuse him to a greater or lesser degree with the Surrealists, in short, to make of him a sort of man in revolt against or rather in flight from [...] reality'] – Michel Leiris, 'Toiles récentes de Picasso' ['Picasso's recent paintings'] in *Documents*, no. 2 (March, 1933), pp. 62–64.

109 André Breton, 'Pablo Picasso – Picasso dans son élément' (1933) in *Œuvres Complètes*, IV, p. 484 – my italics.

> a relationship whose variations, in terms of the benefit to mankind, may well be considered the essential motivating force of artist creation.[110]]

He then went on to imagine how the addition of flies to the painting would substantially improve it[111] even despite the fact that in the *Second Manifeste* of 1929 he had denounced Bataille for being an 'excrement philosopher', openly declaring that 'M. Bataille aime les mouches. Nous, non'[112] ['Mr Bataille loves flies. Not we'[113]]. Moreover, on the issue of artistic creation he referred to the relationship between the 'unassimilated' and 'the assimilated' which sounded uncannily similar to that of the 'heterogeneous' and the 'homogeneous', the terms which Bataille had used in expounding his philosophy of heterology. In this philosophy, the 'heterogeneous' was expounded as the rejected Other, as what was fundamentally alien to humanity; it was frequently scatological or base in nature and represented as the object of humanity's contempt.

The precise intention behind Breton's pastiche is difficult to surmise. The passages read as an ironic tribute to a viewpoint he once considered alien and undesirable though, given their singularity within the writings of Breton, it may appear rather presumptuous or hasty to ascribe a specific meaning or intention to them. More significant perhaps is that through his involvement with *Minotaure*, Breton was inexorably led to the domain of untamed instincts and base desire – in other words, to those preoccupations which reflected a greater affinity with Bataille. Irrespective of how much credence he wanted to give to Bataille's ideas in this article, he had nonetheless agreed to collaborate with the writers and artists associated with *Documents* (such as Leiris, Picasso and Giacometti) whose respective philosophical outlooks encompassed a recognition of sexuality in its baser manifestations. Moreover, he had actively promoted Maurice Heine's studies of Sade and been bound in his editorship to unify the journal around the image of the Minotaur, with its associations of unbridled Sadistic desire and instinct.

110 André Breton, 'Pablo Picasso in his element' (1933) in *Surrealism and Painting*, p. 114 – my italics.

111 Breton, *Œuvres Complètes* IV, pp. 484–485.

112 Breton, *Manifestes du Surréalisme*, p. 134.

113 Breton, *Manifestoes of Surrealism*, p. 184.

Transgression, Sade and Black Humour

In *L'Érotisme* (1957), Bataille charted the transition of *Homo sapiens*' from his animal origins on the horizontal plane to his emergence as a 'civilised' human being on the vertical plane. In assuming an upright posture, and becoming more remote from the baseness of the earth, the human species had developed 'la sexualité avec honte'[114] ['sexuality with shame'[115]]. Such shame was, in Bataille's view, one of the basic modalities of 'eroticism' and resulted from (wo)man's increasing awareness and interrogation of his/her own mortality and sexual desire. He identified both work and religion as having contributed towards the increasing regulation of sex and death, which in turn led to the establishment of taboos around the two most important areas of life.

In a number of areas, Bataille's view of modern (wo)man evoked Freud's account of the progressive domestication of our instinctual life. Bataille's reference to human feelings of shame over sexuality paralleled what Freud called 'reaction-formation' or the cultivation of a puritanical self-reproof in response to one's sexual (and other base) instincts. The subject of taboo formation in the area of human sexuality was similarly taken up by Freud in *Totem and Taboo* (where he suggested that it was incestuous-Oedipal in origin) and in *Civilisation and Its Discontents* where taboos were presented as a corollary to a repressive civilisation. The increasing regulation of sexuality by work posited by Bataille was associated by Freud with the constraints of the reality principle (later to be renamed by Marcuse as a work-induced 'performance principle'). The transition of (wo)man to the upright posture was associated by both men with the onset of civilisation. In Freud's writings many of these ideas contributed to his picture of a civilisation underpinned by repressive sublimation.

114 Georges Bataille, 'L'Érotisme' in *Œuvres Complètes* (Paris: Gallimard, 1987), vol. X, p. 35.

115 Georges Bataille, *Erotism: Death & Sensuality*, trans. by Mary Dalwood (San Francisco, CA: City Lights Books, 1986), p. 31.

For his part, Bataille seemed to be developing Freud's view of civilisation one stage further by suggesting that the very experience of the 'erotic' was predicated upon shame, guilt, morality and sublimation; in other words, upon all of those things which are fundamental to civilised life and distinguishable from animal behaviour.[116] The experience of the erotic was heightened when those pleasures considered shameful (and ordinarily sublimated or repressed) were indulged in and the moral codes which regulated them were violated. He also outlined how transgression could operate as a rupture from the ordered routine of daily living, his ultimate example of this being the orgy, that 'négation des limites de la vie qu'ordonne le travail'[117] ['denial of the limits set on life by work'[118]].

Given the popular image of Breton as an avant-gardist who paid lip service to perversion but whose own homogenising Puritanism occasioned a certain level of intolerance, one might have imagined that such talk of orgies and transgression was at variance with his thinking; in fact, his comments struck a much more conciliatory tone than is often acknowledged. Whereas he may have been more priggish in his youth, in 1959, by way of an introduction to the International Surrealist Exhibition (whose overarching theme was eroticism), Breton wrote not only in support of

116 Bataille therefore rejects a regression to animality and what he terms a 'back to nature attitude' as a predicate to eroticism: 'Les images érotiques, ou religieuses, introduisent essentiellement, chez les uns les conduits de l'interdit, chez d'autres, des conduits contraires. Les premières sont traditionelles. Les secondes elles-mêmes sont communes, du moins sous forme d'un prétendu retour à la nature, à laquelle s'opposait l'interdit. Mais la transgression diffère du "retour à la nature" : *elle lève l'interdit sans le supprimer*. Là se cache le ressort de l'érotisme, là se trouve en même temps le ressort des religions' – Bataille, *Œuvres Complètes* X, p. 39 – Bataille's italics. ['Erotic or religious images draw forth behaviour associated with prohibitions in some people, the reverse in others. The first type is traditional. The second is common at least in the guise of a so-called back-to-nature attitude, the prohibition being seen as unnatural. But a transgression is not the same as a back-to-nature movement; it suspends a taboo without suppressing it. Here lies the mainspring of eroticism and religion too' – Bataille, *Erotism*, p. 36].

117 Bataille, *Œuvres Complètes* X, p. 113.

118 Bataille, *Erotism*, p. 112.

transgressive desire but of philosophy's indebtedness to Georges Bataille for his insights into the subject:

> [en citant Bataille] 'L'expérience intérieure de l'érotisme demande de celui qui la fait une sensibilité non moins grande à l'angoisse fondant l'interdit, qu'au désir menant l'enfreindre.'
>
> Cet interdit, de caractère immémorial et qui continue à s'imposer, sous toutes les latitudes, des prétendus 'sauvages' aux prétendus 'civilisés', est, en effet, le véritable point de mire de l'érotisme.
>
> Nous estimons qu'il se précisera d'autant mieux qu'on parviendra à le dégager de l'immense broussaille de préjugés qui le recouvre. Toutefois, il serait vain de vouloir avancer ici en pleine lumière. Qui se flattera de braver à la fois, sans sourciller, le préjugé et l'interdit se trouvera hors d'état de traiter de l'érotisme, dont il aura méconnu, à travers sa propre conscience, le besoin fondamental de *transgression.*[119]
>
> [[quoting Bataille] 'The inner experience of eroticism demands from the person involved an equal sensitivity towards the anguish which provides the basis for interdiction and the desire which tends to violate it.'
>
> This interdiction, which has existed since time immemorial and continues to hold sway in every latitude over so-called 'savage' and so-called 'civilised' races alike, is the true target at which eroticism aims its arrow.
>
> I have no doubt that it will become increasingly explicit to the extent that we succeed in disentangling it from the dense undergrowth of prejudices which cover it. However, it would be idle to hope to advance here in the full light of day. Anyone who flatters himself on having braved prejudice and interdiction simultaneously, without turning a hair, will find himself disqualified from dealing with eroticism, since his own consciousness has failed to realise eroticism's fundamental need for *transgression.*[120]]

119 Breton, 'Introduction à l'Exposition Internationale du Surréalisme' (1959) in *Recherches sur la Sexualité (Janvier 1928 – Août 1932)*, ed. by José Pierre (Paris: Gallimard, 1990), pp. 208–209 – Breton's italics.

120 André Breton, 'Introduction to the International Surrealist Exhibition' (1959) in *Surrealism and Painting*, pp. 378–389 – Breton's italics.

Breton, like Bataille, seemed to view the 'repressive' sublimation of civilised society as something to be violated, and, correspondingly, as eroticism's direct complement. Moreover, Breton insisted that to confront the true nature of erotic desire an open-mindedness was required about its transgressive basis. This necessitated the overcoming of one's own prejudices – an assertion which seemed altogether different in tone from the young Breton's rather more judgemental pronouncements about certain forms of sexual behaviour (for example, homosexuality and unquestioning libertinism[121]).

This view of Breton, who, despite the obvious lapses into intolerance which characterised his youth, nonetheless maintained (and developed) a certain openness of spirit toward alterity, is one which is quite frequently downplayed by critics. There was little indication here of Breton, the idealising romantic, who disdained Bataillean thought for its single-minded defence of the erotic and the base. Indeed, he had started his introduction by paying homage to Bataille 'qui, au terme d'une instante et souvent pathétique interrogation à ce sujet, est le mieux parvenu à nous faire appréhender l'érotisme pour ce qu'il est, à savoir un "aspect immédiat de l'expérience intérieure, s'opposant à la sexualité animale"'[122] ['who, in the course of an urgent and often moving investigation of the subject, has succeeded best in making us apprehend eroticism for what it is, that is to say an "immediate aspect of inner experience, opposing itself to animal sexuality"'[123]].

It was certainly significant (though unsurprising) that Breton should have openly endorsed one of the cornerstones of late Bataillean philosophy 'the inner experience'. For Bataille, 'inner experience' – of which eroticism was one major form – was an abstract term referring to emotions and

121 Examples of such attitudes are to be found in *Recherches sur la Sexualité* and the English translation *Investigating Sex – Surrealist Discussions 1928–1932*, ed. by José Pierre, trans. by Malcom Imrie (London: Verso, 1992). In these discussions Breton famously inveighed against homosexuality (*Recherches sur la Sexualité*, p. 39, p. 68, p. 173; *Investigating Sex*, p. 5, pp. 27–28, p. 132) and unquestioning libertinism (*Recherches sur la Sexualité*, p. 75; *Investigating Sex*, p. 32).

122 Breton, *Recherches sur la Sexualité*, p. 208.

123 Breton, *Surrealism and Painting*, p. 377.

sensations which stimulated our inner life to help overcome the 'discontinuous' (i.e. finite, alienated) nature of our existence. He stressed that the erotic aspect of inner experience was, moreover, elective in nature, relying on the personal taste of the subject or 'des goûts personnels du sujet' and answering 'the *innerness* of desire'[124] ('l'intériorité du désir'[125]). These aspects of the erotic were again to be distinguished from animal desires, which were devoid of such discernment. The theory of inner experience raised the erotic to the level of the sacred, contrasting sharply with the asceticism of organised religion.

One can see why the thinking of Breton and Bataille might have started to converge on these points. Bataille had, on the one hand, moved away from notions of direct immersion in base desire and perversion (which one might associate with 'the animalistic') to present a more thoughtful approach to eroticism which valorised the inner life and the elective (so prized by Surrealism since its inception) and showed open contempt for the Christian church by re-defining the parameters of the sacred. Breton on the other hand had been obliged to confront questions of sexuality via a number of Surrealist projects: the group discussions about sexuality (1928–1932), the creation of symbolic-erotic objects (from about 1932), the programme for a revolt in moral values in *Contre-Attaque* (in 1935) and the erotic-themed post-war exhibition to which he wrote the introduction (and eulogy of Bataille). Moreover, the vicissitudes of Breton's own life (as well as those of his Surrealist friends), which had seen partners come and go and endured the ravages of two world wars, undoubtedly attuned him to the complexities and ambivalences surrounding human relationships.

In an interview which was conducted in the 1950s, Breton, quoting Valéry, admitted frankly that 'l'érotisme n'est jamais loin des véridiques'[126] ['the truth sayers are never strangers to eroticism'[127]]. He spoke also of the Surrealists' determination to break down sexual taboos and penetrate that

124 Bataille, *Œuvres Complètes* X, p. 33.
125 Bataille, *Erotism*, p. 29.
126 Breton, 'Entretiens' (1952) in *Œuvres Complètes* III, pp. 518–519.
127 Breton, *Conversations*, p. 111.

'infracassable noyau de nuit'[128] ['the unshatterable kernel of darkness'[129]] in which such taboos were shrouded.

As mentioned previously, the Surrealists were famously led to the figure of Sade in their quest to apprehend the kernel of the night. The figure of Sade (and the attempt to define his revolutionary value) can again be viewed as a reference point in establishing Breton's stance on transgression and whether and how it met that of Bataille's (even though the Marquis is more usually cited by commentators as a source of contention between both writers).

Sade's role in their early polemics, which did indeed set the writers against each other, has been well-documented. In an article entitled 'Le Langage des Fleurs' in *Documents*, Bataille had insisted on the fundamental vulgarity of the flower, with its slimy roots submerged in the feculent baseness of the earth and the deceptive beauty of its petals oriented toward the sky destined to wither and perish. The article, which was pivotal in illuminating his theory of base materialism, also provided the opportunity of reclaiming the Marquis as an anti-hero and defender of the base (from the mythologised Romantic figurehead which the Surrealists had made him to be). Bataille therefore concluded the article with an image of 'le geste confondant du marquis de Sade [...] se faisant apporter les plus belles roses pour en effeuiller les pétales sur le purin d'une fosse'[130] ['the disconcerting gesture of the Marquis de Sade' who 'has the most beautiful roses brought to him only to pluck off their petals and toss them into a ditch filled with liquid manure'[131]].

In the *Second Manifeste* Breton objected to the vulgar mundanity of Bataille's description of Sade, claiming that it reduced him to the level of a staid librarian (like Bataille) rather than depicting him as the defender of social and moral freedom he truly was.[132] Breton attempted to undermine Bataille's view of the Marquis by observing that Sade's plucking of petals from a rose could equally have signified an assault on poetic convention

128 Breton, *Œuvres Complètes* II, p. 359 and *Œuvres Complètes* III, p. 519.
129 Breton, *Conversations*, p. 111.
130 Bataille, *Œuvres Complètes* II, pp. 51–52.
131 Bataille, *Visions of Excess*, p. 14.
132 Breton, *Manifestes du Surréalisme*, p. 136; Breton, *Manifestoes of Surrealism*, p. 186.

and the clichéd 'finer feelings' associated with the offering of the flower.[133] The vitriol of Sade's act could thus be seen as a challenge to the moral worth accorded to the rose by a toothless poetic idolatry, a challenge which, in Breton's words, sought to help the human spirit unshackle itself from its metaphorical chains.[134]

Bataille, in his turn, would remark that this made Sade a 'moralising idealist'[135] and that the Surrealists' adulation of him was comparable to the (misguided) admiration of the Catholics for Jesus.[136] More generally, he considered the Surrealists' preoccupation with 'insalubrious' themes as inauthentic because of their transposition into the literary, which by definition made very real perverse impulses anodyne and remote from their origins. He believed that this applied particularly to the Surrealists' treatment of Sadean desire, which had become neutered in its incorporation into a poeticised reality.

One frequently overlooked fact is, however, that Bataille's early disdain for Breton's poeticisation of Sade eventually yielded to an attitude of recognition and respect:

> Le surréalisme a mis en avant sous une forme parfois discrète et maintient en avant un élément noir qui lui est lié d'une façon indiscutable [...]. Il ne s'agit pas seulement d'une eau noire, de sang noir, mais de cœur noir et toujours cet élément noir domine, l'emporte, assure je ne sais quel arrachement au monde qui nous avait dominé autrefois. [...] les idées de rompre le passé dominent le sort qui a été fait par le surréalisme pour la première fois à la figure parfaitement noire de Sade.[137]

> [Surrealism has brought to the fore and maintained, in a sometimes discreet form, a black element which characterises it indisputably [...]. It is not a matter of black water or black blood, but of a black heart; and this black element always dominates, carries off, and ensures some tearing away from the world which we once dominated.

133 *Ibid.*
134 *Ibid.*
135 Bataille, *Œuvres Complètes* II, p. 103.
136 Georges Bataille, 'Les propositions contenues ici' (circa 1930) in *Œuvres Complètes* II, p. 73.
137 Bataille, *Œuvres Complètes* VII, pp. 384–385.

> [...] the ideas of breaking with the past dominate the destiny prepared by Surrealism for the first time in the perfectly black figure of Sade.[138]]

By this time in his career, Bataille had revised his view of the movement as spinelessly evading reality in literary transpositions of the real; he now approved the scandalous impact of its imaginative reworkings of Sade and similarly iniquitous motifs. Underpinning Surrealism's subversive basis, he identified a 'black' current to which such motifs, as well as the figure of the Marquis, were attached.

The black current of Surrealism had in fact become more pronounced throughout the 1930s and culminated in Breton's *Anthologie de l'Humour Noir* (1940). This text has received little attention with respect to Breton's view of Sade, who within the work was given his own entry amongst a list of dark thinkers and humorists.[139] He began the entry by stressing the full force of 'civilised' society's repression of the Sadean œuvre, the consequence of a 'tabou d'une interdiction presque totale'[140] ['taboo of an almost total ban [interdiction]'[141]]. He also wrote of the strenuous efforts needed to overcome the prejudice against the Marquis, and the necessity to liberate his basic aspirations from the realm of thought.

138 Bataille, *Absence of Myth*, p. 74.

139 In its exposition of darker themes in literature, it is perhaps comparable with Bataille's later work *La littérature et le mal* [*Literature and Evil*] which begins with a recognition of the importance of Surrealism: 'La génération à laquelle j'appartiens est tumultueuse. Elle naquit à la vie littéraire dans les tumultes du surréalisme. Il y eut, dans les années qui suivirent la première guerre, un sentiment qui débordait. La littérature étouffait dans ses limites. Elle portait, semblait-il, en elle une révolution' ['The generation to which I belong is tumultuous. It awoke to the literary world set in the tumults of surrealism. There was in the years which followed the First World War, a feeling of going over the edge. Literature was suffocating from its own limits. It seemed to carry within it a revolution'] – Georges Bataille, 'La littérature et le mal' (1957) in *Œuvres Complètes* (Paris: Gallimard, 1979), vol. IX, p. 171.

140 Breton, *Œuvres Complètes* II, p. 890.

141 Breton, *Anthology of Black Humour*, p. 18.

Although Breton's discussion of the Marquis was still to a large degree rooted in the literary and even the fantastical, his approach was perhaps more realistic and less poetic than in the *Second Manifeste*, for quite significantly he was quick to underline Sade's value as a transgressive thinker. His recourse to the fantastical served not to romanticise Sade but to show how the potential for transgression was increased through a more meticulous elaboration of multitudinous debauched acts in the imagination, whereby 'le réel, le plausible sont délibérément transgressés'[142] ['the real, the plausible are deliberately transgressed'[143]].

He claimed Sade to be an authentic predecessor of Freud and called for the establishment of a 'véritable science de mœurs'[144] ['a science of [moral values/] mores'[145]] to complement the project of psychoanalysis. In so doing, he again paid tribute to Sade's biographer, Maurice Heine, for his scientific exposition of perversion and Sadean desire. The success of such a science (marked by its capacity to promote a genuine understanding of sexual alterity) would, in Breton's view, depend on the conditions of revolution[146] (echoing the demand for a 'revolution in morals' first put forward by Heine in *Contre-Attaque*).

Perhaps the most subversive aspect of the *Anthologie* was the claim that Sade's writing was in any way humorous. Yet for Breton, Sade's 'black humour' was reflected in his final testament in which he speaks of his own death in the most matter-of-fact, if not flippant terms; and in a letter from Sade to his wife, in which he appears to mock both her 'prattling' style as he does his own internment.[147]

Breton's discussion of Sade for his comedic value represented one major point of convergence with Bataille who likewise elaborated a theory of humour with reference to the Marquis. For Bataille, humour like the radical alterity of Sadean pleasure (which is rejected by most people) resembled

142 Breton, *Œuvres Complètes* II, p. 891.
143 Breton, *Anthology of Black Humour*, p. 19.
144 Breton, *Œuvres Complètes* II, p. 891.
145 Breton, *Anthology of Black Humour*, p. 18.
146 Breton, *Œuvres Complètes* II, p. 891.
147 *Ibid.*, p. 897; Breton, *Anthology of Black Humour*, p. 27.

excretory discharge. As Bataille affirmed in the second part of his essay 'La valeur d'usage de D.A.F. de Sade', the object of humour corresponds not only to the body's expelled waste products (i.e. faeces or bodily fluids) but also to the unwanted, heterological by-products of ideology:

> Lorsque les éclats de rire se produisent, il faut donc admettre que la décharge nerveuse qui aurait pu normalement être libérée par l'anus (ou par les organes sexuels voisins) est libérée par l'orifice buccal. Mais dans le rire l'excrétion cesse d'être positivement matérielle : elle devient idéologique.[148]
>
> [When there are bursts of laughter, one must therefore admit that the nervous discharge which could normally have been liberated via the anus (or the neighbouring sexual organs) is liberated via the oral cavity. Though in laughter excretion ceases to be positively material: it becomes ideological.]

The humour of 'ideological expulsion' arises from that which is fundamentally other to the self. As one's own constitution is confirmed as homogenous, what is different to it is excluded or forcibly removed:

> En effet, dans la mesure où la merde provoque l'hilarité elle peut être regardée comme analogue à d'autres *corps étrangers* qui la provoquent, tels que les parasites du corps, les personnages éminents (en tant qu'objet des caricatures), les fous, les mal adaptés et surtout les mots introduits d'une certaine façon dans les phrases qui les excluent.[149]
>
> [In effect, to the extent that shit provokes hilarity, it can be regarded as any other *foreign body* which provokes the same effect, such as bodily parasites, distinguished personalities (as the targets of caricature), mad people, the maladjusted and above all the words introduced into sentences in such a way as to exclude them.]

For Bataille, Sade was the *corps étranger* par excellence for his life and work resembled the type of excrement 'dans lesquels on n'aime le plus souvent que le plaisir rapide (et violent) de les évacuer et de ne plus les voir'[150] ['from which one mostly derives only the short-lived (and violent) pleasure of expelling them and no longer seeing them'].

148 Bataille, 'La Valeur d'usage de D.A.F. de Sade' (1930) in *Œuvres Complètes* II, p. 71.
149 Bataille, *Œuvres Complètes* II, 72 – Bataille's italics.
150 *Ibid.*, p. 70.

Although Breton would almost certainly have avoided the terminology of excretion to elucidate the notion of humour, he nonetheless drew attention to its heterological basis. This heterological exposition of humour began in Breton's preface to the *Anthologie*, where he cited Baudelaire, who defines humour as 'émanation, explosion, dégagement de comique'[151] ['emanation, explosion, comic release'[152]] suggesting something similar to the scatalogical eruption of Bataille. Another of Breton's references was to Freud, who remarked that humour is 'l'invulnérabilité du *moi* qui s'affirme victorieusement'[153] ['the *ego*'s victorious assertion of its own invulnerability'[154]]. Breton further developed this view to expound a notion of humour which was almost Sadistic in nature and which he defined as:

> une revanche du principe du plaisir attaché au surmoi sur le principe de réalité attaché au moi [...]. L'agressivité du surmoi hypermoral envers le moi passe ainsi au soi totalement amoral et donne toute licence à ses tendances destructives. L'humour, comme processus permettant d'écarter la réalité en ce qu'elle a de trop affligeant, ne s'exerce plus guère ici qu'aux dépens d'autrui.[155]
>
> [the revenge of the pleasure principle (attached to the superego) over the reality principle (attached to the ego) [...]. The hostility of the hypermoral superego toward the ego is thus transferred to the utterly amoral id and gives its destructive tendencies free reign. Humour, the process that allows one to brush reality aside when it gets too distressing, is exercised here almost exclusively at others' expense.]

These comments again pointed to a heterological view of humour, confirming the integrity of the self against the awkward presence of a distinct 'other' who becomes the source of derisive mockery for what (s)he is not.

I do not want to suggest that there is absolute parallelism between Breton and Bataille concerning Sadean humour. Breton for example also quoted Freud's reference to humour as '[ayant] quelque chose de

151 Breton, *Œuvres Complètes* II, p. 867.
152 Breton, *Anthology of Black Humour*, p. xiii.
153 Breton, *Œuvres Complètes* II, p. 872 – Breton's italics.
154 Breton, *Anthology of Black Humour*, p. xviii – Breton's italics.
155 Breton, *Œuvres Complètes* II, pp. 1055–1056.

sublime et d'élévé'[156] ['fine [or sublime] and elevated'[157]]. Bataille would almost certainly have denied that humour was in any way 'elevated' and, if 'sublime', then one suspects only in its terrorising, vertiginous aspect. Breton's reliance on Hegel for his concept of objective humour may also have been problematic for Bataille, being derived from a system of thought presumed to be idealist. Notwithstanding such divergences, both men's engagement with Sade as the source of humour does appear to shed light on a number of shared concerns which modern scholarship has left unexamined.

The most compelling example of this sympathy of ideas was another reference from Breton's introduction of the *Anthologie* to a lesser known author, Armand Petitjean, who stated that 'le rire, en tant que l'une des plus fastueuses prodigalités de l'homme, et jusque la débauche, est au bord du néant en nantissement'[158] ['laughter, as one of humanity's most sumptuous extravagances, even to the point of debauchery, stands at the lip of the void, offering itself as surety'[159]]. While it cannot be presumed that in quoting an author Breton necessarily shared the entirety of his ideas, the fact that the quotation featured so prominently within the work's introduction and supported its basic arguments, suggested at the very least a marked interest in (if not sympathy for) Petitjean's formulation. Significantly, the quotation evokes aspects of Bataille's thinking on humour when elaborated in the register of inner experience, as one of the products of the nothingness left behind by the death of God:

> … quand je ris, il y a dans mon objet quelque chose d'incomparable. […] D'ailleurs dans mon esprit je faisais de cet objet du rire un substitut de Dieu, je n'y voyais rien de moins qu'un principe de l'univers. Ce qui se révélait à moi avec une violence qui

156 Breton quoting Freud – *Ibid.*, p. 872.

157 Breton, *Anthology of Black Humour*, pp. 212–213.

158 Breton quoting Armand Petitjean in *Œuvres Complètes* II, p. 868 – original quotation taken from Armand Petitjean, *Imagination et Réalisation* (Paris, 1936).

159 Breton quoting Armand Petitjean in *Anthology of Black Humour*, p. xiv. Translation modified by me: the phrase 'offers us the void as a pledge' has been changed to 'offering itself as surety'.

me renversait, c'était que dans le monde et dans le vide inconcevable qu'il ouvre, il n'était rien qui ne soit violemment risible.[160]

[… when I laugh there is something incomparable in the object of my laughter. […] Besides, in my mind, I made the object of this laughter a substitute for God; here I saw nothing less than a principle of the universe. What was revealed to me, with a violence that astounded me, was that in the world and in the inconceivable void that it opens up, there is nothing that is not violently laughable.[161]]

Bataille and Petitjean both seemed to consider laughter as a tonic that assuaged the trials of living in a meaningless and Godless universe, a universe resembling a void. They believed that through a consciousness of our plight, the absurd and risible nature of things would become self-evident, and that our reaction subsequently would be to embrace the experience of laughter. Given the vain and tragic circumstances of our existence, the laughter embraced was of a markedly dark and hysterical nature. Whilst Breton would not have shared the nihilistic aspect of this outlook, it appeared that this dark narrative of humour appealed to him sufficiently to make it one of the underlying premises of his anthology.

* * * * * * * *

My intention in this chapter has not been to elide what were fundamental differences in outlook and disposition in Breton and Bataille, but in many instances simply to muddy the waters of firm assumption and enquire into some of the commonalities of their ideas which history has overlooked.

Székely has stated that hauntedness is one of the hallmarks of the works of Breton and Bataille.[162] One might say that both men were in

160 Georges Bataille, 'Notes – Conférences 1951–1953 – 2. L'Athéologie' in *Œuvres Complètes* (Paris: Gallimard, 1976), vol. VIII, p. 568 – Bataille's italics.

161 Georges Bataille, 'Aphorisms for the "System" – 2. Plans and Notes for "Atheology"' (1952) in *The Unfinished System of Non-Knowledge*, trans. by Michelle and Stuart Kendall (Minneapolis: University of Minnesota Press, 2001), p. 160 – Bataille's italics.

162 Michael Székely, 'Text, trembling: Bataille, Breton and Surrealist eroticism' in *Textual Practice*, 19:1 (2005), p. 126 (pp. 113–129).

actuality haunted by one another. Perhaps it was for this reason that Bataille in *Méthode de Méditation* would remark, 'je situe mes efforts à la suite, à côté du surréalisme'[163] ['I situate my efforts as a result of and alongside Surrealism'] and Breton would muse that 'je m'amuse d'ailleurs à penser qu'on ne peut sortir du Surréalisme sans tomber sur M. Bataille'[164] ['I am amused, moreover, to think that one cannot leave Surrealism without running into Mr Bataille'[165]].

Bernard Noël writes that there was 'within Breton an unrecognised Bataille: one can sense it behind *Nadja* and in which the spark of poetry is revealed outside the beautiful moments it achieves and in its failure but this Bataille then continues to pass unnoticed, even if now and again his Other is recognised'.[166] In Bataille, Noël similarly discerned 'a Breton who is recognised and rejected, like a double on the point of being reconciled to itself'.[167]

It would seem that by the mid-forties and 1950s, the determination of both writers to reject each other had transformed into mutual recognition – and a realisation that for Surrealism to be the movement it was, composed of myriad contradictions, their relative viewpoints had defining roles to play. In this post-war era Bataille considered the movement as 'l'exigence que j'ai subie et comme l'insatisfaction que je suis'[168] ['the demand to which I have submitted and as the dissatisfaction I exemplify']. Furthermore, Bataille praised Breton for 'guaranteeing authenticity':[169] 'qu'un écrivain parle au nom du destin positif de l'homme, s'en soucie du fond du cœur, avec rage, comme le fanatique de la gloire de Dieu, c'est ce qui paraissait suspendu'[170] ['for a writer to speak in the name of the positive destiny of mankind, about

163 Georges Bataille, 'Méthode de Méditation' (1947) in *Œuvres Complètes – La Somme Athéologique* I (Paris: Gallimard, 1974), vol. V, p. 193.

164 Breton, *Manifestes de Surréalisme*, pp. 132–133.

165 Breton, *Manifestoes of Surrealism*, p. 183.

166 Bernard Noël, *Change*, no. 7 (1970) – quoted in Surya, *An Intellectual Biography*, p. 229.

167 *Ibid.*

168 Bataille, *Œuvres Complètes* XI, p. 31.

169 Georges Bataille, 'Le Surréalisme et sa Différence avec l'Existentialisme' (1945) in *Œuvres Complètes* XI, p. 74; Georges Bataille, 'Surrealism and how it differs from Existentialism' (1945) in *Absence of Myth*, p. 60.

170 Bataille, *Œuvres Complètes* XI, p. 73.

which he cares for with his whole heart, with a sense of rage, as the fanatic speaks of the glory of God – this is what seems so striking'[171]].

In the following chapter I examine the implications of Breton's more positive stance towards eroticism and transgression for his understanding of sublimation, which, perhaps somewhat perplexingly, also became a concern of his in the 1930s. To account for this apparent contradiction in his preoccupations, I will argue that he viewed sublimation as a validation and extension of sexual desire beyond its proper ends, which were not, in the process, forfeited for some higher good. Since this view eschews the repression of Freudian sublimation, I relate it to Marcuse's non-repressive conceptualisation of the term, which as in Surrealism postulates a close connection between the open expression of desire and an improved social reality (consisting of freer and better adjusted individuals). In this respect, a re-consideration of Breton's view of art will also be pivotal in showing how desire and instinct are liberated in Surrealist work and in its defining aesthetic of convulsive beauty.

171 Bataille, *Absence of Myth*, p. 60.

CHAPTER 3

Breton's Non-Repressive View of Sublimation and Art

In the previous chapter, I attempted to qualify the ostensible roles of Bataille and Breton as exponents of desublimation and sublimation respectively, by showing that the latter actively promoted an understanding of eroticism, elective love, Sade, transgression and black humour through theoretical enquiry, historical research (Heine's studies of sexual behaviours), eroticised art forms and a proposed revolution of moral values (in *Contre-Attaque*). Yet at the same time Breton advocated sublimation in his theoretical writings. There remains, then, a discrepancy which needs to be accounted for. This chapter will postulate that Breton's view of sublimation was non-repressive in nature and therefore converged with major aspects of Herbert Marcuse's thought, in particular his musings on 'non-repressive sublimation'.

In fact, the common ground shared by Breton and Marcuse was considerable and based on a number of compelling factors.[1] Firstly, Marcuse's Marxian-inflected sociology shared broadly the same aims as Surrealism in that it similarly supported the overturning of repressive political regimes (capitalist, fascist and communist) in favour of an egalitarian society in which the psychical wellbeing of the individual was central. In the catalogue of the *100th Anniversary of Hysteria International Surrealist Exhibition* in Milwaukee (1978), Franklin Rosemont proposes that 'Marcuse's principal works should be regarded above all as contributions to the Surrealist critique'.[2] Secondly, Marcuse referred to the movement in his letters, writings and theoretical texts between 1955 and 1971 in a way which shows that

1 The implications of comparing Breton's thought with Marcuse's have barely been considered by most existing scholarship on Surrealism. One major exception to this, which explores the intellectual affinities between Marcuse and Surrealism, is Franklin Rosemont, 'Herbert Marcuse and Surrealism' in *Arsenal* 4 (1989), pp. 31–38.

2 *Ibid.*, p. 33.

he found confirmation of his own ideas in Surrealist works and attempted to explore these affinities further. He betrayed an intimate knowledge of the writings of Breton and Péret and broadly supported their revolutionary endeavours on both a social and a linguistic level.[3] Thirdly, Marcuse's ties with Surrealism had a relevance to his own life, in that he had corresponded with the Surrealist artists of Chicago.

The foregoing points demonstrate why a comparison of both writers is apt to be so fruitful. The chapter thus begins by outlining some of the commonalities in how Breton and Marcuse conceived of sublimation, above all in how they considered it an expansion of desire into working life and creative activity rather than its enforced negation. It will then be demonstrated how this non-repressive aspect of sublimation underpins Breton's view of art as well as his concept of convulsive beauty with its regular incursions into the paroxysmal (such as orgasm or hysteria), the taboo-ridden and the liminal. Finally, the function of Eros and Thanatos in Surrealist art will be considered, and I will argue that they have their sublimated correlates in 'the erotic veiled' and 'the explosive fixed' (two of the defining terms of convulsive beauty).

Breton with Marcuse: A Non-Repressive Conception of Sublimation

With respect to the central ideas of psychoanalysis, Breton and Marcuse can be considered as having had a common outlook which contrasted with that of Freud. For Marcuse, Freud's outlook upon civilisation – and how it was conveyed in *Civilisation and Its Discontents* (1930) – represented submission to what he termed 'repressive sublimation'. The latter contributed in large measure to the individual's sense of alienation, subjecting him/her to a life of labour – that is to say, necessary but unpleasurable toil – at the

3 *Ibid.*, pp. 31–33.

expense of the libido's gratification. He was overtly critical of Freud for recognising only the imperiousness of a repressive reality principle whilst failing to provide an alternative to its dehumanising aspect and reclaim what was pleasurable about life: 'The notion that a non-repressive civilisation is impossible is a cornerstone of Freudian theory.'[4]

Eros and Civilization (1955) constituted Marcuse's lengthy counter-proposal to Freud's narrative of an unhappy civilisation:

> Freud repeatedly emphasized that the lasting interpersonal relations on which civilization depends presuppose that the sex instinct is inhibited in its aim [...]. The full force of civilised morality was mobilised against the use of the body as mere object, means, instrument of pleasure [...]. With the emergence of a non-repressive reality principle, with the abolition of the surplus-repression necessitated by the performance principle, this process would be reversed [...]. No longer used as a full-time instrument of labour, the body would be resexualised.[5]

In the same treatise he put forward an alternative non-repressive view of sublimation. The aim of doing so was to provide a much more affirmative account of Eros than Freud (who had presented it as anti-civilisational) as well as to address the problem of personal transformation (of how to create psychically emancipated and well-adjusted individuals) which must accompany social transformation. This was a question which had long been neglected by Marxism as well as Freud.

As we saw in the introduction, Breton, like Marcuse, opposed the notion of a repressive civilisation which he likened to a 'monstrous oppressive organism'[6] though his main concern was to elaborate a notion of sublimation suited to the artistic projects which formed the basis of so much Surrealist activity. He believed that a genuinely free and uncensored form of art (as expounded via successive Surrealist manifestoes) would be the best guarantor of a forward-thinking, non-repressive society.

While Breton's comments about psychoanalytic concepts were not specifically directed at Freud, as had been the case with Marcuse, they

4 Marcuse, *Eros and Civilization*, p. 17.

5 Marcuse, *Eros and Civilization*, p. 201.

6 Breton, *Les Vases Communicants*, p. 146; Breton, *Communicating Vessels*, p. 126.

did reveal discrepancies in how Breton had understood and applied them (vis-à-vis their original use in Freudian theory). These discrepancies reflected Breton's determination to employ psychoanalysis as a means of fostering unhampered artistic expression and better supporting (/understanding) the inner life. Sublimation, for example, was adapted to those aspects of Breton's thought which focussed on creative self-expression, in particular to his vision of convulsive beauty. In the *Second Manifeste* he paid tribute to 'this Freudian concept', before subsequently defining sublimation as '[le] souci de créer, de détruire artistiquement'[7] ['the concern to create, to destroy artistically'[8]]. The addition of a destructive quality to sublimation, considered here in its application to art, was significant: firstly as it appeared to mirror his view of compulsive beauty as 'explosive-fixed' (as will be further discussed below); and secondly as it represented a departure from any normalising use of the term, drawing on the aggressive instincts of the id to produce art in rupture with the status quo. This was further reinforced by Breton's exhortation that artists should practise sublimation in order to 'suppléer par une auto-observation […] à ce qui laisse d'insuffisant la pénétration des états d'âme dits "artistiques" par des hommes qui ne sont pas artistes mais la plupart médicins'[9] ['to perform an act of self-observation […] to compensate for what is insufficient about the penetration of so-called "artistic" states of mind by men who for the most part are not artist but doctors'[10]]. Breton clearly rejected the curative ends of medicine and art therapy as well as empirical explanations of art-making. His aim was for Surrealist art to analyse more incisively the interactions of the psychic and the social and thereby to challenge people's complacency about reality.

In the sphere of art Breton proposed that sublimation could mobilise the repressed components of the *id* in such a way as to serve the ego ideal in enriching the creative capabilities of the artist:

7 Breton, *Manifestes du Surréalisme*, pp. 109–110.
8 Breton, *Manifestoes of Surrealism*, pp. 160–161.
9 Breton, *Manifestes du Surréalisme*, p. 110.
10 Breton, *Manifestoes of Surrealism*, pp. 160–161.

> Le mécanisme de sublimation qui intervient [...] et que la psychanalyse a mis en évidence, a pour objet de rétablir un équilibre rompu entre le 'moi' cohérent et les éléments refoulés. Ce rétablissement s'opère au profit de l' 'idéal du moi' qui dresse contre la réalité présente, insupportable, les puissances du monde intérieur, du 'soi', communes à tous les hommes et constamment en voie d'épanouissement dans le devenir.[11]
>
> [The process of sublimation, which here comes into play [....] and whose existence has been revealed by psychoanalysis, tries to restore the broken equilibrium between the coherent 'ego' and its repressed elements. This restoration works to the advantage of the 'ego ideal' which marshals against the unbearable present reality all those powers of the inner world, of the 'id', which are common to all men and ever poised for an enriching self-expression in the future.[12]]

The idea that sublimation did not compromise psychic well-being represented a radical departure from Freud's thinking. For the latter, the formation of the ego ideal was entirely distinct from the process of sublimation as well as serving the super ego[13] in a manner which exacerbated repression rather than attenuating it.[14] The notion that the *id* could be brought into play either to foster creative sublimation or support the crusade of the inner life against reality was an idea peculiar to Breton. The process was, moreover, conceived by him to be restorative as if to promote the psychical health of the subject and counter the effects of a repressive society.

11 Breton, *Œuvres Complètes* III, p. 686.

12 Breton, *What is Surrealism?*, 2, p. 185 – translation modified extensively by me in order to account for the mistranslations of Freudian terminology into English and other shortcomings which estrange the translation from the original.

13 Freud comments that in serving the super ego it is 'the vehicle of the ego ideal by which the ego measures itself, which it emulates, and whose demand for ever greater perfection it strives to fulfil [...] the precipitate of the old picture of the parents, the expression of admiration for the perfection which the child then attributed to them' – Freud, 'New Introductory Lectures' in *Complete Psychological Works* XXII, pp. 64–65.

14 'the formation of an ego ideal and sublimation are quite differently related to the causation of neurosis. As we have learnt, the formation of an ideal heightens the demands of the ego and is the most powerful factor favouring repression' – Freud, 'On Narcissism: An Introduction' in *Complete Psychological Works* XIV, p. 95.

The reparation afforded to the *id* through artistic sublimation was also discussed in very similar terms in Breton's 'Situation Surréaliste de l'Objet' (1935), in which he associated art with the subordination of the ego to the *id* as well as the ascendency of the pleasure principle over the reality principle.[15] In his writings, Breton took up the discussion of Freud's two principles on multiple occasions to stress the importance of harnessing pleasure to the detriment of reality. This was not just an artistic imperative but helped counter the effects of an impoverished personal and social reality. In 'Conférences de Mexico' (1938), for example, he underlined the necessity for Surrealism to 'cut the cord with' and 'transgress' the reality principle[16] in an attempt to promote the pleasure principle and 'faire du désir le maître du monde'[17] ['to make desire the master of the world']. This was a bold claim, which nonetheless provided an insight into Surrealism's principal ambitions.

In *Eros and Civilization*, Marcuse similarly affirmed that artistic work grew out of a non-repressive instinctual constellation[18] and was exceptional in the pleasure it afforded the individual, in particular as compared to all other forms of work. Such was the delectation associated with art-making that, according to Marcuse, the term 'sublimation' might require modification[19] (indirectly suggesting, again, the need for a non-repressive variant).

15 'En art, la recherche nécessairement de plus en plus systématique de ces sensations travaille à l'abolition du moi dans le soi, s'efforce par suite de faire prédominer de plus en plus nettement le principe du plaisir sur le principe de réalité' – André Breton, 'Situation Surréaliste de l'Objet' (1935) in *Œuvres Complètes* II, p. 490 ['In art the necessarily more and more systematic search for these sensations works toward the dissolution of the *ego* in the *id*, and consequently it endeavours to make the pleasure principle hold clearer and clearer sway over the reality principle' – André Breton, 'Surrealist Situation of the Object' (1935) in *Manifestoes of Surrealism*, p. 273. The words 'abolition of the ego by the id' in the original translation have been replaced by the 'dissolution of the *ego* in the *id*' in my translation]. Breton would repeat these ideas in a later text entitled 'Trait d'Union' (or 'Hyphen' in English) in *Œuvres Complètes* IV, p. 852.

16 Breton, *Œuvres Complètes* II, 1261 – Breton's italics.

17 *Ibid.*

18 Marcuse, *Eros and Civilization*, p. 84.

19 *Ibid.*

He went on to assert that psychoanalysis had a significant role to play in the investigation of art's erotic origins though these stemmed as much from the sensuousness of the artwork itself as from the psyche of the artist.[20] Art expressed the 'order of sensuousness', an order which challenged the prevailing order of logic as well as pitting 'the logic of gratification' against that of repression:[21] 'Behind the sublimated aesthetic form, the unsublimated content shows forth: the commitment of art to the pleasure principle'.[22] Like Breton, he believed that such art actively countered the reality principle[23] and resulted from the mining of the subconscious: 'the opposition of phantasy to the reality principle is more at home in such sub-real and surreal processes as dreaming, daydreaming, play, the "stream of consciousness"'.[24] Thus Marcuse also envisaged a form of sublimation which was non-normalising in so far as it drew on the subconscious and the pleasure principle to counter reality.

In Marcuse's œuvre, sublimation was mostly presented as a corollary of work (and work was at all times associated with Freud's reality principle). Apart from the obvious exception of artistic activity, Marcuse insisted that the work undertaken by most people was repressive in nature and led to both unfreedom and unhappiness. Many of his musings were, again, a direct response to Freud's *Civilisation and Its Discontents*, in which the latter had highlighted the difficulties of the majority, 'who work under the stress of necessity',[25] in finding satisfaction in their working life. For Freud, then, sublimation offered little or no pleasure to the majority of working men and women. Marcuse's solution of non-repressive sublimation would thus manifest itself 'in contradiction to the

20 *Ibid.*, p. 185.
21 *Ibid.*
22 *Ibid.*
23 Marcuse, *Eros and Civilization*, p. 105.
24 Marcuse, *Eros and Civilization*, pp. 145–146.
25 Freud, *Complete Psychological Works* XXI, p. 80 – on the same page, Freud does concede that 'professional activity is a source of special satisfaction if it is a freely chosen one – if, that is to say, by means of sublimation, it makes possible the use of existing inclinations, of persisting or constitutionally reinforced instinctual impulses' yet he acknowledges the difficulties of the majority in finding such pleasurable employment.

entire sphere of social usefulness; [...] it is the negation of all accepted productivity and performance'[26] and provide the foundation of a freer and more playful society.

Breton was similarly derisive about work and characterised it as that perennial obligation which weighed down upon (wo)man and crushed him or her.[27] He lamented the 'nécessité de l'asservissement de l'homme par l'homme, le souci d'exploiter d'une manière inavouée le besoin impérieux de transformation sociale au profit de la seule oligarchie financière et industrielle'[28] ['necessity of man to enslave man, the careful underhanded exploitation of the urgent need to transform society for the sole profit of a financial and industrial oligarchy'[29]]. *In La Révolution Surréaliste*, in an article headed 'La Dernière Grève' ('The Last Strike'), Breton presented workers as being the allies of artists and intellectuals in that they were all the dispossessed victims of the same exploitative system. He defended their right to fight for freedom by striking, an action which would form the prelude to wider social agitation. Only this sort of protest against working conditions could assure the overcoming of 'unpleasure', 'the triumph of the spirit', the 'freedom of thought', the realisation of 'individual and collective will' as well as the free 'play of human inclinations'.[30]

In their projects for a freer and more pleasure-oriented society both Marcuse and Breton suggested that sublimation need not entail the diversion of libidinal energy away from its primary aims; indeed, it could be re-integrated into all societal functions and most notably that of work. The mechanism of sublimation could offer the subject additional means of creative expression and psychical relief without sacrificing libidinal energy in the process. Marcuse believed that alienating labour would thus give way

26 Marcuse, *Eros and Civilization*, p. 208.

27 Breton, *Œuvres Complètes* II, p. 226; Breton, *What is Surrealism?*, p. 113.

28 Breton, 'Position politique de l'art d'aujourd'hui' (1935) in *Œuvres Complètes* II, pp. 416–417.

29 Breton, 'Political Position of Today's Art' (1935) in *Manifestoes of Surrealism*, p. 213.

30 André Breton, 'La Dernière Grève' in *La Révolution Surréaliste*, 2 (1925), pp. 1–3.

to playful work.[31] In the process, the body itself would become 'an object of cathexis [...] an instrument of pleasure'[32] with libidinal energy being redistributed throughout the body in such a way that all erotogenic zones would become activated and the genital supremacy of sexuality would be transcended. Marcuse named this process the 'the self-sublimation of sexuality' and the more diffuse form of libido in which it resulted 'Eros'. Both concepts were, moreover, fundamental to non-repressive sublimation.

Like Marcuse, Breton seemed to predicate a new world order upon a recognition of the subject's libidinal life and its claim to free expression (indeed, this was one of the major commonalities in the thinking of both writers). In *Arcane 17* he declared that 'la vie humaine est à repassioner'[33] ['human life must be re-impassioned'[34]] and in the fourth *Conférence d'Haïti* (1946) he sought a more elaborate philosophical basis for this statement by considering a number of theoretical frameworks for the establishment of freedom.[35] These included ideas about how the sexual instincts might find gratification not only in the personal domain but in the assumption of a social utility in the world beyond. He reserved particular praise for Charles Fourier who posited the existence of twelve passions which could be given full expression in society according to their nature and function. There were five passions of the senses (touch, taste, hearing, sight and smell); four of the soul (friendship, love, ambition and parenthood); and three that he called distributive (*la Papillone* or the love of variety, *la Cabaliste*, the desire for rivalry and competition, and *la Composite*, a combination of passions). On account of their diverse nature and unexplored capacity for playfulness, Breton asserted that these passions would establish widespread

31 In *One Dimensional Man* Marcuse gives more concrete examples of playful work, for example handicrafts as opposed to products manufactured on the assembly line, the home-baked loaf as opposed to factory-produced bread. See Marcuse, *One Dimensional Man*, p. 73.

32 Marcuse, *Eros and Civilization*, p. 201.

33 Breton, *Arcane 17*, p. 197.

34 Breton, *Arcanum 17*, p. 149.

35 In the *Conférence* he spoke also of the intention to publish a critical anthology of freedom but, in fact, this never made it to print; only the groundwork for it appeared in this speech.

social harmony.[36] He also maintained that if these passions were liberated rather than repressed, finding a positive outlet in the subject's immediate environment, the dangers of regression (expressed as a recourse to vice) would diminish:

> Les passions, selon Fourier, sont universelles et sont bonnes ; l'ascétisme se trompe en les niant, et c'est sur les passions que doit s'établir la société future. C'est précisément le refrènement – on dirait aujourd'hui le refoulement – des passions qui en fait des vices. Ces vices disparaîtront dans une bonne organisation sociale où les passions ne seront plus combattues, mais encouragées et où il sera veillé à leur judicieuse utilisation.[37]
>
> [Passions, according to Fourier, are universal and good; asceticism is deceived in denying them, and it is on the passions that future society must be founded. It is precisely the reigning in – one would say today the repression – of the passions which makes vices of them. These vices will disappear in a good social organisation where the passions will no longer be fought, but encouraged and where their judicious employment will be carefully tended to.]

Breton and Marcuse both denied that a wide-scale unshackling of the instincts would pose a threat to society. Marcuse's specific claim was that the genitofugal redistribution of libidinal energies across the body[38] would not result in a society of sex maniacs, for the process would involve 'a spread rather than explosion of libido [...] the free development of transformed libido within transformed institutions, while eroticising previously tabooed zones, time, and relations, would *minimise* the manifestations of *mere* sexuality by integrating them into a far larger order',[39] an order which straddled the personal and the social, leisure and work.

36 Breton, 'Entretiens 1913–1952' in Œuvres Complètes III, p. 598; André Bretons, *Conversations – The Autobiography of Surrealism* (New York: Marlowe & Co., 1993), p. 206.

37 Breton, *Œuvres Complètes* III, p. 265. Breton's italics.

38 Marcuse defined genitofugal libido as moving '*away* from genital supremacy toward the erotization of the entire organism'. Significantly, he also outlined the possibility of such libido being channeled into '"cultural" expression, *without* external repressive modification'. Marcuse's italics. See *Eros and Civilization*, p. 208.

39 Marcuse, *Eros and Civilization*, pp. 201–202. Marcuse's italics.

For Breton, Eros would, in an egalitarian society, reach similar ends. In *L'Amour Fou* – and in paraphrasing Friedrich Engels – he declared that the freeing of humanity from any social and economic constraints within the personal domain would not result in a regression to "disordered" sexual relations'[40] but that, for the first time in history, genuine monogamous relationships could be realised.

Despite the discrepancies between Breton's beliefs and Freud's, he adduced the latter to underscore the value of Eros in strengthening (rather than debasing) society and in forging cohesive bonds between disparate social classes and cultures. He specifically highlighted Freud's claim that Eros dismantles the hierarchies and barriers which keep races, nations and social groups apart.[41] Unlike the latter, he did not, however, believe in the eventual conflict of interests which might arise between the libidinal expenditure of individuals in the private sphere and the forging of collective bonds upon which civilisation was predicated.[42] Freud had warned that the sublimation required for communal bonds would inevitably entail a desexualising cathexis for the individual, a prospect which Breton would have clearly rejected. He was unwilling to see desire, elective love or any form of creative energy residing within the self sacrificed in the name of civilisation or other collective entities. This more life-affirming view underlines again the difference in outlook between Freud and Breton, a difference which was also apparent in the latter's hopes to reclaim the subject's personal life:

40 Breton, *L'Amour Fou*, p. 112; Breton, *Mad Love*, p. 77.

41 Breton, *L'Amour Fou*, p. 112 – Breton's italics; Breton, *Mad Love*, p. 77 – Breton's italics.

42 See Marcuse, *Eros and Civilization*, pp. 82–83 and Freud, *Complete Psychological Works* XXI, pp. 108–109: 'Reality shows us that civilization is not content with the ties we have so far allowed it. It aims at binding the members of the community together in a libidinal way as well and employs every means to that end. It favours every path by which strong identifications can be established between the members of the community, and it summons up aim-inhibited libido on the largest scale so as to strengthen the communal bond by relations of friendship. In order for these aims to be fulfilled, a restriction upon sexual life is unavoidable'.

> Il est inadmissible que dans la société nouvelle la vie privée, avec ses chances et ses déceptions, demeure la grande distributrice comme aussi la grande privatrice des énergies. Le seul moyen de l'éviter est de préparer à l'existence subjective une revanche éclatante sur le terrain de la connaissance, de la conscience sans faiblesse et sans honte.[43]
>
> [It is inadmissible that in the new society private life, with its ups and downs, should remain the great distributor and also the great depriver of energies. The only way of avoiding this is to prepare for subjective existence some stunning revenge on the terrain of knowledge, of consciousness without weakness and without shame.[44]]

The quotation was a reaffirmation of Breton's conviction that the emergence of a 'new society' would be premised upon the shaking up of established knowledge through a more profound engagement with the inner life (which in turn would occasion the means and understanding by which it could be better sustained). The 'stunning revenge' Breton speaks about would entail a thoroughgoing re-examination and rebalancing of the inner life based upon the insights obtained. For Breton political struggle would therefore have to be accompanied by the reclamation of the individual's subjectivity and, to use Marcuse's term, *Innerlichkeit* ('inwardness' / 'interiority').

Subjectivity and Artistic Autonomy

In *Les Vases Communicants*, Breton referred to subjectivity as 'la royauté de la nuit'[45] ['the royalty of night'[46]] but bewailed the fact that this richest of all terrains, as he referred to it, had been left 'uncultivated'.[47] He claimed that the history of the subjective had lost out to theology and that the

43 Breton, *Vases Communicants*, p. 152 – my italics.
44 Breton, *Communicating Vessels*, pp. 130–131 – my italics.
45 Breton, *Vases Communicants*, p. 167.
46 Breton, *Communicating Vessels*, p. 144.
47 Breton, *Vases Communicants*, p. 166; Breton, *Communicating Vessels*, p. 142.

exploration of the subjective outside of religious discourse had been greatly neglected. In any other domain – such as literary history – its treatment had never been more than piecemeal and unsatisfactory.[48]

The recuperation of the subjective was, then, a vital aspect of Surrealism's mission. The term 'subjectivity' encompassed many of the movement's preoccupations, such as dreams, the emotional and instinctual life, the unconscious, the range of mental states which constitute human experience (from sanity to madness), the function of thought and the imagination. Breton's reference to universal subjectivity as 'the royalty of night' suggests, however, that it was dreams (with their close connection to the subconscious and the instinctual) which epitomised subjective self-expression for the Surrealists. This was also reflected by the privileged position it was accorded in Breton's reinterpreted dialectic of inner life and exterior reality, which in *Les Vases Communicants* frequently became the interplay of dream life and material reality.

Breton's goal in presenting these two realities as dialectical was to show how dreamwork afforded a reparation to waking consciousness[49] by inducing the epiphanies needed to overcome the problems and tensions of everyday life and thus to spur the subject to constructive action. He prized the utility of dreams in the social sphere rather than just their interpretation for curative ends (as would be the priority in Freudian doctrine) and thus opposed the Freudian hypotheses 'which see in dreaming a hallucinatory satisfaction, made possible by a regression to repressed perceptions (an entirely asocial satisfaction which is even, most of the time,

48 Breton, *Vases Communicants*, p. 168; Breton, *Communicating Vessels*, p. 145.

49 'Puisque l'activité pratique de veille entraîne chez l'homme un affaiblissement constant de la substance vitale qui ne trouve à se compenser partiellement que dans le sommeil, l'activité de réparation qui est la fonction de celui-ci ne mériterait-elle pas mieux que cette disgrâce faisant de presque tout homme un dormeur *honteux* ?' – Breton, *Vases Communicants*, p. 166. ['Because the actual activity of waking [consciousness] entails a constant drain on man's vital substance which can be partially compensated for only in sleeping, doesn't the restorative activity that is sleep's function deserve better than this disgraceful attitude that makes almost any sleeper *ashamed*?' – Breton, *Communicating Vessels*, p. 142]. Breton's italics.

incomprehensible for the dreamer)'.[50] For Breton, accessing repressed affects via the dream state was not asocial but allowed the subject to rework day residues, which in turn led to an active re-examination of his or her reality. The analysis of one's own dreams could, therefore, be a significant catalyst for a change.

Harris points out that Breton's view of the inner life reflected 'an imperative shared by many revolutionary intellectuals in the 1930s to make thought active, to relate the hitherto separate spheres of thought and action, action and dream, a separation that had been understood to be the hallmark of a separate, modernist art and literature since the time of Baudelaire'.[51] For this reason, the Surrealists considered the world of dreams and fantasies a complement to social engagement with the dialectical interdependency of dream and action abetting rather than contradicting the dialectical materialism of Marxism. At a time when fascism was gaining ever more support across Europe, the Surrealists viewed the defence of thought and the inner life as essential to maintaining the momentum of a Marxist revolution and, thereby, to realising their hope of wide-scale personal emancipation:

> que pour nous, surréalistes, les intérêts de la pensée ne sauraient cesser d'aller de pair avec les intérêts de la classe ouvrière. Que toute menace aux libertés, toute entrave à l'émancipation de la classe ouvrière et à plus forte raison toute attaque contre elle à main armée est par nous ressentie comme une tentative d'empoisonnement de la pensée.[52]

> [for us surrealists, the interests of thought cannot cease to go hand in hand with the interests of the working class, and that all attacks on freedom, all fetters on the emancipation of the working class and all armed attacks on it cannot fail to be considered by us as attacks on thought likewise.[53]]

Breton also explained that the liberation of thought was dependent on the ability of the individual to reconnect with and express the contents of his/

50 Jean-Pierre Morel and Philip Lewis, 'Breton and Freud' in *Diacritics*, vol. 2, no. 2 (Summer, 1972), p. 23.

51 Harris, *Surrealist Art and Thought*, p. 2.

52 Breton, *Œuvres Complètes* II, p. 261.

53 Breton, *What is Surrealism?*, 2, pp. 140–141.

her imagination, the very locus of the inner life and the subjective. There existed a direct correlation between the degree to which the imagination (in itself a site of the concretisation of subconscious instincts and desires) could be translated into reality and the overcoming of repression. Giving artistic form to the imagination was one way of achieving this; above all, it brought about a more authentic form of communication which expressed the truth of the subject's interiority on its own terms 'en dehors de toute préoccupation esthétique ou morale'[54] ['exempt from any aesthetic or moral concern'[55]], one of the founding principles of Surrealist practice as articulated in Breton's first manifesto. Personal and political autonomy therefore played an essential role in guaranteeing such authentic self-expression.

The terms with which Breton described the imagination in his manifestoes effectively anthromorphised it as an anarchical insurgent who desires freedom from servitude. In the *Premier Manifeste*, he speculated that the imagination might be on the verge of reclaiming its rights[56] and in *Pour un art révolutionnaire indépendant*, Trotsky and he explicitly affirmed the rights of the imagination to operate without external constraint in all matters of artistic creation.[57] In the *Second Manifeste*, he qualified the philosopher's stone of the alchemists as 'rien autre que ce qui devait permettre à l'imagination de l'homme de prendre sur toutes choses une revanche éclatante'[58] ['nothing more or less than that which was to enable man's imagination to take a stunning revenge on all things'[59]]. The language which he employed to defend the imagination had taken on an increasingly fervid tone, reflecting the increasing importance he had attached to it and its revolutionary potential.

This characterisation of the imagination as restive was broadly reflective of the defiant outlook of many avant-garde movements, who, since the fin-de-siècle, had sought to make their dreams of a free society reality with

54 Breton, *Manifestes du Surréalisme*, p. 36.
55 Breton, *Manifestoes of Surrealism*, p. 26.
56 Breton, *Manifestes du Surréalisme*, p. 20; Breton, *Manifestoes of Surrealism*, p. 10.
57 Breton, *Œuvres Complètes* III, p. 687; Breton, *What is Surrealism?*, 2, p. 185.
58 Breton, *Manifestes du Surréalisme*, p. 124.
59 Breton, *Manifestoes of Surrealism*, p. 174.

their visionary programmes for the future. Movements such as Symbolism and Decadence (from which the Surrealists drew much of their inspiration) gave new momentum to anarchistic conceptions of art first conceived by nineteenth-century thinkers such as Pierre-Joseph Proudhon and Peter Kropotkin.[60] The discussions of the latter (groups and thinkers) about this new anarchistic (or radical left-libertarian) art form centred around a number of common themes: that it should be non-elitist, collectivist, spontaneous, anti-authoritarian and, above all, free from external control. 'Nous ne sommes originaux, nous n'attestons notre liberté et notre personnalité que par notre faculté d'art'[61] ['we are only original, we only bear witness to our freedom and our personalty though the faculty of art'] wrote Proudhon, the first man to call himself an anarchist. Elucidating the function of Symbolism, the poet Remy de Gourmont affirmed that the movement could be translated by the word 'Liberty' (or as 'Anarchy' for the violently inclined) and that it sought nothing more than the personal development of the aesthetic individual.[62] It is not difficult to see the remblances with the ideas put forward by Breton and Trotsky in *Pour un art révolutionnaire indépendant*, a tract which advocated 'toute licence en art' ['complete freedom for art'], a precept which, they maintained, could only be fulfilled through an anarchy of individual liberty co-existing alongside a more centralised socialist regime.[63]

60 For more on the development of this anarchic strain of European thought, the reader is referred to: Patrick McGuinness, *Poetry and Radical Politics in Fin-de-siècle France from Anarchism to Action Française* (Oxford: OUP, 2015) and André Reszler, *L'Esthétique anarchiste* (Paris: Presses Universitaires de France, 1973).

61 Pierre-Joseph Proudhon, 'Du principe de l'art et de sa destination sociale (Nouvelle édition)' in *Œuvres posthumes de P.-J. Proudhon* (Paris: Librairie internationale, A. Lacroix & ce, 1866–1875), p. 12.

62 Remy de Gourmont, 'Le Symbolisme' in *La Revue blanche* (25 juin 1892), pp. 322–323.

63 Breton, *Œuvres Complètes* III, 687; Breton, *What is Surrealism?*, 2, p. 185. Walter Benjamin pithily described the double-edged nature of Surrealist revolt as between an 'anarchistic *fronde* and a revolutionary discipline' – see Walter Benjamin, 'Surrealism – The Last Snapshot of the European Intelligentsia' (1928) in *Reflections – Essays, Aphorisms, Autobiographical Writings*, trans. by Edmund Jephcott, ed. by Peter Demetz (New York: Schocken Books, 1978), p. 177.

On the potential of the imagination to engage in anarchic activity and help foment a social revolution, Marcuse's thought concurred with that of Breton's. In an interview published in the *New York Times Magazine*,[64] Marcuse discussed the New Left and the social upheaval of 1968, commenting that:

> the most interesting aspect of the events of May [was] the coming together of Marx and André Breton. Imagination in power: that is truly revolutionary. It is new and revolutionary to try to translate into reality the most advanced ideas and values of the imagination. This proves that people have learnt an important lesson: that truth is not only in rationality, but just as much and perhaps more in the imaginary [...]. And this is why I believe that the student movement, whatever its immediate results, is a real turning point in the development of contemporary society.[65]

The imagination afforded the artist and his/her audience visions of an alternative future purged of social injustice and critically helped incite the protest required to make this prospect a reality. Even when the imagination conceived of the future as haunting and dystopic, it often prompted the corresponding level of resistance against the development of such a reality. In this regard, Breton defined the role of the artist as revealing 'à la conscience collective ce qui *doit être* et ce qui *sera*. L'œuvre d'art n'est pas valable qu'autant que passent en elle les reflets tremblants du futur'[66] ['to the collective consciousness what *must* be and what *will* be. A work of art is valuable only if it is traversed by luminous tremors of the future'[67]]. In *Eros and Civilization* Marcuse again took up these themes, praising Surrealism for allying the artistic imagination with revolution, and specifically for having gone beyond psychoanalysis to demand that the dream be realised as the future reality without compromising its content:

> The truth value of imagination relates not only to the past but also to the future: the forms of freedom and happiness which it invokes claim to deliver the historical reality.

64 *New York Times Magazine* (27th October 1968).

65 *Ibid.*

66 Breton, *Œuvres Complètes* II, pp. 447–448 – Breton's italics.

67 Breton, *What is Surrealism?*, 2, p. 184 – Breton's italics.

> In its refusal to accept as final the limitations imposed upon freedom and happiness by the reality principle [...] lies the critical function of phantasy.[68]

Above all, he considered this form of resistance to be a decisive move against repression, or, borrowing from A. N. Whitehead, it was the 'Great Refusal', when conceived as the 'protest against unnecessary repression, the struggle for the ultimate form of freedom – "to live without anxiety."'[69] Surrealism's Great Refusal was a concept Marcuse was to return to time and again to underline what he saw as being its primary message.

In addition to prefiguring the future, Surrealist art also functioned as a seismograph for the impact of contemporaneous reality upon it; and, in the process, reflected the truth of this reality back into the world for others to learn from. Such a process was also envisaged as having the greatest transformative, and indeed subversive, effect. With these thoughts in mind, Marcuse in *The Aesthetic Dimension* set out his vision of subjectivity as a dissenting social force:

> With the affirmation of the inwardness of subjectivity, the individual steps out of the network of exchange relationships and exchange values, withdraws from the reality of bourgeois society [...]. Indeed, this escape from reality led to an experience which could (and did) become a powerful force in *invalidating* the actually prevailing bourgeois values, namely, by shifting the locus of the individual's realisation from the domain of the performance principle and the profit motive to that of the inner resources of the human being: passion, imagination, conscience. Moreover, withdrawal and retreat were not the last position. Subjectivity strove to break out of its inwardness into the material and intellectual culture. And today, in the totalitarian period, it has become a political value as a counter-force against aggressive and exploitative socialisation.[70]

The value Marcuse ascribes to the subjective as invalidating bourgeois values evidently contradicts the claim that a preoccupation with interiority is necessarily accompanied by an idealist standpoint, and thus a flight from material reality. In my view, the Surrealists' appropriation of subjectivity

68 Marcuse, *Eros and Civilization*, pp. 148–149.

69 *Ibid.*, pp. 149–150.

70 Marcuse, *Aesthetic Dimension*, pp. 4–5.

can be understood particularly in the light of this invalidating function. Artists' subjective representations revealed the deficiencies of the inner life and the social reality which moulded it; as a result, they played a vital role in exposing the repressive structures of institutions (such as church, state and bourgeois morality) which determined their lives.

In *Pour un art révolutionnaire indépendant*, Breton claimed that the collision between the thinking individual and the social forms of capitalism made allies of the artist and the revolutionary Marxist.[71] He also believed that given art's capacity to liberate the instinctual life, it was able to disrupt and to shatter conventional perceptions and consciousness. This, in turn, had great potential to unsettle the sphere of social relations, again without the risk of wide-scale social regression:

> [la recherche des sensations des couches les plus profondes de l'appareil psychique] tend à libérer de plus en plus l'impulsion instinctive, à abattre la barrière qui se dresse devant l'homme civilisé, barrière qu'ignorent le primitif et l'enfant. La portée d'une telle attitude, étant donné [...] le bouleversement général de la sensibilité qu'elle entraîne (propagation de charges psychiques considérables aux éléments du système perception-conscience) [...] est socialement incalculable.[72]

> [This search [for sensations in the deepest layers of the psychic mechanism] tends more and more to liberate instinctive impulses, to break down the barrier that civilised man faces, a barrier that primitive people and children do not experience. Given [...] the general disruption of sensibility that it brings on (through the communication of quite large psychic charges to the elements of the perception-consciousness system) [...] the import of such an attitude is socially incalculable.[73]]

Breton's thoughts about artistic expression invite comparison with Marcuse's theory of aesthetics, especially in its capacity to critique the norms of capitalist society and foster a consciousness amongst the general public which is amenable to revolutionary action. In *The Aesthetic Dimension*, Marcuse defined 'aesthetic sublimation' as the process of giving aesthetic form to material circumstance. The work of art thus created would take

71 Breton, *Œuvres Complètes* III, p. 686; Breton, *What is Surrealism?*, 2, p. 185.

72 Breton, *Œuvres Complètes* II, p. 490.

73 Breton, *Manifestoes of Surrealism*, p. 273.

on a life of its own and transcend immediate reality. This is because, in art, the objectivity of established social relations gives way to the interpretative subjectivity of the individual; even if the individual depicts actual, historical or social circumstances, they are still interpreted subjectively. According to Marcuse, art was a sphere which contained its own truth: in reshaping reality and giving it aesthetic form, art penetrated deeper into the heart of reality (this he called the sublation of the familiar and the unfamiliar[74]). Critically, this also presumed the work's autonomy: 'The work of art can attain political relevance only as an autonomous work. The aesthetic form is essential to its social function. The qualities of the form negate those of the repressive society'.[75]

In *Pour un art révolutionnaire indépendant* Breton expressed similar ideas about art, calling upon artists to assimilate and reinterpret the tensions of their social and personal environment with the faculties of their inner life:

> … l'artiste ne peut servir la lutte émancipatrice que s'il est pénétré subjectivement de son contenu social et individuel, que s'il en a fait passer le sens et le drame dans ses nerfs et que s'il cherche librement à donner une incarnation artistique à son monde intérieur.[76]

> [… the artist cannot serve the struggle for freedom unless he subjectively assimilates its social and individual content, unless he feels in his very nerves its meaning and drama and freely seeks to give artistic form to his own inner world.[77]]

We may recall that in the *Second Manifeste du Surréalisme* (1930), Breton had qualified sublimation as the artist's act of self-observation, unearthing the verities of the unconscious through automatic art. To this he had, rather significantly, added that in performing such acts of self-analysis Surrealism had required of artists to help bring about a new 'consciousness'.[78] Surrealist

74 Marcuse, *Aesthetic Dimension*, p. 41.
75 *Ibid.*, p. 53.
76 Breton, *Œuvres Complètes* III, p. 688.
77 Breton, *What is Surrealism?*, 2, p. 186 – translation modified by me.
78 Breton, *Manifestes du Surréalisme*, pp. 109–110 – Breton's italics; Breton, *Manifestoes of Surrealism*, p. 160 – Breton's italics.

works thus aspired to create a counter-consciousness to everyday lived experience, the artist's symbolic, desire-laden language of the subconscious contrasting sharply with the firm assumptions of mundane reality.

For Marcuse, art which, as in Surrealism, was rooted in subjectivity of the self, actively negated a realistic-conformist mind-set. Far from promoting bourgeois 'false consciousness' (as traditional Marxist aesthetic theory held) it 'accused' reality. Dominant norms, needs and values were invalidated and art became a dissenting social force. Upon confronting this type of art, the individual was more inclined to seek the dissolution of repressive institutions and norms as well as to subvert the social management of Eros and Thanatos. Marcuse referred to this process as 'desublimation' (i.e. the breaking up of dominant norms and values in society – not to be confused with 'desublimation' as the infusion of base sexuality into art).

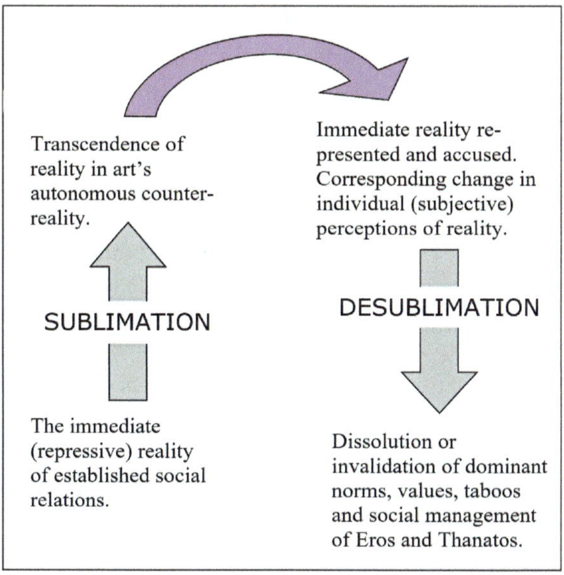

Figure 3.1: Marcuse's model of sublimation and desublimation as applied to the interrelationship between art and society in *The Aesthetic Dimension* (1979).

Marcuse's model of aesthetic sublimation and desublimation (see Figure 3.1) – with its emphasis on art challenging individual consciousness and dominant norms, ideas and institutions – had parallels with Surrealism's endeavours to produce works which counteracted the repressive features of society (a point to which I shall return presently).

Like Marcuse, Breton believed in the political importance of art and in its capacity to break down the fixed norms and values of an inequitable society. As well as insisting on art's independence in *Pour un art révolutionnaire indépendant*, he also underscored its capacity to stoke up a general desire for social reconstruction by drawing attention to humanity's needs and deficits: 'L'art véritable [....] s'efforce de donner une expression aux besoins intérieurs de l'homme et de l'humanité d'aujourd'hui, ne peut pas ne pas être révolutionnaire, c'est-à-dire ne pas aspirer à une reconstruction complète et radicale de la société'[79] ['True art insists on expressing the inner needs of man and of mankind in its time – true art is unable not to be revolutionary, not to aspire to a complete and radical reconstruction of society'[80]]. In 'Political Position of Today's Art' (1935) he even quoted C. Day Lewis in order to show how a bankrupt social reality became encoded into the symbolic language of art and poetry:

> The poet gives his universe, and translates into his own language, the language of individual truth, the coded messages that he receives. In a capitalist regime these materials cannot help but have a capitalist tinge. But if this regime is dying, or as you would have it, is already dead, its poetry is bound to point this out.[81]

His remarks appear to be made in anticipation of a Marcusean 'desublimation' of fixed ideas and social structures especially when the latter could be identified as moribund and antagonistic to humanity's basic needs.

In an interview with the socialist journal 'Indice' (1935) Breton remarked upon the 'undeniability' of there being two currents of art in history – one which was closely linked to the dominant classes, the other

79 Breton, *Œuvres Complètes* III, p. 687.

80 Breton, *What is Surrealism?*, 2, p. 184.

81 Breton quoting C. Day Lewis, *Manifestoes of Surrealism*, p. 226. Text originally in English.

non-conformist.[82] He aligned Surrealism and its nineteenth-century progenitors such as Baudelaire and Rimbaud with the latter class. Authors whose works were written and conceived under the capitalist system (or were simply the product of an elite sphere of culture) were not, however, rejected outright by Breton or Marcuse. For Marcuse, works of 'high culture' represented one of the primary means of aesthetic sublimation – namely the expression of the social in the particular. The individual's fate was recoded as a literary work showing him to be at the mercy of forces which were both extrinsic (such as class struggle) and intrinsic (such as Eros and Thanatos, other impulses which governed his behaviour as a lover, scoundrel, fool and so on). Contrary to established Marxist aesthetic theory, which would consider any such abstraction from class struggle to be decadent and elitist, he underlined the value of the transhistorical, universal truths expressed in existing canonical works. For him, the consciousness embodied within this literature stood apart from the consciousness promoted by capitalist society, appealing to and developing the life-enhancing faculties of any mind which became increasingly attuned to the injustices and depredations of reality. Such literature and art would not necessarily change the world of itself but could, according to Marcuse, contribute to changing the consciousness and drives of those individuals who might oppose aspects of the world from the resultant maturation of their thinking. The study of high-brow art and literature was, therefore, desirable in any future praxis of liberation.

Breton similarly believed that, rather than hamper the path to social transformation, so-called 'bourgeois art' could help promote the sort of knowledge which might spawn an appetite for a radical change in society. He recognised the value of high culture in mediating transhistorical truths

82 'Interview d' "Indice"' in *Œuvres Complètes* II, 445; Breton, 'Interview with "Indice"' in *What is Surrealism?*, 2, p. 144 – Breton considers this non-conformist wing of culture to have reached its ascendancy in the nineteenth century in the literary works of Baudelaire, Courbet, Rimbaud and Lautréamont; and in the contemporary art of Ernst and Picasso which expresses 'une émotion d'ordre révolutionnaire', *Œuvres Complètes* II, p. 448 ['an emotion of a revolutionary nature', *What is Surrealism?*, 2, p. 146].

which appealed to all classes and allowed them to better understand the world in its complexity. Far from resulting in the complete exaltation of culture beyond the concerns of material reality, high culture could thereby foster revolutionary consciousness. In a speech made to the 'Leftist Front' of Prague, Breton's use of quotations provided ample evidence of this belief, among them a reference to an English text by Stephen Spender which contended that the high art of past epochs was on no account anti-revolutionary:

> ... bourgeois art is not bourgeois propaganda, but simply the depiction of that phase of our society when the bourgeois class possessed culture [....]. It might seem much closer to the truth to maintain that bourgeois art has played a large part in the downfall of capitalist society, but this opinion would be as erroneous as the one I have just mentioned: art has merely placed already existent forces working to pull the regime down into contact with each other [....] art may allow revolutionary militants to see clearly those events in history that have the most political meaning, in the deepest sense of the word.[83]

Like Marcuse, Breton differed from those revolutionary Marxists who considered canonical literature as bourgeois self-indulgence. In the same speech, he therefore eulogised Shakespeare, Goethe and Baudelaire for their exceptional aptitude for self-expression and for allowing the interpretative subjectivity of the artist to be presented as a reality in its own right:

> Le don d'expression exceptionnel d'un Shakespeare, d'un Goethe ou d'un Baudelaire est chose non moins universellement reconnue. Les hommes de toutes conditions, de toutes classes, qui trouvent dans leurs œuvres une justification éclatante, qui y puisent une conscience passagèrement triomphante du sens de leurs douleurs et de leurs joies, ne perdent pas de vue qu'un privilège unique permet, de loin en loin, à la subjectivité artistique de s'identifier à la véritable objectivité.[84]

> [The exceptional gift of expression of a Shakespeare, of a Goethe or of a Baudelaire is something which is no less recognised on a universal scale. Men of all conditions, of all classes, who find a splendid justification in their works – who find in them a

83 Breton, *Manifestoes of Surrealism*, p. 227.
84 Breton, *Œuvres Complètes* II, p. 426.

> temporarily triumphant awareness of the meaning of their joys and sorrows – do not lose sight of the fact that a unique privilege every now and then allows artistic subjectivity to become identical with true objectivity[85]].

The context in which Breton's speech was made was not insignificant – and in particular with regard to the issue of artistic autonomy. At a time when he had still been seeking an alliance with the PCF, he had hoped, by his comments, to persuade the Left of the righteousness of Surrealism's basic principles. Given the growing tendency of the Stalinist USSR to regulate cultural output, he had set out to strengthen the case for artistic autonomy and the role of the subjective. Breton's speech had thus been an opportunity for him to insist on the soundness of his core beliefs, which had met with a great deal of scepticism after the publication of *Les Vases Communicants*. Quoting directly from the book, he reaffirmed Surrealism's ambition to continue to ('unir [....] cette activité de transformation à cette activité d'interprétation'[86] ['unite [....] this activity of transformation [of the world] with this activity of interpretation'[87]]).

By underlining the centrality of art's interpretative capacities in transforming the world, he was again endorsing the value of subjective self-expression. As will now be demonstrated, this type of self-expression manifested itself particularly in the convulsive nature of Surrealism's artworks. As the Surrealists probed the depths of their inner psyche, they unleashed the powers of Eros and Thanatos, those two fundamental instincts of the human psyche which helped to define Surrealism's aesthetic of convulsive beauty. It was these instincts which – when exploited for artistic purposes – best succeeded in accusing the repressive structures of reality and disconcerting the beholder of Surrealist works.

85 Breton, *Manifestoes of Surrealism*, p. 221.
86 Breton, *Œuvres Complètes* II, p. 430.
87 Breton, *Manifestoes of Surrealism*, p. 225.

Convulsive Beauty: Eros and Thanatos Unbound

The term 'convulsiveness' is an apt *leitmotiv* for Surrealism's most important concerns: hysteria, paroxysms of orgasmic bliss, sudden or sporadic revolutionary actions, the convulsions of space-time which engineer the synchronistic encounters between future lovers. All of these phenomena serve on the whole not to promote civilisation but to undermine it and to allow human passion and creativity to flourish in all its guises.

In Foster's major work on Surrealism *Compulsive Beauty* instances of Surrealist 'convulsiveness' are re-interpreted as repressive 'compulsion' (hence the title of Foster's book). In the remainder of this chapter I wish to reconsider his understanding of Bretonian Surrealism, which attributes the actions and motives of its main players to the effects of repression, by considering also those occasions when they were reacting against these effects. In examining Breton's literary works (*Nadja*, *Les Vases Communicants* and *L'Amour Fou*), Foster sometimes provides a symptomatic reading of their content and casts the narrator (Breton) into the role of a traumatised patient:

> As Freud theorised in 1926 (almost contemporaneously with Nadja), anxiety in Bretonian Surrealism is a signal (Angstsignal), a repetition of a reaction to a past trauma triggered by a perception of a present danger. Repressed, the trauma is subsumed by the signal, just as in the uncanny the referent is subsumed by the sign. The enigma of the signal, then, attests not to a lack of signification to be filled in the future but an overdetermination produced in the past. This is why Breton is an 'agonised witness' of these signals...[88]

Most of Breton's motives and actions – including his chance encounters with the female characters of these works, his passion for locating unusual and discarded objects – are attributed to repression, which, Foster affirms, engenders an uncanny compulsion to repeat. Given the Surrealists' strident opposition to established thought forms, I want to suggest that this yoke of repression was not always accepted quite so passively.

88 Foster, *Compulsive Beauty*, p. 31.

As will be demonstrated in this section, Surrealist works often functioned as a counterpoint to social reality by expressing those buried passions, unconscious desires and neurotic fears which accused the restrictive socio-political structures around them. This was particularly evident in those Surrealist paintings which embodied the notion of convulsive beauty: their haunting iconography had the potential to destabilise and unsettle the thoughts and sensations of their spectatorship by drawing attention to the inadequacies of material reality and the fate of the individual within it. Thus, the subjective dimension of these works did not so much estrange the Surrealist artist from reality as it helped him/her to subvert it.

Convulsiveness hardly appeared to promote conventional Freudian sublimation (of the type Foster attributes to Surrealism) if this entailed a surrender to the established order of things. Indeed, this would have contradicted Freud's analysis of the supporting role of sublimated pleasures in upholding civilisation: 'at present we can only say figuratively that such satisfactions seem "finer and higher." But their intensity is mild as compared with that derived from the sating of crude and primary instinctual impulses; it does not convulse our physical being'.[89] This sedate, non-convulsive formulation of pleasure articulated by a mature Freud again seemed to put his psychoanalytical project at odds with the ambitions of Surrealism, and above all with Breton, for whom 'la beauté sera convulsive ou ne sera pas'[90] ['beauty will be convulsive or will not be'[91]] and for whom sublimation and pleasure were not mutually exclusive.

Breton later qualified this definition of convulsive beauty in *L'Amour Fou* with the formula 'la beauté convulsive sera érotique-voilée, explosante-fixe, magique-circonstancielle ou ne sera pas'[92] ['veiled-erotic, fixed-explosive, magic-circumstantial or will not be'[93]]. His principal example of this concept was the image of an abandoned locomotive in a forest, an image which embodied all three facets of convulsive beauty: the implicit

89 Freud, *Complete Psychological Works* XXI, pp. 79–80 – my italics.
90 André Breton, *Nadja* (Paris: Gallimard, 1964), p. 190.
91 André Breton, *Nadja*, trans. by Richard Howard (London: Penguin, 1999), p. 160.
92 Breton, *L'Amour Fou*. p. 26.
93 Breton, *Mad Love*, p. 19.

phallic eroticism of the locomotive's form and motion (veiled-erotic); the explosive potential of kinetic energy and its arrestment in nature (explosive-fixed); and the poetic fatefulness of the train's displacement from the industrial world into a forest (magic-circumstantial). This was a form of beauty, then, which had great potential to disrupt everyday lived experience.

Breton's assertion that convulsive beauty gave expression to both the 'veiled-erotic' and the 'explosive-fixed' suggested that the convulsive forces of Eros and Thanatos were deeply imbricated within those works which exemplified the concept. This was also reinforced by Breton's definition of sublimation in *Le Second Manifeste* as a process of creating and destroying artistically[94] (another clear departure from Freudian thinking) and was, as we have already seen, accompanied by the exhortation to artists to self-observe and channel something of their unconscious into their paintings. One of the major aims of recuperating the unconscious in art was to lay bare the nature of Eros and Thanatos as a source of knowledge to others and as a challenge to society. This was commented upon in depth by Breton and Marcuse.

Marcuse's theorisations again mirrored those of Breton for he believed the subjectivity of art and literature (which arose from 'aesthetic sublimation') necessitated 'the ingression of the primary erotic-destructive forces which explode the normal universe of communication and behaviour'.[95] His interest lay again in the capacity of these forces to shatter established modes of thinking and perception and he identified many of Surrealism's literary forebears as having achieved this, including Baudelaire, Mallarmé and Poe[96] (a list to which the Surrealists could have been justly added).

Eros and Thanatos expressed artistically both had the potential to unsettle normal modes of communication, though while Thanatos did so in a quite an overt and unambiguous manner, Eros could be more subtle or complex. Both Marcuse and Breton theorised extensively on the details of the latter point. To begin with, both considered the sensuousness of

94 Breton, *Manifestes du Surréalisme*, pp. 109–110; Breton, *Manifestoes of Surrealism*, pp. 160–161 – full quotation in the introduction to this chapter.

95 Marcuse, *Aesthetic Dimension*, p. 20.

96 *Ibid.*, p. 19.

art as mediating aspects of erotic experience which frequently remained stifled in reality. For Marcuse this sensuousness was to be found in art's aesthetic qualities: 'the sensuous substance of the Beautiful is preserved in aesthetic sublimation.'[97] His characterisation of art as sensuously beautiful invites comparison with Freud's view, which explicitly drew attention to the sexual origins of the beautiful and according to which: 'visual impressions remain the most frequent pathway along which libidinal excitation is aroused'.[98] Freud explained that the word 'reizvoll' in German (commonly used to mean 'beautiful') had its origins in the designation of erotic sensations: 'There is to my mind no doubt that the concept of "beautiful" has its roots in sexual excitation and that its original meaning was "sexually stimulating."'[99]

Unlike Freud, Marcuse was ever fixated on exploring the socio-political ramifications of art's sensuous and erotic qualities, believing the latter to be the guarantor of art's autonomy as well as having great potential political impact.[100] Specifically, the stark contrast between art's 'beautiful appearance (*schöner Schein*) and the nature of social reality helped to throw the shortcomings of the latter into relief:[101] 'the work of art is beautiful to the degree to which it opposes its own order to that of reality – its non-repressive order'.[102] Art therefore countered the substance of reality, which was repressive and unsatisfying with that of fiction, which was pleasurable, bold and sensuous. Art as such was antagonistic to the status quo: 'the encounter with the fictitious world restructures consciousness and gives sensual representation to a counter-societal experience'.[103]

For Breton, the sensuousness of art became tangible through a personal reaction to those works which embodied convulsive beauty and,

97 *Ibid.*, p. 66.

98 Sigmund Freud, 'Three essays on the theory of sexuality' (1905), trans. by James Strachey, in *On Sexuality: "Three Essays on the Theory of Sexuality" and Other Works*, ed. by Angela Richards (Harmondsworth: Penguin Books, 1977), p. 69.

99 Freud, *On Sexuality*, p. 69.

100 *Ibid.*, p. 66.

101 Marcuse does, however, leave the question of beauty's definition open.

102 Marcuse, *Aesthetic Dimension*, p. 63.

103 *Ibid.*, p. 44.

like Marcuse, he also believed that it played a role in changing thinking or consciousness. Asked by Claude Levi-Strauss about the forceful nature of his reactions to such art, he responded:

> Je cède en effet tour à tour [...] à deux entraînements très distincts : le premier me porte à rechercher dans l'œuvre d'art une jouissance (c'est le seul mot juste [...] car l'analyse de ce sentiment chez moi ne me livre que des éléments para-érotiques) ; le second [...] me porte à l'interpréter en fonction du besoin général de connaissance.[104]
>
> [I do in fact fall prey to [...] two very distinct forces by turns: the first induces me to seek within a work of art a heightened sense of sensual pleasure [jouissance] (this is the only fitting expression [...] for the analysis of this feeling within me supplies only para-erotic sensations); the second [...] induces me to interpret it [the artwork] in accordance with a general need for knowledge.]

Of interest here is the liberation of 'para-erotic' sensations and feelings of *jouissance* (intense pleasure, frequently sensual or sexual in nature) imparted to the subject by the work of art on the one hand, and the desire for the expansion of knowledge on the other. Both of these phenomena contributed to an illuminating moment peculiar to Breton, which seemed both to satisfy a sensual longing within him and broaden his epistemic horizons beyond the limits of a prosaic and rational reality.

Breton had already made reference to para-erotic sensations when describing his experiences of artistic appreciation in *L'Amour Fou*, where he acknowledged 'un trouble physique caractérisé par la sensation d'une aigrette de vent aux tempes susceptible d'entraîner un véritable frisson. Je n'ai jamais pu m'empêcher d'établir une relation entre cette sensation et celle du plaisir érotique et ne découvre entre elles que des différences de degré'[105] ['a physical sensation in me, like the feeling of a feathery wind brushing across my temples to produce a real shiver. I could never avoid establishing some relation between this sensation and that of erotic

104 André Breton, 'Réponse à une note de Claude Lévi-Strauss' ['Response to a note by Claude Lévi-Strauss'] in *Œuvres Complètes* III, p. 118.

105 Breton, *L'Amour Fou*, pp. 12–13.

pleasure, finding only a difference in degree'[106]]. In the same passage, moreover, we learn that such an experience contributed to his overcoming of repression, for according to Breton the sensation stemmed from 'my most profoundly repressed instincts'[107] where 'la sexualité seule y préside'[108] ['sexuality alone presides'[109]]. Breton's reaction to the stirring qualities of art and their impact upon his innermost instincts did not reveal any inhibitions on his part, appearing to differ from Foster's view of him as 'orderly, parsimonious, obstinate... in a classic reaction-formation against his own anal eroticism'.[110]

Breton's statements are not only significant for betraying his personal reactions to these artworks; they also tell us about the artistic processes employed to elicit such a feeling, specifically, how the convulsive potential of Eros was harnessed in Surrealist art for emancipatory ends. In *L'Amour Fou* Breton affirmed that the compulsive beauty of Surrealist works reached such ends since they were '"envisagée exclusivement à des fins passionnelles"'[111] ['envisaged exclusively for passion-inspiring purposes'[112]]. This suggested that they aimed at inciting feelings of both passion and provocation.

One striking example of a work which elicited both was the film *L'Âge d'Or*, directed by Luis Buñuel (and co-written by the latter and Salvador Dalí). The film told the story of a love between a man and a woman which didn't succeed in being consummated because of the untimely interventions of the middle classes and the church. The public reaction at the time of the film's release in November 1930 is well-documented: incensed audiences threw bottles of ink at the screen, dropped stink bombs and defaced Surrealist paintings in the cinema's vestibule. The film was subsequently

106 Breton, *Mad Love*, p. 8.

107 Breton, *L'Amour Fou*, p. 13; Breton, Mad Love, p. 8 – My translation since the translation of Mary Ann Caws ('repressed feelings') lacks the emphatic tone of the original.

108 Breton, *L'Amour Fou*, p. 13.

109 Breton, *Mad Love*, p. 8.

110 Foster, *Compulsive Beauty*, pp. 111–112.

111 Breton, *L'Amour Fou*, p. 12.

112 Breton, *Mad Love*, p. 8 – I have modified Mary Ann Caws's translation 'envisaged exclusively to produce passion'.

banned and the Surrealists themselves were subjected to the severest rebuke by press, publishers and patrons alike. So 'if proof were necessary, the incident demonstrated the gulf between Surrealism at its most radical and what the Surrealists regarded as the highly repressive institutions of bourgeois society'.[113]

The film was also commented upon extensively by Breton, who in *L'Amour Fou* described it as:

> la seule entreprise d'exaltation de l'amour total tel que je l'envisage et les violentes réactions auxquelles ses représentations de Paris ont donné lieu n'ont pu que fortifier en moi la conscience de son incomparable valeur. L'amour [...] ne s'est jamais manifesté d'une manière aussi libre, avec tant de tranquille audace.[114]
>
> [the only enterprise of the exaltation of total love such as I envisage it, and the violent reactions which its showings occasioned in Paris have only strengthened my awareness of its incomparable value. Love [...] has never shown itself so freely, with so much tranquil audacity.[115]]

It is easy to see why the film's basic meaning and controversial reception appealed to Breton. On the one hand, it critiqued the bourgeois morality of capitalism (through a radical artistic counter-consciousness), provoking in the spectator a *frisson* of horror or sympathetic desire. On the other hand, as a project in artistic sublimation, it was non-repressive, revealing the omnipotence of Eros and encouraging its full expression.

The film was important as it was the first ever to portray explicitly the collisions of Eros and the death drive within the human psyche, as embodied by the lead male role of the film who was shown at the mercy of uncontrollable urges to both lust and violence. In Breton's introduction to the film – a text also entitled *L'Âge d'Or*, which accompanied the film's release – the subheading read 'L'Instinct Sexuel et L'Instinct de Mort' ('The Sexual Instinct and the Death Instinct').[116] The essay is of

113 Mundy, *Surrealism: Desire Unbound*, p. 43.
114 Breton, *L'Amour Fou*, p. 113.
115 Breton, *Mad Love*, p. 78. Translation modified by me.
116 Breton, *Œuvres Complètes* I, pp. 1025–1027.

particular significance for the present discussion since Breton identified Buñuel's film as an exercise in sublimation, and began his essay with a directive similar to the one given in the *Second Manifeste*:

> Il est, pensons-nous, de leur devoir le plus élémentaire [en tant qu'artistes], de soumettre l'activité qui résulte pour eux de cette sublimation d'origine mystérieuse, à une critique aiguë et de ne reculer devant aucune outrance apparente, dès lors qu'il s'agit avant tout de desserrer le bâillon dont nous parlions.[117]
>
> [It is, we believe, their most basic duty [as artists] to submit the activity which results for them from this sublimation of mysterious origins to a very incisive critical analysis and not to shrink back from any apparent scandal, so long as it is a question of loosening the gag of which we have spoken.]

If sublimation was to be employed as a mechanism which would permit self- observation and lead to the creation of a new consciousness,[118] Breton had found in the film a laudable example of the concept's application as he had envisaged it.[119] The depiction of the protagonist at the mercy of Eros and Thanatos certainly reflected an honest confrontation with (and observation of) the intrapsychical conflicts of the inner self. As such, it was indeed responsible for 'loosening the gag' ('desserrer le bâillon') of those repressive forces, both personal and social, which ordinarily inhibited the expression of potent psychical instincts and included everything from the

117 Breton, *Œuvres Complètes I*, p. 1026.

118 Breton, *Manifestes du Surréalisme*, pp. 109–110; Breton, *Manifestoes of Surrealism*, p. 160.

119 It is here that I differ from Steven Harris when he claims that the quotation reflects Breton's mistrust of sublimation which 'equals enslavement to the existing order of things, as well as conformity' and which needs to be countered by 'research posed against the naive production of sublimated works of art, in order to recover the sexual bases of creativity' – Harris, *Surrealist Art and Thought*, p. 12. He seems to overlook the fact that the *L'Âge d'Or* text was written in the same year as the *Second Manifeste* (1930), in which Breton explicitly identifies sublimation as being integral to the working practices of Surrealist artists as a form of auto-observation they engage in to forge a new consciousness (p. 110). These statements are parodied almost word for word in the *L'Âge d'Or* text.

banning orders imposed upon Surrealist works to the prevailing taboos around sexual matters in society.

Breton had elsewhere underlined the important role which Surrealist works played in overcoming opposition to the expression of unconscious drives which could, he claimed, potentially deal a death blow to bourgeois society:

> Il s'agissait de déjouer, de déjouer pour toujours la coalition des forces qui veillent à ce que l'inconscient soit incapable de toute violente éruption: une société qui se sent menacée de toutes parts comme la société bourgeoise pense, en effet, à juste titre, qu'une telle éruption [inconsciente] peut lui être fatale.[120]
>
> [It was a question of foiling, foiling forever the coalition of forces that seek to make the unconscious incapable of any sort of violent eruption: a society that feels itself threatened on all sides, as bourgeois society does rightly think that such an eruption may be the death of it.[121]]

He affirmed that in the film Eros and the death instincts had been allowed to co-mingle in an open display of passion which could favour not only the free expression of love but the revolt against a conservative mind-set in the grip of 'anti-Eros': 'à la violence dont nous voyons la passion amoureuse animée chez un être, nous pouvons juger de sa capacité de refus'[122] ['from the violence with which a being's most amorous passion is roused, we can judge his capacity for refusal]. Thus, the strength of an individual's passion was commensurate with his/her determination to refuse the yoke of social conformity. Breton stated that the Surrealists did not recognise any art forms other than those which attested to the 'frenzy' of this passion and that their own artistic endeavours represented 'the new and dramatic limit of compromise'[123] with society, a compromise which was dependent upon the unconditional disimprisonment of passion as represented in *L'Âge d'Or*.

120 Breton, *Œuvres Complètes* II, p. 438.
121 Breton, *Manifestoes of Surrealism*, pp. 231–232.
122 Breton, *Œuvres Complètes* I, p. 1027.
123 Breton, *Manifestoes of Surrealism*, pp. 231–232 – Breton's use of the term of 'compromise' may seem odd for suggesting an acceptance of reality. When read in context, however, it is clear that the term is not used to signify resignation but a raising of

Although the death instincts were originally characterised as life-denying in nature and the source of potential regression (this had been Freud's view), Breton always found a certain utility for them within society. On the one hand, the dynamic-aggressive aspect of Thanatos could be put at the service of Eros by fomenting the social upheaval necessary for its liberation (therefore serving radical socio-political ends). On the other hand, the 'explosive-fixed' could, along with its aesthetic counterpart, the 'erotic-veiled', be harnessed in art to epistemological ends: the 'explosive-fixed' yielded a more profound understanding of the death drive and the destructive-kinetic forces in nature, whereas the 'erotic-veiled' helped uncover the mysterious nature of Eros and the instinct to life. We can see how Surrealist art served both of these ends (the socio-political and the epistemological) by examining the works of Matta and Masson as well as Breton's comments about them.

In their early career both artists used automatism in order to tap into these primal states of Eros and Thanatos. For Breton, automatism involved a journey inwards into the wellspring of contrary meanings and sensations deep within the artist's unconscious:

> Une œuvre d'art ne peut être tenue pour surréaliste qu'autant que l'artiste s'est efforcé d'atteindre le champ psychophysique total (dont le champ de conscience n'est qu'une faible partie). Freud a montré qu'à cette profondeur 'abyssale' règnent l'absence de contradiction, la mobilité des investissements émotifs dus au refoulement, l'intemporalité et le remplacement de la réalité extérieure par la réalité psychique, soumise au seul principe du plaisir. L'automatisme conduit à cette région à droite ligne.[124]

> [In the whole field of art, a work can be considered surrealist only in proportion to the efforts the artist has made to encompass the whole psychophysical field (in which the field of consciousness constitutes only a very small segment). Freud has demonstrated that at these unfathomable depths there reigns the absence of contradiction, the relaxation of emotional tensions due to repression, a lack of the sense of time, and the replacement of external reality by a psychic reality obeying the pleasure principle alone. Automatism leads us in a straight line to this region.[125]]

---

the stakes in terms of what should be considered acceptable in respect of the free pursuit of passion and relationships.

124 Breton, *Œuvres Complètes* IV, p. 432.

125 Breton, *Surrealism and Painting*, p. 70.

The quotation is significant in underlining the role of automatic art in unearthing repressed sensations, exposing a psychical space governed by pleasure and in gaining greater insight into those abysmal regions of the soul, where the antithetical states of being are united. My view of this operation again diverges from that of Foster, who associates automatism and compulsion in humans with a behaviour redolent of death and the return of the repressed: 'Surrealist automatism suggests not liberation but compulsion, so Surrealism in general may celebrate desire only, in the register of the uncanny, to proclaim death'.[126] While I agree that automatism can certainly evoke death, I believe that the prospect of a life reduced to an unthinking, automated demi-existence can – and did for many Surrealists – equally inspire people to pursue their will to life and to live out their desires in defiance of the deathly.

The latter argument seems further corroborated in Breton's writings on Matta in which he characterises Thanatos not as an instinct which negates life but as one which abets Eros in its struggle for ascendency:

> A l' 'instinct de mort' qui se donna ces dernières années toute licence, [...] devait, en effet, s'opposer avec une vigueur non moins accrue l'instinct sexuel qui veut que 'le penchant à la destruction affecte toujours et dans tous les cas la forme d'un penchant de dérivation, au service d'Eros'. Jamais œuvre plastique n'avait encore montré si clairement, et comme analytiquement, ces deux instincts aux prises.[127]

> [During these last few years, the 'death instinct' has permitted itself every abuse of freedom [...]. It was essential that this 'death instinct' should be opposed with equally increased vigour by the sexual instinct and its insistence that 'the urge towards destruction should always and in every case assume the form of a channel diverting this urge to the service of Eros'. No one else's painting has, so far shown so clearly and almost analytically these rival instincts in conflict with one another.[128]]

126 Foster, *Compulsive Beauty*, p. 11.

127 Breton, *Œuvres Complètes* IV, pp. 580–581.

128 André Breton, 'Matta' (1947) in *Surrealism and Painting*, p. 191 – translation somewhat modified by me. The expression 'aux prises' translated as 'at grips' in the original has been rendered by me as 'in conflict with one another'.

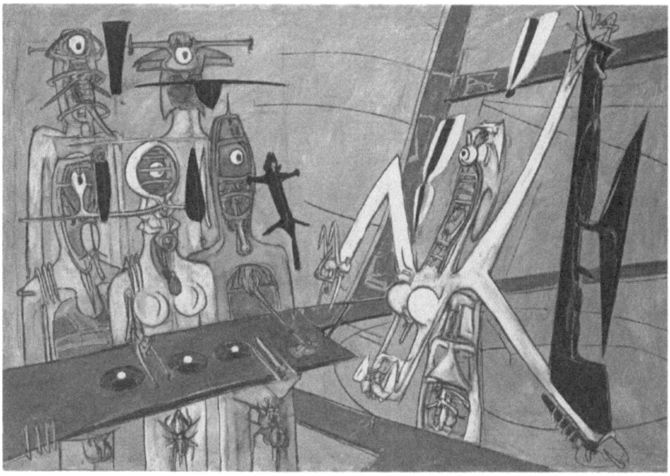

Figure 3.2: Roberto-Sebastian Matta Echaurren, *L'Octrui* (1947)
© Roberto-Sebastian Matta Echaurren/ADAGP. Copyright Agency, 2018.

Breton discussed the intersections of Eros and Thanatos as embodied in the figures of one of the artist's paintings, *Octrui* (1947; Figure 3.2). These figures were 'hottés de herses, cravatés d'arbalètes [...] et qui n'en entretiennent pas moins un commerce lingual et génital'[129] ['carrying harrows on their backs and wearing crossbows round their necks [...] but who nevertheless maintain a frenzied lingual and genital commerce'[130]]. Representations of the complicity between Eros and Thanatos typified much of Matta's iconography and captured very convincingly the spirit of the favoured Surrealist simile (taken from Lautréamont) 'like a chance encounter on a dissecting table of a sewing machine and an umbrella'. Similarly we are made to think of Freud's admission that 'the two kinds of instinct [Eros and the death drive] seldom – perhaps never – appear in isolation from each other, but are alloyed with each other in varying and very different proportions and so become unrecognisable to our judgement'.[131]

129 Breton, *Œuvres Complètes* IV, p. 581.
130 Breton, *Surrealism and Painting*, p. 191.
131 Freud, *Complete Psychological Works* XXI, p. 119.

When examining *Octrui* we are bound to wonder whether Breton's claim about the death instincts operating in support of Eros holds true. From a cursory inspection of the painting one might reasonably assume the contrary given that the future depicted appears to negate the impulse to life. On the other hand, as Breton observed, the painting depicts elements of 'lingual and genital commerce', suggesting at least the potential for sexual congress beyond the confines of a repressive and mechanised reality. The painting evokes Marcuse's statement that 'Eros and Thanatos are lovers as well as adversaries. Destructive energy may be brought into the service of life to an ever higher degree – Eros itself lives under the sign of finitude, of pain'.[132] Upon seeing the painting, we are obliged to consider an evolutionary course which transforms working individuals into dehumanised biomechanical forms that are barely distinguishable from the production line upon which they operate. Faced with such an inhuman vision of the world, we are more inclined to commit ourselves to a future which abets Eros in its self-actualisation.

According to Breton, Matta provides a vision '*à l'avant* dans la quête d'une solution qui intéresse aujourd'hui l'humanité entière, de ce qui fait qu'elle est passion et action tout ensemble – une âpre volonté s'exprime ici de ressaisir au plus tôt les leviers de commande'[133] ['so firmly *in advance* in the search for a solution encompassing the whole of humanity today, one which must therefore be compounded of passion and action' reflecting 'a keen determination to regain possession as soon as possible of the control levers'[134]]. Indeed, the iconography of his paintings has sometimes seemed so much in advance of contemporaneous humanity that it has been construed by some to be science-fiction. However, Matta himself commented that 'an artist will only be actual if his work enters the two-way traffic of receiving from his people the consciousness of needs they have detected in themselves, and as an artist, charges this consciousness of needs with an intuition of important emotion, thus sending it back to widen their picture

132 Marcuse, *Aesthetic Dimension*, p. 69.

133 Breton, *Œuvres Complètes* IV, p. 581 – Breton's italics.

134 Breton, *Surrealism and Painting*, p. 192 – Breton's italics.

of reality'.[135] Matta sought, then, to capture the concerns of the present as well as of the future (in many works there was a clear interrelation between both time frames). As Matta depicted alienating and dystopic views of humanity's prospective future, he drew attention to the many exploitative working practices which already defined the present age and reduced the essential function of the worker to a cog in a machine.

In *Octrui* the functional and mechanised depiction of the sexual instincts evoked the 'erotic-veiled' whereas the 'explosive-fixed' was mediated through the furious yet regulated clamour of a highly industrialised, cybernetic reality. Matta also conveyed the 'explosive-fixed' through representations of the potency of universal energies which were captured and made static within painting. Aesthetic instantiations of such energies, which typified the nature of convulsive beauty, were described by Breton at the beginning of *L'Amour Fou* and included the image of an abandoned train in a forest (as already discussed), a stalagmite covered with iridescent drops of water and the lustre of crystalline structures.

If we examine Matta's painting *Science, Conscience et Patience du Vitreur* (*Science, Conscience and Patience of the Glazier*, 1944; Figure 3.3), the meandering lines mediate a strong sense of the kinetic, despite appearing as frozen within the imagery of Matta's 'inscape' (a portmanteau term coined by the artist to denote the infusion of psychical interiority into external morphology). Here again, the reference to glass-making evokes Breton's 'explosive-fixed' and the natural structures he described (stalagmite, crystal) which similarly hold nature's energies in check.

By arresting natural forces, we are better able to study them; and, for this reason, Matta's paintings supported the epistemological ends of convulsive beauty. Given the abstraction of the painting and its function as an inscape,

135 Roberto da Matta, 'On Emotion' in *Manifesto: A Century of isms*, ed. by Mary Ann Caws (Lincoln, NE: University of Nebraska, 2001), p. 493. Cf. Breton's words in another text on Matta where he refers to 'la source d'un des désirs humains les plus communs et les plus impérieux, de rien moins même que de celui qui tend à s'épanouir dans l'art' – André Breton, 'Matta' (1944) in *Œuvres Complètes* IV, p. 581 ['the source of one of the commonest and most urgent of human desires […] the desire to expand its [or one's] consciousness through art' – André Breton, 'Matta' (1944) in *Surrealism and Painting*, p. 137].

that is to say as a portrait of psychical interiority, we are inclined to believe that it pertains more to human consciousness and the impact of science upon it. Both the coldness of the glacial panes of glass and the fiery heat suggested by the reddish flecks (also evocative of blood and red flesh) point to a lingering pain in the subject's consciousness, possibly brought about by intensive industrial conditioning. The images of the wrought dehumanised cybernetic organisms only seem to reinforce this vision of life as pain and restriction. Taken as a whole, the painting evokes the adverse effects of a narrow and imprisoning technocratic reality, yet the emanative lines of energy which also traverse the painting give cause for further reflection. As a source of ingenuity and resourcefulness, such energy can be enlisted to the self-serving causes of instrumental reason and technological progress but the painting equally highlights its universality and interdependence with sentient life, as reflected by its radiating presence around the organic forms depicted. At a time when energy forms were (and still are) studied purely for their advantage to science and industry, and even to war, Matta's painting pointed to a more profound and incisive view of the universe in which vital energy is seen as underlying human consciousness and endeavour.

Similarly preoccupied by the two strands of convulsive beauty expressed in the 'explosive-fixed' and 'erotic-veiled' was André Masson, who remarked that 'l'érotisme et la mort sont toujours coexistants'[136] ['eroticism and death are always co-extensive']. In Breton's 1939 text on the artist, he related Masson's painting, *La Métamorphose des Amants*, to the convulsiveness of Eros.[137] The painting (Figure 3.4) does indeed present us with a scene of erotic encounter but under the guise of carnal butchery. A peculiar form of metamorphosis has dissolved the identity of the two lovers into a gallimaufry of libidinal fragments and dissected flesh. They now appear as ravaged, their identities no longer distinct from one another or their environment. Thus, Masson also appeared to show how the destructive instincts of the unconscious could operate in tandem with Eros.

136 André Masson, *Entretiens avec Georges Charbonnier* (Marseille: André Dimanche, 1995), p. 80.

137 André Breton, 'André Masson' (1939) in *Œuvres Complètes* IV, 535; André Breton, 'André Masson' (1939) in *Surrealism and Painting*, p. 154.

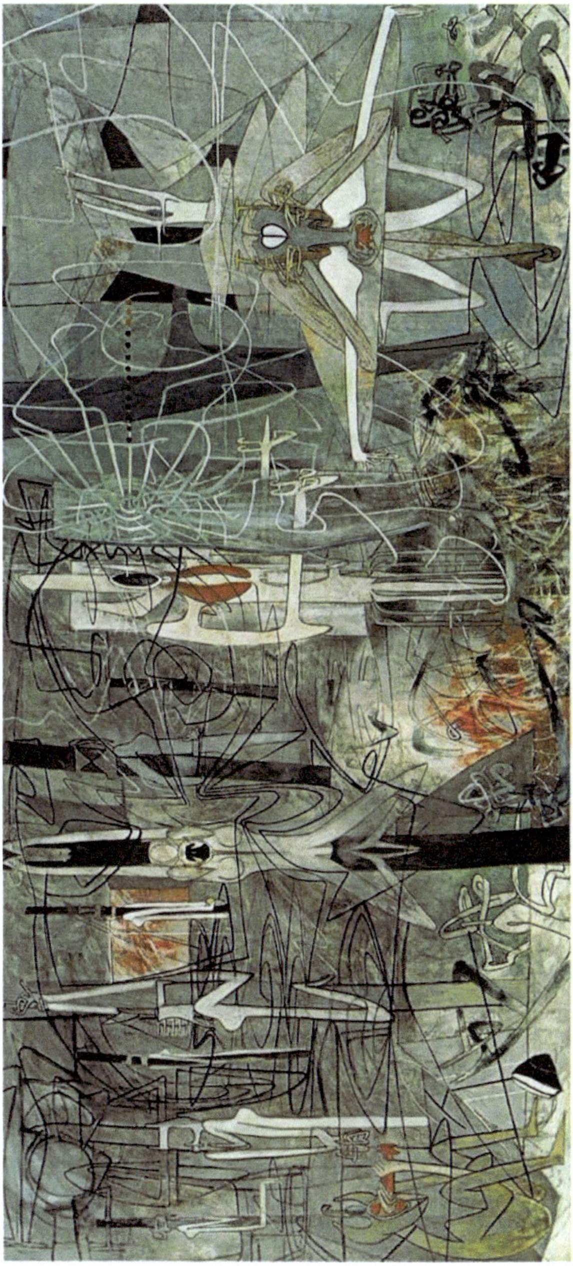

Figure 3.3: Roberto-Sebastian Matta Echaurren, *Science, conscience et patience du Vitreur* (*Science, Conscience and Patience of the Glazier*) (1944)

The theme of metamorphosis, which was recurrent within the artist's œuvre, was situated by Breton within a dialectical interplay of life's dawn when 'l'être *prend connaissance*'[138] ['the living being *achieves consciousness*'[139]] and life's dusk when 'l'être perd connaissance'[140] ['that same being loses consciousness'[141]]. In these two processes we are exposed to the raw emotions of convulsive human experience, with life's dawn implying the pains of child birth and life's dusk the pangs of death.

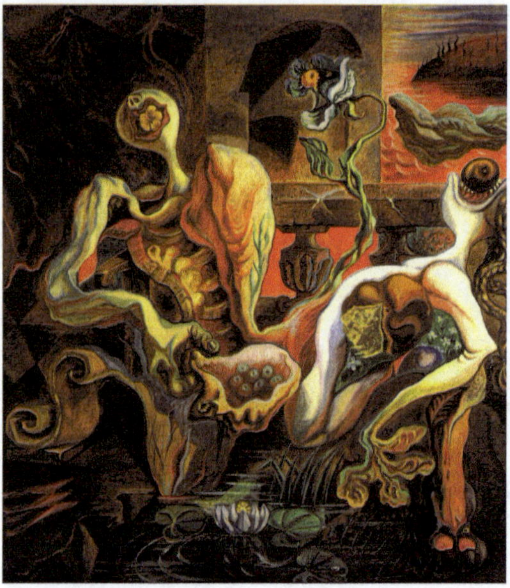

Figure 3.4: André Masson, *La Métamorphose des Amants* (*The Metamorphosis of Lovers*) (1938) © Andre Masson/ADAGP. Copyright Agency, 2018.

138 Breton, *Œuvres Complètes* IV, p. 535. Breton's italics.

139 Breton, *Surrealism and Painting*, p. 154. Breton's italics.

140 Breton, *Œuvres Complètes* IV, p. 535 – Breton further qualifies the dialectics of Masson's working practices as a 'a chemistry of the intellect' (a term borrowed from Poe to denote the novel admixtures of beauty and deformity) in 'Le Surréalisme et la Peinture' (1928) in *Œuvres Complètes* IV, p. 392 as well as a hermetic interdependency of high and low, inner and outer states in *Œuvres Complètes* IV, p. 430. This anticipates the importance of Hermeticism in Surrealist painting, as discussed in the following chapter.

141 Breton, *Surrealism and Painting*, p. 154.

Despite the inherent savagery of Masson's works, Breton saw in the metamorphoses of his paintings qualities which were poetic and life-affirming: 'la peinture d'André Masson n'a cessé de procéder de ces phénomènes de germination et d'éclosion saisis à l'instant où la feuille et l'aile, qui commencent à peine à se déplier, se parent du plus troublant, du plus éphémère, du plus magique des lustres'[142] ['André Masson's painting has always developed out of these phenomena of germination and blossoming captured at the moment when the leaf and the wing are only just beginning to unfold, and are shimmering with the most disturbing, evanescent and magical glow'[143]]. It is thus the impulse to life and consciousness which Breton emphasised most in Masson's work.

While this view of Masson's work may seem puzzling, it is perhaps more plausible when considered as a flourishing of the instinctual life. In *La Métamorphose des Amants*, for example, the sheer ferocity of the instincts seems to efface the spirit and personality of the lovers. Their bodies appear as pupal remains following the metamorphosis they underwent in an all-consuming passion, a passion which resided in a violence of feeling as much dependent on the destructive instincts as on Eros. Breton referred to Masson's preoccupation with hatching or 'éclosion', which for him marked the (re)birth of the individual in the passion of love, an interpretation which seems more credible still when we consider the level of pain which accompanies any birth.

Moreover, the painting would have had the potential to raise many questions in the mind of its beholder. Was passion a self-defeating and annihilative experience or was it, on the contrary, desirable to lose one's identity in such an emotional maelstrom? Had the lovers transcended the materiality of their passion or had they reached a point of self-exhaustion? Did the painting signify the beginning or the end of love?

Not only could the painting bring the spectator to ponder the violence of the instincts (and his/her own relationship towards them), but it was able more generally to serve as a channel for destructive energies, which lent themselves to intellectual analysis. The violence and metamorphoses

142 Breton, *Œuvres Complètes IV*, p. 535.

143 Breton, *Surrealism and Painting*, p. 154.

of certain organisms had already provided the Surrealists with a fertile ground for scholarly enquiry, with some even writing articles on the curious nature of their findings. Masson's painting may for example have been at least partially informed by the studies of Roger Caillois, a fellow contributor to *Minotaure*, who had published two highly influential articles in the journal. The first article was on the mating habits of the female praying mantis, which devours the male's head prior to fertilisation;[144] the second on the tendency of certain organisms within nature toward mimicry and the inevitable blurring of subject and environment which this entails.[145]

Thus, another possible interpretation of *La Métamorphose des Amants* is that the lovers have consumed one another (figuratively or quite literally) in the act of love; the effects of this consumption being further compounded by an environment hungry to appropriate both protagonists. Given the interplay of subject and environment, we might also consider whether the social and cultural circumstances of their relationship had not played a role in the extermination of the lovers.

In *Minotaure*, Dalí had postulated 'the cannibalism of objects' as the basis of a new era of Surrealist art which he had inaugurated with the declaration that 'la beauté sera comestible ou ne sera pas'[146] ['beauty will be edible or will not be'] (a parody of Breton's formulation of convulsive beauty). Dalí's theory of a cannibalistic genre of art found expression in a large number of Masson's paintings of the late thirties (*Pygmalion*, 1938; *Le Fauteuil Louis* XVI, 1938; *Gradiva*, 1939; *Paysage à la mante religieuse*, 1939) with their accumulation of menacing anthropomorphic furniture, gaping castrative orifices, brutalised anatomies and contorted sexual symbolism.

In producing these works, Masson would frequently intone support words (like 'transmutation', 'fall', 'whirling') which helped evoke his innermost emotions and bring about the necessary state of consciousness for their execution; if unsatisfied with a canvas he would hurl himself at it and

144 Roger Caillois, 'La mante religieuse. De la biologie à la psychanalyse' ['The praying mantis. From biology to psychoanalysis'] in *Minotaure*, no. 5 (1934), pp. 23–26.

145 Roger Caillois, 'Mimétisme et psychasthénie légendaire' ['Mimicry and Legendary Psychasthenia'] in *Minotaure*, no. 7 (1935), pp. 5–10.

146 Dalí, *Minotaure* 3–4, p. 76.

pierce it with the lashes of a knife. Such working procedures cast a very distinctive new light upon Breton's term 'explosive-fixed'; for in channelling his aggressive instincts into art, Masson was stabilising forces which were potentially (self-)destructive and affirming the creative processes which made life more endurable.

We are reminded here too of Van Gogh who, like Matta, captured the vital and kinetic forces of nature in his paintings and, like Masson, went about harnessing his own impulses to (self-)destruction. In the third *Conférence d'Haïti*, Breton nominated Van Gogh as the painter who best fitted the title 'convulsionary', stating that along with Gauguin and Cézanne he represented the route of the 'great adventure' in art.[147] This was because he was the inheritor of an Impressionist tendency which operated a visual revolution on the nature of perceived objects, showing that in the field of representation it was no longer a question of showing how objects were ('*l'être des objets*'[148]) but what instead they were becoming ('*leur devenir*'[149]). This mediation of becoming undoubtedly appealed to the Surrealists on account of their strivings to bring about renewal and change in the world. Breton even characterised Van Gogh's working processes in terms of energy and vitalism:

> Tout ce que touche son pinceau, tout ce qu'il modèle par hachures pareilles à des flammèches, à des serpenteaux de feu, acquiert une extraordinaire valeur animique.[150]
>
> [Everything that touches his paintbrush, everything that he shapes from hatchings which resemble flying sparks and serpentine fireworks, acquires an extraordinary animistic value.]

He made these remarks with reference to the work *La Nuit Étoilée* (*The Starry Night*; Figure 3.5) of which the markings seemed to epitomise so well the nature of the 'explosive-fixed', where this is understood in its more general sense of dynamic natural forces which are stabilised through painting.

147 *Ibid.*, p. 236.
148 *Ibid.*
149 *Ibid.*
150 *Ibid.*

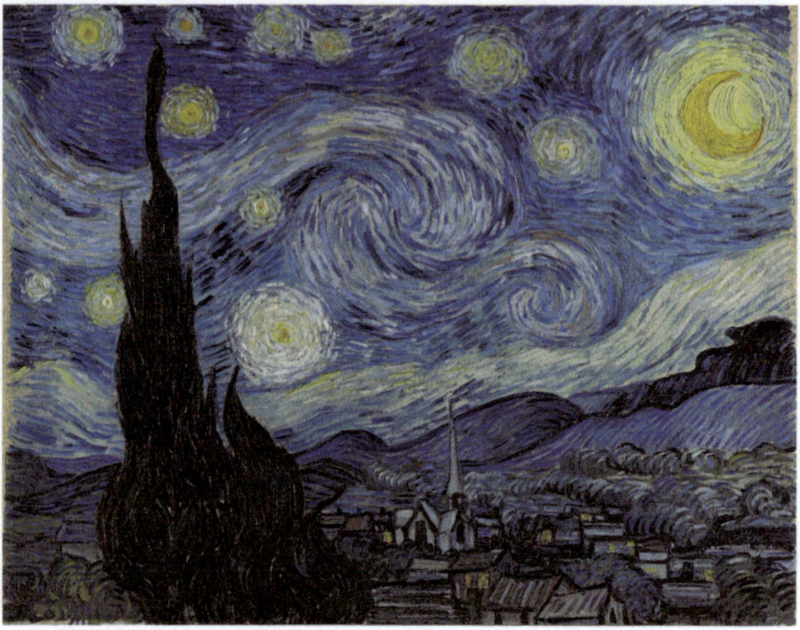

Figure 3.5: Vincent Van Gogh, *The Starry Night* (1889).

Although not a Surrealist himself (or even a typical precursor), Van Gogh's manner of painting did correspond to Surrealism's goal of releasing and artistically fixing latent forces buried deep within nature and the unconscious mind.

In the 'explosive-fixed', Breton found a more wholesome application of the aggressive instincts than did Bataille in his concept of *altération*. As we saw in Chapter 2, the latter was the destructive, disfiguring processes involved in art-making, which in Bataille's view spoiled a blank canvas by reproducing an imperfect copy of the artistic subject upon it and the urge to which he considered the source of Van Gogh's self-mutilation. Breton and Bataille both identified the same aggressive energies underlying artistic activity though established different ends to which this energy could be put. As the life and works of Van Gogh seemed to demonstrate, however, the dividing line between the canalised aggression of the explosive-fixed and the violence of *altération* was sometimes thin.

* * * * * * *

In *Le Surréalisme et la Peinture* Breton stated 'je repousse de toutes mes forces les tentatives qui, dans l'ordre de la peinture comme de l'écriture, pourraient avoir étroitement pour conséquence de soustraire la pensée de la vie, aussi bien que de placer la vie sous l'égide de la pensée'[151] ['I reject categorically all initiatives in the field of painting, as in that of literature, that would inevitably lead to the narrow isolation of thought from life'[152]]. Surrealist works, such as those we have examined, frequently sought to celebrate the flourishing of the life instincts and Eros in external reality and celebrate the dynamism of nature. This could be achieved directly by highlighting the ineluctability of Eros as in *L'Âge d'Or* or even when, quite paradoxically, Eros and Thanatos seemed to share a complicitous relationship. Even when Surrealist paintings depicted the ravages of Thanatos or disquieting visions of a dystopic future in which Eros had been actively subjugated, Thantatos and the 'explosive-fixed' always reinforced the need for a liberation of the sex instincts and freedom in the personal sphere. These paintings thus helped to forge the counter-consciousness to everyday lived experience which was largely governed by the repressive practices of Western societies. Clearly, works of convulsive beauty were not confined to the realm of thought but had a pragmatic role to play in material reality, actively militating against repression and any social impediments to the unchastened expression of the instincts.

Concerning Breton's appropriation of alchemy, which I discuss in the next chapter, I argue that he conceived this as the process whereby the interiority of the self would be transformed to emancipatory ends. A key aspect of Breton's non-repressive conceptualisation of sublimation was that it was alchemical in nature though this pertained to the psychological transformation of the inner life rather than to material or metallurgical transformation, and complemented the Surrealists' mission of remoulding external reality through social revolution.

151 Breton, *Œuvres Complètes* III, p. 404.
152 André Breton, 'Surrealism and Painting' (1928) in *Surrealism and Painting*, p. 46.

CHAPTER 4

Surrealism's Inner Alchemy: Perturbing the Senses, Awakening the Spirit

The chapter will begin by showing that Breton and other Surrealists conceived alchemical sublimation as a trope for the transformation of the inner life, especially when conceived as the necessary complement to wide-scale socio-political transformation. The alchemical and hermetic notions absorbed by the movement was not motivated by any spurious promise of eternal life, gold procurement or becoming transfigured in some mystical beyond but functioned as a symbolic language which described the operations of the human psyche. It will be demonstrated that these notions have become an integral aspect of Surrealism's legacy and, as such, are still both vehemently defended and critiqued today. Of significance here is that Surrealism's contemporary exponents still reaffirm the movement's aspirations for alchemical change – with its critical emphasis on inner transformation – to underline its ambitions of freeing the subject from repression.

I therefore attempt to tease out the hermetic aspect of Breton's conception of sublimation both in *Le Second Manifeste* and *L'Art Magique* (1957), a compendium of art examined under its transmutative and operational aspect throughout the ages and his last major treatise. In relation to the former work, I show how he appropriates Rimbaud's 'alchemy of the word' in his endeavours to free language and thus aid the development of the counter-consciousness which sought to undermine the repressive instruments of society. In my discussion of *L'Art Magique* I focus on his analysis of the paintings of Hieronymus Bosch for here he revealed an understanding of alchemical sublimation as the transformational aspect of an *élan vital* which inhabits the cosmos and strives *in perpetuum* towards renewal and regeneration. This *élan vital* does, I believe, mirror the strivings of Surrealism, with its tenet of perpetual revolt and its ongoing campaign to renew social reality.

The discussion of Bosch brings me to the pictorial aspect of hermeticism, which I identify as a central strand within Surrealism's visual lexicon. I examine in some depth the works of Max Ernst, one of the movement's foremost exponents of the hermetic who, in his own words, sought to realise 'the alchemy of the image'. His interest in art as transmutation was reflected not only in his working practices, for example in the creation of montages and collage novels out of disparate cuttings and illustrations, but also in the hermetic and alchemical themes which pervade his works. I show particularly how the simple binaries of noble love and base desire were problematised by the artist through unusual inversions of the high and the low. These inversions were, of course, of special significance to hermeticism, which was inaugurated by the affirmation of Hermes Trismegistus that 'what is on high mirrors what is below'.

Finally, I consider the writings of Bataille, Desnos and Leiris for I believe that these point to a number of the convergences between Surrealism and the *Documents* group in relation to alchemy and hermeticism, revealing a common belief in the capacity of both to liberate desire and challenge established ways of thinking.

The Mistrust of Alchemy

In terms of its function, alchemy was perhaps an ideal complementary framework to a Marxist-inspired mission to 'change the world'. The transformative potential which alchemy carried, specifically for inner change, would operate in tandem to the action-orientated campaign of Marxism and was a necessary component within the dialectics of interior and exterior states, which Breton had presented in *Les Vases Communicants*.

As I established in Chapter 1, Surrealism was as much a juxtaposing of diverse philosophies and thought systems as it was of incongruent imagery (Surrealism itself did not appear to embody any one philosophy *per se*). Marxism and alchemy were then two of several theoretical frameworks Breton favoured in support of his campaign of absolute refusal and which were incorporated into the syncretistic whole of Surrealism.[1] In the early nineteen seventies, the movement was, however, derogated by *Tel Quel* for its interest in alchemy and its estrangement from true Marxist principles. Pierre Rottenberg pointed to the discrepancy between André Breton's revival of a discipline as discredited as alchemy in *Arcane 17* and his apparent endorsement of Marx, who had qualified Hegelian idealism as a putrescent *caput mortuum* (Latin for 'dead head') debased by precisely the sort of charlatanry which alchemists were associated with:

> Arcane 17 sera, pour une part, le livre salvateur. Dans ces années d'après-guerre, notamment, 'l'alchimie' produit, donc, une réalité dans un texte réel, résultat de la 'pratique matérielle' (Marx, *Idéologie Allemande*) de Breton. Marx, dans un passage décisif marque comment au lieu d'une chimie scientifique, le système hégélien produit en Allemagne, en 1840–1844, une fausse chimie, donc bien une sorte d'alchimie. Termes de Marx: 'caput mortuum' restes, résidus, résidu d'une distillation.[2]

> [Arcane 17 will be, in the first instance, the redeeming work of literature. In these post-war years, 'alchemy' is therefore made a reality within a real text as a result of the 'material practice' (Marx, *The German Ideology*) of Breton. Marx, in a critical passage, indicates how in place of scientific chemistry, the Hegelian system generated a false chemistry in Germany between 1840 and 1844, thus a sort of alchemy. In the words of Marx: 'caput mortuum', remains, residues, residue of distillation.]

Caput mortuum is an alchemical term referring to a distilled or sublimated residue. It was originally considered to be of no subsequent value within the great work of metallurgical alchemy (that elaborate and arcane set of processes purportedly leading to the creation of the philosopher's stone, which transformed base metals into gold). Its use in the above quotation clearly indicates that the 'Hegelian system', that is to say Hegelian idealism, is also expendable and worthless. Notwithstanding the fact that

1 A number of other philosophical and theoretical frameworks, which are also explored within this book, such as Sadism, Fourierism, Luciferianism, were similarly mobilised in the name of revolt.

2 Rottenberg, *Tel Quel* 46, p. 43 – Rottenberg's italics.

Marx within *The German Ideology* was more interested in considering the impact of gold-trafficking upon class dynamics than impugning alchemy, Rottenberg dismisses all neo-Hegelian and Romantic writers originating from Germany at the time of Marx as peddlers of an inauthentic philosophical gold. The fantastical literature of the writer E.T.A. Hoffman is cited as evidence that 'on fait de l'or'[3] ['people are making gold'] across the literary and philosophic worlds of Germany, with 'gold' representing not only the Romantic world view but its supposed corollary 'le terrain refoulé, où le sexuel'[4] ['the repressed terrain, or the sexual']. With Surrealism being considered by Rottenberg to be neo-Romantic, the movement was necessarily condemned as the latest incarnation of a questionable and repressive philosophical lineage.

Rottenberg's negative characterisation of the sublimate as *caput mortuum*, that is to say as a seemingly worthless residue, evokes again the prevailing mistrust of sublimation as a concept throughout the second half of the twentieth century which – as was discussed in Chapter 1 – was first affirmed by the young Bataille and subsequently absorbed by the *Tel Quelists* and October group.

Despite Rottenberg's use of *caput mortuum* purely in its negative aspect, many alchemical commentators have noted that its perishability and worthlessness are only apparent in nature:

> The fact that it is called caput or head indicates a paradoxical reversal of opposites. The worthless becomes the most precious, and the last becomes first.[5]

Indeed, in alchemy, the residue which was designated *caput mortuum* and was formed after an initial process of distillation was frequently considered essential for the completion of the great work.

The figurative *caput mortuum* of Surrealist art and poetry can similarly be seen not as a vain pursuit (generating apparently subjective or

3 *Ibid.*

4 *Ibid.*

5 Edward F. Edinger, *Anatomy of the Psyche – Alchemical Symbolism in Psychotherapy* (La Salle, IL: Open Court Publishing, 1985), p. 167.

inaccessible works) but an essential preliminary exercise in effecting wider change within society. Walter Benjamin in his essay 'Surrealism – The Last Snapshot of the European Intelligentsia' (1928) suggested that an integral part of Surrealism's revolutionary agenda was in the unearthing of forgotten, 'outmoded' and apparently worthless objects – and exposing, reviving or elevating these through art – as they 'bring the immense forces of "atmosphere" concealed in things to the point of explosion'.[6]

In describing the mythological significance of the alchemical *caput mortuum*, Edinger also states that 'it was the head of the black Osiris or Ethiopian that, when boiled, turned into gold [...]'.[7] Osiris is the Egyptian God who was famously dismembered only to be put back together by his wife (Isis) and resurrected; the head is singled out here since it represents the most developed and complete part of the body, its severance betokening the extraction of the self's quintessence from the sensorial body. The association between *caput mortuum* and black Osiris can also be related to the thinking of Breton who famously ended *Arcane 17* with the words 'Osiris est un dieu noir'[8] ['Osiris is a black god'[9]]. This statement is significant since, as one Surrealist exegete explains, Osiris symbolised renewal experienced through resurrection and metamorphosis.[10] We are thus presented here with another link to the themes of personal and psycho-social transformation, so dear to the Surrealists. *Arcane 17* took up precisely these themes with Breton expatiating on the value of resurrection and metamorphosis in the following terms:

> L'homme voit trembler cette aile qui est, dans toutes les langues, la première grande lettre du mot Résurrection. Oui, les plus hautes pensées, les plus grands sentiments peuvent connaître un déclin collectif et aussi le cœur de l'être humain peut se briser et les livres peuvent vieillir et tout doit, extérieurement, mourir, mais une puissance qui n'est en rien surnaturelle fait de cette mort même la condition du renouveau.

6 Benjamin, *Reflections*, p. 182.

7 Edinger, *Anatomy of the Psyche*, p. 167.

8 Breton, *Arcane 17*, p. 159.

9 Breton, *Arcanum 17*, p. 121.

10 Marc Eigeldinger, 'Poésie et langage alchimique chez André Breton' in *Mélusine – Occulte-Occultation* (Lausanne: L'Age d'Homme, 1981), vol. II, p. 33.

> Elle assure au préalable tous les échanges qui veillent [...] à ce qu'à travers les obscures métamorphoses, de saison en saison, le papillon reprenne ses couleurs exaltées.[11]

> [Man sees this trembling wing which is, in all languages, the capital letter that begins the word Resurrection. Yes, the highest thoughts, the greatest sentiments can undergo a collective decline and the human heart can also break and books can age and all things must, on the outside, die, but a power that is not at all supernatural makes death itself the basis for renewal. To begin with, it guarantees all the exchanges that make sure [...] that, through its obscure metamorphoses from season to season, the butterfly again puts on its exalted colours.[12]]

Retracing Breton's thoughts on these matters is important in that they reveal the value in bearing out the agonies of (metaphorical) rebirth or resurrection – in other words, of the symbolic aspects of the Osirian dead head. Critically, there is little indication here of the static, neutered ideality which Rottenberg and Krauss impute to him, nor such hollow concepts as the *caput mortuum* in its negative interpretation. His thoughts attribute a much more affirmative role to the processes of inner transformation showing them to be forces for positive change. One wonders therefore whether the alchemical 'gold' of the Surrealists and neo-Romantics was quite the 'repressed terrain' the *Tel Quelists* made it out to be, especially given the life-denying implications that this claim has (which are in contradiction to Breton's own comments). Moreover, in re-examining the alchemical basis of sublimation in Surrealist art and thought, we can further attest to its dynamic nature and supporting role in the promotion of a non-repressive, emancipatory world view.[13] This is a view which is documented in many

11 Breton, *Arcane 17*, pp. 128–129.

12 Breton, *Arcanum 17*, p. 104.

13 This chapter extends the very valuable work already conducted by scholars who, having intuited the value of the *caput mortuum,* have considered the ideational and iconographic richness that alchemy and the hermetic arts have brought to Surrealism. These include David Hopkin's *Marcel Duchamp and Max Ernst: The Bride Shared* (1998), M. E. Warlick's *Max Ernst and Alchemy: A Magician in Search of Myth* (2001), Celia Rabinovitch's *Surrealism and the Sacred: Power, Eros, and the Occult in Modern Art* (2002), Susan Aberth's *Leonora Carrington: Surrealism, Alchemy and Art* (2004), M. E. Warlick's *Magic, Alchemy and Surrealist Objects* (2007),

of the contemporary analyses of Surrealism written by French scholars, analyses which are little known in the English-speaking world, yet show how fundamental this conception of alchemical sublimation was in defining Breton's thought and Surrealism's *raison d'être*.

Surrealism's Forgotten Legacy: An Alchemical and Promethean Movement

The esoteric and hermetic aspects of Surrealist thinking marked indelibly the opinions of the late Surrealists of the 1950s and 1960s as to the beliefs and values of the movement. This becomes particularly clear when reading the contemporary French reception of Surrealism, much of which originates from these latter-day Surrealists and includes names such as Vincent Bounoure, Michel Carrouges, Guy DuCornet, Michael Löwy and José Pierre. In offering their assessments of Surrealism, these 'second-generation' Surrealists remember the late Breton, who befriended both Eugène Canseliet, a disciple of the alchemist Fulcanelli, and René Alleau, the then head of the *Société Alchimique* of France.

In a radio interview which was conducted in remembrance of Breton shortly following his death in October 1966, some of the most distinguished names associated with Surrealism (including Marcel Duchamp, Gérard Legrand, Vincent Bounoure and Pierre Naville) attempted to assess the importance of Breton's legacy. Bounoure remarked that through Breton:

> L'ambition poétique, formatrice de cités nouvelles, reprend à son compte la volonté révolutionnaire, formulation d'une morale des relations humaines [...]. C'est de manière analogue que l'alchimiste suscite et constate les faits des influences universelles sur les matières qu'il entend transformer. Le langage, qui libère de tout contrôle les puissances du microcosme humain, devient alors aux yeux de Breton une matière

---

Tessel M. Bauduin's *Surrealism and the Occult: Occultism and Western Esotericism in the Work and Movement of André Breton* (2015).

> première justiciable des opérations de sublimations par lesquelles les alchimistes comptaient transformer leur vie en même temps que les matières du grand œuvre. De la notion toute intuitive d'alchimie du verbe, de la séduction extrême qu'il ressentait à la lecture de Nicolas Flamel, Breton passe à une tentative concertée de transmutation de la parole poétique, laquelle ne saurait passer pour la pierre des alchimistes sans une radicale transformation de l'esprit. Ce voyage initiatique, [n'a] jamais [été] aussi justifié en raison que lorsque Breton se saisit de la férule des grands hérésiarques et des voleurs de feu, [il] dispose pour l'avenir de toutes les chances que réserve encore la parole à ceux qui en ont fini avec la littérature.[14]
>
> [Poetic ambition, the creator of new cities, regains its revolutionary will, being the elaboration of a moral code for human relationships [...]. In an analogous manner, the alchemist elicits and records the effects of mundane influences upon the matter which he intends to transform. In Breton's eyes, language, which liberates the powers of the human microcosm from all control, thus becomes a *prima materia* requiring the operations of sublimation through which alchemists hoped to transform their life at the same time as the matter of the great work. From the highly intuitive notion of the alchemy of the word and the extreme seductiveness of reading Nicolas Flamel, Breton proceeded to a concerted attempt at transmuting the poetic word, which could not pass for the philosopher's stone without the radical transformation of the spirit. This voyage of initiation has never been as defensible for the reason that when Breton seizes the ferula of the heresiarchs and the stealers of fire, all future chances of keeping the floor reserved for those who have discarded literature are his.]

Of significance here is that Breton's appropriation of concepts such as sublimation, transmutation, poetry, spirit are remembered neither for their repressive associations nor for reflecting an insulation from the world. Rather, they are embedded within an alchemical discourse, wherein alchemy is again understood as seeking to reinvigorate and free the human spirit as well as poetic language and thought.

Equally important is the notion of Promethean heresy (indicated by the description of Breton as 'stealer of fire') for, as Bounoure indicates, this reflects the Surrealists' disavowal of traditional forms of literature in favour of new modes of poetic expression which draw on the

14 *Pour saluer André Breton*, radio transmission produced by Maurice Nadeau and Jean Schuster in October 1966 on France Culture.

unconscious. Fire is the central image of Bounoure's thoughts for it links the notion of the alchemist's fire as the agent of change and basis of sublimation to the fire of divine knowledge, which is expropriated from the realms of the Gods and dispersed among mortals. The ferula too is a reference to Prometheus for it was within the stout, hollow stem of a ferula plant that the latter was said to smuggle the divine fire which was subsequently transferred to humanity. Rather germanely, for Freud, the phallic shape of the ferula represented the fire of sexuality and carnal knowledge.[15] This interpretation seems to accord with some of Surrealism's principal aims, which, in addition to seeking hermetic truth, attempted to recuperate a knowledge of sexuality (also in defiance of God).

In a recent French-language publication entitled *Surréalisme & Athéisme*, Guy Ducornet reaffirmed the hermetic and atheistic basis of Surrealism, citing Breton's anticlerical tract 'À la niche les glapisseurs de Dieu' (1948) (To Your Kennels, Curs of God) in which the latter had stated:

> Les Églises, d'ailleurs, depuis qu'elles ont perdu les secrets qu'elles ont pu momentanément usurper – encore que dans le domaine religieux les véritables dépositaires de secrets fussent généralement des hérétiques (avec lesquels la pensée surréaliste accepte de se reconnaître certains points de contact) – ne maintiennent plus leur ascendant sur le monde des idées qu'à l'aide d'escroqueries de ce genre.[16]
>
> [What's more, ever since churches lost those secrets they had for some time managed to usurp – even though within the sphere of religion, the true depositaries of such secrets were most often heretics (with whom Surrealism recognises some common ground) – they have maintained their influence in the world of ideas only by these sorts of fraudulent means.[17]]

15 Sigmund Freud, 'The Acquisition and the Control of Fire' (1931) in *Complete Psychological Works* XXII, p. 188.

16 André Breton, 'À la niche les glapisseurs de Dieu!' in Guy Ducornet, *Surréalisme et Athéisme 'À la niche les glapisseurs de dieu!'* (Paris: Gingko Éditeur, 2007), p. 103.

17 My translation since the English translation given in Ducornet's work suffers from inaccuracies and omissions – see André Breton, 'To your kennels, curs of God', trans. by Guy & Rikki Ducornet, in Ducornet, *Surréalisme & Athéisme*, p. 220.

The 'usurped' secrets were the belief systems of esoteric groups – such as the Knights Templar, alchemists, Cathars and Luciferians – in which the Surrealists took a keen interest above all for their heretical status vis-à-vis established Catholic doctrine.[18] Not only did Surrealism feel a sense of kinship with these groups on account of their heresy, but according to Guy Ducornet, borrowed their ideas in an attempt to challenge religious orthodoxy. In his view, the movement focussed particularly on alchemical concepts though also drew its inspiration from ancient magical belief systems which defied the facticity of established thinking (based on notions such as 'sin' and 'redemption'). Ducornet states that:

> Breton élabore progressivement le Surréalisme comme humanisme libérateur et mode de vie, une conception de l'homme dont la présence dans le monde s'affirmerait par [...] un retour aux sources, avant que la civilisation occidentale [...] ne lui ait imposé de contraignants et factices modes de pensée – péché, rédemption, salut, etc.[19]
>
> [Breton progressively elaborates Surrealism as a liberatory humanism and a way of life, a conception of man whose presence in the world is affirmed by [...] a return to his sources, before Christian civilisation [...] imposed upon him restrictive and artificial ways of thinking – sin, redemption, the hailing of the Lord, etc.]

The pre-Christian sources to which he alludes suggest the magico-primitive world views of ancient civilisations, including those of Hellenistic Egypt from which hermeticism originates.

Significantly, the release of *Surréalisme & Athéisme* coincided with the centenary of secularism in France and a campaign on the part of those still-active Surrealists (of whom Ducornet was one) to re-energise secularism's basic tenets 'à l'heure où l'on menace de rétablir le délit de blasphème et de sacrilège dans la République française'[20] ['at a moment where the threat of restoring the offences of blasphemy and sacrilege in the French Republic

18 Alchemy itself has been read as an allegorisation of cosmological and spiritual principles which proliferated at the time of the Inquisition – see Barbara G. Walker, *The Woman's Encyclopedia of Myths and Secrets* (San Francisco, CA: Harper & Row, 1987), pp. 18–22 and pp. 436–449.

19 Ducornet, *Surréalisme et Athéisme*, p. 126.

20 *Ibid.* – back cover.

lingers']. For this reason, Breton's tract 'À la niche les glapisseurs de Dieu' was counter-signed in 2006 by 175 Surrealists from differing countries in order to reignite those debates which Breton had helped to bring to the forefront of French intellectual life. The tract itself was translated into nine languages, including English (into which it had not previously been translated), with a view to making the campaign for secularism not merely a 'French' concern, but a global one. In doing so the signatories once again underscored the function of unorthodox or heretic disciplines such as hermeticism in liberating (wo)mankind from the demands of organised religion.

Although the words and actions of these critics postdated the original Surrealist movement by many years, I believe they were significant for showing an absolute fidelity to the values of Bretonian Surrealism and for demonstrating that, far from being a moribund debate, the question of sublimation's meaning and function within Surrealism has been kept very much alive.

The Alchemical Dimension of Bretonian Sublimation

The move toward a more esoteric definition of sublimation, and the divergence from Freudian thinking which this entailed, had already been apparent since the publication of the *Second Manifeste*. For even though Breton had originally come by the term via Freudian theory, he did in a footnote of the manifesto qualify the concept as a form of 'transmutation';[21] a term which was distinctly un-Freudian and redolent of alchemy. In *L'Anthologie de l'Humour Noir* he referred to sublimation as an alchemical process which separated the subtle from the dense and identified Benjamin Péret's poetics as an exemplum of alchemical sublimation operating on a verbal plane (an analysis of this claim follows

21 Breton, *Manifestes du Surréalisme*, p. 110; Breton, *Manifestoes of Surrealism*, p. 160.

later in this section). Breton may have received the idea of sublimation as a form of alchemical transmutation from René Allendy, who made the association in a published Sorbonne lecture of early 1924.[22] According to Elizabeth Legge, the lecture provided the Surrealists with an understanding of psychoanalysis as 'the new alchemy'.[23]

Breton's esoteric understanding of sublimation reflected a general interest amongst Surrealists in so-called magical practices. Irrespective of the credibility and merit one accords to magic, it shared a common goal with Surrealism in that it too aspired to make thought active and thereby effect change in the physical domain. Moreover, magic seemed not to buttress a repressive civilisation but rather to militate against it, for as Breton explained in *L'Art Magique* magic 'suppose la protestation, voire la révolte; l'orgueil, certes, aussi du fait qu'elle admet pour principe que l'homme "dispose"'[24] ['supposes protestation, and even revolt; indubitably hubris too, for it [magic] admits of the principle which states that man is "self-determining"']. Magic was to be contrasted with religion which supposed 'une grande part de résignation'[25] ['a large proportion of resignation'].

One can imagine that if Jung had found greater currency in France,[26] the Surrealists may have acknowledged the validity of his critique of Freud for defining sublimation as a support to civilised, bourgeois society:

> *Sublimatio* is part of the royal art where the true gold is made. Of this Freud knows nothing, worse still, he barricades all the paths that could lead to true

22 The lecture appeared in written form as 'A précis' and was published in *La Vie des Lettres et des Arts*, 19 (1924), p. 91.

23 Elizabeth M. Legge, *Max Ernst: The Psychoanalytic Sources* (Ann Arbor: UMI Research, 1989), p. 87.

24 Breton, *L'Art Magique*, p. 27.

25 *Ibid.*

26 Roudinesco suggests that the French reticence about Jung can be traced to national pride in rationalism which made them hostile to the irrationalist trend of his thought. She argues that Surrealism was the most obviously fertile ground for Jungian ideas in France but that its rejection of the *au-delà* meant that it too steered clear of them – Roudinesco, *Histoire de la Psychanalyse*, pp. 27–28.

> *sublimatio*. This is just about the opposite of what Freud understands by sublimation. It is not a voluntary and forcible channelling of instinct into a spurious field of application, but an alchymical transformation for which fire and *prima materia* are needed. *Sublimatio* is a great mystery. Freud has appropriated this concept and usurped it for the sphere of the will and the bourgeois, rationalistic ethos.[27]

Jung deplored Freud's repressive use of the term sublimation as well its expropriation of the term from the discipline of alchemy into psychoanalysis. Like Breton, Jung believed sublimation to be an alchemical operation when this was to be understood in its meditative, symbolic (rather than literal) aspect. Moreover, his belief in the manufacture of 'true gold' via alchemy and *sublimatio* greatly resembled Breton's understanding of the reconciliation of antinomies.[28]

In a manner which evoked Jung far more than Freud, Breton, in an interview held in 1950, also characterised the accomplishment of the great alchemical work as the 'interior revolution' of humanity. This came about when the individual uncovered new poetic forms of knowledge which transcended ordinary cognition.[29] In the *Second Manifeste* Breton formally aligned the goals of Surrealism with those of alchemy, whereby the quest for the philosopher's stone became an allegory for that which transforms the artist-poet's way of thinking and imagining. Specifically, the philosopher's stone freed the latter from rationalist-conformist thinking by acting on and actively destabilising the senses. This harks back to the previous chapter in which we saw works of compulsive beauty achieve precisely this and, in which, we examined a part of the same key section on alchemy from the *Second Manifeste* in which Breton likened the imagination to an anarchical malcontent:

27 Carl Jung, *Letters*, ed. By G. Adler and A. Jaffé (Princeton: Princeton University Press, 1974), vol. 1, p. 171.

28 Carl Jung, 'The Visions of Zosimos' in *The Collected Works of C.G. Jung*, Vol. 13, Alchemic studies, ed. by Herbert Read and others, trans. by R.F.C. Hull (Princeton: Princeton University Press, 1967), pp. 57–108.

29 Breton, *Œuvres Complètes* III, pp. 616–617.

> Je demande qu'on veuille bien observer que les recherches surréalistes présentent, avec les recherches alchimiques, une remarquable analogie de but : la pierre philosophale n'est rien autre que ce qui devait permettre à l'imagination de l'homme de prendre sur toutes choses une revanche éclatante et nous voici de nouveau, après des siècles de domestication de l'esprit et de résignation folle, à tenter d'affranchir définitivement cette imagination par le 'long, immense raisonné dérèglement de tous les sens' [...][30]
>
> [I would appreciate your noting the remarkable analogy, insofar as their goals are concerned, between the surrealist efforts and those of the alchemists: the Philosopher's Stone is nothing more or less than that which was to enable man's imagination to take a stunning revenge on all things which brings us once more, after centuries of the mind's domestication and insane resignation, to the attempt to liberate once and for all the imagination by the 'long, immense, reasoned derangement of the senses' [...][31]]

Breton's reference to the 'derangement of the senses' was taken from Rimbaud, one of a succession of allusions to the poet, whom he venerated as an alchemist-poet and whom he quoted in the process of elaborating Surrealism's own alchemical basis. Surrealism's proposed derangement of the senses is comparable to the concept which Walter Benjamin defined as the Surrealists' main ambition, that of 'profane illumination',[32] an intoxication of the senses by secular means and to socially radical ends.

Breton's call to free the mind from its 'domestication' and 'resignation' and to 'derange' the senses seemed an incitement against the status quo, with art and poetry becoming the natural means by which an audience was subjected to a sensory impact which transformed and destabilised. As Michael Löwy has stated 'What interests them [the Surrealists] in so-called "primitive" practices, in occultism, in alchemy and the other hermetic arts, is the immense poetic charge which these disciplines carry. In the most explosive sense of the term, they serve to

30 Breton, *Manifestes du Surréalisme*, p. 124.
31 Breton, *Manifestoes of Surrealism*, pp. 174–175.
32 Benjamin, *Reflections*, p. 179.

energise the established cultural order and its positivistic conformism'.[33] Surrealist propaganda from the interwar years made use of alchemical language to exhort individuals to tune into this poetic charge: 'Vous qui avez du plomb dans la tête / Fondez-le pour en faire de l'or surréaliste'[34] ['You who have lead in your heads / Melt it down and turn it into surrealist gold'].

In *L'Art Magique*, Breton distinguished between 'discursive knowledge', the conventional dialogical knowledge which aims at establishing clear conclusions; and 'lyrical consciousness', based on a recognition of 'the powers of the Word'.[35] He believed there was a clear collusion between this lyrical consciousness, with its veneration of the Word and its capacity to forge new artistic and poetic forms, and the operations of magical transformation: 'C'est sur l'acceptation très haute [...] à ce mot de Verbe que ceux qui vouent à la poésie et à l'art tombent d'accord avec ceux qui proclament l'efficacité des opérations magiques proprement dites'[36] ['It is on the basis of this very great acceptance [...] of the notion of the Word that devotees of poetry and art fall into agreement with those who affirm the efficacy of magical operations in the true sense of the term']. Breton's preoccupation with the Word is again partially attributable to his admiration for Rimbaud, who coined the phrase 'alchemy of the word', a term which Breton also co-opted in the *Second Manifeste* to promote new poetic forms. He specifically praised Rimbaud's *Une Saison en Enfer* as a work exemplifying the 'alchemy of the word' and considered it therefore a seminal experiment in Surrealist writing.

As we can see, the terminology of alchemy (including concepts such as 'sublimation', 'transmutation', 'great work') became for the Surrealists a symbolic language which defined in figurative terms their working

33 Michael Löwy, 'Magie proti posvátnu'['Magic against the sacred'] in *Analogon* (Prague, 1999), p. 8. Translated from Czech – my translation.

34 Surrealist leaflets, Paris, 1924 – one of nine small leaflets issued by the Bureau de Recherches Surréalistes, with texts by Tristan Tzara and Paul Éluard.

35 Breton, *L'Art Magique*, p. 34.

36 *Ibid.*

practices especially under that aspect which aimed at reconfiguring the interiority of (wo)man. Another expression Breton borrowed from alchemy was 'prima materia' or 'primal matter', which in its original sense designated the raw material used at the start of the great work and thus in the creation of the philosopher's stone. Given Breton's interest in the Word, the *prima materia* was unsurprisingly language itself in its purest and most unrarefied form (when unmodified by conscious thought). Mining this language in the subconscious, would invariably lead to the discovery of the philosopher's stone (the reaching of the imagination's full potential) with the ensuing changes in self-awareness helping to bring about the great work, defined by Breton as the 'interior revolution' of humanity.[37]

The 'alchemy of the verb' thus metaphorised particularly the transformation of the primal matter of language (the preconscious flux of words and ideas) into poetry. In *Du Surréalisme en ses Œuvres Vives* (1953), Breton was explicit in identifying the source of this alchemical poeticisation, stating that 'le tout, pour le surréalisme a été de se convaincre qu'on avait mis la main sur la "matière première" (au sens alchimique) du langage'[38] ['the whole point, for Surrealism, was to convince ourselves that we had got our hands on the "prime matter" (in the alchemical sense) of language'[39]]. In a radio interview conducted in the same period he further qualified this verbal *prima materia* as the 'latent content' of poetry and art.[40] The idea of words and forms being 'latent content' was inspired by Freud's use of the term with reference to dreams. The latter believed that the 'manifest content' of dream symbolism could be decoded and reduced to pre-verbal impulses and desires of a vague and unconscious nature, in other words, to a latent meaning. For Breton, such latent content (which mostly consisted of unconscious notions and desires) was also buried within poetry, having been assisted in its externalisation by the alchemy of the word.

37 Breton, *Œuvres Complètes* III, pp. 616–617.
38 Breton, *Manifestes du Surréalisme*, p. 167.
39 Breton, *Manifestoes of Surrealism*, p. 299.
40 Breton, *Entretiens*, p. 258.

Verbal alchemy was a concept which was embraced by many of the literary names who first associated with Breton, a fact which was reflected not only in the poetry they wrote but also in the themes they adopted. Desnos, for example, was adept at teasing out the homonymic and calligrammatic playfulness of language in trance-like states. In his early volumes of poetry one finds evidence of this in 'Langage Cuit' (1923) or 'Baked Language', implying a process of alchemical transformation occurring on a verbal plane; or in 'Rrose Sélavy' (1922–1923), the title of which was a homophone of 'Éros, c'est la vie' (Eros is life) and which contains pithy musings whose meanings are similarly contained within their homonymic qualities:

> 39. Rrose Sélavy propose que la pourriture des passions devienne la nourriture des nations.
>
> 59. Rrose Sélavy proclame que le miel de sa cervelle est la merveille qui aigrit le fiel du ciel.
>
> 61. Apprenez que la geste célèbre de Rrose Sélavy est inscrite dans l'algèbre céleste.[41]
>
> [39. Rrose Sélavy proposes that the putrescence of passions becomes the nourishment of nations.
>
> 59. Rrose Sélavy proclaims that the honey of her mind is the marvel which envenoms the gall of the heavens.
>
> 61. Understand that the famous gesture of Rrose Sélavy is inscribed in algebra celestial.]

The selection above seems significant in exploring the sublimatory aspects of Eros. Aphorism 39 suggests a misdirection of the impulses of the *id* into nation-building (with the negative repercussions this can have of war and imperialism). Aphorisms 59 and 61 are more hermetic, with the first corresponding to Breton's notion of the alchemical imagination taking flight (guided by a Promethean spark that places it at odds with the Gods) and the second evoking the hermetic axiom that 'what is below is like what is

41 Robert Desnos, 'Rrose Sélavy' (1922–1923) in *Corps et Biens* (Paris: Gallimard, 1953), pp. 31–46.

on high' (the latter, which was ostensibly written by Hermes Trismegistus in the Emerald Tablet or Tabula Smaragdina, is the foundational principle of Hermetic thought and highlights the symmetrical relationship between microcosm and macrocosm).

Benjamin Péret shared many of the poetic and hermetic interests of Desnos and was considered by Breton to be the poet who has 'pleinement réalisé sur le *verbe* l'opération correspondante à la "sublimation" alchimique qui consiste à provoquer l' "ascension du subtil" par sa "séparation d'avec l'épais"'[42] ['fully performed on the *word* the operation corresponding to alchemical "sublimation," which consists in provoking the "ascension of the subtle" via its "separation from the dense."']. Here 'the dense' was explained by Breton as being the very narrow, utilitarian use of words which characterised everyday speech. The tendency towards the 'subtle' (meaning in Breton's sense, the most direct expression of the unconscious) was indeed embodied in Péret's works – such as the aptly titled 'Je Sublime' or 'I sublime' of 1937 – where each poem read as a profusion of richly evocative images and bizarre new verbal associations, having been automatically manufactured in the subconscious layers of the psyche. In the introduction to the poem mundanely entitled 'Le Carré de l'Hypoténeuse' ['The Square of the Hypotenuse'] Péret wrote:

> Première fleur du marronnier qui s'élève comme un œuf
> dans la tête des hommes de métal
> dur comme une jetée
> quand
> dans la pluie d'encre qui me transperce de miroirs
> tes yeux magiques comme un arbre égorgé
> crient sur tous les tons
> Je suis Rosa
> je t'aime comme la fougère d'autrefois aime la pierre qui l'a faite équation
> je t'aime à tour de bras
> je t'aime comme un poêle rouge dans une caverne
> Que ta robe de fil de fer barbelé
> me déchire avec un grand bruit de vaisselle tombant dans l'escalier

42 Breton, *Œuvres Complètes* II, p. 1133.

je t'aime comme une oreille emportée par le vent
qui siffle Attends.[43]

[First flower of the chestnut-tree which ascends like an egg
in the heads of metal men
hard as a jetty
when
in the ink-rain which cuts through me with mirrors
your magical eyes like a topped tree
cry out in all pitches
I am Rosa
I love you as the fern once loved the stone with which it stood in equation
I love you by the outlines of your arms
I love you like a red stove in a cavern
May your barbed-wire dress
tear me to pieces with the loud clatter of crockery falling on the stairway
I love you like an ear which has been carried away by the wind
murmuring Wait.]

The poem lends itself to a close analysis for, in addition to freeing language from its conventional function (and thus performing the alchemy of the word), it also makes use of alchemical ideas and symbols (the egg and the stove as sites of transformation, the recognition of fern and stone as sentient and the merging of the sexes). The meaning of the poem seems to be conveyed in two of its central images: that of the self-actualisation of (wo)man through the freeing of his/her imagination (which has hitherto been metal); and that of the blossoming of (wo)man through the experience of love. In its vivid and indeed violent imagery, the poem assails and unsettles the senses as well as foregrounding Thanatos and the 'explosive-fixed' of compulsive beauty. Péret commented that such imagery might be construed by some to be 'visionary' and that as such it had a specific role to play in countering religious indoctrination, as it had already done since the Middle Ages.[44] The poet's natural ally was thus the magician rather

43 Benjamin Péret, 'Je Sublime' in *Œuvres Complètes* (Paris: Terrain Vague, 1971), vol. II, p. 135.

44 Benjamin Péret, 'La Parole est à Péret' in *Benjamin Péret*, ed. by Jean-Louis Bédoin (Poitiers: Pierre Seghers, 1972), p. 163.

than the priest for 'le commun dénominateur unissant le sorcier, le poète et le fou ne peut être que la magie. Elle est la chair et le sang de la poèsie'[45] ['the common denominator uniting the sorcerer, the poet and the madman can only be magic. It is the flesh and blood of poetry'].

The references to the faceless Rosa, which permeate *Je Sublime* and evoke Desnos' 'Rrose', seem not only to betoken the omnipotence of Eros but the ability of artistic and poetic forms to express the full extent of sexuality and desire. In the introduction to *L'Anthologie de L'Amour Sublime* Péret recognised the 'l'universalité du désir' ['universality of desire'] and its 'signification cosmique'[46] ['cosmic significance']. In Breton's writings he had underscored the quasi-sexual chemistry of verbal interplay when he stated that 'les mots font l'amour'[47] ['words make love'] affirming that 'la poésie se fait fans un lit comme l'amour'[48] ['poetry is made in a bed like love'] and that 'l'étreinte poétique comme l'étreinte de chair / tant qu'elle dure / défend toute échappée sur la misère du monde'[49] ['the poetic embrace like the embrace of the flesh / as long as it endures / forbids all vistas on the misery of the world']. These statements highlight the liberatory nature of the creative act when expressed in the sensuousness of poetry and art.

In *L'Art Magique* Breton showed how art under its transformative aspect has sometimes assumed a similar function to the alchemical poetry above, creating rich new visual experiences from conjunctions of miscellaneous visual fragments. He also revealed how the transformation of sexuality (both its sublimation or desublimation) can be manifested in such art. One individual in particular captured his attention for achieving both such forms of transformation, namely the late medieval painter and Surrealist precursor Hieronymus Bosch.

45 *Ibid.*, p. 164.

46 Benjamin Péret, 'Le Noyau de la Comète' in *L'Anthologie de L'Amour Sublime* (Paris: Albin Michel, 1956), p. 21.

47 André Breton, 'Les mots sans rides' in *Littérature, 2e série,* n° 7 (Décembre, 1922), p. 14.

48 André Breton, 'Sur la route de San Romano' (1948) in *Œuvres Complètes* III, p. 419.

49 Breton, *Œuvres Complètes* III, p. 421.

Breton on Bosch: Alchemy and Metamorphosis in the Works of a Surrealist Precursor

According to Louise Tythacott, the Surrealists' interest in Bosch reflected a more general interest in Medievalism as a time before the segregation of the pathological from the rational-minded, as well as the mind/body dualism of Descartes.[50] By extension, many of those antinomies which made up the rationalist discourse of the modern age were at this time not considered as being distinct from one another; and for this reason the Surrealists, with their practice of merging all contrary states, felt a natural affinity for the medieval period. The same period in history also saw a proliferation of alchemical texts, in which the fusion of contrary states (such as sulphur and mercury, red king and white queen, *sol* and *luna*) were represented.

In *L'Art Magique*, Breton identified the paintings of Hieronymus Bosch as depicting this movement towards reconciliation. Bosch himself was greatly interested in alchemy, with the iconography of his paintings frequently making use of alchemical ideas and processes. The triptych *The Garden of Delights* (Figure 4.1) is one of the most ambitious of his works and vividly depicts intricate scenes of heaven (in the left-hand panel), earth (in the centre) and hell (in the right-hand panel). The inferno to the right features the slaying of humans and a multiplicity of alchemical allusions. In Laurinda Dixon's *Alchemical Imagery in Bosch's Garden of Earthly Delights*, this panel has been interpreted as a process of 'putrefaction', in others as an alchemical operation which occurs early in the great work and involves the chemical decomposition of a substance.[51] Putrefaction corresponds to the *nigredo* phase of alchemy (reflecting the blackness of decaying matter) and has been described by Edinger in psychological terms as:

50 Louise Tythacott, *Surrealism and the Exotic* (New York: Taylor & Francis, 2003), p. 61.

51 See Laurinda S. Dixon, *Alchemical Imagery in Bosch's Garden of Earthly Delights* (Ann Arbor, MI: UMI Research, 1981).

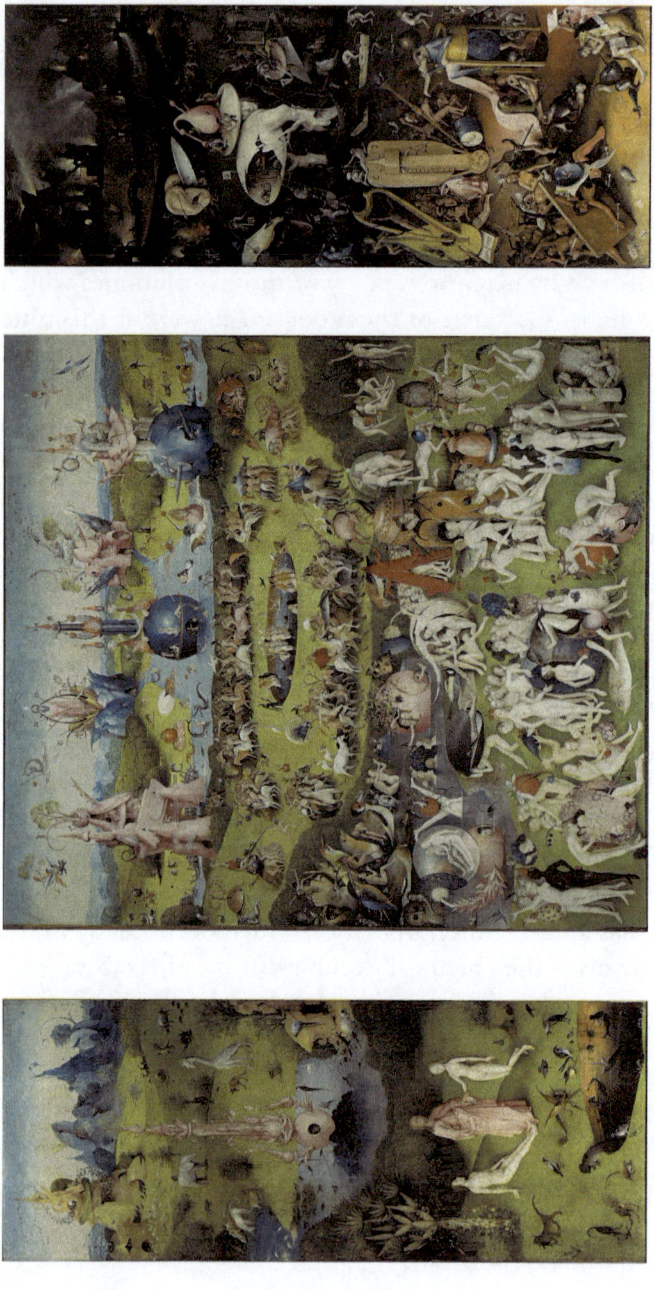

Figure 4.1: Hieronymus Bosch, *The Garden of Earthly Delights*, 1503 and 1515.

> the most negative operation in alchemy. It has to do with darkness, defeat, torture, mutilation, death and rotting. However, these dark images often lead over to highly positive ones – growth, resurrection, rebirth ...[52]

This is also the phase of the great work that gives rise to the *caput mortuum* which, we recall, was a residue that appeared worthless but was, in actuality vital to subsequent alchemical operations and closely associated with rebirth and regeneration. Given the further intimations of rebirth throughout the triptych (the eggs as sites of creation, the transformative fires, the intimacy of the nudes, and the sense of metaphysical progression from heaven to hell and back), the reading of *nigredo* as rebirth seems particularly pertinent to Bosch's work.

Breton himself considered the painting's central meaning to reside in that symbol of resurrection and transformation which is the Orphic egg: 'dans cette atmosphère de rêve, c'est l'œuf orphique qui règne, le principe des métamorphoses'[53] ['in this dreamlike atmosphere, it is the Orphic egg which reigns, the principle of metamorphoses']. In the Greek Orphic religion, the egg (Figure 4.2) gave birth to the universe as well as to the hermaphroditic deity, Phanes (*phanaô* meaning bringer of light in Greek), who infused the cosmos with light (and by extension knowledge and understanding). A coiled serpent – which is commonly depicted around the egg and deity – evokes the snakes of the hermetic caduceus, also a symbol of transformation.

It is no coincidence that Breton used the symbol of the Orphic egg to explicate the meaning of Bosch's painting for in surveying all three panels of the triptych we are confronted with numerous eggs and egg-shaped vessels. Furthermore, as Breton himself remarked, the central panel is filled with hermaphroditic and hybridic couplings which are suggestive of Phanes. The paleness of the figures, the white egg shells and the lustre which – in the absence of sunlight – illuminates all three panels (in particular the inferno) suggest that all three scenes have been touched by the Orphic light.

52 Edinger, *Anatomy of the Psyche*, p. 148.
53 Breton, *L'Art Magique*, p. 179.

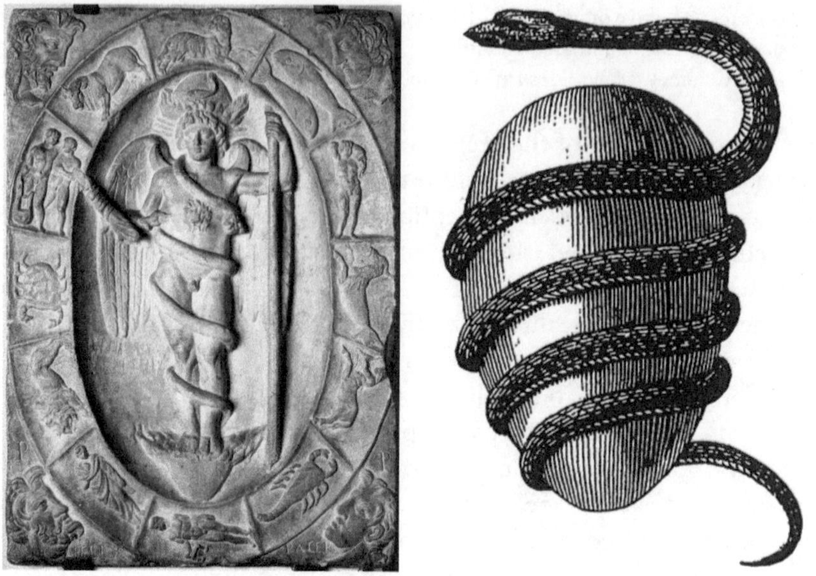

Figure 4.2: Symbols of birth and transformation (two aspects of Phanes, the hermaphroditic deity). (Left) Phanes, the hermaphroditic deity entwined with a serpent and (Right) the Orphic (or Cosmic) egg from whence Phanes hatched (Jacob Bryant, 1774).

We can see how the notion of the egg as life-giving and emanative would have resonated with one of Surrealism's central goals: that of transforming the world by pioneering new forms of thinking. The image of light (when symbolising knowledge) is a recurring one within the œuvre of Surrealism, as we have seen, in the Promethean theft of fire from the Gods as well the widespread interest in Luciferianism.[54]

Breton further explicated the painting's theme of metamorphosis with another comparison. He compared the triptych with Flaubert's *Tentation de Saint Antoine*, specifically the end of the play script, when

54 The interest in Prometheus developed particularly in the aftermath of the Second World War. Breton alluded explicitly to Luciferianism in *Arcane 17* – see Breton, *Arcane 17*, p. 104, pp. 173–174; Breton, *Arcanum 17*, p. 90, pp. 131–132.

the saint has surmounted those temptations with which the devil has attempted to bait him. At this point he experiences a vision of the plenitude of creation, in which the boundaries between all things animate and inanimate dissolve. He senses within him the same vital force which inhabits and moves all entities as well as the constant metamorphoses to which they are subjected:

> Il va pour marcher sur un galet: une sauterelle grise bondit. Des insectes, pareils à des pétales de roses, garnissent un arbuste. [....] Des cailloux ressemblent à des cerveaux, des stalactites à des mamelles, des fleurs de fer à des tapisseries ornées de figures. Dans des fragments de glace, il distingue des efflorescences, des empreintes de buissons et de coquilles– à ne savoir si ce sont les empreintes de ces choses-là, ou ces choses elles-mêmes.[55]
>
> [He goes forward to tread on a pebble: a grey grasshopper leaps up. Insects resembling rose petals adorn a bush. [...] Stones appear as brains, stalactites as breasts, iron flowers as tapestries decorated with figures. In fragments of ice, he distinguishes efflorescences, imprints of shrubs and shells–so that he hardly knows whether these are the imprints of these things, or the things themselves.]

In Bosch's *The Garden of Earthly Delights*, the parallels with Flaubert's work are to be found firstly in the focus on the plenitude of creation: individual souls appear to be incarnated in any one of creation's multitudinous forms, whether in heaven, hell or earth, whether as sinner or saint, human, plant or animal. Secondly, and as in the Flaubert quotation, the chaotic representation of terrestrial life shown in the central panel reveals the delineations between life-forms to be quite fluid.

Far from pointing to an inert, unchanging ideality which underlies creation, Breton's interest in the animistic (as reflected in his Flaubert quotation) seemed to encapsulate the very notions of vitality and kinetic dynamism, which we have already seen expressed in Surrealist works of convulsive beauty and seemed so fundamental to Surrealism's defence of human freedom:

55 Breton (quoting Flaubert), *L'Art Magique*, p. 179.

Les aspirations de l'homme à la liberté doivent être maintenues en pouvoir de se recréer sans cesse; c' est pourquoi elle doit être conçue non comme état mais comme *force vive* entraînant une progression continuelle. C'est d'ailleurs la seule manière dont elle puisse continuer à s'opposer à la contrainte et à la servitude, qui, elles, se recréent continuellement et de la manière la plus ingénieuse.[56]

[Humanity's aspirations for liberty must always be given the power to recreate themselves endlessly; that is why it must be thought of not as a state but as living [/vital] force bringing about continual progress. Besides, that is the only way in which it can continue to oppose constraint and servitude, which themselves are continually recreated in the most ingenious fashion.[57]]

For Breton such a vital, transformative force helped promote self-realisation and the unhindered expression of the human spirit. As such, the *élan vital* of Breton's animism also acquired a certain social utility when allied to a will to take one's destiny into one's own hands. It certainly seems no less significant that the work, *Arcane* 17, from which the quotation comes and which marked for Breton a more pronounced move to esoteric subject-matter, has been described as 'un hymne à la liberté, sa profession de foi libertaire la plus lucide et la plus passionnée'[58] ['a hymn to liberty, his most lucide and passionate profession of libertarian faith'].

The notion of endlessly recreating oneself and its relevance to Bosch's triptych is one that Breton took up again with reference to another quotation from Flaubert's *La Tentation de Sainte Antoine*. This is again to be found in the story's denouement when, after despairing about the futility of life and its manifold contradictions, the Saint is overcome with a pantheistic frenzy as he reconnects with Creation:

Je voudrais avoir des ailes, une carapace, une écorce, souffler de la fume, porter une trompe, tordre mon corps, me diviser partout, être en tout, m'émaner avec les odeurs, me développer comme les plantes, couler comme l'eau, vibrer comme le son, briller

56 Breton, *Arcane 17*, p. 165 – Breton's italics.

57 Breton, *Arcanum 17*, p. 126.

58 Victor Crastre, 'André Breton et la liberté' in *André Breton*, ed. by Marc Eigeldinger (Neuchâtel: Editions de la Baconnière, 1970), p. 149.

> comme la lumière, me blottir sous toutes les formes, pénétrer chaque atome, descendre jusqu'au fond de la matière, être la matière![59]
>
> [I would like to have wings, a shell, a coat of bark, to breathe out smoke, to have a trunk, to writhe like a serpent, to parcel myself out everywhere, to be in everything, to be released as an odour, grow like a plant, run like water, vibrate like sound, shine like light, nestle under all manner of forms, penetrate each atom, descend to the depths of matter – to be matter!]

Flaubert is showing us that the mutual dependency of spirit and matter, life and death are to be found in the bounty of earthly creations. Such a world view seems then in no way to repress the material or corporeal aspect of existence but points again to its vital, living nature. The saint's spiritual ecstasy is after all derived from an immersion within matter itself.

The fact that Breton quoted these passages in interpreting Bosch's painting is significant for he believed that antinomical states such as spirit and matter also became fused together in the *Garden of Earthly Delights*. He remarked that the painting had deliberately obscured the traditional delineations of this world and the world beyond by depicting Earth as a Blakean 'marriage of heaven and hell'[60] (as represented in the central panel). According to Breton, this strategy was reflected by the use of colour in the panels, for earth is dominated by reddish hues whereas as dark blue covers a large part of the infernal panel. Moreover, although the Edenic panel on the left seems already contaminated by 'worrying germinations', in the right-hand panel the physiognomies of the damned bare an expression of pre-Adamite serenity.

Having advocated sublimation in his theoretical writings, one might have supposed Breton to have explicitly approved those metamorphoses within creation which signified a movement from low to high (as is often presupposed by the process of sublimating); and conversely, that the movement from high to low would be met by a corresponding

59 Breton (quoting Flaubert), *L'Art Magique*, pp. 179–180.
60 Breton, *L'Art Magique*, p. 178.

amount of disapprobation. Yet through his reading of Bosch, we are led to believe that the painting is founded on a complete relativisation of good and evil, noble and base – and that Breton himself submitted fully to such a view:

> il n'est plus question aujourd'hui de se demander si le rocher pense, si la fleur souffre, moins encore d'envisager le monde matériel comme un carrefour d'âmes prisonnières, les unes entraînées dans un processus de chute, les autres dans un processus d'ascension : l'animisme actuel s'est pour cela trop bien dégourdi des boues glaçantes du péché.[61]

> [it is no longer a question today of asking oneself whether the rock thinks or the flower suffers, and even less of envisaging the material world as a crossroads of imprisoned souls, one lot being dragged down towards perdition and the other lot wafted up towards salvation: animism, at the present time, is too thoroughly thawed out to leave any place for the ice-cold mud-bath of sin.[62]]

He specifically rejected the idea that we can impute the coltish figures of Bosch's painting with any degree of sinfulness when the persons represented are simply facing 'la conséquence de la découverte de l'universelle sexualité [...]. En "psychanalysant" la matière, ils se sont reconnus'[63] ['the consequences of the discovery of universal sexuality [...]. In "psychoanalysing" matter, they recognised themselves']. As such, they were neither embracing debauchery nor repudiating matter to pursue a life of spiritual self-abnegation. Instead, Breton informed us, they were simply bearing witness to an incipient awareness of their own materiality. Their view of creation could, moreover, only be amoral in nature, making evil no longer a question of religious dissent, but a fundamental aspect of (wo)man's experience, caught up as it was between the celestial and the infernal:

61 Breton, *Œuvres Complètes* IV, pp. 573–574.
62 Breton, *Surrealism and Painting*, p. 186.
63 Breton, *L'Art Magique*, p. 180.

> Alchimie et sexualité ne serait-elle pas pour lui [Bosch] les moyens d'une investigation encore plus audacieuse, qui supprimerait le "Mal" religieux en en dispersant la cause ou le support, qui est l'homme?[64]
>
> [Wouldn't alchemy and sexuality be for him [Bosch] the means for an even more audacious investigation, which would do away with religious 'evil' by dissipating its cause or its contributory agency, which is man?]

One of Breton's principal reasons for bringing up Flaubert's dramatic portrayal of Saint Anthony in his discussion of Bosch is that the latter produced two works which also explored the trials of the saint. Bosch painted one triptych (circa 1505) and one panel (approximately a decade later), both of which were entitled *La Tentation de Sainte Antoine.* The first (Figure 4.3) is an oneiric and fantastical representation of the saint's visions of temptation, in which the borders between inner and outer life have been completely dismantled. These visions are replete with both alchemical and sexual symbolism, as Breton explained: 'la symbolisme alchimique fait son apparition. Elle se combine aux calembours profanes [...] pour donner à l'œuvre un caractère sexuel accentué'[65] ['alchemical symbolism makes its appearance. It is accompanied by a profane play on words [...] to give the work a pronounced sexual character'].

He then went on to remark that 'chaque animal, chaque objet peut devenir une allusion ésotérique, un aveu'[66] ['each animal, each object is a potential esoteric reference, a confession'] with 'confession' here referring to thoughts of sexuality and sin. As evidence of a 'profane play on words' (calembours) he identified the troll at the far left of the left-hand panel who plays a bagpipe, which resembles both an alchemical alembic and a scrotum. As Breton noted, the saint's gaze suggests a detachment from the bacchanalia which surround him; an idea which is repeated in the right-hand panel where his pious readings prevent him from observing a nude emerging from behind an oak tree in front of him.

64 *Ibid.*, p. 179.
65 *Ibid.*, p. 176.
66 *Ibid.*

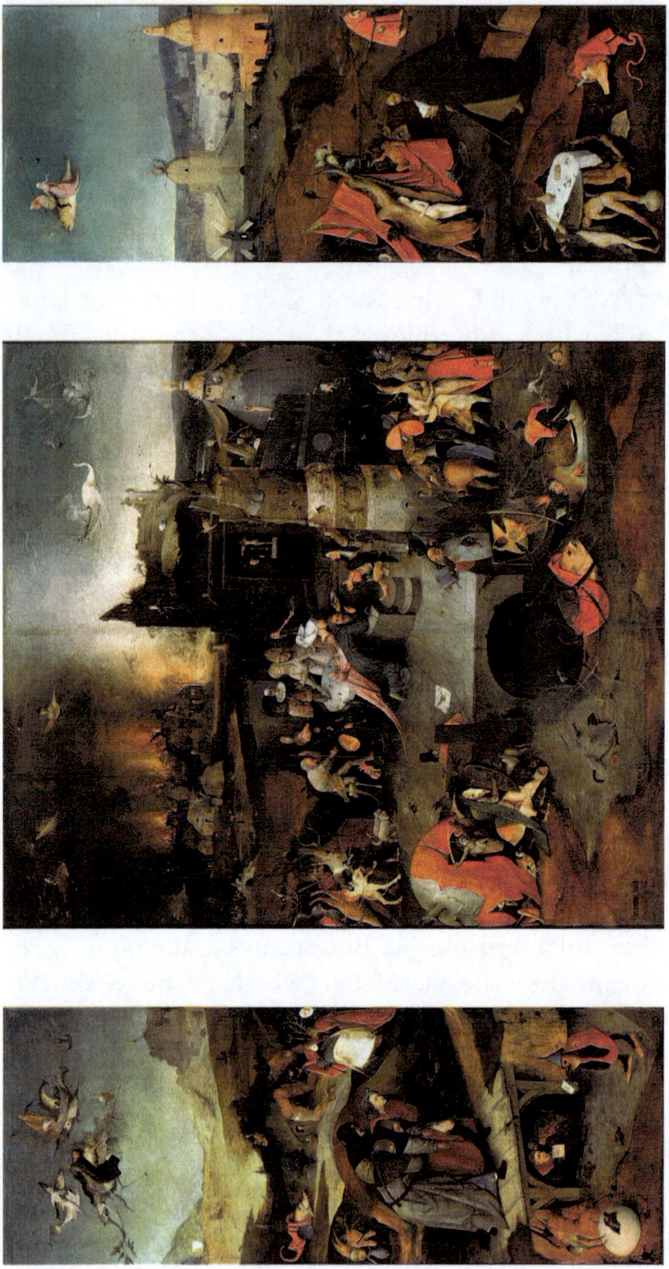

Figure 4.3: Hieronymus Bosch, *The Temptation of Saint Anthony*, triptych, 1505.

On the central panel, a toad-like figure near the Saint holds up an egg. The latter may symbolise the alchemical incubation of that which the saint really desires, here the philosopher's stone as a means of surmounting temptation. This seems reinforced by the egg's proximity to the royal couple who represent a harmonisation of the opposing forces which threaten to destabilise the saint, and are a striking counter-model to the other libidinal enticements which offer themselves within the painting. Alongside the libidinal snares, we see a number of hybrid grotesques, demons and inauspicious birds which mediate a sense of ruin, decay and excess, the nature of which is further expressed in alchemical symbolism (such as the large, decomposing tomato in the foreground panel, which signifies putrescence). In many respects, the saint epitomises those intrapsychical conflicts which so interested the Surrealists, being poised between sexual allurements and degeneracy on the one hand, and the redeeming qualities of balance (particularly of the sexes), erudition and contemplation on the other. One might almost say that the painting offers a visual dramatisation of the competing demands of the *id* and the super ego. Furthermore, this probing of the unconscious life to visual ends can be considered a prime example of Surrealism *avant la lettre.*

As Breton pointed out, the triptych contrasts starkly with the panel on the same theme which Bosch paints in the final years of his life (Figure 4.4). This offers a realistic depiction of the Saint's temptation in which the fantastical imaginings of the triptych as well as the encounters with demonic germinations are barely hinted at (only a small number of indeterminate figures within the paintings remind one of Bosch's hallmark hybrid creations). In this depiction of the saint, he is situated in a natural setting where he meditates beside a river.

Breton explained this surprising move towards realism as follows:

> Cette toile apparemment 'réaliste' marque au contraire le comble de l'intériorisation de la vision par Bosch. Elle réduit la présence de la magie dans l'univers à quelques simulacres, parce que cette magie, loin d'être 'expurgé' par une thérapeutique de sublimation abortive a été *réintégrée* en l'homme, qui s'est reconnu matière et sang ; mais comme le dira Nietzsche 'le sang est l'esprit'.[67]

67 *Ibid.*, p. 180 – Breton's italics.

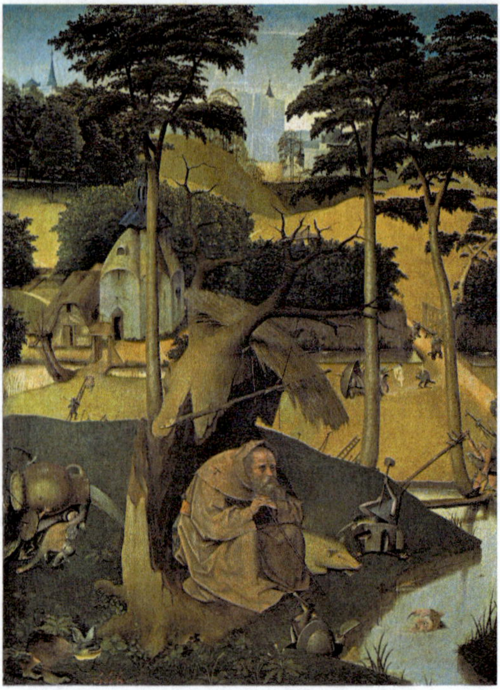

Figure 4.4: Hieronymus Bosch, *The Temptation of Saint Anthony*, panel.

[This apparently 'realistic' canvas marks by way of contrast the fullness of the interiorisation of the vision that Bosch had painted. It reduces the presence of magic in the universe to a few simulacra, because this magic, far from having been 'expurgated' by a therapy of abortive sublimation, has been *reintegrated* into man, who has recognised himself as matter and blood; after all, as Nietzsche would say 'blood is the spirit'.]

Breton's use of the term 'abortive sublimation' was very telling. In fact it seemed closely allied to the repressive dimension of Freudian sublimation when the subject is required to renounce or suppress the physicality of his/her being in order to adapt to reality. Breton was explicit in signalling that the saints' fantasies have not been repressed (or aborted) but linger on in a vision of the world in which body and spirit are regarded as consubstantial with one another, adducing Nietzsche to show that in this world view blood is synonymous with spirit.

In his exploration of antonymic and hybrid states as well as in his preoccupation with hermetic and alchemical themes, Bosch may be considered one of the great (and unacknowledged) antecedents of Surrealism. Moreover, Breton's engagement with Bosch is illuminating in how it reveals so much of his world view and, in particular, his opinions on primacy of materiality over spirituality. Artists such as Max Ernst as well as the contributors to *Documents* similarly explored how the sexuality underlying organic life could be given meaningful expression in visual works. As we shall see, they frequently conveyed their ideas with reference to a hermetic world view which demonstrated a reciprocity between the high and the low; and in which, quite radically, the 'low' sexuality of human desire and the 'high' or sublime magnitude of the universe were accorded equal worth.

Visual Alchemy and Hermeticism in the Works of Max Ernst

Operating in parallel to the alchemy of the word, as practised by the Surrealist poets, there was within Surrealism an alchemy of the image, which was characterised by its ability to distinguish itself from a tradition of mimetic illusionism and had – with some notable exceptions[68] – dominated artistic practice since the Renaissance.[69] Ernst was without doubt one of the foremost pioneers of this visual alchemy.[70] Breton wrote of him that 'son

68 According to S. Lee Hager, the Northern Renaissance artists such as Bosch, Dürer, Bruegel and Jan van Eyck incorporated alchemical principles into their paintings in the manner of the Surrealists – see S. Lee Hager 'Surrealism, Alchemy and the Northern Renaissance' (University of California, 2000), <http://www.csuchico.edu/art/contrapposto/Contrapposto97/Pages/Lee1.html> (now available only as archive: <http://archive.li/0bY0K>) accessed 1 April 2001.

69 Carlo Sala, *Max Ernst et la Démarche Onirique* (Paris: Klincksieck, 1970), p. 53.

70 Ernst did experiment also with verbal alchemy, writing Surrealist poems (which sometimes accompanied his paintings) and concocting collage words such as 'phalustrade' – an amalgam of the words *autostrada*, ballustrade and phallus.

œuvre graphique a été tendue dans le sens d'une toujours plus grande émancipation de la vue'[71] ['his graphic work has always been directed towards an ever-increasing emancipation of vision'[72]]. In another of Breton's articles on Ernst, he had compared the painter to the Renaissance magician Cornelius Agrippa, who, like Ernst, came from the environs of Cologne.[73] This was a particularly apt comparison to make for Ernst betrayed a great interest in magic and hermeticism – a fact which has been borne out by reappraisals of his work and most notably in M.E. Warlick's *Max Ernst and Alchemy* (2001) which charts the enduring influence of hermetic and alchemical ideas upon the artist.

Central to Ernst's notion of alchemy was collage for as the artist stated in 'Au-delà de la peinture' (1936) collage was 'l'alchimie de l'image visuelle'[74] ['the alchemy of the visual image'[75]]. This visual alchemy was in many respects analogous to the 'alchemy of the word'. It similarly depended on the *prima materia* of pre-existing images (rather than words) as the starting point of its *magnum opus* and, via numerous intricate operations, it also ended with an entirely new and ostensibly more valuable artefact. Like the alchemy of the verb, the alchemy of the image helped transform consciousness. Ernst acknowledged the subversive and destabilising qualities of alchemical montage within the same text of 1936, qualifying it as:

> un composé alchimique de deux ou plusieurs éléments hétérogènes, résultant de leur rapprochement inattendu, dû, soit à une volonté tendue – par amour de la clairvoyance – vers la confusion systématique et le *dérèglement de tous les sens* (Rimbaud), soit au hasard, ou à une volonté favorisant le hasard.[76]

71 André Breton, 'Max Ernst – Œuvre Graphique' (1950) in *Œuvres Complètes* IV, p. 552.
72 André Breton, 'Max Ernst – Graphic Works' (1950) in *Surrealism and Painting*, p. 168.
73 André Breton, 'Max Ernst' (1942) in *Œuvres Complètes* IV, 542; André Breton, 'Max Ernst' (1942) in *Surrealism and Painting*, p. 159.
74 Max Ernst, 'Au-delà de la peinture' (1936) in *Max Ernst : Œuvres de 1919 à 1936* (Paris: Éditions des Cahiers d'art, 1937), p. 28.
75 Max Ernst, *Beyond Painting* (New York: Wittenborn, Schultz, Inc., 1948), p. 12.
76 Ernst, *Au-delà de la peinture*, pp. 38–40.

> [an alchemical composition of two or more heterogeneous elements, resulting from their unexpected reconciliation owing either to a firm will which – from a love of clear sightedness – is directed towards systematic confusion and the *derangement of all the senses* (Rimbaud) or to chance, or to a will favourable to chance[77]]

Again, Ernst's comments seem analogous to Breton's statement about the alchemy of the verb occasioning a 'derangement of the senses'. As we shall now see, his collages frequently depicted vividly oneiric yet disjointed scenes, which like Rimbaldien poetry or Surrealist automatism, had a destabilising effect on their audience.

A compelling example of such a collage was Ernst's photomontage novel, *La Femme 100 Têtes* (1929), which consisted of diverse illustrations taken from works of nineteenth-century fiction, and in which the mundane was rendered absurd through the addition of incongruous visual elements. As such, those repressive social structures which were ordinarily dismissed as being part of life were suddenly exposed as a risible charade. Disquieting spectacles, foreboding gestures and depictions of panic or frustration were juxtaposed with the genteel unreality of bourgeois life, which discarded or repressed the unseemly impulses of the human psyche as it did the disaffection of the lower classes.

In one of the book's collages entitled 'Chaque émeute sanglante la fera vivre pleine de grâce et de vérité' ['Each bloody riot will help her to live in grace and truth'] (Figure 4.5), we see a young woman perched as though in the gods of a theatre, which are, however, located in the middle of a street where soldiers are firing upon a crowd (evoking the Paris Commune or the French Revolution of 1848). The fact that she appears so detached from the events around her (like an Olympian Goddess looking down upon the lives of mortals), and is apparently unmoved by the fate of those massacred before her, is a clear indictment of the bourgeois mores she represents.

77 My translation. Cf. Ernst, *Beyond Painting*, p. 16.

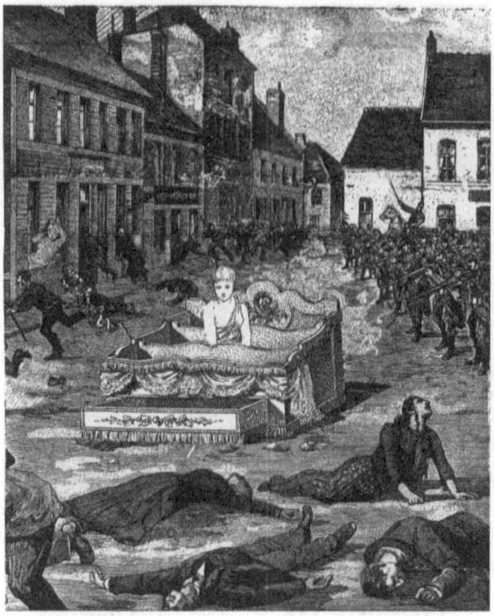

Figure 4.5: Max Ernst, 'Chaque émeute sanglante la fera vivre pleine de grâce et de vérité' ('Each bloody riot will help her to live in grace and truth'). Illustration from collage novel *La Femme 100 Têtes* (1929) © Max Ernst/ADAGP. Copyright Agency, 2018.

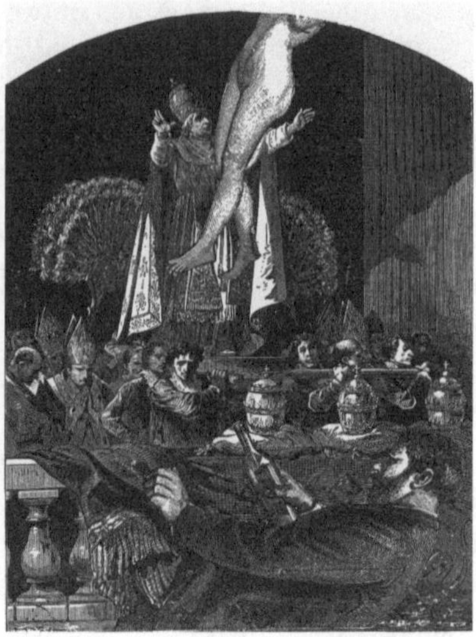

Figure 4.6: Max Ernst, 'Rome'. Illustration from collage novel *La Femme 100 Têtes* (1929) © Max Ernst/ADAGP. Copyright Agency, 2018.

More generally, the novel assumes an accusatory tone for throughout the work there are references to anticlericalism and oblique criticisms of the notions nationhood and family. In the final chapter we see a panel entitled 'Rome' (Figure 4.6) which depicts a papal procession, though the earnestness of the occasion is completely overturned by the inclusion of a nude who hovers before the pope; and a drunkard in the foreground, who beholds the papal cavalcade. The pope is shown with raised arms as though he were performing a ritual to exorcise the nude's body from his sight; she, in turn, appears to be drifting upwards (her head is already cut off from the picture), elevated, sanctified and removed from the sphere of terrestrial concerns. Only the drunk, who points a phallic bottle in her direction, appears to recognise her presence. The uneasy combination of these disparate elements within the picture recalls the precarious foundations of civilised life and makes a mockery of those gestures (here the

Catholic ritual) which attempt to conceal and repress the demands of the subject's instinctual life.

Within this work and the more alchemical collage novel *Une Semaine de Bonté* ('A Week of Kindness'), which he was to publish five years later, reality is subverted by the eruption of obscure unconscious impulses into the lives of the protagonists. As this occurs, the instinctual life comes fully into play – as Carlo Sala explains, 'cette liberté de rapports, cette liberté de symboles, est toujours présente dans les meilleures œuvres de Ernst qui peuvent être d'ailleurs conçues comme des songes à yeux ouverts où, par un procédé de désublimation, les désirs et les pulsions se révèlent avec toute leur charge affective'[78] ['this freedom of relations, this liberty of symbols is always present in the best works of Ernst and can moreover be conceived as a waking dream, where, via a process of desublimation, desires and impulses are revealed with all of their emotional force'].

'Desires and impulses' certainly feature very prominently within *Une Semaine de Bonté* in which, as M.E. Warlick has shown, the great work is re-enacted via a great many vicissitudes.[79] Again, the 'great work' is to be understood symbolically; whereas for Breton, it was the 'interior revolution' of humanity, for Ernst it was the making of the self through the experiences of love and desire. The early chapters of his work are filled with fragments of nudes and characters which seem more animal than human. In their lubricity, the images of *Une Semaine de Bonté* remind one of Adorno's description of Surrealism: 'Breasts that have been cut off, mannequin's legs in silk stockings in the collages – these are mementos of the objects of the partial drives that once aroused the libido'.[80]

As a representation of the great work, this novel reveals the tortuous early phases necessary to the discovery of the self and the Other. Thus, *Une Semaine de Bonté* is perhaps best understood as an exposition of love and its necessary (and more earthy) constituents. The structure of the

78 Sala, *Démarche Onirique*, p. 53.

79 M. E. Warlick, 'Max Ernst's Alchemical Novel: "Une Semaine de bonté", in *Art Journal*, vol. 46, no. 1, *Mysticism and Occultism in Modern Art* (Spring, 1987), pp. 61–73.

80 Theodor W. Adorno, 'Looking Back on Surrealism' (1956) in *Notes to Literature*, trans. by Shierry Weber Nicholsen (New York: Columbia University Press, 1991), vol. I, p. 89.

photomontage proceeds from 'mud' (or earth), the 'element' associated with the first chapter ('Sunday'), progressing through other elements in subsequent chapters and then culminating in 'desire' or the 'great one times one'[81] in the final chapter ('Saturday'). This progression is reflected to some degree by the imagery of the chapters: the first is filled with the beasts of untamed licentiousness as symbolised by lions' heads (Figure 4.7). These are the raw materials of the great work, the necessary ingredients in the creation of the final product, a more rarefied form of ecstatic desire, which in the final chapter is metaphorised as a series of figures who are suspended in mid-air and appear to be lost in the supreme elation of love (Figure 4.8).

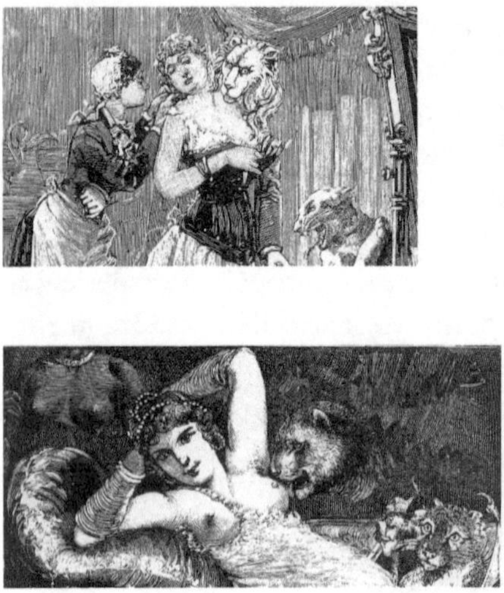

Figure 4.7: Max Ernst, 'images (untitled)'. Illustrations from Chapter 1 (Sunday – Mud) of collage novel *Une Semaine de Bonté* (1934) © Max Ernst/ADAGP. Copyright Agency, 2018.

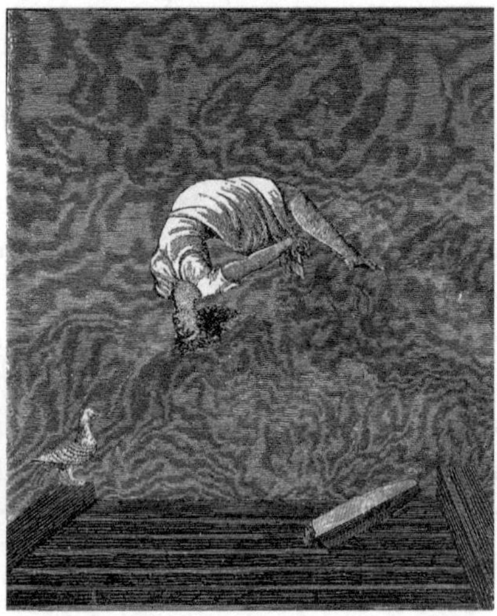

Figure 4.8: Max Ernst, 'image (untitled)'. Illustration from Chapter 7 (Saturday – Desire or the great one times one) of collage novel *Une Semaine de Bonté* (1934) © Max Ernst/ADAGP. Copyright Agency, 2018.

81 These were the revised headings given to the final chapter in the German publication of the work (1963) – see *Une Semaine de Bonté: Die weisse Woche: Ein Bilderbuch von Güte, Liebe und Menschlichkeit* (Berlin, 1963).

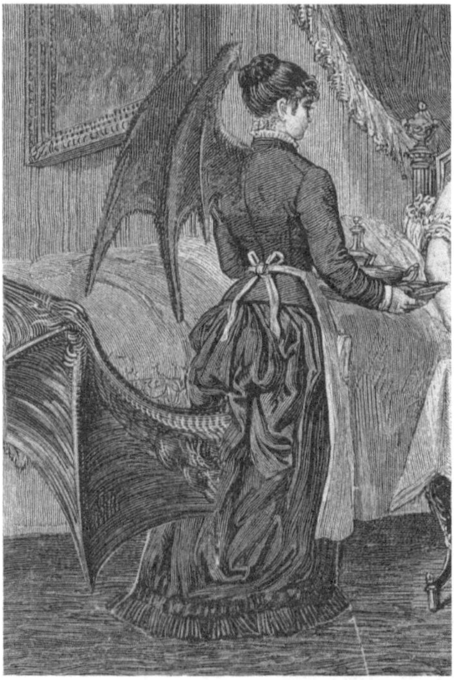

Figure 4.9: Max Ernst, 'image (untitled)'. Illustration from Chapter 3 (Tuesday – Fire) of *Une Semaine de Bonté* (1934) © Max Ernst/ADAGP. Copyright Agency, 2018.

Presented in these two chapters are the opposing ends of love, with the chapters (or days) in between portraying the various forms of satisfaction and dismay which can arise between these two extremities. For example, Tuesday, corresponding to the element of fire, depicts a series of winged characters (as in Figure 4.9) which symbolise the attempt at volatilisation (or sublimation) of fixed or unrefined matter (in the context of the novel therefore, the bestial desire of the preceding chapters). This volatilisation is confirmed also by the presence of serpents which, according to Warlick, symbolise primal matter,[82] that is to say, the matter to be worked upon and transmuted (for Ernst, the baseness of desire). The images of Wednesday show that the volatilisation of the humans of the previous day has failed

82 Warlick, *Art Journal,* 46(1), p. 67.

to transmute them into pure spirit; instead, they have become grotesque hybrid creations consisting of a bird's head and a human body (Figure 4.10). Unable to take flight and ascend to the heights of spiritual ecstasy which love can afford, they are earthbound and still a victim of their animal passions (as reflected by the scenes of struggle and agitation they are depicted in). On the following day (Thursday) these bird men are replaced by masked characters (Figure 4.11) unable to find their way to love from which they are apparently excluded (in the entire chapter the female subject acknowledges only one unmasked man with a human head).

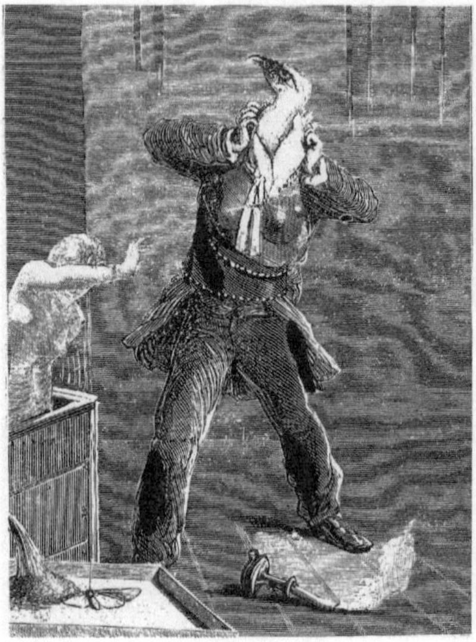

Figure 4.10: Max Ernst, 'image (untitled)'. Illustration from Chapter 4 (Wednesday – Blood) of *Une Semaine de Bonté* (1934) © Max Ernst/ADAGP. Copyright Agency, 2018.

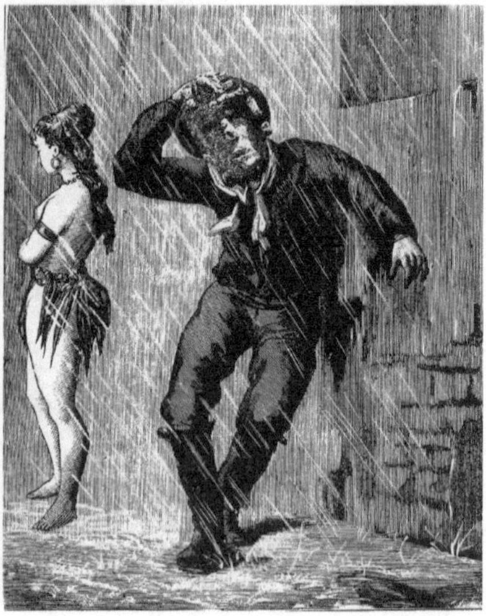

Figure 4.11: Max Ernst, 'image (untitled)'. Illustration from Chapter 5 (Thursday – Blackness) of *Une Semaine de Bonté* (1934) © Max Ernst/ADAGP. Copyright Agency, 2018.

I believe that the interest of this novel lies in these intermediate chapters since they problematise the nature of desire, poised as it is between sublimatory and desublimatory impulses (and thereby reflecting one of the most salient conflicts from within Surrealism itself). Love's fulfilment is shown to be preceded by a vexed and arduous journey in which the subject must balance base and noble pleasures, distinguish truth from fiction and endure conflict and disappointment. If, like the alchemist in his quest for gold, (s)he is able to conclude these many complex and testing processes, (s)he stands a chance of attaining the 'spiritual gold' of Surrealism – the reciprocation of love and the mystical union with the other. It is to this state of grace which the great work of *Une Semaine de Bonté* leads the subject via a succession of detours and erotic (mis)adventures; though the ambiguous postures of the characters in the final chapter (Figure 4.8), which suggest both a falling to earth and an ascent to the heavens, leaves sufficient doubt about the finality of this state.

Within the same period that Ernst compiled these collage novels, he also explored hermetic themes in a number of paintings – of which the most famous is arguably *Les Hommes n'en sauront rien* (*Men Shall Know Nothing of This*, 1923; Figure 4.12). The painting evokes at once the hermetic axiom of 'what is on high is like that which is below'. How exactly the symmetry between high and low operates within this painting does, however, require closer examination, for as Ernst stated in the poem which accompanied the painting 'the picture is odd in its symmetry. The two sexes balance each other there'.

The work's most obvious complementarity is between the sun and the moon, and the legs of the copulating couple. Within hermetic philosophy the conjunction of sun and moon has always represented the coming together of the king (or the man) and the queen (or the woman).[83] As Jung affirms 'since antiquity, the main traditional astrological and alchemical correspondence to marriage has been the *coniunctio Solis et Lunae*'.[84] This is mirrored by an image of the Earth which is suggestive of a vagina (and covered by a woman's hand) and a phallic whistle immediately below. Both images are aligned to the sun and moon, and the couple's legs, which loom over them.

Despite this complementarity, the painting does from a hermetic perspective represent a curious inversion, for the microcosm (i.e. (wo)man, here represented only metonymically by the two pairs of legs) assumes the

83 These are also interpreted as the merging of philosophical sulphur (the active principle) and philosophical mercury (the passive principle) within alchemy.

84 C. G. Jung, *Synchronicity – An Acausal Connecting Principle*, trans. by R.F.C. Hull (Princeton, NJ: Princeton University Press, 1973), p. 38.

huge proportions of the macrocosm (i.e. the universe, symbolised here by a series of planets which are considerably smaller than the couple's legs). The low (and the base) have therefore taken the place of the high.

This depiction of the couple's legs suggests an exaltation of terrestrial love,[85] especially when conceived against the depredations of reality. The decaying remains below, and the orbital motion of the celestial bodies, remind us of the passage of time and the ineluctability of decay; and therefore endow the image of the legs with a greater significance. For the ecstasy of what appears a quasi-mystical union offers, if not a complete release from, then a mitigation of the ravages of time and the transience of life. The exaltation specifically of an act of copulation reflects the general importance which the Surrealists attached to the free pursuit and realisation of love (in its physical and not just its emotional aspects).

On a more esoteric level, the union may also refer to the restoration of the primordial androgyne, which Breton calls for in *Du Surréalisme et ses Œuvres Vives* (1953)[86] or the tantric merging of Shakti and Shiva.[87] When taken as distinct entities, the Goddess Shakti ushers in periods of bounty, fertility and creation whereas the God Shiva presides over cycles of destruction. The combining of the two thus creates a cosmic harmony which overcomes the vicissitudes of creation and destruction.[88] The comparison between Ernst's

85 I use the term terrestrial love both to distinguish it from the love of a higher power (such as a love of the divine) and to denote love in its sexual, romantic and elective (i.e. human and earthly) aspects, in other words, those aspects which were especially prized by the Surrealists and are exalted in the painting to the level of a divine or cosmic agency.

86 Breton, *Manifestes du Surréalisme*, p. 170; Breton, *Manifestoes of Surrealism*, p. 302.

87 For information on the correspondences between Surrealism, alchemy and Tantrism, see Arturo Schwarz, 'L'Amour est l'Érotisme – De Quelques Correspondances entre la Pensée Surréaliste et Celles de l'Alchimie et du Tantrisme' in *Mélusine – Le Livre Surréaliste*, ed. Henri Béhar (Lausanne: L'Age d'Homme, 1982), vol. 4, pp. 179–202.

88 These notions are also found in Allendy's commentary on the emerald tablet in which the sun, like Shiva, is characterised as 'desiccating, burning, sterilising' though completed by the moon, which has the inverse properties: 'The Astrologers regard the Sun as being rather sterile, but the Moon represents the plasticity that enables solar energy to be fertile' – René Allendy, *La Table d'Eméraude* (Paris: Chacornac, 1921), p. 24. The joining of Shakti and Shiva can also signify the merging of the female and

work and Tantrism seems apt as Breton himself described Ernst as appearing as a 'dieu lamé d'or entre les six bras de sa Çakti'[89] ['gold-spangled God between the six arms of his *Shakti*'[90]], the gold-spangled God suggesting Shiva.

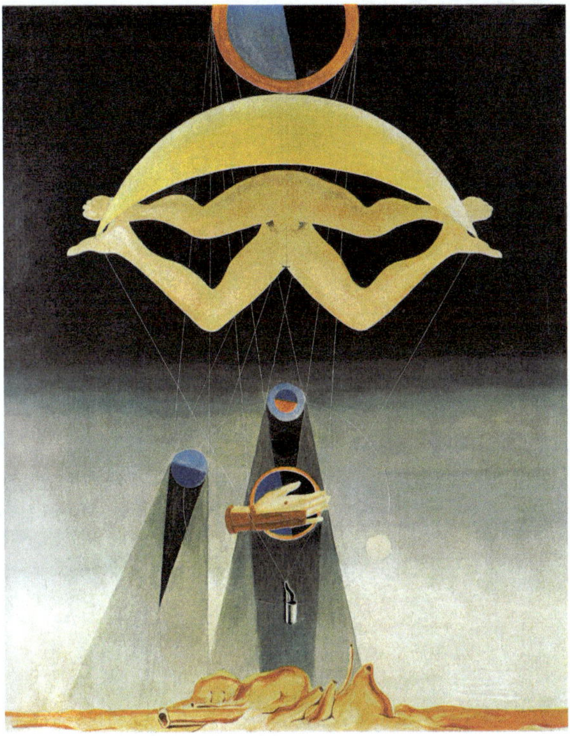

Figure 4.12: Max Ernst, *Les Hommes N'en Sauront Rien* (*Men Shall Know Nothing of This*) (1923) © Max Ernst/ADAGP. Copyright Agency, 2018.

Ernst's painting can be compared to a seventeenth-century painting which was well known to the Surrealists, and may have inspired Ernst: Juan de Valdés Leal's *Finis Gloriae Mundi* (1660) (Figure 4.13). Breton referred to it

male aspects of the psyche which is achieved by a sublimatory yogic practice known as Kundalini yoga, whereby the libido (Shakti) is guided to the head (Shiva).

89 Breton, *Œuvres Complètes* IV, p. 548.

90 Breton, *Surrealism and Painting*, p. 164.

as 'le chef d'œuvre de l'alchimie'[91] ['the masterpiece of alchemy']. Although the painting does not depict any planetary bodies, its layout and purport are comparable to that of *Les Hommes N'en Sauront Rien*. Instead, the decaying remains of a bishop are shown at the base of the painting, though beside him lies what appears to be a Templar Knight, who on the basis of his initiatory knowledge is spared from decay. The painting seems to announce the victory of the heretic over the orthodoxy of the Church, a fact which is further reinforced by the celestial scales bearing the words 'nimas' (neither more) and 'nimenos' (nor less), suggesting that their respective fates have been judged and sanctioned by higher powers. Both Ernst's and Leal's painting offer the promise of redemption from an annihilative material reality on the basis of initiatory knowledge; this resides in the Surrealist cult of love in the first, and in the absorption of the hermetic mysteries in the second.

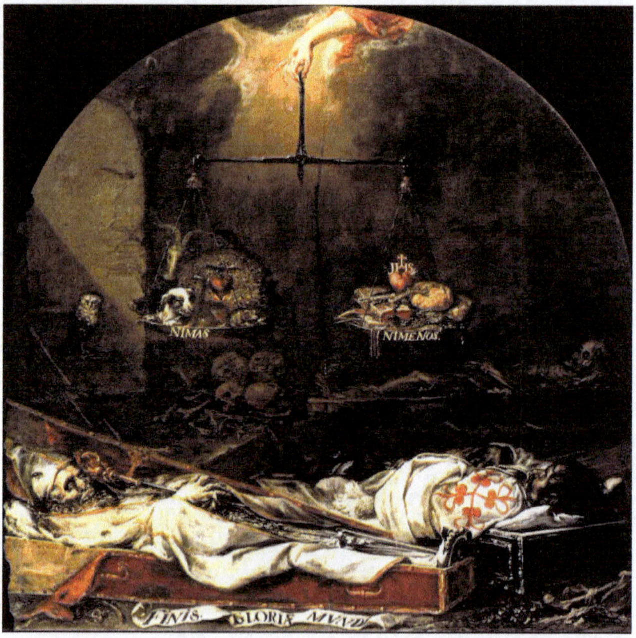

Figure 4.13: Juan de Valdés Leal, *Finis Gloriae Mundi* (*End of the World's Glory*) (1660).

91 Breton, *L'Art Magique*, p. 167.

Such hermetic imagery, and its association with the impulse for life and sexual fulfilment, was also to be found in the writings of Bataille and the dissident Surrealists in *Documents*. The journal not only elaborated the phenomena of sexuality in the register of the base but also related sexuality to hermetic transformation as well as to the themes of death and putrescence. For this reason, the putrescent dead head or *caput mortuum* of alchemy – that is to say the sublimated yet worthless remains of the *nigredo* phase of the great work – came to the attention of the journal, in which it was defended in a manner which remained true to the ethos of *Documents* whilst evoking those ideas about the Surrealist counter-consciousness which had been promoted by Breton.

The Return of the *Caput Mortuum*: Hermeticism and Veiling in the Writings of the *Documents* Group

Bataille's writings made frequent allusions to esoteric practices (manipulation of the pineal gland, gnosis, tantra, the blowing out of the self) and amongst them was one which reaffirmed a secret complicity with the Surrealists – namely an interest in alchemy. In the Bibliothèque Nationale Bataille had taken an interest in the original treatises of Robert Fludd[92] (as had Breton) and elaborated his philosophies with reference to Breton's reconciliation of antinomies.[93] The latter, according to Michael Richardson and Andrew Hussey,[94] embodied the hermetic principle according to which 'what is below is like what is on high and what is high is like what is below' (highlighting the symmetry between microcosm

92 Urszula Szulakowska, 'The Paracelsian Magus in German Art: Joseph Beuys and Rebecca Horn' in *Art & Alchemy*, ed. by Jacob Wamberg (Copenhagen: Museum Tusculanum Press, 2006), p. 173.

93 See Bataille, *Œuvres Complètes* IX, p. 186.

94 Michael Richardson, *Georges Bataille* (London: Routledge, 1994), p. 26 and Hussey, *The Inner Scar*, p. 29

and macrocosm). Breton actually referred to the principle himself in *Du Surréalisme en ses Œuvres Vives* (1953) in which he described the creative impulse of Surrealism as a momentary realisation of the hermetic adage.[95] According to Richardson, Bataille was no less doubtful of the axiom's veracity: 'there can be no question that Bataille accepted this principle as the basis of his thought. Without it his thinking as a whole makes little sense'.[96]

As early as 1927 Bataille included alchemical references in his writings.[97] Moreover, in the aftermath of the Second World War, when Breton and Bataille had overcome their differences, Bataille responded positively to Breton's *L'Art Magique*, specifically to a questionnaire which the latter had sent him concerning the status (and possible interconnectedness) of art and magic and, in doing so, made use of alchemical concepts. Whilst we find in his response some recognition of potential differences of outlook, we also find a thoughtful attempt at engaging directly with Breton's notion of *art magique* rather than ridiculing it:

95 'il [l'esprit] vérifie alors, fragmentairement il est vrai, du moins *par lui-même*, que "tout ce qui est en haut est comme ce qui est en bas" et tout ce qui est en dedans est comme ce qui est en dehors' – Breton, *Manifestes du Surréalisme*, p. 171 ['the mind then proves to itself, fragmentarily of course, but at least *by itself*, that 'everything above is like everything below' and everything inside is like everything outside' – Breton, *Manifestoes of Surrealism*, pp. 302–303]. Breton's italics.

96 Richardson, *Georges Bataille*, p. 26 – Richardson's claim rests upon a comparison between Bataillean thought and the writings of Pierre Mabille. He explains that both posit a view of the individual which is deeply intertwined with the existence of society, and by extension, the universe itself – with human life emerging as a sort of scientific 'precipitate' or 'compound' from the mass of human life within both.

97 In *L'Anus Solaire*, for example, he stated that 'la combinaison ou transformation mécanique' ['the mechanical combination or transformation'] of such movements as rotation (planetary, physical, mechanical) and sexual movement were what 'les alchimistes recherchaient sous le nom de pierre philosophale' – Georges Bataille, 'L'Anus Solaire' (1927) in *Œuvres Complètes* I, 82) ['alchemists sought as the philosopher's stone' – Georges Bataille, 'The Solar Anus' (1927) in *Visions of Excess*, p. 6].

> Il me semble que cette valeur [de voir dans l'œuvre d'art une possibilité de conséquence dans le monde réel], qui est pour vous comme pour moi la *pierre philosophale* à la recherche de laquelle nous vivons, ne peut être aperçu que sans mystère, dans le pur effet sensible, lié seulement aux réactions–affectives ou actives–qu'il a commandé.[98]
>
> [It seems that this value [of seeing in the work of art a possibility of having a consequence in the real world], which is for you as it is for me the *philosopher's stone* and whose recovery we are engaged in, can only be perceived without mystery, in its purely sensible effects, being linked only to those reactions – affective or active – which it has commanded.]

His comments are interesting for underlining a fundamental area of kinship between Bataille and Breton as seekers of the philosopher's stone and as art critics who look to artworks to provide tangible and rousing sensations. Breton, we recall, had defined the philosopher's stone as the 'le long, immense raisonné dérèglement de tous les sens' ['the long, immense, reasoned derangement of the senses'] and, as the previous chapter established, was sensitive to the 'para-erotic sensations' elicited by certain artworks. In his letter, Bataille now also affirmed that the philosopher's stone was nothing more than the sensible effects or 'effet sensible' of art upon the real world.

Bataille's journal *Documents* reflected this preoccupation with hermetic practices as well as an ambition to use them and other esoteric thought systems to challenge established ways of thinking and feeling. The journal was not merely a voice-piece for base materialism but operated rather more generally as a 'machine de guerre contre les idées reçues'[99] ['war-machine against received ideas']. As such it juxtaposed all manner of themes within one volume ranging from avant-garde art and music, extreme or violent phenomena (such as the workings of slaughterhouses) to ethnographic and esoteric anomalies. Desnos and Leiris, two of the so-called dissident Surrealists, wrote extensively on aspects of alchemy and hermeticism, frequently drawing their inspiration from the same esoteric writers as Breton

98 Bataille in Breton, *L'Art Magique*, p. 265 – Breton's/Bataille's italics.

99 Michel Leiris, 'De Bataille l'impossible à l'impossible Documents' (1963) in *Critique* (195–196), p. 689.

(Nicolas Flamel, Robert Fludd, Grillot de Givry, Paracelsus and William Blake).

Within the fifth edition of *Documents* (1925), Desnos published an article entitled 'Le Mystère d'Abraham Juif' ('the Mystery of Abraham the Jew') which outlined the mysterious tale of Nicolas Flamel's discovery of an ancient alchemical manuscript, the title and author of which were only identifiable by the words 'The Book of Abraham, the Jew, Prince, Levite, Astrologer, Philosopher to the Nation of Jews' and which Flamel spent approximately twenty years decoding. The fruits of his enquiries were set out in *Exposition of the Hieroglyphic Figures*, which interpreted Abraham's teachings, and purportedly instructed the reader on how to manufacture the philosopher's stone. Flamel claimed to have followed these steps himself in order to transmute mercury into gold.

The illustrations of *Exposition of the Hieroglyphical Figures* included images that Breton would describe in *Le Second Manifeste* to provide the ultimate examples of Surrealist imagery:[100] the encounter of Saturn and Mercury and the slaying of innocents. By a remarkable coincidence, Desnos, within his article, published two variations of the same images which had also been produced by Flamel (Figure 4.14). He claimed that the illustrations would allow alchemists of honest intent to find the philosopher's stone, whilst thwarting the efforts of disingenuous alchemists, whom he associated with modern chemists. He designated the latter as 'puffers', a decidedly pejorative term, referring to those (al)chemists who sought material gain through a number of transmutative operations without regard for the spiritual aspects of alchemy. Thus, Desnos effectively presents the inverse argument to that of *Tel Quelist* Pierre Rottenberg (quoted at the start of the chapter), who claimed the ascendency of chemistry over what he perceived to be its ignominious bastardisation, alchemy.

100 Having briefly described replicas of the same images as printed in Desnos' article, Breton asks 'Ne dirait-on pas *le* tableau surréaliste?' – Breton, *Manifestes du Surréalisme*, p. 125 ['Doesn't this sound like *the* Surrealist painting?'– Breton, *Manifestoes of Surrealism*, p. 175]. Breton's italics.

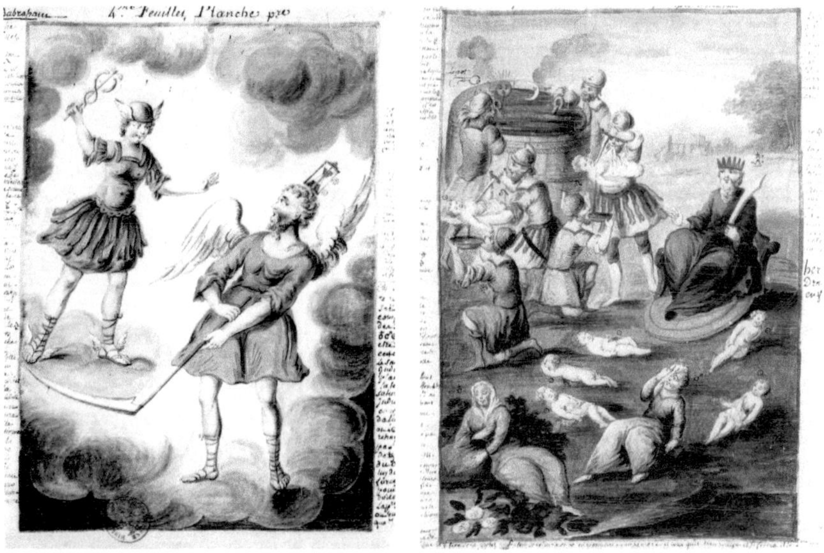

Figure 4.14: Illustrations of Flamel's *Exposition of the Hieroglyphical Figures*, reproduced in Robert Desnos' article 'Le Mystère d'Abraham Juif' (*Documents*, 1925).

At a time when Surrealism had appeared riven by dissension, Breton, in the *Second Manifeste*, was compelled to acknowledge this area of kinship with his former ally who had now become a self-professed dissident.[101] Although Desnos refrained from commenting on this coincidence, he did assess the value of these images in such way as to suggest an unspoken sympathy for Breton's ideas (and which would similarly situate him at the antipodes of the *Tel Quelists*). He similarly considered the philosopher's

101 'Il est hors du doute [...] que Desnos et moi, vers la même époque, avons cédé à une préoccupation identique, alors que pourtant, nous agissons *en toute indépendance extérieure* l'un de l'autre [...] Avec Desnos ce n'est pas la première fois que pareille aventure nous arrive' – Breton, *Manifestes du Surréalisme*, p. 124. ['There can be no doubt [...] that Desnos and I, at about the same time, were involved in the same experiment, although we were *acting completely independently* from each other [...] This is not the first time that something of this kind has happened to Desnos and me' – Breton, *Manifestoes of Surrealism*, p. 174]. Breton's italics.

stone as a work of the imagination, as having the capacity to refashion language into new poetic forms. He designated the modern heir of Flamel's alchemical doctrine as Gérard de Nerval '[le] parfait alchimiste du verbe, possesseur de la pierre philosophale de toute poésie'[102] ['[the] perfect alchemist of the word, possessor of the philosopher's stone of all poetry']. Along with Rimbaud, Gérard de Nerval was for Breton also one of those poets who embodied the Surrealist spirit *avant la lettre* having mined the depths of his unconscious and reworked his episodes of psychosis into mythopoeic narratives.

Like Desnos, Michel Leiris similarly had a keen interest in the occult. He had for a long time been an intermediary between Breton and Bataille before participating in the publication of *Documents*, where he nonetheless continued to write about topics which typically were Surrealist in flavour. He identified poetry and fiction as expressions of the marvellous, a term which he in turn associated with 'revolt' and 'rupture':

> Poésie et fictions reposent essentiellement sur cette ruse inconsciente, leur but le plus général consistant précisément en cette rupture des relations qui engendre le Merveilleux, aveuglant météore de révolte.[103]

> [Poetry and fiction basically depend on that ruse of the unconscious, their most general aim consisting of precisely that rupture of relations which engenders the Marvellous, the blinding meteor of revolt.]

Leiris was effectively still giving credence to the counter-consciousness which Breton established in opposition to rationalist thought, taking exception both to the narrow logic of hard science and to the inhumane, stultifying machinery of capitalist society. A number of his other statements in *Documents* reflected this critical view. For example, he considered the marvellous as that which temporarily reconnects the subject with a sense of the absolute and in so doing disrupts all normal

102 *Ibid.*

103 Michel Leiris, 'A propos de "Musée des sorciers"' in *Documents*, no. 2 (1929), p. 109.

relations, rejecting 'logique stupide' ['stupid logic'] and escaping 'cette atroce féodalité des causes qui décime ses fiefs humains à grands coups d'édits rationnels et de potences pragmatiques'[104] ['the atrocious feudality of causes which decimates its human fiefs with great weapons of rational edicts and pragmatic potencies']. The absolute stood not for a transcendent Godhead but for the fiery zeal of a person's heart or 'essence', which, when harnessed, allowed the individual to project something of him- or herself onto external circumstances.[105] Leiris considered the eruption of the absolute through the marvellous to be both esoteric and subversive, and the fascination it exercised upon (wo)men to be universal.

Given the manifold virtues of the marvellous, Leiris maintained that occult treatises (when uncontaminated by obvious charlatanry) merited more serious attention than they had hitherto received from sceptics and occultists alike. He reviewed (what he considered) a more credible compendium of occult lore compiled by Grillot de Givry, *Le Musée des Sorciers* ('The Museum of Sorcerers'), which was also one of Breton's favourite esoteric reference works. In particular, he analysed its hermetic and alchemical content. In so doing, he not only uncovered unexpected correspondences between high and low (in particular, the divine and the sexual) but also considered the extent to which this content prefigured modern thinking, including psychoanalytical concepts.

In the second part of his article, Leiris discussed in detail one of the images printed in *Le Musée des Sorciers*, an illustration originating from the English physician and alchemist, Robert Fludd, entitled *Le Jour et la Nuit du Microcosme*[106] (*The Day and the Night of the Microcosm*; Figure 4.15).

104 *Ibid.*

105 *Ibid.*

106 This image is also reproduced in a later edition of Breton's *L'Art Magique* as published within *Œuvres Complètes* IV, p. 223.

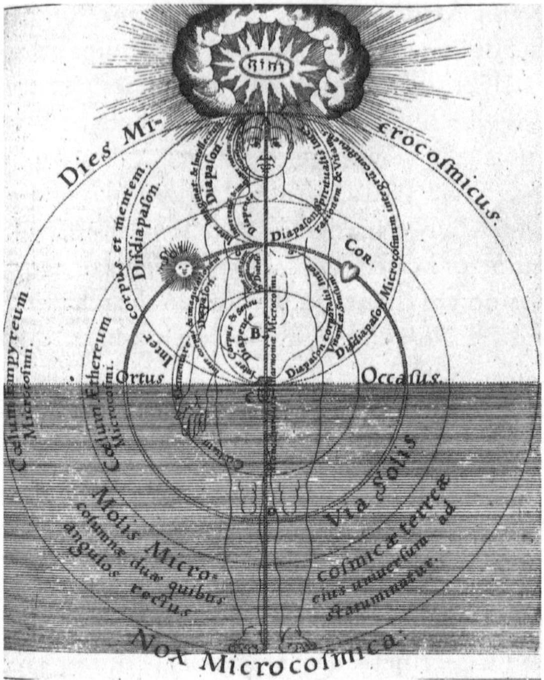

Figure 4.15: Robert Fludd, *The Day and Night of the Microcosm* (1617–1619), reproduced in Grillot de Givry's *Le Musée des Sorciers, Mages et Alchimistes* (1929).

Fludd's diagram reflected a belief in the symmetry between macrocosm and microcosm, and specifically that the various parts of the human body were influenced by events in the cosmos, particularly the movement of the planets. Superimposed upon the figure were concentric circles emanating from his genitalia, with an additional circle drawn in to connect them with the top of his head (which touches a cloud bearing the four letters of 'sacred tetragrammation', in other words the name of God as designated by the Hebrew letters י ה ו ה). The circles served to establish correspondences between different parts of the body as well as between these and the planets. The most striking correspondence, however, was between the sexual organs and the divine, which highlighted the underlying complicity of both.

Leiris remarked that the common element of conceptions of the microcosmic body (of which Fludd's illustration was a prime example) was the role of the genitalia in mediating between the baseness of nature and the 'higher' faculties of (wo)man. He further explained that within several occult systems (kabbalistic, religious, Rosicrucian, Paracelsan and Agrippan) the genitals were conceived as the 'principe générateur' ['generative principle'] which straddled both the divine and the terrestrial life, and were symbolised by the phallic-shaped letter yodh (י) in Hebrew:

> En hébreu, la lettre *iod*, qui exprime le principe générateur ou, dans le tétragramme sacré, Dieu le Père, est un symbole phallique. [....] Cornelius Agrippa, dans sa *Philosophie occulte*, indique comme correspondant à la lettre *iod* Lucifer dans le monde infernal et la pierre philosophale dans le monde élémentaire. Paracelse, dans une des figures du *Liber Azoth (Practiva lineæ vitaæ)*, donne la même signification phallique au *iod*, ou point générateur [....]. Enfin cette importance primordiale de l'élément sexuel est également vérifiée par le rôle capital que joue le serpent, autre symbolique phallique, dans un grand nombre de religions.[107]

> [In Hebrew, the letter *yodh*, which expresses the generative principle or, in the sacred tetragram, God the Father, is a phallic symbol. [...] Cornelius Agrippa, in his *De occulta philosophia*, indicates how the letter *yodh* corresponds to Lucifer in the underworld and the philosopher's stone of the elemental world. Paracelsus in one of the illustrations of *Liber Azoth (Practiva lineæ vitaæ)*, accords the same phallic meaning to the *yodh*, or the generative point [....] Finally the primordial importance of the sexual element is equally corroborated by the preeminent role occupied by the serpent, another phallic symbol, in a great number of religions.]

It is important to note again the ends to which Leiris puts these examples within the article for, as expected, his intention is not to provide an apologia of religious faith but to establish conceptual linkages between historical conceptualisations of sexuality in esoteric writing and the modern (Freudian) theory of libido.

One example of this is in Leiris' comparison of Fludd's *The Day and Night of the Microcosm* and an illustration taken from Gichtel's *Theosophica Practica* (1736; Figure 4.16), in which the bowels and genitalia of the central figure are depicted in dark, infernal colours but also show thick fleshy pathways running from these regions to the head. The pathways seem to

107 Leiris, *Documents* 2, p. 116.

anticipate those channels to which Freud refers in *Three Essays on Sexuality* (1905) whose purpose is to accomplish the displacement of the erotic instincts but of which 'very little is as yet known'.[108]

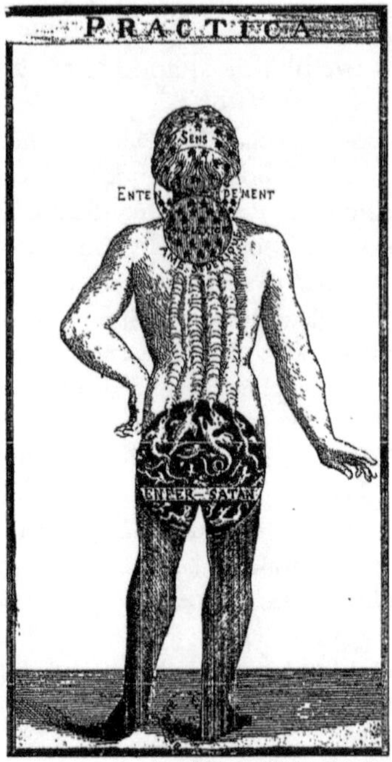

D'après l'édition de la Bibliothèque Rosicrucienne

THEOSOPHIA PRACTICA DE GICHTEL

Figure 4.16: Images from Gichtel's *Theosophia Practica* (1736), reproduced in *Documents*, no. 2 (1929).

For Leiris, these illustrations offered 'mythological' explorations of the origins of sexuality that anticipated key aspects of psychoanalytic theory, establishing 'à quel point la vie psychologique de l'homme est liée à sa sexualité'[109] ['the extent to which the psychological life is linked to sexuality'].

108 Sigmund Freud, 'Three Essays in Sexuality – II Infantile Sexuality' (1905) in *Complete Psychological Works* VII, p. 206.

109 *Ibid.*

Moreover, they made one believe that God was nothing more than the transposition of the ultimate paternal or phallic signifier to the ideal plane.[110] This appeared a direct echo of Freud's assertion about the function of sublimation within religion:

> genitals were the pride and hope of living beings; they were worshipped as Gods and transmitted the divine nature of their function to all newly learned human activities. As a result of the sublimation of their basic nature there arose innumerable divinities [...]. In the course of cultural development so much of the divine and the sacred was ultimately extracted from sexuality that the exhausted remnant finally fell into contempt[111]

Leiris reached the same conclusion as Freud: that the sexual component of human life fell into ignominy during the course of cultural evolution. Significantly, Leiris built upon this observation by assigning the culpability for such repressiveness to the 'intellectualism' and 'le rationalisme étroit qui [...] s'obstinant à nier l'influence des "parties basses" sur la pensée, afin de préserver de ce qu'il jugeait être un attentat sur la dignité humaine'[112] ['narrow rationalism which [...] laboured stubbornly to deny the influence of the "lower regions" upon thought, in order to preserve human dignity from what it considered an assassination attempt'].

Despite pleading for a revalorisation of the physical (and sexual) dimension of human experience, Leiris seemed here to caution against a myopic, introverted scientism preferring instead a 'science de l'homme, faite par l'homme et pour l'homme'[113] ['science of man, made by man, for man'] which would include the study of all those phenomena of the Surrealist counter-consciousness, such as dream-life, the mytho-symbolic world of poetry and the occult, and the life of the unconscious in which all cathected

110 *Ibid.*

111 Sigmund Freud, 'Leonardo da Vinci and a Memory of his Childhood' (1910) in *Complete Psychological Works* XI, 97 – Leiris' observation can also be compared to Freud's assertion that 'the roots of the need for religion are in the parental complex; the almighty and just God, and kindly Nature, appear to us as a grand sublimation of father and mother' – Freud, *Complete Psychological Works* XI, p. 123.

112 Leiris, *Documents* 2, p. 116.

113 *Ibid.*

sexual impulses are contained, or as Leiris put it 'le reflet dans la tête des hommes des déterminations instinctives et cachées'[114] ['the reflection in the heads of men of instinctual and hidden determinations'].

In another article Leiris expressed the hope that the alterity of states considered mystical, erotic, poetic or insane would be employed at the service of a monism which overcame the old dualities of body and spirit, in a manner which again evoked Surrealism:

> une des seules tâches valables qu'un homme puisse se proposer d'accomplir est l'abolition, par quelque moyen que ce soit (mysticisme, folie, aventure, poésie, érotisme…), de cette insupportable dualité établie […] entre le corps et l'âme, la matière et l'esprit.[115]
>
> [one of the only tasks which are worth being accomplished by a man is the abolition, by whichever means possible (mysticism, madness, adventure, poetry, eroticism …) of the insupportable duality established […] separating the body and soul, matter and spirit.]

In an attempt to reconcile both the material and mystical, Leiris, within the same article, presented a reinterpretation of the *caput mortuum*, with reference to disguise on the one hand and fetish on the other, though in both cases delineated in alchemical terms. As the *caput mortuum* signifies a 'dead head', his starting point was the negation or effacement of the head, especially when imposed by culture, by means of veils and disguises. For Leiris these concealments, which emphasised the body at the expense of the head, could result in a profound emotional climax (or *jouissance*), erotic and mystical in nature with both aspects being 'sous le signe de la complète exaltation'[116] ['under the sign of complete exaltation']. The force of such a concealment of the face also resulted in the liberation of the subject from the (social, moral) confines under which he ordinarily laboured. It was 'un moyen de sortir de soi, de briser les liens que vous imposent la morale, l'intelligence et les coutumes, une manière aussi de conjurer les

114 *Ibid.*
115 Michel Leiris, 'Le "Caput Mortuum" ou la Femme de l'Alchimiste' in *Documents*, no. 8 (1930), p. 461.
116 *Ibid.*

forces mauvaises et de braver Dieu ou ses succédanés'[117] ['a means of escaping from the limits of the self, of cutting the binds which are imposed upon you by morality, intelligence and tradition, it is also a manner of warding off evil forces and of standing up to God or his substitutes']. Concealment of a woman's face constituted 'lèse divinité'[118] since, Leiris affirmed, woman was constructed in the image of God.

Leiris concluded his article by relating the *caput mortuum* to the philosophy of Kant, claiming it to resemble 'une sorte de *chose en soi* obscure, tentante et mystérieuse – résidu suprême qu'on peut colorer de la valeur aussi bien la plus idéale que la plus sordidement matérielle'[119] ['a sort of obscure *thing in itself*, tempting and mysterious – supreme residue which one can invest with the most ideal value as well as with the most sordidly material value']. He then reminded us of the alchemical origins of the *caput mortuum* and where it occurred within the great work, 'cette phase [...] où tout semble pourri quand tout est régénéré'[120] ['that phase [...] where everything appears rotten when it has all been regenerated']. Contrary to the *Tel Quelists*, he draws attention to some of the complexities of the *caput mortuum*, not only in its capacity to bring about salutary renewal from an apparent state of decay, but in a figurative sense in its equivocal position between the erotic and the deathly.

In highlighting the transformative aspect of the *caput mortuum*, Leiris could also be compared to Ernst, whose collage novel *La Femme 100 Têtes* (or 'Hundred-Headless Woman') played with the homophonic ambiguity of the words 'sans' (meaning 'without') and 'cent' (meaning 'one hundred'). As the title of the work suggested, feminine identity within the novel was both negated and amplified in such a way as to highlight the omnipotence of (masculine) unconscious desire (in a manner similar to Desnos' *Rrose Sélavy* or Péret's Rosa). In many of the book's plates, nudes are represented in unexpected, unsettling poses mediating an uncanny sense of mystery and foreboding, the female subjects appearing as libidinal traces, buried

117 *Ibid.*, p. 466.
118 *Ibid.*, p. 465.
119 *Ibid.* – Leiris's italics.
120 *Ibid.*

memories and forgotten fragments of the subconscious, whose presence in everyday reality serves to disturb and disrupt. In some of the plates, they are represented as headless, the woman's head being typically situated beyond the limits of the illustration or concealed behind other objects.

In one of the book's plates (Figure 4.17, right-hand image) and in a later painting entitled *The Robing of the Bride* (1940; Figure 4.17, left-hand image) Ernst depicted female nudes whose heads were completely submerged by avian plumage. It has been suggested that the painting, which is replete with alchemical symbolism, represents the inversion of the alchemical operation known as 'the unrobing of the bride'[121] which preceded the marriage of opposites – the mid-point of the great work.

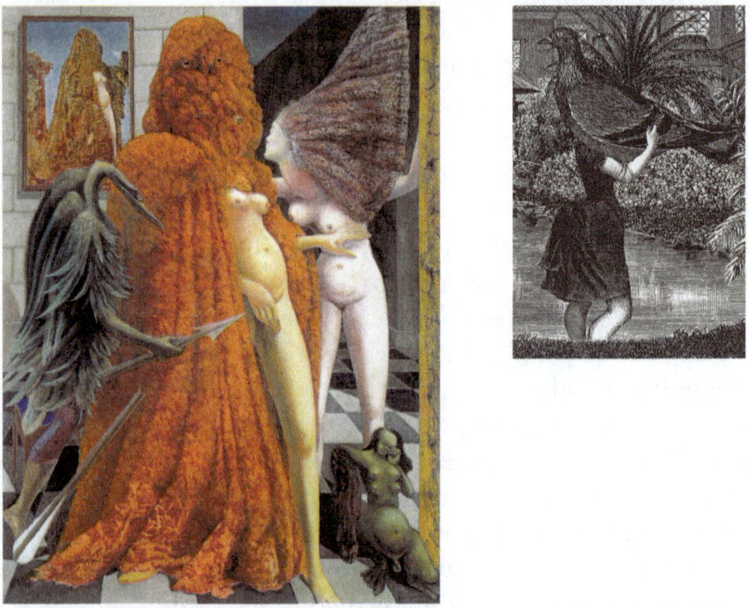

Figure 4.17: Max Ernst, *The Robing of the Bride* (1940) © Max Ernst/ADAGP. Copyright Agency, 2018 and, right, an illustration with a similar motif, Max Ernst 'Loplop et la Belle Jardinière' ('Loplop and the Beautiful Gardener'). Illustration from collage novel *La Femme 100 Têtes* (1929) © Max Ernst/ADAGP. Copyright Agency, 2018.

121 See Nadia Coucha, *Surrealism and the Occult* (Oxford: Mandrake, 1991), p. 118.

This 'marriage of opposites' can be considered in its more mystical interpretation as the union of male and female principles through matrimony, or in more general terms, the restoration of the primordial androgyne. Ernst, however, presents us with the outright failure of such a union, especially in its sexual aspect, for the green hermaphroditic figure in the bottom right is shown to be pregnant, yet unable to give birth because of its lower anatomy, which resembles that of a man. This sexual failure seems further reinforced by the broken arrow, whose head is clasped by a creature which is half-human, half bird; a clear phallic reference betokening a thwarting of desire. Like the *caput mortuum*, the painting points to the inefficacy of desire which has here become stymied in an unproductive and unnatural union yet which, according to the values of Surrealism, still holds promise for the future. For the birds which veil the female protagonists underline the obscure nature of the desired object suggesting to the onlooker that its truth has yet to be discovered.

The engagement of Leiris and Ernst with the *caput mortuum* brings us full circle within this chapter. I hope to have qualified in some measure Pierre Rottenberg's argument (cited in the introduction) that the *caput mortuum* and alchemy were of an unavailing nature. For Surrealists from both Bretonian and Bataillean camps considered alchemical transmutation to be an apt metaphor for their own working practices when these recuperated the worthless and repressed contents of the psyche in a way which frequently exposed the gaping inadequacies of our own reality. Of special significance within the metaphor of the great work was the focus on regeneration and the omnipresence of sexuality (showing us that is was not simply the 'repressed terrain' which Rottenberg claimed). This brings us to the role of love within Surrealism more generally, and thus to the subject of the next chapter, in which the Surrealist's valorisation of terrestrial love will be shown to be a site both of sublimation and (in its divergence from divine love and emphasis on the elective) of transgression.

CHAPTER 5

The Surrealist Cult of Love: Extolling the Forbidden Fruit

'tout ce qui est en haut est comme tout ce qui est en bas' et tout ce qui est dedans comme ce qui est en dehors.[1]

['everything above is like everything below' and everything inside is like everything outside[2]]
— André Breton, 'Du Surréalisme en ses Œuvres Vives' (1953)

The previous chapter showed that in exploring alchemy and Hermeticism, the Surrealists were better able to understand the complicity between the high and the low (including the material and the rarefied), and, in so doing, developed a more profound notion of sublimation (a sublimation which recognised matter and desire). They invariably became drawn to the hermetic adage 'as above, so below', though frequently high and low were subject to the most curious inversions (showing that one could not assume the primacy of one term over another). More generally, the preoccupation with these opposing orientations reflected the Surrealist fascination with antinomies (how they interacted and how they could merge) though precluded their appropriation into an overarching philosophy. Illustrative of this is the philosophical bricolage of the opening quotation which combines Hermetic thought (what is above and what is below) with its own interpretation of dialectics (of interior and exterior states).

1 Breton, 'Du Surréalisme en ses Œuvres Vives' (1953) in *Manifestes du Surréalisme*, p. 171.
2 Breton, 'On Surrealism and its Living Works' (1953) in *Manifestoes of Surrealism*, pp. 302–303.

The latter dialectic of internal and external states has, in fact, accompanied us from the beginning of our enquiry, from Breton's exposition of the interplay of interior and exterior states to the destabilising impact of Surrealist works upon the outer world when conceived under the banner of non-repressive sublimation. This chapter will therefore provide a valuable, and indeed necessary, addition to the previous analyses of this dialectic, considering its implications for the realisation of love and desire in the Surrealists' immediate social environment and how this too constituted a direct engagement with physical reality rather than a willed insulation from it. Moreover, the theory used to understand this interplay – which will be derived from Lacan – shows the consequences of the non-repressive sublimation posited by Marcuse and will reflect again the divergence of Surrealist thought from that of Freud.

In this chapter I draw on Lacanian theory to present an alternative view of the sublimated which is derived from external reality rather than the wellspring of the libido interior to the self. For Lacan sublimation was not synonymous with the neutered existence upon which society's 'highest cultural successes'[3] were predicated as Freud had held, but was instead conceived as the recourse to any activity or object which could be used to fill the emotional void inherent in the human condition (experienced particularly when humans are deprived of romantic and sexual ties). The objects which could achieve this were both human and inanimate artefacts of special symbolic value (such as those of sexual or perverse form) and exercised upon the Surrealists such mystery and seduction that they found themselves cajoled into the external world in a never-ending quest for signifiers of love.

When the love and desire depicted in Surrealist works are read through Lacanian theory, we are again confronted with a counter-model to Freudian renunciation: rather than being inhibited in their aims, the instincts circumvent any sense of lack and find satisfaction in the real. Before proceeding with such a reading, however, I will provide a brief overview of Lacan's theory on sublimation to demystify the principal terms he uses in its elaboration.

3 Freud, *Complete Psychological Works* XI, p. 54.

Demystifying Lacanian Sublimation

Associating the phenomena of love and sublimation was never an immediate concern to Freud, which is in some ways surprising, since the rawer manifestations of love, the erotic instincts, formed the basis of the sublimatory process as he had conceived it.[4] In his rather pessimistic view of civilisation, love was mainly discussed in terms of its non-fulfilment. For Lacan, on the other hand, the possibility of allying love and sublimation started to impress itself upon him in the early thirties when he became exposed to the psychoanalytically inflected writings of the Surrealists and actively collaborated with them on the publication of the journal *Minotaure*. At this time he began to synthesise psychiatry, psychoanalysis and Surrealism;[5] and when he ultimately put forward his own theory of sublimation in the seventh seminar of *The Ethics of Psychoanalysis*, he adduced Surrealist theory and literature to substantiate his claims. He showed that sublimation was not merely, as Freud had maintained, a deflection of libidinal energy situated in the *id* into 'some achievement which is no longer sexual but has a higher social or ethical valuation'[6] which 'makes it possible for higher psychical activities, scientific, artistic or ideological, to play such

4 The only suggestion Freud makes of being able to reconcile love and sublimation is by pointing to the potential for self-sacrifice in a relationship, 'afforded by the state of being in love, whether in a sexual or sublimated manner, which goes so far as involving a sacrifice of the self' – Sigmund Freud, 'An Autobiographical Study' in *Standard Edition of the Complete Psychological Works – An Autobiographical Study, Inhibitions, Symptoms and Anxiety, the Question of Lay Analysis, and Other Works*, trans. by James Strachey in collaboration with Anna Freud (London: Hogarth Press, 1959), vol. XX, p. 56.

5 Roudinesco, *Histoire de la Psychanalyse 2*, p. 126; Roudinesco, *Jacques Lacan & Co*, p. 111.

6 Sigmund Freud, 'Two Encyclopaedia Articles' – 'B- The Libido Theory' (1922) in *The Standard Edition Of The Complete Psychological Works of Sigmund Freud – Beyond the Pleasure Principle, Group Psychology, and Other Works*, trans. under editorship of James Strachey in collaboration with Anna Freud (London: Hogarth Press, 1955), vol. XVIII, p. 256.

an important part in civilised life'.[7] Lacan claimed that sublimation did not always serve civilisational ends; instead, it resulted from an attitude toward the love object, which he qualified as 'overvaluation', an emotional over-investment in (and fixation upon) the object of interest which stood in relief to the relative desolation and uncertainty of the individual's social reality. Sublimation was not however limited to the treatment of the love object as an intangible literary ideal, or the avoidance of physical relations in favour of more selfless, socially utilitarian acts.

In finding examples for his theory, he evoked not only the Surrealists but the *troubadours* of the Middle Ages[8] (for him both were part of the same lineage of love poets). Lacan explained that both groups of poets had sought solace, meaning and order in love at those times when external (historical or social) circumstances appeared at their most arbitrary and chaotic. They had thus practised sublimation as a process of what he termed 'creation *ex nihilo*': this was the concentration of desire (and the creative activity inspired from it) against the backdrop of a sprawling void or *nihil* – here, the turbulent or directionless socio-historical circumstances in which the poets found themselves in.

For Lacan the term creation *ex nihilo* denoted the process of meaning being created out of empty spaces and represented one of the defining features of sublimation. He found abundant applications of the concept in the artistic and personal realm: the creation of a painting upon an empty canvas; the shaping of a vase on a potter's wheel; the writing of poetry in the absence of love[9] (it is here where his conceptualisation of the term comes to resemble Freud's); and, as a form of emotional investment, the commitment to an individual that helps overcome the feeling of being

7 Freud, *Complete Psychological Works* XXI, p. 97.

8 Lacan specifically identifies Breton, Péret and Éluard as poets belonging to this lineage – Jacques Lacan *The Seminar of Jacques Lacan, Ethics of Psychoanalysis* (1959–1960), ed. by Jacques-Alain Miller (London: Routledge, 1992), vol. VII, pp. 148–154; Jacques Lacan *Le Séminaire de Jacques Lacan – L'Éthique de la Psychanalyse* (1959–1960), ed. by Jacques-Alain Miller (Paris: Seuil, 1986), pp. 177–184.

9 For Lacan the 'empty space' of the woman is also to be understood as the vagina (Séminaire VII, p. 193; Lacan, *Seminar* VII, p. 163).

incomplete. The latter example is particularly important since, for Lacan, the most fundamental type of *nihil* was what he termed the ego's 'l'Autre préhistorique'[10] ['prehistoric Other'[11]] – commonly perceived as the subject's 'other half' – without which the individual labours with a certain sense of existential vacuity. Another name given to this prehistoric Other by Lacan was '*das Ding*' (the German word for 'the thing'), a concept whose meaning and function was later extended under the new name of *petit objet a*. Much of a subject's behaviour could be explained by an unconscious desire to retrieve *das Ding* or, more specifically, an object which might represent or stand in for it. Such an object allowed the individual to feel as though his/her existence was completed and that the unspecified sense of psychic lack had been overcome.

Das Ding was, moreover, central to Lacan's understanding of sublimation which he further defined as the raising of the object 'à la dignité de la Chose'[12] ['to the dignity of *das Ding*'[13]]. This involved an undue exaltation of and emotional investment in the Other; in others words, the putting of one's beloved upon a metaphorical pedestal. From identifying a desirable 'something' in the external world, the subject mythologised and refashioned it into the signifier of its complementary Other with the implications of dreamlike romance and irrational over-attachment this entails. For Freud, however, this process would undoubtedly have sounded too much like 'idealisation' which, he was keen to stress, was not to be confused with sublimation.

'*Das Ding*' recalls Kant's term 'das Ding an sich' ('the thing in itself') – the object whose existence is defined (and limited) by spatio-temporal modalities and can thus only ever be partially known through sense perception. It is the noumenon whose true 'essence' evades cognition.[14] Lacan effectively expropriates the term '*Ding*' from

10 Lacan, *Séminaire* VII, p. 69.
11 Lacan, *Seminar* VII, p. 56.
12 Lacan, *Séminaire* VII, p. 133.
13 Lacan, *Seminar* VII, p. 112.
14 'The term [*das Ding*] has a long philosophical history from Aristotle to Heidegger and is the term highlighted in Kant's "das Ding an sich," "the thing in itself," which

epistemological discourse to apply it to the realm of human psychology. This almost certainly accounts for his assertion that *das Ding* 'se présente toujours comme unité voilée'[15] ['always presents itself as a veiled entity'[16]] and that it relates to 'quelque chose qui est bien au-delà du domaine de l'affectivité, mouvant, confus, mal repéré'[17] ['something far beyond the domain of affectivity, something moving, obscure and without reference points'[18]].

It is assuredly no coincidence that, as we saw in the previous chapter, Leiris refers to the veiled love object (when considered under the guise of *caput mortuum*) as an obscure 'thing in itself' ('une sorte de *chose en soi* obscure'[19]), tempting and mysterious, and defined as much by its sordidness as its ideal value. Ernst's illustrations of women who are veiled or whose identities are obscured by birds as well as of 'the hundred-headless woman' also seem to exemplify the veiled nature of the Other as *das Ding*. If we consider Breton's statement in *Du Surréalisme en ses Œuvres Vives* that the restoration of the primordial androgyne was amongst Surrealism's central aims[20], we can see how this too might refer to the recouping of an abstract, timeless entity, which universally completes the individual. As Lacan pointed out, the works which emerged from movements such as Surrealism and the troubadours playfully explored all forms of absences and voids which served as a metaphor for a particular type of creation *ex nihilo*, the ultimate example being the vagina as reflective of a desire with

---

lies beyond phenomenal appearances and is unknowable in itself' – John Muller, 'Lacan's View of Sublimation' in *American Journal of Psychoanalysis*, 47:4 (1987), p. 315. Muller remarks that Heidegger's essay 'The Thing' (1950), and its treatment of the potter's clay jug, was a particularly strong influence on Lacan's conception of sublimation. Freud also mentions '*das Ding*' briefly in his essays 'Project' (1895) and 'On Negation' (1925), though not in relation to sublimation.

15 Lacan, *Séminaire* VII, p. 142.

16 Lacan, *Seminar* VII, p. 118.

17 Lacan, *Séminaire* VII, p. 124.

18 Lacan, *Seminar* VII, p. 103.

19 Leiris, *Documents* 8, p. 466.

20 Breton, *Manifestes du Surréalisme*, p. 170; Breton, *Manifestoes of Surrealism*, pp. 301–302.

an emptiness at its core. Sublimatory works could, albeit paradoxically, therefore broach subjects that were taboo.

Lacan believed sublimation to be the mechanism which allowed the subject's libido to fixate on any number of love objects, ever in the hope of recuperating the prehistoric Other or '*das Ding*' which was by definition 'lost' and impossible to recover: 'c'est de sa nature que l'objet est perdu comme tel. Il ne sera jamais retrouvé. Quelque chose est là en attendant mieux, ou en attendant pire, mais en attendant [...] Ce n'est pas lui que l'on retrouve, mais ses coordonnées de plaisir'[21] ['[*das Ding*] is to be found at the most as something missed. One doesn't find it, but only its pleasurable associations'[22]]. He therefore viewed the fulfilment of human desire as circular and circuitous. This is significant since Freud similarly stated that human desire consisted of a certain type of circularity whereby libidinal energy flowed from the self to the object(s) and back again.[23] Although he did not specifically relate this process to sublimation, it is undoubtedly the main point of contact between Lacanian and Freudian thinking.

The Detours of Love's Fulfilment

The path to finding gratification was in Lacan's eyes a meandering one. Indeed, he characterised human life as the succession of detours undertaken in the quest for the lost object or the absolute Other of the subject: 'Le principe du plaisir gouverne la recherche de l'objet, et lui impose ces détours qui conservent sa distance par rapport à sa fin'[24] ['The pleasure principle governs the search for the object and imposes detours which

21 Lacan, *Séminaire* VII, p. 65.

22 Lacan, *Seminar* VII, p. 52.

23 'All through the subject's life his ego remains the great reservoir of his libido, from which object-cathexes are sent out and into which the libido can stream back again from the objects' – Freud, *Complete Psychological Works* XX, p. 56.

24 Lacan, *Séminaire* VII, p. 72.

maintain the distance to *Das Ding* in relation to its end'[25]]. In the lives of the Surrealists such detours frequently characterised the pursuit of the desired love object, leading them off the path of conventional social mores to the site of transgression. Descriptions of these aleatory escapades featured particularly in the writings of three of the founding members of Surrealism, Breton, Péret and Éluard. Lacan considered the three writers to be modern incarnations of the troubadours and some of their works to be exemplifications of his ideas on sublimation, in particular where they exalted and overvalued the Other. It was their determination to do this (to find someone worthy of being exalted beyond all others) which led the three of them into an inexhaustible pursuit of love, which ultimately could not rest at one person and therefore defied the sanctity of Christian marriage. The prodigious value the three men attached to the experience of what might be termed free (or elective) 'terrestrial' love, with its emphasis on the personal and the sexual, and unencumbered by the constraints of marriage, placed them at the antipodes of the prevailing Christian mores of 1930s France, under which the enticements of extra-conjugal relationships were taboo. Yet these encounters were at the cornerstone of the Surrealist social revolution and thus led them to denigrate the church for its repressive influence upon society. In the two manifestoes of Surrealism, Breton had promised to restore meaning to the notion of love in defiance of its detractors,[26] inciting the reader to 'tue, vole plus vite, aime tant qu'il te plaira'[27] ['kill, fly faster, love to your heart's content'[28]]. The manifestoes were in many respects a rallying cry for society to break the boundaries established by an all-pervasive Christian conservative morality.

For Breton the serendipitous process whereby the subject is guided to the desired object, future soul mate or new idea consisted of 'la forme de manifestation de la nécessité extérieure qui se fraie un chemin dans l'inconscient humain'[29] ['the form of making manifest the exterior necessity

25 Lacan, *Seminar* VII, p. 58.

26 Breton, *Manifestes du Surréalisme*, p. 130; Breton, *Manifestoes of Surrealism*, p. 181.

27 Breton, *Manifestes du Surréalisme*, p. 23.

28 Breton, *Manifestoes of Surrealism*, p. 13.

29 Breton, *L'Amour Fou*, p. 35.

which traces its path into the human unconscious'[30]]. The force responsible for such serendipity he termed '*le hasard objectif*' or objective chance, which orchestrated uncanny yet life-changing encounters pregnant with meaning for the parties concerned yet completely arbitrary for the disinterested onlooker. Breton affirmed that these encounters were in some way motivated by a preconscious desire which, via a series of 'precautions' and 'ruses', led the desiring subject to what he or she wants – at which point the preconscious becomes conscious.

For Lacan *le hasard objectif* – and the resulting encounter with a desirable Other – lent credence to the idea that sublimation is a process of creation *ex nihilo*: the events of this objective chance seemed to occur in a beyond-of-the-causal, not merely because the subject sensed the void of *das Ding* but because the circumstances leading to a chance encounter (particularly while on a Surrealist *flânerie*) seemed entirely arbitrary. Lacan specifically qualified *le hasard objectif* as a 'drôle de configuration signifiante'[31] ['a strange signifying configuration'[32]] before addressing its importance in Breton's *L'Amour Fou* and asking:

> qui comprendra, à relire ces choses sans leur contexte, dans un siècle ou deux, que le hasard objectif veut dire les choses qui arrivent avec un sens d'autant plein qu'elles se situent quelque part où nous ne pouvons saisir aucun schème rationnel, ni causal, ni rien qui en justifie d'aucune façon le surgissement dans le réel ? Autrement dit, c'est aussi à la place de la Chose que Breton fait surgir l'amour fou.[33]

> [who, a century or so from now, without reading these things in context, will understand that objective chance means that things occur and are all the richer in meaning because they take place somewhere where we are unable to perceive either rational, or causal, or any other kind of order, that can justify their emergence in the real? In other words, it is once again in the place of the Thing that Breton had the madness of love emerge[34]]

30 Breton, *Mad Love*, p. 23 (translation slightly modified).
31 Lacan, *Séminaire* VII, pp. 183–184.
32 Lacan, *Seminar* VII, p. 154.
33 Lacan, *Séminaire* VII, pp. 183–184.
34 Lacan, *Seminar* VII, p. 154 – in the first line the word 'on' in the official translation has been replaced by 'without'.

Le hasard objectif guides the narrative of *L'Amour Fou* and two other of Breton's semi-autobiographical works: *Nadja* and *Les Vases Communicants.* In the first of these three works, he attributes his initial encounter with his second wife, Jacqueline Lamba, to objective chance; in the second, he similarly ascribes his meeting with his psychiatrically vulnerable lover, Nadja, to the same phenomenon; and in *Les Vases Communicants* Breton wanders the streets of Paris in anticipation of yet another fortuitous encounter following his break-up with lover Suzanne Muzard. The works begin by imparting a sense of aimless despair, depicting his restless peregrinations through the French metropolis in the absence of love and set against the backdrop of the uncertain, contingent and austere times which defined the interwar period. In other words, these narrative openings highlight the very absence of what Lacan describes as 'rational', 'causal' and 'ordered' circumstances and thus provide the optimal conditions for a romantic chance encounter.

All three works foreshadow such encounters by means of portents which mostly take the form of *trouvailles*, the arbitrarily located bric-a-brac which on account of their highly personal and symbolic import become a complement of the psyche. The term *trouvaille*, which means 'found object', is derived from the French verb 'trouver' – to find. Lacan sees in the act of searching and finding a defining characteristic of the courtly love tradition, for as he explains, the word *troubadour* itself comes from the Provençal word 'trobar', to find.[35] It is to these found love objects to which we now turn our attention.

Signifying Love Objects

'Ce qui est trouvé est cherché, mais cherché dans les voies du signifiant'[36] ['What is found is sought, but sought in the paths of the signifier'[37]], Lacan tells us, explaining that such a signifier is the embodiment of desire

35 Lacan, *Séminaire* VII, p. 143; Lacan, *Seminar* VII, p. 118.

36 Lacan, *Séminaire* VII, p. 143.

37 Lacan, *Seminar* VII, p. 118.

and serves to represent *das Ding*. This signifier may assume the form of an idealised love interest or of a crude and primitive object, as in the case of the Surrealist *trouvailles*. Ironically then, the sublimatory process may lead to the discovery of artefacts which take the form of the 'low' (in simplistic terms, denoting the function of the reproductive organs) and not the highly valued intellectual or artistic works which we have to associate with Freudian sublimation.

To illustrate this principle, Lacan tells of Jacques Prévert's obsession with collecting matchboxes during the war and threading the draws of each into the case of another to create a long, decorative ribbon. This had brought out the signifying presence, the 'thingness' of the matchbox and, in particular, its copulatory force. As I noted above, for Lacan meaning is created around empty spaces (whether anatomical or artistic) and as such forms the crux of sublimation as creation *ex nihilo*.

One of the central paradoxes which emerges with respect to the found love object or *trouvaille* is that in representing or filling the emptiness of *das Ding* (whether animate or inanimate) it frequently has an empty space incorporated into its design. Lacan highlights some of the most striking instances of this paradox, using the example of the vase to show how such a primordial form 'n'est signifiant, dans son essence de signifiant [...] de rien de particulièrement signifié [...] c'est bien le vide qu'il crée, introduisant par là la perspective même de le remplir'[38] ['is in its signifying essence a signifier of nothing [...] it creates the void and thereby introduces the possibility of filling it'[39]]. The vase and by extension any object fashioned around a hollow space can therefore be considered a metaphor of the possibility of creation – from the cosmogonic nothingness from which the universe was forged to the woman's womb from which human life emerges.

The portents in *L'Amour Fou*, which anticipate Breton's first encounter with his new love and future wife, are of particular significance in this regard. Toward the start of the work Breton describes his peregrinations around Paris which lead him to a flea market where he acquires a thick wooden spoon (Figure 5.1). In the first instance he sees it as a substitute for

38 Lacan, *Séminaire* VII, p. 145.
39 Lacan, *Seminar* VII, p. 120.

the sculpture of Cinderella's slipper which Breton had asked Giacometti to make for him but which the latter had omitted to do. The tale of Cinderella's missing slipper is of particular interest to Breton as an allegory of a quest for the lost phallus and, by extension, for the sexual fulfilment which was missing from this period of his life. The slipper-spoon is in his own words a 'magnification' or 'dramatisation' of the void he feels, the void of *das Ding*, and indeed 'le contenu latent, sexuel, est assez transparent'[40] ['the latent sexual content is quite transparent'[41]].

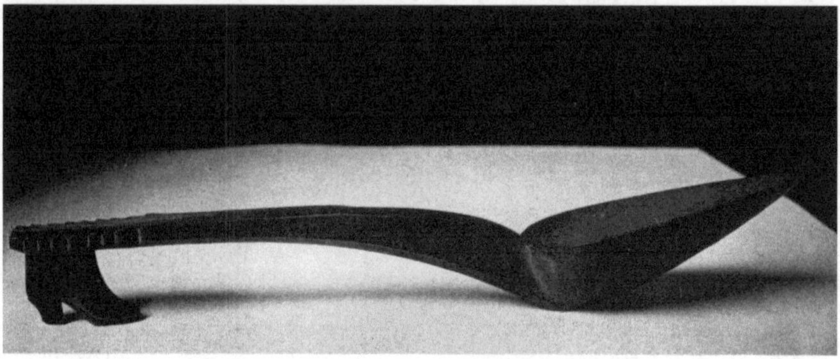

Figure 5.1: Man Ray, Photo of wooden spoon in the novel *Nadja* by André Breton (1928) © MAN RAY TRUST/ADAGP. Copyright Agency, 2018.

The attachment to the slipper-spoon responds to an unconscious desire which is made manifest only at the climax of *L'Amour Fou*: the desire for the full consummation of love with the Other. The moment is allegorised as an ascent into the mountains (specifically, Mount Teide in Tenerife; Figure 5.2) and the attainment of '*le point sublime*', the exalted vantage point of a bucolic and sublime landscape which represents the fulfilment of one's every desire. Although the sexual detail of this experience is to a large degree poeticised, Breton is compelled to recognise, and even venerate 'le délire de la présence absolue'[42] ['the delirium of absolute

40 Breton, *L'Amour Fou*, p. 54.
41 Breton, *Mad Love*, p. 37.
42 Breton, *L'Amour Fou*, p. 108.

presence'[43]] of which carnal love and its more perverse aspects are an indispensable component:

> Amour, seul amour qui sois, amour charnel, j'adore, je n'ai jamais cessé d'adorer ton ombre vénéneuse, ton ombre mortelle. Un jour viendra où l'homme saura te reconnaître pour son seul maître et t'honorer jusque dans les mystérieuses perversions dont tu l'entoures.[44]

> [Love, only love that you are, carnal love, I adore, I have never ceased to adore your lethal shadow, your mortal shadow. A day will come where man will be able to recognise you for his only master, honouring you even in the mysterious perversions that you surround him with.[45]]

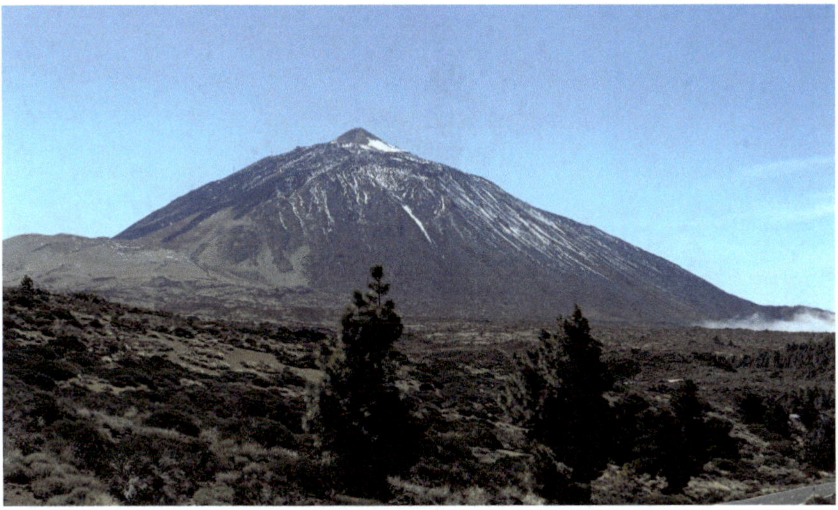

Figure 5.2: Allegory of the 'Sublime Point': Mount Teide, Tenerife.

The moment is also significant as it represents a transient yet potent experience which is brought into relief by an otherwise contingent life. It is the concretisation of Breton's desire (previously foreshadowed by the

43 Breton, *Mad Love*, p. 76.
44 Breton, *L'Amour Fou*, p. 108.
45 Breton, *Mad Love*, p. 76.

appearance of *trouvailles*) in what Lacan would call a process of 'anamorphosis'. This term, which stems from the Renaissance (and the artistic practices of this period), originally designated the corrected reflection of an image painted in an apparently distorted manner as viewed on the cylindrical mirror of an 'anamorphoscope' (Figure 5.3). Lacan extends the term's conventional meaning to denote the moment at which an intangible, elusive desire is temporarily realised. From the chaos of social relations emerges the image of the beloved which has long been yearned for. We might therefore consider 'anamorphosis' to be the visual or manifestational aspect of creation *ex nihilo*. In so far as it relates to signifying love objects appearing in place of *das Ding*, anamorphosis also helps to define the sublimatory process.

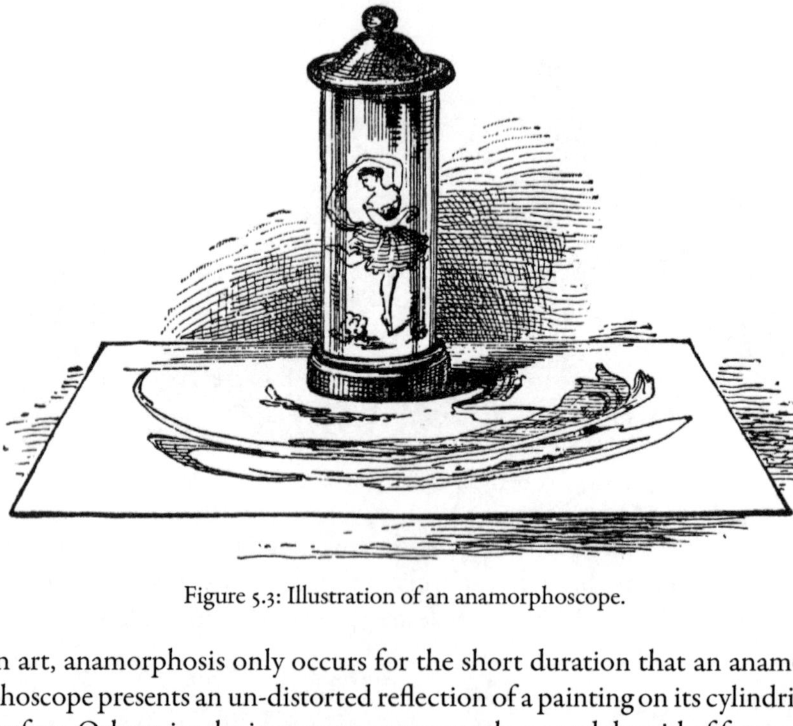

Figure 5.3: Illustration of an anamorphoscope.

In art, anamorphosis only occurs for the short duration that an anamorphoscope presents an un-distorted reflection of a painting on its cylindrical surface. Otherwise the image appears amorphous and devoid of form and meaning. So too the presence of the Other as loved one may only appear to us for a short duration; with the full force of desire being transitory in nature. This process applies particularly to Breton whose attainment of a profound desire often appears ephemeral. His experience of love, as he tells us at the start of the work, is compromised by 'égarements' – instances of 'losing one's way', of falling to the mercy of those detours occasioned by the experience of love.

No sooner is the relationship with Lamba consummated than Breton admits to peculiar and uncanny misgivings about it. He looks to the stars only to observe the 'les méfaits de la discorde'[46] ['toxic effects of conflict'[47]] which afflict him at the very centre of love and concludes by recognising the vanity of any attempt to linger at the sublime point : 'Il eut [...] à partir de là, cessé d'être sublime et j'eusse, moi, cessé d'être un homme'[48] ['It would [...] from then on have ceased to be sublime and I should, myself, have ceased to be a person'[49]]. Although one hopes the sublimation of the Other to be enduring, circumstances collude to bring a perfect image out of focus. Breton is thus impelled from one love object to the next, ever in the hope of recuperating the zenith of desire and the ideal other through which this might be accomplished.

In *Nadja* as in *L'Amour Fou*, Breton's *égarements* first lead him to the flea market, where again his unconscious desires begin to crystallise:

> J'y suis souvent, en quête de ces objets qu'on trouve nulle part ailleurs, démodés, fragmentés, inutilisables, presque incompréhensibles, pervers au sens où je l'entends et où je l'aime.[50]

> [I go there often, searching for objects that can be found nowhere else: old-fashioned, broken, useless, almost incomprehensible, even perverse – at least in the sense I give to the word and which I prefer.[51]]

46 Breton, *L'Amour Fou*, p. 144.
47 My translation. See also Breton, *Mad Love*, p. 99.
48 Breton, *L'Amour Fou*, p. 171.
49 Breton, *Mad Love*, p. 114.
50 Breton, *Nadja* (Fr), p. 62.
51 Breton, *Nadja* (Eng), p. 52.

It is unsurprising that Breton attributes to these objects a perverse or fetishistic quality[52] as it is these, which according to Lacanian theory, come to take the place of the self's complementary Other. As Mona Gauthier states 'l'objet pulsionnel n'est jamais que *métonymie*, que substitut de l'objet du désir éternellement manquant'[53] ['the object upon which the drive is fixated is only ever *metonymy*, only ever the substitute for the eternally missing object of desire']. This particular feature of Breton's narratives which deals with metonymy is significant, for it challenges the claim made by critics such as Lechte (cited in Chapter 2) that Bataille's writings more usually employ metonymy (as associated with the horizontal plane) while Breton's writings favour metaphor (and the vertical plane). Clearly this distinction does not always hold true.

More evidence of this comes when Breton, again perusing the curiosities of a flea market, acquires a semi-cylindrical device for measuring demographic change in a city, a device which he considers perverse on account of its form. Both exquisitely yet bizarrely unique *and* representative of a hollow-full dynamic, it fulfils the same portentous function as the spoon-slipper of *L'Amour Fou*, expressing a veiled desire for a similarly unique love object.

A few pages later Breton's attention is once again directed to an object which signifies lack – a pair of women's gloves whose fetishistic appeal enchant him and which he describes in the same nostalgic terms that he employed about the spoon in *L'Amour Fou*. The gloves are located on the hands of a lady he encounters arbitrarily in Paris and he teasingly asks her to devote them to the *Centrale Surréaliste*. As she is about to agree to his request, Breton ceases to importune her since the thought of the glove without its owner suddenly becomes unbearable to him. He again seems

52 Breton also alludes to fetishism in *Recherches sur la Sexualité* : 'J'ai une conception toute fétichiste de l'amour d'une façon générale. J'ai un grand goût cérébral pour le fétichisme en matière d'objets' – *Recherches sur la Sexualité*, p. 48 ['I have an entirely fetishistic view of love in general. Intellectually, I am strongly inclined to fetishise objects' – *Investigating Sex*, p. 11].

53 Mona Gauthier, *La Jouissance Prise Aux Mots Ou La Sublimation Chez Georges Bataille* (Montréal: L'Harmattan, 1996), pp. 129–130 – Gauthier's italics.

to recoil from the notion of the void, preferring at all times some kind of signifying presence to fill the hollow form, with all the implications this has – from personal and sexual to existential.[54]

The choice of a glove may seem rather commonplace yet Breton is keen to highlight its specificity – a sky blue glove fitted to one particular woman's hand at one particular time. He is attracted to objects for their singularity rather than their value as mass-produced commodities (or, in the case of people, their mundane, conventional nature). This attitude will also determine to a large degree his relationship with others; and it is in this manner that he develops an attraction to Nadja.

Other portents appear in the novel which point to the fact that Breton is subconsciously seeking a woman who defies all standards of convention in her uniqueness. He attends a play by Joseph Babinski et Pierre Palau, entitled 'Les Détraquées' (in English, 'Headcases') the virtues of which for him are incomparable with any other theatrical work (despite its emphasis on the pathological). The theme of the play foreshadows his encounter with Nadja who in her own words is 'l'âme errante'[55] ['the errant soul'[56]]. From the time Breton worked as a medical orderly in World War I and bore witness to the mental disturbances of soldiers, he had become preoccupied with the aberrant and all of its mysterious attractions – a fact which also presages his attraction to the neurodivergence of Nadja.

At a later point in the novel a *trompe l'œil* painting (or *tableau changeant*) is shown to him: in a manner similar to anamorphosis, this painting reveals itself to Breton as both an angel and a vase, depending on the angle from which he views it. The significance of these two images as being created around a void is not lost upon us. Lacan describes both woman and vase as signifiers of *das Ding*, referring to the latter as 'le

54 See also *Recherches sur la Sexualité / Investigating Sex* in which Breton claims that the receipt of women's pants without any trace of their owner would be unbearable. – Breton, *Recherches sur la Sexualité*, p. 183; Breton, *Investigating Sex,* p. 146.

55 Breton, *Nadja* (Fr), p. 82.

56 My translation. Replaces Howard's translation of 'the soul in limbo' – Breton, *Nadja* (Eng), p. 71.

premier signifiant façonné des mains de l'homme [...]. C'est à partir de ce signifiant façonné qu'est le vase, que le vide et le plein entrent comme tels dans le monde'[57] ['the first of such signifiers fashioned by human hand [...]. It is on the basis of this fabricated signifier, this vase, that emptiness and fullness as such enter the world'[58]]. The image of the female angel again evokes the idea of the extolled woman created around an empty space, be it out of a need to fashion a myth in the face of existential desolation or on account of the hollowness of her sexual organs.

The illusion painting thus evokes the Lacanian anamorphosis of Breton's desire for Nadja. For a certain time, he exalts Nadja as an angel and invests in their relationship all the romantic love he can muster. Their kindred natures are expressed in a mutual interest in art, in the contemplation and appreciation of alternative mind states as well as a willingness to explore the psycho-geography of Paris. Breton even weeps at the prospect of never seeing Nadja again. Yet when considered in the light of the transient, the contingent and the unique – in brief, the components of creation *ex nihilo* and anamorphosis – an altogether different picture emerges.

The relationship with Nadja proves merely to be a short, poignant affair with a very unusual person, resulting from a highly arbitrary encounter. As with Lamba, the romantic interlude with Nadja represents another momentary coming into focus of desire. She is one signifying love object of many which Breton temporarily overvalues in order to overcome the emptiness of *das Ding*. Or as Walter Benjamin expresses it 'The Lady, in esoteric love, matters least. So too for Breton. He is closer

57 Lacan, *Séminaire* VII, p. 145 – Lacan then refers to the dual orientation which Heidegger attributes to it, namely that of receiving something from the heavens and (through its manufacture) raising up the materials of the earth. Such an image is, I think, a fitting metaphor for sublimation's function within Surrealism, which acquired the wisdom of lofty cultural elites though used it to try to improve the lot of the common (wo)man on earth. Moreover, the metaphor is almost certainly chosen by Lacan to better illustrate the nature of sublimation itself.

58 Lacan, *Seminar* VII, p. 120.

to the things that Nadja is close to than to her'[59]. The image of the angel thus invariably reverts to that of the emptiness of the vase. Lacan affirms that there is no limit to the number of persons or objects sought by the subject to fill the void which is integral to our psychical apparatus. Guided by the pleasure principle, the subject is led 'from signifier to signifier' even though, as Lacan has forewarned us, the object as such is lost and cannot be recovered.

It is, perhaps, for this reason that Breton frequently refers to the women he has known as a changing set of signifiers or 'substitutes' representing the feminine ideal. His concluding comments in *Nadja* makes this quite clear, for his rapturous adulation of the lover who supersedes Nadja (Suzanne Muzard) reads more like an address to the eternal feminine, of which no woman could in fact be considered to be the sole expression:

> tu t'es substituée aux formes qui m'étaient les plus familières, ainsi qu'à plusieurs figures de mon pressentiment.[60]
> [you have taken the place of the forms most familiar to me, as well as several figures of my foreboding.[61]]

and again:

> cette substitution de personnes s'arrête à toi, parce que rien ne t'est substituable[62]
> [this substitution of persons stops with you, because nothing can be substituted for you[63]]

Here Breton is addressing the woman of his affections with '*toi*'. For Lacan, 'toi', when employed as a pronoun of interpellation or devotion, reflects 'la tentation d'apprivoiser l'Autre, l'Autre préhistorique, l'Autre inoubliable qui risque tout d'un coup de nous surprendre et de

59 Benjamin, *Reflections*, p. 181 – for a feminist perspective of this quotation (and Breton's treatment of the female subject), the reader is referred to Natalya Lusty, *Surrealism, Feminism, Psychoanalysis* (Aldershot: Ashgate, 2007).

60 Breton, *Nadja* (Fr), p. 186.

61 Breton, *Nadja* (Eng), p. 157.

62 Breton, *Nadja* (Fr), pp. 186–187.

63 Breton, *Nadja* (Eng), p. 158.

nous précipiter du haut de son apparition'[64] ['the temptation to tame the Other, that prehistoric, that unforgettable Other, which suddenly threatens to surprise us and to cast us down from the height of its appearance'[65]]. Lacan warns, however, that in reality this 'toi' is merely 'de vaine incantation, de vaine liaison'[66] ['"you" of vain incantation and fruitless connection'[67]], taming nothing. It is, however, precisely this that Breton seeks to do to perpetuity – engage with the Other in a vain attempt to tame it. The vanity of so doing may even be apparent to Breton who acknowledges that this 'toi' has all the characteristics of a chimera, corresponding to an ideal of beauty.[68]

According to Lacan the individual is temporarily duped by his or her own psyche into believing that a particular object, person or circumstance can be relied upon to satisfy his or her needs in a stable and enduring manner whereas, in fact, it can never be retrieved under the same circumstances. So too Breton leans on the surety of relocating the love object according to his prior expectations and is inevitably disappointed:

> J'étais, dis-je, dans l'état d'un homme qui, croyant avoir tout fait pour conjurer le sort contraire à l'amour, devait se rendre à cette évidence que l'être qui lui avait été longtemps le plus nécessaire s'était retiré, que l'objet même qui, pour lui, avait été *la pierre angulaire du monde matériel* était perdu.[69]
>
> [I was, I tell you, in the position of a man who, believing that he had done everything to ward off a fate unfavourable to love, was forced to bow before the evidence that the being who, for a long time, he had needed most of all, had departed, that the very object which for him, had been *the bedrock of the physical world* was lost.[70]]

Here, in *Les Vases Communicants*, Breton relates how, following the break-up of his relationship with Suzanne Muzard, he enters a period of

64 Lacan, *Séminaire* VII, p. 69.
65 Lacan, *Seminar* VII, p. 56.
66 Lacan, *Séminaire* VII, p. 69.
67 Lacan, *Seminar* VII, p. 56.
68 Breton, *Nadja* (Fr), pp. 185–186; Breton, *Nadja* (Eng), p. 158.
69 Breton, *Vases Communicants*, pp. 82–83.
70 My translation. See also Breton, *Communicating Vessels*, p. 68.

melancholy and that in falling victim to the emptiness of *das Ding* he goes to great lengths to replace the lost love object by a number of provisional, makeshift signifiers:

> La tentation absurde mais immédiate, de substituer à l'objet extérieur manquant un objet extérieur qui comblât, dans une certaine mesure, le vide qu'avait laissé le premier, cette tentation se faisait place violemment à certaines heures.[71]
>
> [The absurd yet immediate temptation to substitute the missing external object with another external object which would in some measure fill the void left by the former, this temptation would at times take possession of me with extreme ferocity.[72]]

He then relates how he attempts in vain to replace the lost love object by arbitrarily soliciting women in the streets of Paris, presenting them unexpectedly with a rose or attempting to arrange a *rendez-vous* with them.[73] He also recounts how he gazes wishfully at a number of women on café terraces allowing himself to be mesmerised by their beauty and devising machinations to get to know them better.

In their treatment of the love object's elusiveness Breton's three works are comparable to Éluard's poetry, in which the latter similarly presents derivations of the mysterious archetype of womanhood, each of which is easily substitutable for another:

> Tant de poèmes d'amour sans objet réuniront des amants. D'autres destineront la femme du poète à un autre homme. En tirer une certaine satisfaction, l'objet s'amplifiant. Pour son amant, la femme aimée se substitue à toutes les femmes désirées, elle peut par conséquent être aimée de tous.[74]
>
> [So many love poems without an object will bring lovers together. Other poems will make the poet's wife somebody else's. Gaining a certain satisfaction from this, the object grows in amplitude. For her lover, the beloved woman becomes substituted with all desired women, she can therefore be loved by everyone.]

71 Breton, *Vases Communicants*, p. 85.

72 My translation. See also Breton, *Communicating Vessels*, p. 70.

73 Breton, *Vases Communicants*, pp. 89–90; Breton, *Communicating Vessels*, pp. 74–75.

74 Paul Éluard, 'Physique de la Poésie II' in *Physique de la Poésie* (Paris: Gallimard, 1939), p. 70.

This example seems particularly significant as the object being amplified ('l'objet s'amplifiant') in the mind of the poet seems to express the overvaluation of the love object posited by Lacanian sublimation. Furthermore, the example points to the complicity of writing poetry and loving, as though the existence of an anonymous love object were propped up by the very fact of writing. This idea is even hinted at in Lacan's writings in which he cites one of Éluard's poems as an exemplification of the emptiness of *das Ding*:

> Sur ce ciel délabré, sur ces vitres d'eau douce,
> Quel visage viendra, coquillage sonore,
> Annoncer que la nuit d'amour touche au jour,
> Bouche ouverte liée à la bouche fermée.[75]
>
> [Against this dilapidated sky, these panes of fresh water,
> Which face will appear and, like a sonorous shell,
> Announce that the night of love has turned into day,
> Open mouth joined to a mouth that is closed?[76]]

In this verse, the lover's open mouth and resemblance to a hollow shell accentuate her fundamental emptiness as well as the signifying structures which occur around her vacant centre. Even so, the moment captured seems highly meaningful; the night of love achieves heightened poignancy on account of its immanent end (as further reflected in the anti-sexual image of the closed mouth) and the bleak, chaotic and empty sky, which in Lacanian terms affords an appropriate backdrop for the anamorphosis of desire to occur.

Like Breton then, Éluard writes in a manner which suggests that his lovers are substitutes for the prehistoric Other, representations of *das Ding*. For this reason, the defining features of his love interests do not appear to vary much between one woman and the next:

75 Lacan (quoting Éluard's *Capitale de la Douleur*), *Séminaire* VII, p. 184. Original quotation taken from Paul Éluard, 'Les Petits Justes IX' in *Capitale de la Douleur* (Paris: Gallimard, 1926), p. 81.

76 Lacan (quoting Éluard's *Capital of Pain*), *Seminar* VII, p. 154.

C'est toujours la même jeunesse, les mêmes yeux purs, le même geste ingénu de ses bras autour de mon cou, la même caresse, la même révélation. Mais ce n'est jamais la même femme.[77]

[It's always the same youthfulness, the same pure eyes, the same ingenious gesture of her arms around my neck, the same caress, the same revelation. But it's never the same woman.]

His words 'ce n'est jamais la même femme' ['it's never the same woman'] are of particular significance, for his love of arbitrary encounters was more accentuated than Breton's. As one of Breton's closest allies (in the twenties and thirties), Éluard problematised what it meant to be a 'Bretonian Surrealist' for he did not allow moral scruples to attenuate his appetite for elective love or libertinism (Breton shied away from the latter[78]). In *Recherches sur la Sexualité* he was the sole speaker to advocate the idea of a systemised libertinism for women using the polyandry of Tibet as his example.[79] He argued that 'La sensualité est une chose pure dans laquelle les êtres ne doivent pas être considérés'[80] ['sensuality is something pure in which particular human beings cannot be taken into account'[81]]. This valuation of sexual love for its own sake spawned an eagerness for encounters which could never be exhausted. Indeed, Éluard, like Bataille, frequented the many bordellos of Paris, admitting that:

77 Paul Éluard, 'Les Dessous d'une Vie – La Dame de Carreau' (1926) in *Donner à Voir* (Paris: Gallimard, 1939), p. 12.

78 This view only becomes apparent from a remark he makes which is crossed out in the minutes of the discussion which are taken – 'Je réprouve formellement [le libertinage]' and then crossed out 'sauf au cas où il est mis au service d'une idée très haute de l' amour' – Breton, *Recherches sur la Sexualité*, p. 75 ['I categorically disapprove [of libertinism]' and then crossed out 'except where it serves a very elevated notion of love', Breton, *Investigating Sex*, p. 32].

79 Éluard, *Recherches sur la Sexualité*, p. 159; Éluard, *Investigating Sex*, p. 116. Practising what he preached, he allowed his first wife, Gala, the liberties he accorded himself and famously accepted a *ménage à trois* with her and Max Ernst.

80 Éluard, *Recherches sur la Sexualité*, p. 153.

81 Éluard, *Investigating Sex*, p. 112.

> La vie n'est monotone que si l'on aime pas et les variations du désir et de la satisfaction de ce désir concernant l'amour. On ne peut pas aimer si le désir est toujours semblable.[82]
>
> [Life is only monotonous if one does not love both the variations of desire and the satisfaction of this desire in respect of love. You cannot love if the desire is always the same.[83]]

Here again we are reminded of Lacan's assertion that an ever changing set of signifiers is needed to keep alive the sensation of a desire fulfilled. Éluard's admission that the emptiness of a 'monotonous' life is avoided only then when one varies the object of desire seems confirmed in Lacan's declaration that we can only avoid the emptiness of *das Ding* by a series of detours leading us from one love object to the next.

While Éluard assumed a rather more open stance toward sexual mores than Breton, it did not appear to become a bone of contention between the two of them. They remained united on the essential belief that personal relationships should be pursued in flagrant defiance of the prevailing Christian mores in society. Such a deeply held belief ultimately gave rise to a form of transgression which again highlighted a commonality of outlook between the Surrealists and Bataille, who was similarly cajoled into endless encounters on the basis of an existential 'lack' (or as he referred to it 'le néant'[84] / 'nothingness'). In *L'Anus Solaire*, he stated that 'le mouvement est la figure de l'amour incapable de s'arrêter sur un être en particulier et passant rapidement de l'un à l'autre'[85] ['movement is a figure of love, incapable of stopping at a particular being, and rapidly passing from one to another'[86]] as if to capture what had epitomised the attitudes of avant-gardistes of French society towards desire.

82 Éluard, *Recherches sur la Sexualité*, p. 179.

83 My translation. Takes account of mistranslation in *Investigating Sex*, p. 140.

84 Georges Bataille, 'Annexe 5 – Discussion sur le péché' (1944) in *Œuvres Complètes – La Somme Athéologique II* (Paris: Gallimard, 1973), vol. VI, p. 340.

85 Bataille, *Œuvres Complètes* I, p. 83.

86 Bataille, *Visions of Excess*, p. 7.

Earthly Love and Transgression

In the introduction, I showed how Breton had conceived of Surrealism as a movement whose orientation toward the future and maxim of continual revolt sought to prevent it from becoming inert and ineffectual within the world. It was a movement defined by its refusal to arrive and take its place in society, its members ever engaged in a quest for the next new love object, new challenge, new revolutionary cause. I believe that some of Breton's key notions – *hasard objectif* (objective chance), the quest for the *trouvaille* (found object), elective love and the sublime point, the notion of social revolution as allied to personal transformation – all contributed to the dynamism of the movement, as well as moulding its stance on human relationships. The Surrealists' focus on the ephemeral and the elective in relationships, as defined by the circular quest to recuperate the lost love object, challenged the Christian values of the eternal and the binding and, as such, can be interpreted in relation to the more transgressive aspects of Lacan's *das Ding* as well as Bataillean philosophy.

The question that emerges is how Lacan developed such a transgressive or refractory aspect to concepts such as *das Ding* and sublimation, concepts which we would expect to eschew precisely these qualities. This brings us to what is in essence a theory of transgression within the Lacanian œuvre. Having introduced the notion of the love object as signifier of *das Ding*, he then explains that this signifier is predicated upon interdiction, often being forbidden by law and therefore having a prohibitive or sinful quality about it. Citing those laws which form the very basis of the Judeo-Christian religion, the ten commandments, he enquires:

> Est-ce que la Loi est la Chose ? Que non pas. Toutefois je n'ai eu connaissance de la Chose que par la Loi. En effet, je n'aurais pas eu l'idée de la convoiter si la Loi n'avait dit – Tu ne la convoiteras pas.[87]

87 Lacan, *Séminaire* VII, p. 101.

> [Is the Law the Thing? Certainly not. Yet I can only know of the Thing by means of the Law. In effect, I would not have had the idea to covet it if the Law hadn't said: "Thou shalt not covet it."[88]]

This statement effectively confirms the proverbial tenet that the prohibition of an act makes often it more seductive. Furthermore, Lacan affirms that such laws underpin communication between human beings, regulating and offsetting desire in such a way as to increase man's sense of temptation. With increased temptation comes the potential for increased pleasure or *jouissance* which, in the seventh seminar, he characterises as the excessive excitation that results from a forbidden desire.[89]

Lacan explains that the desire for *jouissance* is not merely premised upon interdiction but upon a concrete punishment, which could even be death. Since the realisation and pursuit of *jouissance* have (at least in the history of Christian society) been considered as evil, he also insists that the terms 'das Ding' and 'sin' might be considered to be kindred notions.[90] To illustrate the point further, he adduces Kant's categorical imperative and his discussion of the man who must decide between the renunciation of a highly pleasurable yet illicit relationship, on the one hand, and, the penalty of death for pursuing the relationship, on the other. Kant surmised that, were the man to act in accordance with the categorical imperative, he would choose to renounce the relationship

88 Lacan, *Seminar* VII, p. 83.

89 In his later work he will bring *jouissance* into even closer proximity to sublimation, advancing the formula 'La Sublimation pour atteindre la jouissance' ['Sublimation for the attainment of pleasure'] – *Le Séminaire de Jacques Lacan – D'un AUTRE à l'autre* (Paris: Seuil, 1968–1969), vol. XVI, pp. 225–226 [English title: 'From one OTHER to the Other', though unpublished in English].

90 'certains d'entre vous au moins se doutent que ce n'est plus moi qui parle. En effet, à une toute petite modification près – *Chose* à la place de *péché* – ceci est le discours de saint Paul concernant les rapports de la loi et du péché, Épitre aux Romains, chapitre 7, paragraphe 7' – Lacan, *Séminaire VII*, 101 ['some of you at least have begun to suspect that it is no longer I who have been speaking. In fact, with one small change, namely "Thing" for "sin" this is the speech of Saint Paul on the subject of the relations between the law and sin in the Epistle to the Romans, Chapter 7, paragraph 7' – Lacan, *Seminar* VII, p. 83].

(the implication being that the alternative would, if applied on a mass scale, terminate the life of all those harbouring illicit desires and annul the rule of law). For Lacan, however, Kant is missing the point – the very reason for the illicit relationship is the stimulus of fear of chastisement and death.

Compare Lacan's theory of desire being predicated upon interdiction with Breton's opinions about transgression and we find a surprising degree of convergence. Firstly, we recall Breton's words about Bataillean transgression as quoted in Chapter 2, where he not only recognised 'le besoin fondamental de transgression [de l'érotisme]'[91] ['eroticism's fundamental need for *transgression*'[92]] but the prohibitions which surrounded illicit desire and eroticism: 'Cet interdit, de caractère immémorial et qui continue à s'imposer, sous toutes les latitudes, des prétendus "sauvages" aux prétendus "civilisés", est, en effet, le véritable point de mire de l'érotisme.'[93] ['This interdiction, which has existed since time immemorial and continues to hold sway in every latitude over so-called "savage" and so-called "civilised" races alike, is the true target at which eroticism aims its arrow'[94]]. One can see that Breton's views on the matter had reached maturation here for in his earlier work of *L'Amour Fou* he had specifically rejected the sinfulness of the forbidden fruit (here a metaphor for carnal knowledge) considering there only to be divine temptation:

> La tentation seule est divine. Éprouver le besoin de varier l'objet de cette tentation, de le remplacer par d'autres, c'est témoigner qu'on est prêt à démériter, qu'on a sans doute déjà démérité de l'innocence.[95]
>
> [Temptation alone is divine. To experience the need to vary the object of this temptation, and to replace it with others, is to attest that one is ready to fall, nay that one has undoubtedly already fallen from grace.[96]]

91 Breton, *Recherches sur la Sexualité*, pp. 208–209.
92 Breton, *Surrealism and Painting*, pp. 378–389.
93 Breton, *Recherches sur la Sexualité*, pp. 208–209.
94 Breton, *Surrealism and Painting*, pp. 378–389.
95 Breton, *L'Amour Fou*, p. 136.
96 My translation. See also Breton, *Mad Love*, p. 93.

Breton at this stage seems not to recognise the immediate interdependency of prohibition and desire, but his statement does point to a number of commonalities with Lacanian thinking. He states for example that temptation depends on a variation of the love object; only in this way can desire be sustained and renewed. The state of grace, as Breton conceives it, is the consumption of the subject through the passion of love, without which he strives to 'retrouver la grâce perdu du premier moment où l'on aime'[97] ['find once more the lost grace of the first moment when one is in love'[98]]. Whenever a state of grace is lost, there emerges a corresponding need to recuperate it, implying in Breton's case the kind of libidinal circularity which in Lacanian theory is so characteristic of human relationships.

Breton's understanding of grace is evidently inscribed within human experience, within the vicissitudes of terrestrial life. God's favour is supplanted by the favour of the desirable Other. In reclaiming the rights of the fallen man – and particularly in his defence of earthly desire and the worth of temptation – we detect more than a trace of his interest in Luciferianism. In *L'Arcane 17*, Breton pays tribute to Lucifer as light-bearer and one who is favoured by love: 'Lucifer, l'intelligence proscrite, enfante deux sœurs, Poésie et Liberté et "l'esprit d'amour empruntera leurs traits pour soumettre et sauver l'ange rebelle"'[99] ['Lucifer, the outlaw intellect, begets two sisters, Poetry and Liberty and "the spirit of love will borrow their features to subdue and save the rebel angel"'[100]]. Not unlike Lucifer, his intention is to usurp the cult of organised religion and replace it with the cult of (free) love. At times we witness his attempts at this through the use of considerable profanity: he proclaims rather provocatively that it is an enduring fantasy of his to make love with a nun in the deepest recesses of the church[101] and appeals to Surrealists to 'vomir leur dégoût à la face de

97 Breton, *L'Amour Fou*, p. 67.

98 Breton, *Mad Love*, p. 44.

99 Breton quoting Auguste Viatte, *Arcane 17*, p. 173 – Viatte's work *Victor Hugo et les Illuminés de son temps* is cited by Breton as an affirmative exposition of the figure of Lucifer within French literature.

100 Breton, *Arcanum 17*, p. 131.

101 Breton, *Recherches sur la Sexualité*, pp. 51–52; Breton, *Investigating* Sex, p. 14.

chaque prêtre'[102] ['to vomit their disgust in the case of *every* priest'[103]]. In these statements he reveals an identification not with the high but with the low – a domain which has so frequently been considered to be the sole province of Bataillean philosophy.

In fact, it is clear from Bataille's writings that his view of the interrelationship of desire, transgression and religious law at times converges with that of Breton and Lacan. He similarly situates erotic transgression in opposition to Christian morality, equating 'the forbidden' with sin and sensuality:[104] 'L'interdit est là pour être violé'[105] ['the taboo [/'the forbidden'] is there in order to be violated'[106]] he affirms in the text 'La Transgression'. His theoretical framework includes a notion similar to *das Ding* as the site of sinfulness and he affirms that: 'le fait de rechercher son néant au-delà de soi-même est déjà un péché'[107] ['the fact of searching for one's empty void outside of oneself is already a sin']. It is worth stating that although Bataille's conceptualisation of *le néant* is more commonly associated with his metaphysics, as a term which denotes an existential laceration that defines yet challenges human life, in the 'Discussion sur le péché' he presents the concept in psychological terms, as an internalised nothingness which impels the subject into the outside world in search of a desirable Other and sinful pleasure: 'En même temps qu'un plein dans l'être, il y a aussi le sentiment d'un vide, puisque c'est ce sentiment du vide

102 Breton, *Manifestes de Surréalisme*, p. 78.

103 Breton, *Manifestoes of Surrealism*, p. 129.

104 Bataille, *Œuvres Complètes* VI, p. 341.

105 Georges Bataille, 'Chapitre V – La Transgression' in *Œuvres Complètes* X, 67 – expressed elsewhere in the chapter as 'La transgression n'est pas la négation de l'interdit, mais elle le dépasse et le complète' (p. 66) ['The transgression does not deny the taboo [the forbidden] but transcends it and complements it' – Bataille, *Erotism*, p. 63] and 'la religion commande essentiellement la transgression des interdits' (p. 72) ['religion is the moving force behind the breaking of taboos [transgression of what is forbidden]' – Bataille, *Erotism*, p. 69].

106 Bataille, *Erotism*, p. 64 – The original does not make reference to taboo, but to 'l'interdit', which means literally 'the forbidden' – hence its enclosure in square brackets.

107 *Ibid.*, p. 340.

qui le rejette vers le dehors'[108] ['As well as a feeling of wholeness within the self, there is also a feeling of emptiness, since it is this feeling of emptiness which sends one back into the world outside']. The ideas presented in this discussion come strikingly close to those of Lacan.

According to Bataille, what is perceived as sin ought not, however, to be considered as distinct from what is sacred (for there was originally no distinction between the two). For him, the Christian teaching of Lucifer's banishment from heaven represents an impoverishment of the divine rather than a necessary segregation. Any modern re-interpretation of the sacred should therefore seek to reunite the qualities of the divine and the diabolical.[109] The thematics of his literary works, such as *Histoire de l'Œil*, make many allusions to acts which are of a blasphemous or diabolical nature including scatology, sexual humiliation, rape, torture, and necrophilia – and it is clear that he is able to appreciate the sacred in a number of these acts. Like Breton, for example, he valorises sexual acts which are performed in churches, albeit those of a more extreme nature (in *Histoire de l'Œil* these focus on the sexual assault and asphyxiation of a priest).

In opposition to religious law, Breton similarly posits the perverse, expressing a preference for 'tout ce qui dans l'amour physique est du ressort de la perversité'[110] ['everything in physical love which pertains to perversity'[111]]. In *Recherches sur la Sexualité*, he approves the practices of free love, sodomy, onanism, semi-exhibitionism, sadism and lesbianism, most of which were considered morally deviant at the time of the *Recherches* (and thus subjected to much greater moral censure). Of all these practices he favours sodomy the most for its moral nonconformity[112] – in other words because of the deviation it represents from sexual protocol in a Christian marriage. Here once again a hidden affinity emerges with Bataille as he too is opposed to Christian marriage

108 Georges Bataille, 'Annexe 5 – Discussion sur le péché' (1944) in *Œuvres Complètes – La Somme Athéologique II* (Paris: Gallimard, 1973), vol. VI, p. 340.

109 Georges Bataille, 'Le Sacré au XXe siècle' (1951) in *Œuvres Complètes* VIII, p. 188.

110 Breton, *Recherches sur la Sexualité*, p. 70.

111 Breton, *Investigating Sex*, p. 29.

112 Breton, *Recherches sur la Sexualité*, p. 186; Breton, *Investigating Sex*, p. 151.

and its requirement that coital sex serve only the propagation of the human species. As Geoffrey Roche explains:

> for Bataille it is the very sinfulness of sexual activity that makes it significant. Without the sin of breaking taboos, according to Bataille, sex is not 'erotic'. Therefore, sex within marriage, where there are no traditional taboos against sex, is not erotic; marriage itself providing only a 'narrow outlet for pent-up violence'[113]

Bataille viewed marriage as the very negation of the erotic, being merely a repository for frustrated or unsublimated aggression. Both Bataille and Breton show how the desire to represent and possess *das Ding* is exacerbated in face of Christian moral imperatives, which threaten to repress rather than liberate the human subject. Lacan's theory of *das Ding* being regulated by the law (specifically moral law) seems therefore confirmed by both men.

Their resistance to moral conformity is also demonstrated in their conceptualisations of women. For Breton, this is reflected by his rejection of sexual propriety or modesty in women ('pudeur') on account of its associations with Christianity. His view of the woman is at least based as much on *la femme-sorcière* ('the woman-sorceress') as *la femme-enfant* ('the woman-child'), his ideal of womanhood, therefore, derived not from the Virgin Mary but from the ghostly vampire women (or succubae) of his dreams[114] and the paintings of Gustave Moreau.[115] Similarly, Bataille's depictions of women are frequently centred around their sinful aspect, claiming prostitutes to be 'fallen creatures' who 'se vautrer comme les porcs'[116] ['wallow like pigs in their own degradation'[117]] and the sight of a woman's

113 Geoffrey Roche, 'Black Sun: Bataille on Sade' in *Janus Head* (Amherst, NY: Trivium Publications, 2006), 9(1), p. 167.

114 Breton, *Recherches sur la Sexualité*, p. 102; Breton, *Investigating Sex*, pp. 59–60.

115 André Breton, 'Gustave Moreau' (1961) in *Œuvres Complètes* IV, p. 787; André Breton, 'Gustave Moreau' (1961) in *Surrealism and Painting*, p. 363 – One of Moreau's most famous paintings which provided literary inspiration for Breton as well as Moreau's contemporaries, such as Huysmans and Wilde, was *Salomé,* who, despite her captivating beauty, infamously had John the Baptist's head served on a plate.

116 Bataille, *Œuvres Complètes* X, p. 136.

117 Bataille, *Erotism*, p. 137.

breasts 'pure incarnation du péché'[118] ['the pure incarnation of sin'[119]]. While clichéd and caricatured, the conceptions of women advanced by both Breton and Bataille are spectral and sinful in nature, being oneiric, mythological, artistic or literary but seldom based entirely within reality.

Lacan comments that such depersonalising characterisations of the female love object are a frequent attribute of (courtly) love poetry, the woman being 'emptied of all real substance' as she is elevated, then becoming 'affolant, un partenaire inhumain'[120] ['terrifying – an inhuman partner'[121]]. Poets who can be aligned with this tradition, including the Surrealists, are (as previously suggested) merely addressing the same lady who is never characterised for any of her real, concrete virtues.[122] For Lacan, this form of depersonalisation is, moreover, one of the defining features of artistic and literary sublimation, though paradoxically such sublimation also has the capacity to debase: 'On ne parle jamais tant en termes d'amour les plus crus que quand la personne est transformée en une fonction symbolique'[123] ['It is only when the person involved is transformed into a symbolic function that one is able to speak of her in the crudest terms'[124]].

Breton's rejection of *pudeur* (decency, modesty, particularly in sexual matters) forms part of his campaign against Christian conditioning more generally. It is *pudeur* which makes him momentarily question the effects of Freudian sublimation, in particular when these are associated with feelings of shame:

> La pudeur est un sentiment à la hauteur duquel il s'agit de ne pas être. C'est un sentiment de gêne absurde à l'égard de toute chose, qui est capable comme on le sait de sublimation, *mais que cela n'excuse guère*. Il n'est jamais inconnaissable et peut toujours se ramener à un schéma élémentaire d'ordre sexuel outre lequel on peut

118 Georges Bataille, *L'Expérience Intérieure* (Paris: Gallimard, 1986), p. 147.
119 Georges Bataille, *Inner Experience*, trans. by Leslie Anne Bolt (New York: Suny Press, 1988), p. 127.
120 Lacan, *Séminaire* VII, p. 180.
121 Lacan, *Seminar* VII, p. 150.
122 Lacan, *Séminaire* VII, p. 180; Lacan, *Seminar* VII, p. 150.
123 Lacan, *Séminaire* VII, p. 179.
124 Lacan, *Seminar* VII, p. 149.

> passer. Ce sentiment n'a pour lui qu'une excuse : il s'inspire de la tristesse qu'un homme peut avoir à considérer la prétendue existence de son corps, je veux dire qu'il est d'ordre chrétien.[125]
>
> [The feeling of modesty in sexual matters is not one which should be aspired to. It is an absurd feeling of awkwardness about all things, which, as we know, may result in sublimation, *but can hardly be excused on this basis*. It never defies explanation and can always be traced back to a basic schema of a sexual nature which can be overcome. It can only be excused as follows: it is inspired by the sadness which a man may feel in considering the apparent existence of his body, in other words, it is a feeling of Christian origin.[126]]

Bataille similarly paints a picture of the subject who blushes awkwardly at the very contemplation of his or her sexuality and whose sheer embarrassment, horror and torment at his or her erotic nature is inescapable: 'A cette horreur, nous ne pouvons nous dérober au point de n'avoir plus à rougir, nous n'en pouvons jouir qu'à la condition d'en rougir encore'[127] ['Such is the horror that we cannot escape our feelings of shame, indeed, we can only extract its pleasures so long as we continue to feel ashamed']. He underlines the universality of this complex, which makes human eroticism a shameful taboo.[128] His association of chastity with horror reads as a diagnosis of the human condition, and like Breton, intimates an underlying resistance to accepting such an unhappy reality.

Although Breton is willing to entertain that (in all matters other than the question of *pudeur*) he is being guided by a higher notion of love, Bataille finds any such suggestion risible. Ironically though, it is at the very site of Breton's sublimated love that he always finds what binds him to Bataille – the inexorable pull of physical desire – which for him is the necessary complement of romantic love. We may recall his homage to carnal

125 Breton, *Recherches sur la Sexualité*, p. 82 – my italics.

126 I have provided my own translation here in an attempt to convey the essence of the French word 'pudeur' in English. Official English-language translation in Breton, *Investigating Sex*, p. 41.

127 Georges Bataille, 'L'Érotisme, Soutien de la Morale' (1957) in *Œuvres Complètes* (Paris: Gallimard, 1988), vol. XII, p. 467.

128 Bataille, *Œuvres Complètes* X, p. 53.

love in *L'Amour Fou* (quoted in the previous section) which coincided with the attainment of the sublime point (the supreme elation of love in the presence of the Other). Ever since the *Manifestes* he had believed that carnal love was not to be distinguished from emotional or spiritual love: 'Il est parfaitement certain que l'amour charnel ne fait qu'un avec l'amour spirituel'[129] ['It is absolutely true that carnal love is at one with spiritual love'[130]].

In highlighting the physical dimension of emotional love, Breton's outlook was similar to that of Benjamin Péret's, a kindred spirit within the movement who, broadly speaking, held many of the same values and beliefs as Breton concerning desire, relationships and religion. Significantly, and as we shall now see, Péret also practised blasphemy and exalted the physical and base components of love as a Bretonian Surrealist, yet to a much greater degree than Breton himself.

Benjamin Péret, Sublime Love and Blasphemy

Péret's role within Surrealism has been defined in terms of supplementing that of Breton's in bringing to the movement a certain combativeness and purposefulness with respect to the outside world.[131] He was a poet

129 Breton, *Manifestes du Surréalisme*, p. 169 – Breton was undoubtedly influenced by Charles Fourier on this point who, like Sade, was extolled for promoting the cult of love and whose utopian view of the world also envisaged the free pursuit of romantic and sexual relationships: 'La nature voulant l'équilibre des deux éléments d'amour, du plaisir sensuel et sentimental' – Charles Fourier 'Le Nouveau Monde Amoureux', in *Œuvres Complètes*, ed. by Simone Debout-Oleszkiewicz (Paris: Anthropos, 1967), vol. VII, p. 34 ['Nature's way is balancing the two components of love, sensual and emotional pleasure'].

130 My translation. Cf. Breton, *Investigating Sex*, p. 41.

131 See Jehan Mayoux, 'Benjamin Péret la fourchette coupante' ['Benjamin Péret the sharp blade'] in *La liberté une et divisible, Œuvres Complètes*, vol. V (Ussel: Éditions Peralta, 1979), p. 103 (pp. 99–128) – 'au sein d'une collectivité qui passe à bon droit

and Surrealist theoretician whose works are little known in the English-speaking world; yet as an exponent of Surrealism's foremost concerns, and a somewhat divisive one at that, his essays provide us with an invaluable insight into the guts of the Bretonian wing of the movement, and the theoretical positionings which came to be elaborated therein. His treatise on love, *Anthologie de l'Amour Sublime* (1956), to which we now turn our attention, reads in parts like a micro-history of love's repression through Christianity as well as charting the campaigns of significant social, literary and religious movements which came to love's defence before Surrealism's time.

Péret's doctrine of sublime love abetted Breton in his attempt to supplant organised religion with the cult of love. Mary Ann Caws remarked that 'in its effort to "*diviniser l' homme*" sublime love must assume the language and the functions of that which it *exactly* replaces'.[132] This statement was certainly true of Péret's anthology in which love is regarded both as 'communion'[133] and 'a state of grace',[134] consisting of 'temptations'[135] as well as 'sacrifices'.[136] The beloved Other appears to the seeker of love as 'a sudden revelation'[137] and his/her seduction consists of 'erotic rituals' and 'ceremonies'.[138] Love itself is 'the source of the spirit',[139] evoking 'sacred

pour combative (le surréalisme), Benjamin Péret assume plus spécialement – mais non exclusivement – les fonctions d'agressivité et de discrimination. [...] on peut dire que Breton a construit le surréalisme de l'intérieur, alors que Péret le définit et le fait connaître en l'opposant à ce qui est autre' ['at the centre of a collective which was legitimately considered to be combative (Surrealism), Benjamin Péret's role was one of exercising especially (though not exclusively) bellicosity and discrimination. [...] one can say that Breton constructed Surrealism from the inside, whereas Péret defined it and disseminated it in opposition to what was other.']

132 Caws, *French Review*, 2 (40), p. 209.

133 Péret, *Amour Sublime*, pp. 31–32 – For the sake of clarity and fluency, only the English will be given for the following quotations.

134 *Ibid.*, p. 67; p. 69.

135 *Ibid.*, p. 69.

136 *Ibid.*, p. 74.

137 *Ibid.*, p. 73.

138 *Ibid.*, p. 42.

139 *Ibid.*, p. 58.

fervour' and 'transfiguring'[140] (though still acknowledging) erotic desire through sublimation.

Péret's strategy reinforces that of Breton's in *L'Amour Fou*, where, as we may recall, he also characterised love as a state of grace and emphasised the centrality of temptation within the experience of desire. Breton had specifically defended the appropriation of religious terminology to describe love *contra* Engels, who had feared it would keep the language of idealism alive.[141] The fact that Breton had challenged such a position in *Surréalisme au Service de la Révolution* (a pro-Marxist journal), while Surrealism was still seeking a *rapprochement* with the PCF, underlines the cult-like status which love had for the Surrealists. Péret, who mirrored Breton's stance, affirmed 'De tous les sentiments, je ne vois de pleinement sacré que l'amour. Si l'amour humain est sacré, c'est qu'en réalité la notion même de sacré découle si directement de l'amour que, sans lui, aucun sacré n'est concevable'[142] ['Of all feelings, I only see love as being fully sacred. If human love is sacred, it's because in reality the very notion of the sacred follows on so directly from love that, without it, the sacred would be unimaginable'].

The recognition of terrestrial love as sacred was of necessity accompanied by a complete repudiation of religious faith and God. For Péret this expressed itself in blasphemous thoughts and behaviours and the violation of religious rites. Like Breton, he admitted to being preoccupied by the notion of making love to a nun, dreamt of 'profaning hosts' and 'depositing excrement in a chalice'[143] and declared in the *Dictionnaire des Contemporains*

140 *Ibid.*, p. 21.

141 'C'est ainsi que l'amour et les rapports sexuels sont élevés à la hauteur d'une "religion" afin que le mot "religion," cher aux idéalistes, ne disparaisse pas du vocabulaire' ['in this way love and sexual relationships are raised to the height of a "religion" so that the word "religion" so dear to idealists, doesn't disappear from their vernacular'] – André Breton quoting Engels, 'La barque de l'amour s'est brisée contre la vie courante' ['The small love boat has been shattered by everyday life'] (1930) in *Œuvres Complètes* II, p. 315.

142 Péret, *Amour Sublime*, p. 72.

143 Benjamin Péret, *Recherches sur la Sexualité*, p. 52; Benjamin Péret, *Investigating Sex*, p. 14.

that his preferred past-time was 'insulter des curés'[144] ['insulting clergymen'] (reputedly he spat at them in the street).

Lacan himself drew on Péret's writings to support his theories and for this reason, the anthology's introduction, 'La Noyau de la Comète' ('The Comet's Nucleus', hitherto untranslated into English), lends itself to further analysis since it is here where all of Péret's ideas about love are contained, as well as the reasons as to why this work may have been of interest to Lacan. Péret's thought begins to intersect with Lacan's when he makes the assertion that sublimation is not just endogenous (libido-based, stemming from within) but exogenous (consisting in a sublimation of the love object external to the self): 'la reconnaissance de l'universalité du désir, de sa signification cosmique et de ses manifestations chez l'homme réclame à la fois sa sublimation et celle de l'*objet de ce désir*'[145] ['the recognition of the universality of desire, of its cosmic significance and its manifestation in man call for its sublimation as well as the sublimation of the *object of this desire*']. As part of a broader discussion on Platonic love, he refers to Freud's distinction in 'Three Essays on Sexuality' between eroticism as a feature of instinct (and hence the inner life) in classical antiquity – and its perception as an external object in modernity.[146] In Péret's view, this modern refocussing of desire upon the object is entirely positive, for he maintains that the 'instinct', when regarded in isolation, becomes moribund and stagnant, compromising the chances of (wo)man for self-realisation. In the case of Platonic love, this too (in his view) results in the neutered expression of instinct through homosocial relations and thereby devalues sexual and romantic relationships between men and women. Whilst this view unnecessarily devalues same-sex relationships, which are as much centred on the external object (or the 'other') as their heterosexual counterparts, Péret's doctrine of sublime love rejects any form of sublimation rooted in Platonic homosexuality on account of being too spiritual or as he puts it 'disembodied'.

144 Quoted in Caws, *The French Review*, 2 (40), p. 205.

145 Péret, *Amour Sublime*, p. 21 – my italics.

146 *Ibid.*, p. 32.

The poet refers with great frequency to the absence of love as 'le vide' (the void) which, like *das Ding*, characterises the human condition and induces humans to search for their complementary Other: 'le désir se propose de combler le vide, inhérent à la condition humaine, par l'être qui lui permettra de former un tout harmonieux'[147] ['the desire presents itself to fill the void, inherent in the human condition, with a being who will permit him/her to form a harmonious totality'] and again '[l'homme] a le sentiment inné de son insuffisance individuelle dérivée de la condition humaine proprement dite [...]. Il est ainsi porté, dès l'origine, à chercher hors de lui ce qui lui fait défaut'[148] ['[man] has the innate feeling of his own inadequacy derived from the human condition itself [...]. He is thus induced, from the very beginning, to search for what he lacks outside of himself']. In outlining the history of love within Western culture, he describes how religious faith has in vain attempted to overcome this innate sense of emptiness, remaining a poor substitute for the experience of sublime love as experienced between a man and a woman.[149] Here again, Péret recalls Lacan who affirms that 'la religion consiste dans tous les modes d'éviter ce vide'[150] ['religion in all its forms consists of avoiding this emptiness'[151]].

Throughout the *Anthologie*, Péret qualifies the sublimation of the love object as 'exaltation', recalling Lacan's formula of the *raising* of the object to the dignity of *das Ding*. Péret's notion of exaltation naturally brings with it 'emotional investment' or 'valuation', in other words, the concepts which Lacan associates with sublimation. Such investment Péret sees as integrating both emotional *and* erotic aspects with sublime love being qualified as 'le lieu géométrique où viennent se fondre en un diamant inaltérable, l'esprit, la chair et le cœur' ['the locus at which the spirit, the flesh and the heart come to be merged in an unspoilable diamond'[152]].

147 *Ibid.*, p. 60.
148 *Ibid.*, p. 22.
149 *Ibid.*, pp. 48–49; pp. 65–66.
150 Lacan, *Séminaire* VII, p. 155.
151 Lacan, *Seminar* VII, p. 130.
152 Péret, *Amour Sublime*, p. 9.

The commonalities which this statement has with Breton's view of love are evident. In celebrating and exalting the physical dimension of love, he similarly underscores his anti-religious stance, a stance which he understands as being central to the Surrealist campaign: 'la réhabilitation de la chair reconnue dans toute sa splendeur et sans laquelle la notion même de l'amour sublime s'évanouit, est justement une des grandes tâches que le surréalisme s'est assignée'[153] ['the rehabilitation of the flesh recognised in all its splendour and without which the very notion of sublime love fades away is precisely one of the big tasks that Surrealism has set for itself']. In its celebration of the flesh, Péret believes sublime love to afford a twofold reparation to the ailing social body, which for too long has been subjugated by the Christian church. This consisted of a reconciliation of man with woman (as well as with his own flesh), rather than a reconciliation of man with the divine. He maintains that Christianity's insistence on humankind establishing a relationship with the divine estranged it from the true source of happiness; and although various movements in history, such as the Cathars, the courtly love poets, the Port Royal school[154] and even the *Précieuses* negotiated a partial mitigation of this estrangement, their inability to effect absolute rupture with social and religious convention meant they were never able to campaign purely in love's name. Péret credits the Romantics and Saint-Simonists[155] as the two movements which first advocated sublime love and sought to overcome the antagonism between mind and body, with the Surrealists becoming their natural successors.

His treatise ends by inscribing Surrealism's campaign within an unhappy reality in which the young person, full of hope for the future, wants only his or her dreams of love to be realised, dreams which are thwarted by a society

153 *Ibid.*, p. 67.

154 A grouping of seventeenth-century Jansenist scholars based at Port-Royal-des-Champs Abbey (southwest of Paris) who rose to fame on account of their works on philosophy and logic.

155 A nineteenth-century philosophical grouping – inspired by the works of Claude Henri de Rouvroy, comte de Saint-Simon – which posited science and industry as the basis of an egalitarian and progressive society.

which transforms him/her into a 'singe dressé'[156] ['trained monkey']. Any endeavour to restore love is undermined and with age (s)he becomes cynical and loses faith in love's ability to bring fulfilment. In an oblique reference to Freud's analysis of repressive civilisation, Péret remarks that 'la civilisation porte la plus grande part dans cette démission'[157] ['civilisation has the largest stake in this resignation']. His view also seems at odds with Freud's assertions within *Civilisation and its Discontents* that the cohesive qualities of Eros, which help to build social bonds and communities, necessitate 'a restriction upon sexual life [which] is unavoidable'[158] and that 'love comes into opposition to the interests of civilisation [...] civilisation threatens love with substantial restrictions'.[159] This differing view of society emerges as Péret sets out Surrealism's role in defying the socialised (wo)man who is content to live by society's strictures and antagonistic to sublime love:[160]

> L'homme social s'oppose à l'être humain, à mesure que se développe la société qui engendre sans cesse de nouvelles contraintes. L'amour sublime doit donc livrer un combat tout à fait inégal à la société qui l'écrase. C'est pourquoi ses cris se confondent si souvent avec les gémissements du désespoir. L'amour sublime ne saurait, en effet, admettre la moindre restriction : tout ou rien ![161]
>
> [The social man becomes opposed to human nature as society develops in such a way as to continually generate new constraints. Sublime love therefore wages a battle which is hardly a match for the society which is crushing it. That is why its cries are so frequently confused with the groans of despair; for in actual fact, sublime love cannot endure the slightest restriction. This feeling is all or it is nothing!]

Péret cites Sade and Rousseau's noble savage as two figures whose scant regard for society is heroic in nature;[162] and throughout the treatise he will

156 *Ibid.*, p. 68.
157 *Ibid.*, p. 68.
158 Freud, *Complete Psychological Works* XXI, p. 109.
159 *Ibid.*, p. 103.
160 As Mary Ann Caws states, 'when Péret says that a human being is the direct opposite of the social man, he speaks for all Surrealist revolutionaries' – Caws, *The French Review*, 2 (40), p. 206.
161 Péret, *Amour Sublime*, pp. 26–27.
162 *Ibid.*, p. 56.

stress the antisocial nature of sublime love.[163] Moreover, such a defiance of social mores does, as the quotation above implies, open the door to transgression, especially when sublime love resists all limitations imposed upon it. I established above that Péret afforded a certain measure of vitriol and bellicosity to Surrealism's campaign. These were qualities which kindled the urge to transgression, a fact which is often reflected within his love poetry and other literary works. The encounter with the Other is, for example, often mediated via copious sexual symbols, highlighting both the desublimatory and sublimatory elements of Péret's sublime love.

'L'Auberge du cul volant' ('The tavern of the flying ass') (1922)' is an oneiric, erotic narrative of absurd proportions which depicts the protagonist's discovery of a vagina organ carved into a rock face. The organ produces a scale of shrill tones as each vagina is touched as well as a series of bizarre by-products, from human limbs to sulphur. A masturbating youth, who then figures in the dream, causes trees, animals and cliffs to reform themselves into a vagina upon ejaculation. In the poem 'Clin d'œil' (in English 'wink' or 'veiled reference') from Péret's collection of poems *Je sublime* (1936), the poet depicts his union with the impersonal Rosa, a mysterious female who recurs throughout the work. The union becomes so intimate that his sense perceptions are lived through her body, which in turn resembles the forces and structures of nature:

Rosa coiffée d'une tribu nègre étagée sur un escalier
où les seins aigus des femmes regardent par les yeux des hommes
Aujourd'hui je regarde par tes cheveux
Rosa d'opale du matin
et je m'éveille par tes yeux
Rosa d'armure
et je pense par tes seins d'explosion
Rosa d'étang verdi par les grenouilles
et je dors dans ton nombril de mer Caspienne
Rosa d'églantine pendant la grève générale
et je m'égare entre tes épaules de voie lactée fécondée par des comètes.[164]

163 For example, 'l'amour sublime reste asocial et parfois même antisocial', *Ibid.*, p. 23 ['sublime love remains socially maladjusted and sometimes even anti-social'].

164 Péret, *Œuvres Complètes* II, p. 125.

[Rosa's head-dress, a black tribe seated on a stairway
where the pointed breasts of women see through the eyes of men
Today I look through your hair
Rosa of morning opal
and through your eyes I am wonder-struck
Rosa of armour
and I think through your explosive breasts
Rosa of the lake coated with green frogs
and I sleep in your Caspian Sea navel
Rosa of sweetbrier during a general strike
and I lose myself between your Milky Way shoulders impregnated by comets.]

The multiple references to spheroid, circular or concave anatomical parts imbue the poem with a voluptuous sensuality and underline the fact that both the carnal and the spiritual are constituents of sublime love. Moreover, the poem evokes Breton's poem 'L'Union Libre' ['Free Union of Love'] (1931) in which he similarly metaphorises the female anatomy as a plethora of natural phenomena:

Ma femme aux seins de taupinière marine
Ma femme aux seins de creuset de rubis
[...]
Ma femme aux fesses de grès et d'amiante
Ma femme aux fesses de dos de cygne
[...]
Ma femme au sexe de placer et d'ornithorynque
Ma femme au sexe d'algue et de bonbons anciens[165]

[My wife with breasts of a marine molehill
My wife with breasts of the ruby's crucible
[...]
My wife with buttocks of sandstone and asbestos
My wife with buttocks of swans' backs
[...]
My wife with the sex of a mining-placer and of a platypus
My wife with a sex of seaweed and ancient sweetmeat][166]

165 André Breton, 'L'Union Libre' (1931) in *Œuvres Complètes* II, pp. 85–87.

166 Michel Ballabriga, *Sémiotique du surréalisme: André Breton ou la cohérence* (Toulouse: Presses universitaires du Mirail, 1995), pp. 153-154.

The two poems and the narrative above can also be related to Lacanian sublimation, in so far as they evoke a series of ring-like forms and empty spaces which are redolent of *das Ding* (vagina, navel, sea, Milky Way, mole-hill, crucible, mining-placer); and by extension, the process of creation *ex nihilo*. Indeed, the creative import of the poems seems to arise from the interplay of hollow absence and signifying presence.

In both poems the substitution of various parts of the female anatomy with a rich array of symbols also reflects a process of metonymy which we saw at work in Breton's recovery of new and unusual (yet sexually suggestive) objects or Bataille's preoccupation with the metonymic self-substitution of eyes, eggs, testicles or bodily fluids in Bataille's novel *Histoire de l'Œil*. This tendency of all three men to repeat references to the female subject (and the parts of her body) reinforce the validity of the Lacanian reading of sublimation, with its emphasis on repetition and replaceability in the face of *das Ding*.

Péret like Lacan realises that the tradition of courtly love poetry conjoined the notions of sublimation and transgression, being 'tantôt un simple rituel de sublimation de la sexualité, tantôt une lubricité dissimulée sous un apparat'[167] ['sometimes a simple ritual of sublimation of sexuality, sometimes the pomp and ceremony of concealed lubricity']. Lacan similarly suggests that the transgression born of prohibition is only the beginning: quite often this can result in the sexual masquerading as the sublimated. To illustrate the point, he cites the verse of the courtly love poet, Arnaud Daniel, in which the allusion is contained to a Lady's courtier having to 'emboucher cette trompette'[168] ['put his mouth to her trumpet'[169]]. This, according to Lacan, is not only an expression of sensuality but 'il déborde [...] les limites de la pornographie, allant jusqu'à la scatologie'[170] ['breaches the boundaries of pornography to the point of scatology'[171]]. Furthermore, it is also evident that the use of a hollow or concave image is – as in the

167 Péret, *Amour Sublime*, p. 43.
168 Lacan, *Séminaire* VII, p. 192.
169 Lacan, *Seminar* VII, p. 162.
170 Lacan, *Séminaire* VII, p. 191.
171 Lacan, *Seminar* VII, p. 161.

poems of Péret and Breton – a metaphor for the vagina (or anus) and reflective of a desire with an emptiness at its core.

Scatology, pornography and blasphemy are quite salient within one of Péret's early texts of 1928 entitled 'Les Couilles Enragées' (in English, 'mad balls' or 'testicles'), a text which on all accounts rivals Bataille's literary works such as *Histoire de l'Œil* in terms of its transgressive force. The story reads as a surreal orgy of carnal indulgence, which pushes the limits of pornography to bestiality. It portrays the sexual exploits of a Sadean aristocrat, *le vicomte Branleur des Couilles-Molles*, his four female accomplices and his two pets, a parrot (whose feathers are used for the purposes of sexual arousal) and a dog. They begin by performing all manner of bizarre acts upon one another in order to reach a sexual frenzy. The orgiastic scenes which build up in the aristocrat's residence are taken on to the streets of the viscount's home town, where throngs of lascivious revellers join the fornicating band; from thence the procession moves toward a church, which they enter to continue their lubricious activities, whilst parodying the sacraments and rituals of Christianity.

The main interest of the story is the supporting role of poetry and religious litany in creating a climate of sexual excess underpinned by extreme blasphemy. The story's narrative is interspersed with verse, which serves as a hymn to concupiscence at the expense of religious piety:

> O grand saint esprit de merde
> vierge enculée de tous les côtés
> mon bock est plein d'eau bénite
> Trempes-y ta bite avant de me l'enfoncer
> Des cons de nénuphar poussent dans le bénitier
> Va donc les peloter avant de m'enculer
> Le Christ n'a pas de queue
> c'est pour cela qu'on l'a cloué
> Coule coule le foutre au fond de nos matrices.[172]
>
> [Oh, holy ghost made of shit
> virgin buggered from all angles

172 Benjamin Péret, *Les Couilles Enragées* (Paris: E. Losfeld 1970), p. 13.

my beer glass is filled with holy water
Soak your cock in it before you penetrate me with it
Water lily cunts are growing in the font
Go and touch them up before somodising me
Christ has no prick
that's why he was nailed to the cross
Let the sperm flow, flow into our womb.]

Such inverted prayer forms are reinforced by a succession of other anti-religious gestures. As the viscount and one of his mistresses enter the church, posteriors and clitorides are crossed with holy water; mass orgies take place in the churchyard whose participants recite salacious incantations; women masturbate with crucifixes and urinate into ciboria and tabernacles; consecrated wine is filled into a woman's vagina and then sealed with a Host.

As one of the few Surrealists who remained true to Surrealism proper his entire life, and who was greatly admired by Breton, Péret also problematises the meaning of 'Bretonian Surrealism'. As has already been shown, Breton considered the poet as having a talent for operating alchemical sublimation upon language, by releasing words from their fixed meanings. Such an operation included the diversion of words away from normalising ends and toward transgression: 'Avec Benjamin Péret [...] cette sorte de "mauvaise conscience" a pris fin, la censure ne joue plus, on excipe du "tout est permis"[173] [With Benjamin Péret [...] this kind of "bad conscience" has come to an end; censorship no longer counts, and one takes it as a given that "everything is permitted."[174]]. It seems no less significant that these words are written in *L'Anthologie de l'Humour Noir*, in which Breton indicates that Péret's works are, as risqué as they appear, a source of unending humour.[175] His comments about black humour representing an unleashing of the (largely

173 Breton, *Œuvres Complètes* II, pp. 1133–1134.

174 Breton, *Anthology of Black Humour*, p. 301 – translation slightly modified by me.

175 Or as Breton puts it, 'l'humour jaillit ici comme de source' ['humour gushes here as if from the source'] – Breton, *Œuvres Complètes* II, 1134; Breton, *Anthology of Black Humour*, p. 301.

destructive) powers of the *id* in defiance of the reality principle and the super ego (as discussed in Chapter 2) seem particularly germane to the writings of Péret.

When reading Péret's more audacious works, it is easy to lose sight of the value of such literature, in particular as a defence of sublime love. For this reason one is bound to remind oneself that the vision of a work such as *Les Couilles Enragées* is not a true reflection of the poet's desired reality. Whilst acknowledging the dangers of ascribing such intentionality to his writings, I believe they represented a socially purposeful transgression (rooted in the need to defy Christian values) rather than a call to outright regression, which would have contradicted Surrealism's main aims as well as the doctrine of sublime love. Despite Péret's claim that sublime love is anti-social, he avows that 'la licence sexuelle sans horizon ne peut que diminuer l'être humain tout autant que les tabous les plus strictes'[176] ['sexual licence without horizons can only diminish human beings as much as the strictest taboos'].

Péret's comment is, I believe, reflective of Surrealism's broader aims, which, on the one hand, sought to subvert social conventions by endowing their works with a certain shock value (and hence bringing to expression the desublimatory) while, on the other hand, not losing sight of the final ends of their revolt: a golden era of elective love in which the pleasure of physical love is heightened (rather than debased or negated), through its free expression and concordance with emotional love. The Surrealists' decision to make love an end in itself, to sustain an unquestioning faith in its value in the face of its incredulous detractors, ensured that their pursuit of the desired Other, the love object, remained energetic and unceasing. This stance more than any other showed Surrealism's view of libertinism to be equivocal, with individual members hoping to rest with one love object but ultimately finding reasons to be inveigled onto the pathways towards yet another encounter. Their sublimation of love was one might say lined with the desublimatory; and in reading Surrealism through Lacan this becomes all too clear.

176 Péret, *Amour Sublime*, p. 64.

* * * * * * * * *

In the preceding exposition of the cult of love, a critical link between Surrealism and the postmodern has been established. For Lacan shows us that through the subject's ongoing quest for signifying love objects, desire is endlessly deferred (a principle not dissimilar to Derrida's concept of *différance,* and the endless deferral of meaning which occurs in language). The interchangeability of the love object is critical, for it underlines the impossibility of a full and satisfying representation of desire. Lacan will develop this idea further in his concept of *le petit objet a*, which he compares to an agalma (a Greek term meaning glory or an ornament, an offering to the gods, or a little statue of a god), a precious object concealed in a relatively worthless container. The subject treats the Other like the agalma in that (s)he attempts to locate within it an object of value (the soul's perfect complement), which disappointingly proves to be evasive and infinitely displaceable.

The fact that the *le petit objet a / das Ding* can be conceived as metonymy (that is can be represented by found objects of fetishistic value) points to the incompleteness and fragmentariness of the object; and, in some senses, complements Lacan's notion of *corps morcelé* (or 'dismembered body'), the sense of division and ambivalence which haunts the subject even after (s)he has identified him/herself as a coherent whole during 'the mirror phase' of infancy.[177] In both of these concepts the idea of the subject and object as coherent entities is questioned; such questioning of the integral self is perhaps one of the defining features of the postmodern. Lacan's contribution to this viewpoint is to have shown in the seventh seminar that the object can only ever fulfil and be known to us partially.

Surrealism's role in exemplifying the latter notions is substantial. This comes about not only because of Lacan's use of Surrealist sources to corroborate his theories. Critically, the movement was perhaps one of the first in European cultural history not only to have acknowledged and to

177 The recognition and assumption of the infant's mirror image at the age of six months, as contrasted with the dismissal of the image as illusory and worthless by a chimpanzee of the same age.

have explored creatively 'the omnipotence of desire' in human behaviour as Freud had postulated it, but also to ask how humans should respond to its potency and to define its function for a new age of greater personal and social freedom. It is clear that Surrealists saw in desire a vital and dynamic force which, in order to flourish, had to be granted free expression and remain object-oriented (being channelled constructively to the outside world). Individuals similarly needed to follow and adapt to desire as it changed its orientation to achieve a sense of self-fulfilment and self-determination. Invariably this involved the passage of desire from one signifying love object to another. Moreover, in an interview in 1946 Breton acknowledged that desire more often than not motivated the Surrealist urge to personal and collective renewal:

> Jean Duché : Vous avez parlé de la toute-puissance du désir, capable de transformer le monde. Est-ce sur le désir que vous appuyez l'action?
>
> André Breton : Le désir, oui toujours.[178]
>
> [Jean Duché: You've spoken of an all-powerful desire, capable of transforming the world. Is it on desire that you base your action?
>
> André Breton: Desire, yes, always.[179]]

As Mary Ann Caws also affirms 'the philosophical "désir" of the Surrealists was a sort of vital force ("sens de la vie") working under the sterile and prudish exterior of the normal world'.[180]

Given today's widespread preoccupation with self-realisation, the constant pursuit of desire (which is endlessly deferred and deflected), the refusal to disregard sexual desire in favour of emotional desire and the eroding of the institution of marriage, one is inclined to see the Surrealist's attitude to love and relationships as portentous of certain

178 Breton, *Œuvres Complètes* III, p. 597.
179 Breton, *Conversations*, p. 206.
180 Mary Ann Caws, 'Péret's "Amour sublime" – Just another "Amour Fou"?' in *The French Review*, No. 2 (Nov, 1966), vol. 40, p. 207.

aspects of modern sexual mores. While love is frequently not regarded as sacred or as the ultimate good to aspire to (as the Surrealists held), and the heteronormative view of relationships is now openly challenged, love in a Western context has been largely uncoupled from any higher moral imperative (as might be ordained by organised religion) and – with its focus on the ephemeral and the elective – it has become a matter for the individual to realise as he or she sees fit. With these thoughts in mind I return to my original thesis that – given their pioneering and at times subversive approach to desire and relationships – the argument of the Surrealists being sublimatory, repressive and idealist seems overstated. In reflecting upon this thesis in relation to the general findings of this book, I now elaborate my concluding comments.

Conclusion

This book has attempted to present a fresh interpretation of Surrealism which reconsiders some of the fundamental assumptions about the movement dating back not only to the *Tel Quel* critiques of the early seventies but to the time of the young Bataille himself. These assumptions have given rise to the prevailing view that, for the Surrealists, sublimation was no more than the corollary of an idealist philosophy which sought to deny the validity of the material and the sexual within existence. One of the primary arguments in favour of this view was that Breton's proposed reconciliation of antinomies mirrored Hegel's belief in a teleological resolution of history in a transcendental beyond (the Absolute Spirit). Upon a closer examination of his written works, however, it has become apparent that his appropriation of Hegel was half-baked for as much as he admired the philosopher, he called for 'l' "avortement colossal"'[1] ['the "colossal abortion"'[2]] of absolute idealism and thus the system of thought which Hegel had represented. The claim that Surrealism could have generally embodied any one system of thought was also problematic on account of Breton's tendency to practise philosophical bricolage.

Far from being a conservative methodology, 'bricolage', like the *informe*, has considerable resonances with the postmodern, having a prodigious capacity to disrupt conventional thought patterns and to generate new and multidimensional ways of engaging with a subject. *The Routledge Companion to Postmodernism* affirms that 'the sense of improvisation that bricolage carries appeals to the postmodern theorist, since it suggests an arbitrary, undetermined quality to creative activity in which the end is not specified in advance'.[3] In *Postmodernism: Foundational essays*, Derrida

1 Breton, *Manifestes du Surréalisme*, p. 89.

2 Breton, *Manifestoes of Surrealism*, p. 140.

3 Stuart Sim, *The Routledge Companion to Postmodernism: Third Edition* (London: Routledge, 2011), p. 237. It should be noted that postmodern ideas have come to

states 'it has even been said that *bricolage* is critical language itself'.[4] The subversive capacity of this unsystematic way of thinking to bring down cherished ideals is not to be downplayed in relation to Surrealism. On account of this bricolage, for example, there arose Breton's unorthodox use of the term dialectics, which was neither entirely Hegelian or Marxist in nature, but inspired by thought systems as diverse as Daoism and alchemy (in addition to dialectical materialism and Hegelianism). Dialectics thus came to refer in a general sense to the interplay of the interior life and external reality in its myriad applications. Significantly, such interplay allowed Surrealists to explore the passage of the instincts and desires of (wo)man's inner reality into the outer world, resulting in the manifestation of uninhibited sexuality both within elective love (of which the physical aspect was prized as much as the emotional aspect) and an abundance of Surrealist works exploring the unconscious life in new and surprising ways.

Qualifying the view of Surrealism as homogeneous and repressive was the profuse and opulent sexual symbolism expressed in these works. This spoke against the claim that Surrealism opposed the direct inscription of sexual desire into its creative works à la Bataille. Although the desublimatory aspect of Surrealist art has been given more attention in recent scholarship, it has either been regarded as marginal to Surrealism (Foster), representative of an underlying sympathy with Bataille (Krauss) or has been discussed without reference to how it might complement rather than contradict Breton's continued interest in sublimation (Harris, Mundy). For this reason I have proposed that these more sexualised art forms were representative of a particular strand of Bretonian Surrealism which deserved to be considered in their own right (having a large number

---

differ from the structuralist theory of Claude Lévi-Strauss, who in *La Pensée Sauvage* (1962) claimed the 'bricolage' was a primitive form of thought, contrasting with the more methodical and precise system of thought embodied in the modern scientist.

4 Jacques Derrida, 'Structure, Sign and Play in the Discourse of the Human Sciences' in Victor E. Taylor, Charles E. Winquist, *Postmodernism: Foundational essays* (London: Taylor & Francis, 1998), p. 511 (pp. 504–520). In this quotation, Derrida is referring to the claims made by G. Genette in 'Structuralisme et critique littéraire' in *L'Arc* (no. 26, 1965).

of exponents from Matta and Masson to Ernst, Bellmer and Dalí). Given that the Surrealists' belief in sublimation was no impediment to the execution of these works, the case for re-reading the movement as one founded on the notion of non-repressive sublimation is invariably strengthened.

A closer examination of Breton's works reveals his growing openness to physical love, perversion and transgression. His statements in later life throw into doubt the commonly held view of him as a romantic who denied the physical dimension of love and execrated certain forms of sexual behaviour (a vice to which he was admittedly prone in his youth). The studies on Sadism and perversion in *Minotaure* and the symbolic objects of Giacometti, Bellmer and Picasso indicate that he did not seek to censor all explicit references to raw sexuality in art and scholarly enquiry. On the basis of his increasing accommodation of these areas as well as his continual engagement with socio-political affairs, a case may be made that he was not quite the 'supereagle' Bataille once described him as, in other words, that he did not simply wish to soar disdainfully above the world and evade the struggles of material reality. A case may equally be made that Bataille did not always conduct himself as an old mole, particularly when he immersed himself in the cultish neo-pagan group Acéphale and incurred the charge of idealism from the Surrealists.

These considerations have been offered in relation to the criticisms of the *Tel Quelists* and October group who have propagated the view that Surrealism was remote from material reality, hostile to baseness and perversion, and thus at the theoretical antipodes of Bataillean thinking. My reconsiderations of this view have not attempted to contradict this view outright but simply to nuance and problematise it. In so doing, I have attempted to respect the deconstructive principles which the October group in particular claims to espouse; and it is hoped therefore that this book contributes to the natural evolution of Surrealism's critical reception.

A prime example of the October group's deconstructive practice can be found in their tome on the history of twentieth-century art, *Art since 1900*, in which they critique Heinrich Wölfflin's *Principles of Art History* for presenting new art movements as antagonistic to their immediate predecessors, and thus ascribing antithetical qualities to successive movements, such as 'linear/painterly, plane/recession, closed/open form, multiplicity/unity; clearness/unclearness'.[5] It is these sorts of binaries which I have sought to avoid and which have been summarised by Marie-Christine Lala in relation to the Breton-Bataille polemic (see Figure 6.1).[6]

« fleur visible » « lumière »	CIEL **HAUT**	TERRE **BAS**	« racines gluantes » « pourriture » « à l'intérieur du sol »
ELEVATION	(idéal) **PUR** **NOBLE** (bien) (amour)	(matières) **IMPUR** **IGNOBLE** (mal) (mort)	**ABAISSEMENT**

Figure 6.1: Table of binaries occurring in Bataillean thought (from Marie-Christine Lala's article 'Bataille et Breton : le malentendu considérable' ['Bataille and Breton: considerable misunderstandings']).

The October group held that Wölfflin's work was ahistorical on account of its binaristic view of art history.[7] While most of Surrealism's critics cannot be accused of being ahistorical, in their insistence on portraying the disagreement between Surrealists and its dissidents as one between materialism and idealism, we are, however, reminded of Jameson when he contends that:

> … I have always been uncomfortable with this kind of opposition between materialism and idealism, considered as it were as suprahistorical positions or eternal forces and tendencies and temptations. […] I'm inclined to wonder, for instance, if 'idealism' is always a reactionary position, or whether under certain circumstances – read in a precise historical context as an ideological move, with a certain determinate social and class content – it may not also have had progressive if not revolutionary consequences […] I guess what I'm tempted to wonder […] about this opposition between materialism and idealism that has become a piece

5 Krauss, Foster et al., *Art Since 1900*, p. 34.

6 Marie-Christine Lala, 'Bataille et Breton : le malentendu considérable' (1992) in *Surréalisme et Philosophie*, p. 54.

7 Interestingly, the October group believed Wölfflin's binarisms to have been inspired by idealist discourse.

> of unexamined Left doxa since the sixties and since Maoism is whether it is not itself just a little bit 'idealistic'.[8]

This reflection recalls some of the hazards involved in being too binaristic in elucidating Breton and Bataille's interactions. Above all, it gives an essential pause for reflection to critics who may be tempted to overlook Bataille's withdrawal from politics into quasi-mystical exaltation and initiatory cults; or Surrealists' endeavours to revolutionise the spheres of the personal and the social.

Both in *Art since 1900* and *Formless* Bataille's *informe* is presented not as a concept or theory, but as an operation, as a term which has been assigned a 'job':[9] 'formless is not simply mess or slime. Its cancellation of boundaries is more structural than that since it involves a voiding of categories'[10] and again 'formlessness results from a blurring of categories'.[11] For this reason, it behoves the critic of Surrealism not to resort to easy categorisations and inflexible boundaries. When applying a structurally rigid and differential approach to the analysis of Surrealism and its rival grouping, the intricacies of a complex and shifting dynamic are invariably overlooked. Such an omission can be compounded by the adoption of a synchronic rather than a diachronic approach, or more precisely, an approach which, in the history of Surrealism, is unduly fixated on the late twenties and early thirties. A nuanced appreciation of the ambivalences which constituted the personalities of Breton and Bataille and their evolving relationship to each other is therefore missed, in particular, the opportunity to 'blur' their usual roles (categories) of super-eagle and old mole. The reluctance to abandon such hard-set dualisms have resulted in Breton continuing to be perceived as 'the simple (paternal)

8 Frederic Jameson, typescript, 1986 – his comments were reproduced in Douglas Crimp, *On the Museum's Ruins* (Cambridge, MA: MIT, 1993), p. 303.

9 Rosalind Krauss, Hal Foster, Yve-Alain Bois, Benjamin H.D. Buchloh, *Art Since 1900: Modernism, Antimodernism, Postmodernism* (New York: Thames & Hudson, 2004), p. 245; Yve-Alain Bois, *Formless*, p. 18

10 Krauss, Foster et al., *Art Since 1900*, p. 247.

11 *Ibid.*, p. 248.

sign of universal homogeneity', 'the priest', the 'castrated lion'.[12] Not all of the criticism levelled at Breton in his early days as Surrealist frontman is unwarranted: he (and other male Surrealists) evinced a notable level of intolerance towards non-heteronormative behaviours and typically represented women in clichéd or schematic terms. On the other hand, the mature and more self-reflexive entities that Surrealism and its leader became from the mid-1930s onward are hardly recognisable in some critical interpretations of the movement.

In the renowned collection of essays on postmodernism, *The Anti-Aesthetic – Essays on Postmodern Culture*, Foster valorises postmodernism as a deconstructive operation (or in his words as a 'counter-practice' or a site of 'resistance'):

> A postmodernism of resistance, then, arises as a counter-practice not only to the official culture of modernism but also to the 'false normativity' of a reactionary postmodernism. In opposition (but not *only* in opposition), a resistant postmodernism is concerned with a critical deconstruction of tradition ...[13]

The history of Surrealist criticism can certainly be considered as a counter-practice, though it is frequently not a 'critical deconstruction', which examines the movement and its figureheads in a more equivocal light. It is on this basis, that I re-affirm the need for this book and reiterate its most significant findings.

Despite – or even because of – the movement's preoccupation with the inner life of (wo)man, it never ceased to establish critical links between the fruits of its introspection and events in the outside world (believing these spheres to be interdependent). Like almost every other grouping on the Left, the Surrealists were unable to translate all of their ideals into social and the political reality. On the other hand, their ability to stir the mind in individual cases both through a strident message of total refusal and thought-provoking works was much more fruitful. For the Surrealists, revolution was, one might say, incremental and never-ending.

12 Krauss, *Formless*, pp. 66–77.

13 Hal Foster, 'Postmodernism: A Preface' in *The Anti-Aesthetic: Essays on Postmodern Culture*, ed. by Hal Foster (Seattle, WA: Bay Press, 1983), p. xii.

In the *Second Manifeste* Breton had called upon Surrealists to make sublimation the basis of a new awareness or consciousness which fell beyond the normalising framework of medicine (including psychoanalysis itself). With reference to Marcuse, we have seen how Surrealist works created a counter-consciousness to the conformist mind-set of capitalism and were therefore able to reflect the essence and injustice of social reality in a manner which destabilised the public. As Marcuse also showed, Eros and Thanatos could also be used to this effect, with Eros imbuing a work with an erotic sensuousness lacking in reality, and the energy of Thanatos being steered away from death and put in the service of Eros. In Surrealism Eros and Thanatos found their sublimated corollaries in the 'erotic-veiled' and 'explosive-fixed' of convulsive beauty, qualities which through their bare instinctual nature likewise had the potential to draw attention to the deficiencies of a repressive reality.

Breton conceived of the new consciousness brought about by this type of artistic sublimation as a form of alchemical transmutation. This consisted in the irruption of words, symbols and ideas from the depths of the unconscious into poetry and art, which were notable by their divergence from ordinary speech patterns or the visual coherence of waking reality (indeed, they might be considered further instances of bricolage). Rimbaud's alchemy of the verb and Ernst's alchemy of the visual image both helped to bring about these new and highly unorthodox modes of expression. Amongst all of the 'factions' within the Surrealist spectrum, artists and poets reworked the hermetic adage 'as above, so below' in a way which frequently problematised the binary of high and low. While Surrealism's critics have always identified Bataille as the anti-Icarian subverter of the high, they have overpassed those artists such as Ernst who were practising this form of subversion from within Surrealism. In Ernst's painting *Of this men shall know nothing* he had exalted the legs of a couple making love to the height of the macrocosm underlining the enormous significance that the Surrealists attached to the elective pursuit of romantic and sexual relationships in disdain of the heavens.

Ernst as well as Leiris conceived of human attraction as something veiled, presenting it in relation to the motif of facial masking. A masked body, they maintained, revealed something of the fundamental truth about desire: that it could occasion a brute instinctual climax and emotional exaltation even as its object (and cause) remained obscure and unknowable. The idea had distinct parallels with Lacan's view of sublimation. This, he defined as an overvaluation of the Other which served to fill one's innate psychical lack (and which was also veiled in nature). He explained that the individual actively sought out objects in the external world which both filled and signified this void; these might take the form of lovers, objects of a fetishistic value, poetry and art. In all cases, the object found or created served in psychical terms as the complement to one's existence.

Lacan's brand of psychoanalysis made a vital and unacknowledged contribution to the discourse on non-repressive sublimation, showing how the latter was exemplified by the Surrealists who were cajoled endlessly into the chaos of urban life to retrieve miscellaneous missing love objects (whether human lovers or *trouvailles*). This unending quest for arbitrary encounters within the social as a means of overcoming lack within the self I interpreted in the light of Surrealism's dialectic of inner and outer states and the endless 'postmodern' deflection of desire from one object to the next. The dynamic nature of this activity reinforced the idea of a movement in perpetual transit, never allowing desire to become impeded in its development, never arriving or finding its place in society. By extension, this implied a refusal to bind sexuality to the conventional order of things. Indeed, through Lacanian theory, it was shown that the Surrealists' pursuit of the lost other exalted the terrestrial in defiance of the divine (and the social and religious values established in its name). Their insistence on elective love (which was opposed to the eternal nature of marriage) was therefore often transgressive in nature, though this sense of transgression was mediated to different degrees in the works of Breton, Bataille and Péret.

The creative works examined in this book have shown how the Surrealists espoused a form of sublimation which was not aim-inhibited, unlike the concept posited by the late Freud in his outline of a repressive civilisation. Rather, it sought to free humanity from the yoke under which it laboured both from a hitherto pervasive Christian-conservative morality and the repressiveness of any one of three political ideologies (capitalism, communism and fascism). In *Les Vases Communicants* Breton postulated the existence of a 'capillary tissue' ('tissu capillaire')[14] which regulated the exchange between inner life and outer reality. I have argued that in terms of permitting instincts and desires to be expressed freely in the outside world, whether in life or art, this capillary tissue was, in the context of Surrealism, much more porous than has frequently been acknowledged. For this reason, the very concept of non-repressive sublimation was a necessary one in the explication of Surrealism, uncovering and rationalising its members' externalisation of the instinctual life without the sacrifice of the libido's primary aim of satisfaction. In *L'Amour Fou* Breton stated, 'Il s'agit de ne pas [...] laisser s'embroussailler les chemins du désir'[15] ['We must not let the paths of desire become overgrown'[16]] – a fitting testament to the Surrealists' determination to overcome the obstacles which impeded the reification of desire in a reality which was fundamentally hostile to it.

14 Breton, *Les Vases Communicants*, p. 161; Breton, *Communicating Vessels*, p. 139.
15 Breton, *L'Amour Fou*, p. 38.
16 Breton, *Mad Love*, p. 25.

Bibliography

Primary Sources
(Surrealist works, works of Georges Bataille, articles in Surrealist and avant-garde journals)

Arnaud, Noël; Blanchard, Maurice; Bocquet, Charles; Bureau, Jacques; Chabrun, J.-F.; Chancel, Paul; Dotremont, Christian; Dumayet, Pierre; Gagnaire, Aline; Hoyaux, Jean; Iche, Laurence; Magritte, René et al., 'Nom de Dieu' (1943) in *Tracts Surréalistes et Déclarations Collectives 1940–1969*, ed. José Pierre (Paris: Terrain Vague, 1982), vol. 2, p. 9.

Bataille, Georges, 'L'art primitif' ('Primitive Art') in *Documents 7* (1930), p. 396.
Bataille, Georges, 'Le Bleu du Ciel' in *Minotaure*, no. 8 (1938), p. 51.

Bataille, Georges, 'Le Gros Orteil' in *Documents*, ed. by Bernard Noël (Paris: Mercure de France, Gallimard, 1968).

Bataille, Georges, 'The Solar Anus' (1927) in *Visions of Excess – Selected Writings 1927–1939*, ed. and trans. by Allan Stoekl (Manchester: Manchester University Press, 1985), p. 6.

———, 'The "Old Mole" and the Prefix Sur in the Words Surhomme [Superman] and Surrealist' (1931) in *Visions of Excess – Selected Writings 1927–1939*, ed. and trans. by Allan Stoekl (Manchester: Manchester University Press, 1985).

———, 'The Practice of Joy before Death' (1939) in *Visions of Excess – Selected Writings 1927–1939*, ed. and trans. by Allan Stoekl (Manchester: Manchester University Press, 1985), pp. 238–239.

Bataille, Georges, *Erotism: Death & Sensuality*, trans. by Mary Dalwood (San Francisco: City Lights Books, 1986)

Bataille, Georges, *L'Expérience Intérieure* (Paris: Gallimard, 1986).

Bataille, Georges, 'The Blue of Noon' in *Inner Experience*, trans. by Leslie Anne Bolt (Albany: State University of New York Press, 1988), p. 78.

———, *Inner Experience*, trans. by Leslie Anne Bolt (New York: Suny Press, 1988), p. 127.

Bataille, Georges, 'L'Anus Solaire' (1927) in *Œuvres Complètes – Écrits posthumes 1922–1940,* ed. by Denis Hollier (Paris: Éditions Gallimard, 1970), vol. I, pp. 82.

———, 'Architecture' (1929) in *Œuvres Complètes – Écrits posthumes 1922–1940*, ed. by Denis Hollier (Paris: Éditions Gallimard, 1970), vol. I, p. 171.

———, 'Les propositions contenues ici' (circa 1930) in *Œuvres Complètes – Écrits posthumes 1922–1940*, ed. by Denis Hollier (Paris: Éditions Gallimard, 1970), vol. II, p. 73.

———, 'La "Vieille Taupe" et le Préfixe Sur dans les Mots Surhomme et Surréaliste' (1931) in *Œuvres Complètes – Écrits posthumes 1922–1940*, ed. by Denis Hollier (Paris: Éditions Gallimard, 1970), vol. II.

———, 'Le masque' (c.1934) in *Œuvres Complètes – Écrits posthumes 1922–1940*, ed. by Denis Hollier (Paris: Éditions Gallimard, 1970), vol. II.

———, 'La Pratique de la Joie devant la Mort' (1939) in *Œuvres Complètes – Écrits posthumes 1922–1940*, ed. by Denis Hollier (Paris: Éditions Gallimard, 1970), vol. I, pp. 553–554.

———, 'En Marge d' «Acéphale» – Programme' in *Œuvres Complètes – Écrits posthumes 1922–1940*, ed. by Denis Hollier (Paris: Éditions Gallimard, 1970), vol. II, p. 273.

———, 'La Valeur d'usage de D.A.F. de Sade' in *Œuvres Complètes – Écrits posthumes 1922–1940*, ed. by Denis Hollier (Paris: Éditions Gallimard, 1970), vol. II.

———, 'Annexe 5 – Discussion sur le péché' (1944) in *Œuvres Complètes – La Somme Athéologique II* (Paris: Gallimard, 1973), vol. VI, p. 340.

———, 'Méthode de Méditation' (1947) in *Œuvres Complètes – La Somme Athéologique I* (Paris: Gallimard, 1974), vol. V, p. 193.

———, 'La Religion Surréaliste' (1948) in *Œuvres Complètes* (Paris: Gallimard, 1976), vol VII, p. 389.

———, 'Notes – Conférences 1951–1953 – 2. L'Athéologie' in *Œuvres Complètes* (Paris: Gallimard, 1976), vol. VIII, p. 568.

———, 'La littérature et le mal' (1957) in *Œuvres Complètes* (Paris: Gallimard, 1979), vol. IX, p. 171.

———, 'Chapitre V – La Transgression' in *Œuvres Complètes* (Paris: Gallimard, 1987), vol. X.

———, 'L'Érotisme' in *Œuvres Complètes* (Paris: Gallimard, 1987), vol. X.

———, 'Le Surréalisme et sa Différence avec l'Existentialisme' (1945) in Bataille, *Œuvres Complètes – Articles 1 1944–1949* (Paris: Gallimard, 1988), vol. XI, p. 74.

———, 'A propos d'assoupissements' (1946) in *Œuvres Complètes – Articles 1 1944–1949* (Paris: Gallimard, 1988), vol. XI, p. 31.

———, 'L'Érotisme, Soutien de la Morale' (1957) in *Œuvres Complètes* (Paris: Gallimard, 1988), vol. XII, p. 467.

Bataille, Georges, 'Surrealism and how it differs from Existentialism' (1945) in *The Absence of Myth – Writings on Surrealism* (London: Verso, 1994), p. 60.

———, 'On the Subject of Slumbers' (1946) in *The Absence of Myth – Writings on Surrealism* (London: Verso, 1994), p. 49.

———, 'The Surrealist Religion' (1948) in *The Absence of Myth – Writings on Surrealism* (London: Verso, 1994), p. 77.

———, 'Notes on the Publication of "Un Cadavre"' (c. 1954) in *The Absence of Myth – Writings on Surrealism*, trans. by Michael Richardson (London: Verso, 1994), p. 32.

Bataille, Georges, 'Programme (Relative to Acéphale)' in *The Bataille Reader*, ed. by Fred Botting and Scott Wilson (Oxford: Blackwell, 1997), p. 121.

Bataille, Georges, *Choix de Lettres* 1917–1962, ed. by Michel Surya (Paris: Gallimard, 1997).

Bataille, Georges, 'Aphorisms for the "System" – 2. Plans and Notes for "Atheology"' (1952) in *The Unfinished System of Non-Knowledge*, trans. by Michelle and Stuart Kendall (Minneapolis, MN: University of Minnesota Press, 2001), p. 160.

Bataille, Georges, 'La Publication d' "Un Cadavre"' (c. 1954) in *Georges Bataille, Michel Leiris – Échanges et Correspondances* (Paris: Gallimard, 2004), p. 76 (pp. 73–80).

Bounoure, Vincent; Dauguet, Aurélien; van Hirtum, Marianne; Lequenne, Michel; Löwy, Michael; Varikas, Eleni; Zimbacca, Michel, 'Hermetic Bird' in *Surrealism Against the Current : Tracts and Declarations*, ed. and trans. by Michael Richardson and Krzystof Fijałkowski (London: Pluto Press, 2001), pp. 79–81.

Breton, André, 'Les mots sans rides' in *Littérature, 2e série,* n° 7 (Décembre, 1922).

Breton, André, 'Le Château Étoilé' in *Minotaure*, no. 8 (1936), pp. 25–39.

Breton, André, *L'Amour Fou* (Paris: Gallimard, 1937).

Breton, André, *Entretiens 1913–1952* (with André Parinaud) (Paris: Gallimard, 1952).

Breton, André, 'D.-A.-F. de Sade' in *Anthology of Black Humour* (1940), trans. by Mark Polizzotti (San Francisco, CA: City Light Books, 1997), p. 18.

Breton, André, *Arcane 17* (Paris: Sagittaire, 1947).

Breton, André, 'The Situation of Surrealism between the two Wars' in *Yale French Studies*, No. 2, Modern Poets (Yale University Press, 1948), pp. 67–78.

Breton, André, *Nadja* (Paris: Gallimard, 1964).

Breton, André, 'Manifesto of Surrealism' (1924) in *Manifestoes of Surrealism*, trans. by Richard Seaver and Helen R. Lane (Michigan: The University of Michigan Press, 1969).

———, 'Second Manifesto of Surrealism' (1930) in *Manifestoes of Surrealism*, trans. by Richard Seaver and Helen R. Lane (Michigan: The University of Michigan Press, 1969).

———, 'Political Position of Surrealism' (1935) in *Manifestoes of Surrealism*, trans. by Richard Seaver and Helen R. Lane (Michigan: The University of Michigan Press, 1969).

——————, 'Surrealist Situation of the Object' (1935) in *Manifestoes of Surrealism*, trans. by Richard Seaver and Helen R. Lane (Michigan: The University of Michigan Press, 1969).

——————, 'On Surrealism and its Living Works' (1953) in *Manifestoes of Surrealism*, trans. by Richard Seaver and Helen R. Lane (Michigan: The University of Michigan Press, 1969).

——————, 'Preface for the New Edition of the Second Manifesto' in *Manifestoes of Surrealism*, trans. by Richard Seaver and Helen R. Lane (Michigan: The University of Michigan Press, 1969), p. 113.

Breton, André, 'Surrealism and Painting' (1928) in *Surrealism and Painting*, trans. by Simon Watson Taylor (London: Macdonald and Co., 1972), p. 35.

——————, 'Pablo Picasso in his element' (1933) in *Surrealism and Painting*, trans. by Simon Watson Taylor (London: Macdonald and Co., 1972), p. 114.

——————, 'André Masson' (1939) in *Surrealism and Painting*, trans. by Simon Watson Taylor (London: Macdonald and Co., 1972), p. 154.

——————, 'Artistic Genesis and Perspective of Surrealism' (1941) in *Surrealism and Painting*, trans. by Simon Watson Taylor (London: Macdonald and Co., 1972), pp. 80–81.

——————, 'Max Ernst' (1942) in *Surrealism and Painting*, trans. by Simon Watson Taylor (London: Macdonald and Co., 1972), p. 159.

——————, 'Matta' (1947) in *Surrealism and Painting*, trans. by Simon Watson Taylor (London, Macdonald and Co., 1972), p. 191.

——————, 'Max Ernst – Graphic Works' (1950) in *Surrealism and Painting*, trans. by Simon Watson Taylor (London: Macdonald and Co., 1972), p. 168.

——————, 'Max Ernst – Œuvre Graphique' (1950) in *Surrealism and Painting*, trans. by Simon Watson Taylor (London: Macdonald and Co., 1972), p. 552.

——————, 'Introduction to the International Surrealist Exhibition' (1959) in *Surrealism and Painting*, trans. by Simon Watson Taylor (London: Macdonald and Co., 1972), pp. 378–389.

——————, 'Gustave Moreau' (1961) in *Surrealism and Painting*, trans. by Simon Watson Taylor (London: Macdonald and Co., 1972), p. 363.

Breton, André, 'What is Surrealism?' (1934) in *What is Surrealism?: Selected Writings* ed. by Franklin Rosemont (New York: Pathfinder, 1978), Part 2, p. 115.

——————, 'Interview with "Indice"' (1935) in *What is Surrealism? : Selected Writings* ed. by Franklin Rosemont (New York: Pathfinder, 1978), Part 2, p. 144.

——————, 'Manifesto for an independent revolutionary art' (1938) in *What is Surrealism?: Selected Writings* ed. by Franklin Rosemont (New York: Pathfinder, 1978), Part 2, p. 186.

Breton, André, 'Manifeste du Surréalisme' (1924) in *Manifestes du Surréalisme* (Paris: Gallimard, 1979).

——————, 'Second Manifeste du Surréalisme' (1930) in *Manifestes du Surréalisme* (Paris: Gallimard, 1979).

——————, 'Avertissement pour la Réédition du Second Manifeste' (1946) in *Manifestes du Surréalisme* (Paris: Gallimard, 1979), p. 63.

——————, 'Du Surréalisme en ses Œuvres Vives' (1953) in *Manifestes du Surréalisme* (Paris: Gallimard, 1979).

Breton, André, *Mad Love* (London: University of Nebraska Press, 1987).

Breton, André, 'Introduction au discours sur le peu de réalité' (1924–1925) in *Œuvres Complètes*, ed. by Marguerite Bonnet (Paris: Gallimard, 1992), vol. II, p. 277.

——————, 'L'Âge d'Or' (1930–1931) in *Œuvres Complètes*, ed. by Marguerite Bonnet (Paris: Gallimard, 1988), vol. I, p. 1025.

——————, 'L'Union Libre' (1931) in *Œuvres Complètes*, ed. by Marguerite Bonnet (Paris: Gallimard, 1992), vol. II, pp. 85–87.

——————, 'Le Message Automatique' (1933) in *Œuvres Complètes*, ed. by Marguerite Bonnet (Paris: Gallimard, 1992), vol. II.

——————, 'Qu'est-ce que le surréalisme?' (1934) in *Œuvres Complètes*, ed. by Marguerite Bonnet (Paris: Gallimard, 1992), vol. II.

——————, 'Contre-Attaque – Union de lutte des intellectuels révolutionnaires' (1935) in *Œuvres Complètes*, ed. by Marguerite Bonnet (Paris: Gallimard, 1992), vol. II.

——————, 'Interview d'"Indice"' (1935) in *Œuvres Complètes*, ed. by Marguerite Bonnet (Paris: Gallimard, 1992), vol. II, p. 445.

——————, 'Position politique de l'art aujourd'hui' (1935) in *Œuvres Complètes*, ed. by Marguerite Bonnet (Paris: Gallimard, 1992), vol. II.

——————, 'Situation Surréaliste de l'Objet' (1935) in *Œuvres Complètes*, ed. by Marguerite Bonnet (Paris: Gallimard, 1992), vol. II.

——————, 'Pour un art révolutionnaire indépendant' (1938) in *Œuvres Complètes*, ed. by Marguerite Bonnet (Paris: Gallimard, 1992), vol. III.

——————, 'Anthologie de l'Humour Noir' (1940) in *Œuvres Complètes*, ed. by Marguerite Bonnet (Paris: Gallimard, 1992), vol. II.

——————, 'Situation du Surréalisme entre les deux Guerres' (1942) in *Œuvres Complètes*, ed. by Marguerite Bonnet (Paris: Gallimard, 1992), vol. III, pp. 723–724.

——————, 'Sur la route de San Romano' (1948) in *Œuvres Complètes*, ed. by Marguerite Bonnet (Paris: Gallimard, 1992), vol. III, p. 419.

——————, 'Entretiens' (1952) in *Œuvres Complètes*, ed. by Marguerite Bonnet (Paris: Gallimard, 1992), vol. III.

———, 'La barque de l'amour s'est brisée contre la vie courante' ['The small love boat has been shattered by everyday life'] (1930) in *Œuvres Complètes*, ed. by Marguerite Bonnet (Paris: Gallimard, 1992), vol. II, p. 315.

———, 'Légitime Défense' in *Œuvres Complètes*, ed. by Marguerite Bonnet (Paris: Gallimard, 1992), vol. II, p. 295.

———, 'Position poétique de l'art d'aujourd'hui' in *Œuvres Complètes*, ed. by Marguerite Bonnet (Paris: Gallimard, 1992), vol. II, p. 431.

———, 'Réponse à une note de Claude Lévi-Strauss' ('Response to a note by Claude Lévi-Strauss') in *Œuvres Complètes*, ed. by Marguerite Bonnet (Paris: Gallimard, 1992), vol. III, p. 118.

———, 'Trois interventions d'Breton, André à Contre-Attaque' in *Œuvres Complètes*, ed. by Marguerite Bonnet (Paris: Gallimard, 1992), vol. II, p. 593.

———, 'Le Surréalisme et la Peinture' (1928) in Breton, *Œuvres Complètes*, ed. by Marguerite Bonnet (Paris: Gallimard, 2008), vol. IV.

———, 'Pablo Picasso – Picasso dans son élément' (1933) in *Œuvres Complètes*, ed. by Marguerite Bonnet (Paris: Gallimard, 2008), vol. IV.

———, 'André Masson' (1939) in *Œuvres Complètes*, ed. by Marguerite Bonnet (Paris: Gallimard, 2008), vol. IV.

———, 'Max Ernst' (1942) in *Œuvres Complètes*, ed. by Marguerite Bonnet (Paris: Gallimard, 2008), vol. IV.

———, 'Matta' (1947) in *Œuvres Complètes*, ed. by Marguerite Bonnet (Paris: Gallimard, 2008), vol. IV.

———, 'Trait d'Union' (1952) (or 'Hyphen' in English) in *Œuvres Complètes*, ed. by Marguerite Bonnet (Paris: Gallimard, 2008), vol. IV, p. 852.

———, 'Gustave Moreau' (1961) in *Œuvres Complètes*, ed. by Marguerite Bonnet (Paris: Gallimard, 2008), vol. IV, p. 787.

Breton, André, 'Introduction à l'Exposition Internationale du Surréalisme' (1959) in *Recherches sur la Sexualité* (Janvier 1928 – Août 1932), ed. by José Pierre (Paris: Gallimard, 1990), pp. 208–209.

Breton, André, *L'Art Magique* (Paris: Éditions Phébus, 1991).

Breton, André et al., *Investigating Sex – Surrealist Discussions 1928–1932*, ed. by José Pierre, trans. by Malcom Imrie (London: Verso, 1992).

Breton, André, *Conversations: The Autobiography of Surrealism – With André Parinaud*, trans. by Mark Polizzotti (New York: Marlowe & Company, 1993).

Breton, André, *Communicating Vessels*, trans. by Mary Ann Caws & Geoffrey T. Harris (Lincoln & London: University of Nebraska Press, 1997).

Breton, André, 'Introduction to the discourse on the paucity of reality' (1924–1925) in *Break of Day* (London: University of Nebraska Press, 1999), p. 18.

——————, 'The Automatic Message' (1933) in *Break of Day* (London: University of Nebraska Press, 1999).
Breton, André, *Nadja*, trans. by Richard Howard (London: Penguin, 1999).
Breton, André, *Arcanum 17* (Los Angeles: Green Integer Books, 2004).
Breton, André, 'À la niche les glapisseurs de dieu!' ['To your kennels, curs of God'] (1948), trans. by Guy & Rikki Ducornet in *Surréalisme & Athéisme : A la Niche les Glapisseurs de Dieu !* (Paris: Gingko éditeur, 2006), p. 220.
Breton, André; Acker, Adolphe; Cahun, Claude; Jean, Marcel; Malherbe, Suzanne; Mouton, Georges; Pastoureau, Henri; Péret, Benjamin, 'La Rupture avec "Contre-Attaque"' in *Tracts Surréalistes et Déclarations Collectives 1922–1939*, ed. by José Pierre (Paris: Le terrain vague, 1980), vol. 1.
Caillois, Roger, 'La mante religieuse. De la biologie à la psychanalyse' ['The praying mantis. From biology to psychoanalysis'] in *Minotaure*, no. 5 (1934), pp. 23–26.
Caillois, Roger, 'Mimétisme et psychasthénie légendaire' ['Mimicry and Legendary Psychasthenia'] in *Minotaure*, no. 7 (1935), pp. 5–10.
Dalí, Salvador, 'De la beauté terrifiante et comestible, de l'architecture Modern Style' ['On the terrifying beauty and edible beauty of Modern Style architecture'] in *Minotaure*, nos. 3–4 (1933), p. 76.
Dalí, Salvador, 'Objets Surréalistes' (1931) in *Oui 1* (Paris: Denoël/Gonthier, 1971), p. 178.
Dalí, Salvador, 'Surrealist Objects' (1931) in *Oui 1*, trans. by Yvonne Shafir (Boston, MA: Exact Change, 1998), p. 136.
Desnos, Robert, 'Le Mystère d'Abraham Juif" in *Documents*, no. 5 (1929), p. 236.
Desnos, Robert, 'Rrose Sélavy' (1922–1923) in *Corps et Biens* (Paris: Gallimard, 1953), pp. 31–46.
Éluard, Paul, 'Les Petits Justes IX' in *Capitale de la Douleur* (Paris: Gallimard, 1926), p. 81.
Éluard, Paul, 'Les Dessous d'une Vie – La Dame de Carreau' (1926) in *Donner à Voir* (Paris: Gallimard, 1939), p. 12.
Éluard, Paul, 'Physique de la Poésie II' in *Physique de la Poésie* (Paris: Gallimard, 1939), p. 70.
Ernst, Max, 'Au-delà de la peinture' (1936) in *Max Ernst : Œuvres de 1919 à 1936* (Paris: Éditions des Cahiers d'art, 1937).
Ernst, Max, *Beyond Painting* (1936) (New York: Wittenborn, Scultz, Inc., 1948).
Ernst, Max, *The Hundred Headless Woman (La Femme 100 Têtes)* (New York: George Brazilier, 1981).
Ernst, Max, *Une Semaine de Bonté* (New York: Dover Publications, 1976).
Gourmont, Remy de, 'Le Symbolisme' in *La Revue blanche* (25 juin 1892), pp. 322–323.

Heine, Maurice, 'Note sur un Classement Psycho-Biologique des Paresthésies sexuelles' ['Note on the Psycho-Biological Classification of Sexual Paresthesias'] in *Minotaure*, nos. 3–4 (1933), p. 36.
Heine, Maurice, 'Rétif de la Bretonne et la Femme Féique' ['Rétif de la Bretonne and the Fairy Woman'] in *Minotaure*, no. 6 (1935), pp. 53–56.
Heine, Maurice, 'Eritis sicut Dii' in *Minotaure*, no. 11 (1938), p. 33.
Leiris, Michel, 'A propos de "Musée des sorciers"' in *Documents*, no. 2 (1929), p. 109.
Leiris, Michel, 'Le "Caput Mortuum" ou la Femme de l'Alchimiste' in *Documents*, no. 8 (1930), p. 461.
Leiris, Michel, 'Toiles récentes de Picasso' in *Documents*, no. 2 (1933), pp. 62–64.
Leiris, Michel, 'De Bataille l'impossible à l'impossible Documents' in *Critique* (1956), p. 689.
Masson, André, *Entretiens avec Georges Charbonnier* (Marseille: André Dimanche, 1995), p. 80.
Matta, Roberto da, 'On Emotion' (1954) in *Manifesto: A Century of isms*, ed. by Mary Ann Caws (Lincoln, NE.: University of Nebraska, 2001), p. 493.
Péret, Benjamin, 'Le Noyau de la Comète' (1955) in *L'Anthologie de L'Amour Sublime* (Paris: Albin Michel, 1956).
Péret, Benjamin, 'Je Sublime' (1936) in *Œuvres Complètes* (Paris: Terrain Vague, 1971), vol. II.
Péret, Benjamin, 'La Parole est à Péret' (1942) in *Benjamin Péret*, ed. by Jean-Louis Bédoin (Poitiers: Pierre Seghers, 1972), p. 163.

Theoretical, Psychoanalytical and Philosophical Works

'Hegelianism' in *Routledge Encyclopaedia of Philosophy* v 1.0 (London: Routledge), CD-ROM.
Adorno, Theodor W., 'Looking Back on Surrealism' (1956) in *Notes to Literature*, trans. by Shierry Weber Nicholsen (New York: Columbia University Press, 1991), vol. I, p. 89.
Agrippa von Nettesheim, Heinrich Cornelius (1531), 'Chapter XLV – Of soothsaying, and phrensy' in *Three Books of Occult Philosophy – Third Book of Magic*, trans. by James Freake (Woodbury, MN: Llewellyn Publications: 1992), p. 616.

Allendy, René, *La Table d'Eméraude* (Paris: Chacornac, 1921), p. 24.
Allendy, René, 'A précis' in *La Vie des Lettres et des Arts*, 19 (1924), p. 91.
Baugh, Bruce, *French Hegel: From Surrealism to Postmodernism* (London: Routledge, 2003), p. 1.
Derrida, Jacques, 'Structure, Sign and Play in the Discourse of the Human Sciences' in Victor E. Taylor, Charles E. Winquist, *Postmodernism: Foundational essays* (London: Taylor & Francis, 1998), p. 511 (pp. 504–520).
Edward F. Edinger, *Anatomy of the Psyche – Alchemical Symbolism in Psychotherapy* (La Salle, Illinois: Open Court Publishing, 1985).
Fourier, Charles, 'Le Nouveau Monde Amoureux', in *Œuvres Complètes*, ed. by Simone Debout-Oleszkiewicz (Paris: Anthropos, 1967), vol. VII, p. 34.
Freud, Sigmund, 'Three Essays on Sexuality – Summary' (1905) in *The Standard Edition of the Complete Psychological Works of Sigmund Freud – A Case of Hysteria, Three Essays on Sexuality, and other Works*, trans. by James Strachey in collaboration with Anna Freud (London: Hogarth Press, 1953), vol. VII, p. 238.
———, 'Three Essays in Sexuality – II Infantile Sexuality' (1905) in *The Standard Edition of the Complete Psychological Works of Sigmund Freud – A Case of Hysteria, Three Essays on Sexuality, and other Works*, trans. by James Strachey in collaboration with Anna Freud (London: Hogarth Press, 1953), vol. VII, p. 206.
———, '"Civilised" Sexual Morality' (1908) in *Standard Edition of the Complete Psychological Works of Sigmund Freud – Jensen's 'Gradiva', and Other Works*, trans. by James Strachey in collaboration with Anna Freud (London: Hogarth Press, 1959), vol. IX, p. 187.
———, 'Five Lectures on Psycho-Analysis – Psychogenic Disturbance of Vision' (1909) in *Standard Edition of the Complete Psychological Works of Sigmund Freud – Five Lectures on Psycho-analysis, Leonardo da Vinci, and Other Works*, trans. by James Strachey in collaboration with Anna Freud (London: Hogarth Press, 1957), vol. XI.
———, 'Leonardo da Vinci and a Memory of his Childhood' (1910) in *Standard Edition of the Complete Psychological Works of Sigmund Freud – Five Lectures on Psycho-analysis, Leonardo da Vinci, and Other Works,* trans. by James Strachey in collaboration with Anna Freud (London: Hogarth Press, 1957), p. 97.
———, 'On Narcissism: An Introduction' (1914) in *Standard Edition of the Complete Psychological Works of Sigmund Freud – On the History of the Psycho-analytic Movement – Papers on Meta-psychology, and Other Works*, trans. by James Strachey in collaboration with Anna Freud (London: Hogarth Press, 1955), vol. XIV.

———, 'The Uncanny' (1919), in *The Standard Edition of the Complete Psychological Works of Sigmund Freud,* trans. under editorship of James Strachey in collaboration with Anna Freud (London: Hogarth Press, 1955), vol. XVII, p. 249.
———, 'Two Encyclopaedia Articles' – 'B – The Libido Theory' (1922) in *The Standard Edition of the Complete Psychological Works of Sigmund Freud – Beyond the Pleasure Principle, Group Psychology, and Other Works*, trans. under editorship of James Strachey in collaboration with Anna Freud (London: Hogarth Press, 1955), vol. XVIII, p. 256.
———, 'The ego and the id' (1923) in *Standard Edition of the Complete Psychological Works of Sigmund Freud – The Ego and the Id, and Other Works,* trans. by James Strachey in collaboration with Anna Freud (London: Hogarth Press, 1961), vol. IXX, p. 46.
———, 'An Autobiographical Study' in *Standard Edition of the Complete Psychological Works – An Autobiographical Study, Inhibitions, Symptoms and Anxiety, the Question of Lay Analysis, and Other Works*, trans. by James Strachey in collaboration with Anna Freud (London: Hogarth Press, 1959), vol. XX, p. 56.
———, 'Civilisation and Its Discontents' (1930) in *The Standard Edition of the Complete Psychological Works of Sigmund Freud – The Future of an Illusion, Civilisation and its Discontents, and Other Works*, trans. by James Strachey (London: Hogarth Press, 1961), vol. XXI.
———, 'Why War?' (1931) in *The Standard Edition of the Complete Psychological Works of Sigmund Freud – New Introductory Lectures on Psycho-analysis and Other Works* (1932–1936) (London: Hogarth Press, 1964.), vol. XXII, pp. 211–212.
———, The Acquisition and the Control of Fire' (1931) in *The Standard Edition of the Complete Psychological Works of Sigmund Freud – New Introductory Lectures on Psycho-analysis and Other Works* (1932–1936) (London: Hogarth Press, 1964.), vol. XXII, p. 188.
———, 'New Introductory Lectures' (1932) in *The Standard Edition of the Complete Psychological Works of Sigmund Freud – New Introductory Lectures on Psycho-analysis and Other Works* (1932–1936) (London: Hogarth Press, 1964), vol. XXII, pp. 64–65.
Freud, Sigmund, 'Three essays on the theory of sexuality' (1905), trans. by James Strachey, in *On Sexuality: 'Three Essays on the Theory of Sexuality' and Other Works*, ed. by Angela Richards (Harmondsworth: Penguin Books, 1977), p. 69.
Gay, Peter, *Freud – A Life for our Time* (London: Norton, 1988), pp. 534–544.
Heidegger, Martin, 'The Thing' (1950) in *Poetry, Language, Thought* (New York: Harper & Row, 1971), pp. 163–186.
Jung, Carl G., *Letters*, ed. By G. Adler and A. Jaffé (Princeton, NJ: Princeton University Press, 1974), vol. 1, p. 171.

Jung, Carl G., *Synchronicity – An Acausal Connecting Principle*, trans. by R.F.C. Hull (Princeton, NJ: Princeton University Press, 1973), p. 38.

Lacan, Jacques, *Le Séminaire de Jacques Lacan – D'un AUTRE à l'autre* (Paris: Seuil, 1968–1969), vol. XVI, pp. 225–226.

Lacan, Jacques, *Le Séminaire de Jacques Lacan – L'Éthique de la Psychanalyse* (1959–1960), ed. by Jacques-Alain Miller (Paris: Seuil, 1986).

Lacan, Jacques, *The Seminar of Jacques Lacan, Ethics of Psychoanalysis* (1959–1960), ed. by Jacques-Alain Miller (London: Routledge, 1992), vol. VII.

Marcuse, Herbert, *Eros and Civilization* (Boston, MA: Beacon Press, 1955).

Marcuse, Herbert, *One Dimensional Man – Studies in the Ideology of Advanced Industrial Society* (London: Routledge & Kegan Paul Ltd., 1964).

Marcuse, Herbert, *The Aesthetic Dimension – Toward a Critique of Marxist Aesthetics* (London: Macmillan Press, 1978).

Marx, Karl and Engels, Friedrich, 'The German Ideology' (1845–1846) in *The Collected Works of Marx and Engels* (New York: International Publishers, 1976), vol. 5.

Marx, Karl and Engels, Friedrich, 'The German Ideology – Extract' (1845–1846) in *Beyond the Body Proper: Reading the Anthropology of Material Life*, ed. by Margaret M. Lock and Judith Farquhar (Durham and London: Duke University Press, 2007), p. 114.

Myers, Frederic W. H., *Human Personality and Its Survival of Bodily Death* (New York: Longmans, Green & Co, 1904).

Pfister, Oskar, *Psychoanalysis in the Service of Education*, trans by Dr Charles Rockwell Payne and Dr F. Gschwind (London: H. Kimpton, 1922).

Proudhon, Pierre-Joseph, 'Du principe de l'art et de sa destination sociale (Nouvelle édition)' in *Œuvres posthumes de P.-J. Proudhon* (Paris: Librairie internationale, A. Lacroix & ce, 1866–1875).

Roudinesco, Elisabeth, *La Bataille de Cent Ans – Histoire de la Psychanalyse en France 2, 1925–1985* (Paris: Seuil, 1986), Part 1.

Roudinesco, Elisabeth, *Jacques Lacan & Co: A History of Psychoanalysis in France, 1925–1985*, trans. Jeffrey Mehlman (Chicago: University of Chicago Press, 1990), Part 1.

Sim, Stuart, *The Routledge Companion to Postmodernism: Third Edition* (London: Routledge, 2011), p. 237.

Walker, Barbara G., *The Woman's Encyclopaedia of Myths and Secrets* (San Francisco: Harper & Row, 1987), pp. 18–22 and pp. 436–449.

Surrealist (and Art) Criticism and History

Audoin, Philippe, *Sur Georges Bataille* (Minneapolis: Actual, 1987), p. 34.

Balakian, Anna Elizabeth, *Surrealism* (Chicago: University of Chicago Press, 1986).

Ballabriga, Michel, *Sémiotique du surréalisme: André Breton ou la cohérence* (Toulouse: Presses universitaires du Mirail, 1995), pp. 153-154.

Baudry, Jean-Louis, 'Pour une matériologie (fin)' in *Tel Quel* 45 (Spring, 1971).

Benjamin, Walter, 'Surrealism – The Last Snapshot of the European Intelligentsia' (1928) in *Reflections – Essays, Aphorisms, Autobiographical Writings*, trans. by Edmund Jephcott, ed. by Peter Demetz (New York: Schocken Books, 1978).

Caws, Mary Ann, 'Péret's "Amour sublime" – Just another "Amour Fou"?' in *The French Review*, No. 2 (Nov, 1966), vol. 40.

Coucha, Nadia, *Surrealism and the Occult* (Oxford: Mandrake, 1991), p. 118.

Crastre, Victor, 'André Breton et la liberté' in *André Breton*, ed. by Marc Eigeldinger (Neuchâtel: Editions de la Baconnière, 1970), p. 149.

Dixon, Laurinda S., *Alchemical Imagery in Bosch's Garden of Earthly Delights* (Ann Arbor, MI: UMI Research, 1981).

Dubief, Henri, 'Témoignage sur Contre-Attaque' in *Textures*, no. 6 (Brussels: Jan, 1970), pp. 56–57.

Ducornet, Guy, *Surréalisme & Athéisme : A la Niche les Glapisseurs de Dieu !* (Paris: Gingko éditeur, 2006).

Eigeldinger, Marc, 'Poésie et langage alchimique chez André Breton' in *Mélusine – Occulte-Occultation* (Lausanne: L'Age d'Homme, 1981), vol. II, p. 33.

Fabre, Gérard, 'Between tame dog and wild wolf a twilight zone' (1987), trans. by R. F. M. Dexter, in *Focus* on *Minotaure*, pp. 173–185.

Foster, Hal, 'Postmodernism: A Preface' in *The Anti-Aesthetic: Essays on Postmodern Culture*, ed. by Hal Foster (Seattle, WA: Bay Press, 1983).

Foster, Hal, *Compulsive Beauty*, Series: October Books (London: MIT Press, 1993).

Gauthier, Mona, *La jouissance prise aux mots ou La sublimation chez Georges Bataille* (Montréal: L'Harmattan, 1996), pp. 129–130.

Hager, S. Lee, 'Surrealism, Alchemy and the Northern Renaissance' (University of California, 2000). <http://www.csuchico.edu/art/contrapposto/Contrapposto97/Pages/Lee1.html> (now available only as archive: <http://archive.li/0bY0K>) accessed 1 April 2001.

Harris, Stephen, *Surrealist Art and Thought in the 1930s: Art, Politics, and the Psyche* (Cambridge: Cambridge University Press, 2004).

Hollier, Denis, *Against Architecture: The Writings of Georges Bataille*, trans. by Betsy Wing (London: MIT Press, 1989).

Houdebine, Jean-Louis, 'Méconnaissance de la Psychanalyse dans le Discours Surréaliste' in *Tel Quel* 46 (Summer, 1971).

Hussey, Andrew, *The Inner Scar: The Mysticism of Georges Bataille* (Amsterdam: Rodopi, 2000).

Krauss, Rosalind, 'Corpus Delecti' in *L'Amour Fou – Photography and Surrealism* (Hong Kong: Cross River Press, 1985), p. 85.

Krauss, Rosalind, 'No more play' in *The Originality of the Avant-Garde and other Modernist Myths* (London: MIT Press, 1987), p. 61.

Krauss, Rosalind E., 'Cadaver' in *Formless : A User's Guide*, written by Rosalind E. Krauss and Yve-Alain Bois (New York: Zone, 1997), p. 66.

Krauss, Rosalind, Foster, Hal, Bois, Yve-Alain, Buchloh, Benjamin H.D., *Art Since 1900: Modernism, Antimodernism, Postmodernism* (New York: Thames & Hudson, 2004).

Lala, Marie-Christine, 'Bataille et Breton : le malentendu considérable' (1992) in *Surréalisme et Philosophie* (Paris: Éditions du Centre Pompidou, 1992).

Lechte, John, 'Surrealism and the practice of writing, or the 'case' of Bataille' in *Bataille – Writing the Sacred*, ed. by Carolyn Bailey Gill (London: Routledge, 1995).

Legge, Elizabeth M., *Max Ernst: The Psychoanalytic Sources* (Ann Arbor: UMI Research, 1989), p. 87.

Legrand, Gérard, 'Breton et l'inauguration philosophique du surréalisme' in *Surréalisme et Philosophie* (Paris: Éditions du Centre Pompidou, 1992), p. 14.

Lindenberg, Daniel, '"Hypermatérialisme" et gnose' in *Surréalisme et Philosophie*, p. 22.

Löwy, Michael, 'Magie proti posvátnu' ['Magic against the sacred'] in *Analogon* (Prague, 1999), p. 8.

Lusty, Natalya, *Surrealism, Feminism, Psychoanalysis* (Aldershot: Ashgate, 2007).

Mahon, Alyce, *Surrealism and the Politics of Eros, 1938–1968* (London: Thames & Hudson, 2005).

Mayoux, Jehan, 'Benjamin Péret la fourchette coupante' ['Benjamin Péret the sharp blade'] in *La liberté une et divisible, Œuvres Complètes*, vol. V (Ussel: Éditions Peralta, 1979), p. 103 (pp. 99–128).

McGuinness, Patrick, *Poetry and Radical Politics in Fin-de-siècle France from Anarchism to Action Française* (Oxford: OUP, 2015).

Morel, Jean-Pierre, and Lewis, Philip, 'Breton and Freud' in *Diacritics*, vol. 2, no. 2 (Summer, 1972), p. 23.

Mundy, Jennifer, 'Letters of Desire' in *Surrealism; Desire Unbound*, ed. by Jennifer Mundy and Dawn Ades (London: Tate Publishing, 2001).

Parijanine, Maurice, 'Mystique Surréaliste' in *Les Humbles* (June, 1933), p. 3–10.

Pierre, José, 'Breton, André and/or "*Minotaure*."' trans. by André Marling, in *Focus on Minotaure: The Animal-Headed Review*, ed. by Charles Goerg (Geneva: Musée d'Art et d'Histoire, 1987), p. 99.

Polizzotti, Mark, *Revolution of the Mind : The Life of André Breton* (London: Bloomsbury, 1995).

Reszler, André, *L'Esthétique anarchiste* (Paris: Presses Universitaires de France, 1973).

Richardson, Michael, *Georges Bataille* (London: Routledge, 1994), p. 26.

Roche, Geoffrey, 'Black Sun: Bataille on Sade' in *Janus Head* (Amherst, NY: Trivium Publications, 2006), 9(1), p. 167.

Rosemont, Franklin, 'Herbert Marcuse and Surrealism' in *Arsenal* 4 (1989), 31–38; see also <http://www.marcuse.org/herbert/pubs/70spubs/73surreal/arsenalindex.htm>.

Rottenberg, Pierre, 'Esquisse Cartographique du Mouvement: Surréalisme', in *Tel Quel* 46

Sala, Carlo, *Max Ernst et la Démarche Onirique* (Paris: Klincksieck, 1970), p. 53.

Schwarz, Arturo, *Die Surrealististen* (Frankfurt am Main: Kulturgesellschaft Frankfurt mbH & Nuove edizioni Gabriele Mazzotta, 1989), p. 22.

Schwarz, Arturo, 'L'Amour est l'Érotisme – De Quelques Correspondances entre la Pensée Surréaliste et Celles de l'Alchimie et du Tantrisme' in *Mélusine – Le Livre Surréaliste*, ed. Henri Béhar (Lausanne: L'Age d'Homme, 1982), vol. 4, pp. 179–202.

Surya, Michel, *Georges Bataille: An Intellectual Biography*, trans. by Krzysztof Fijalkowski and Michael Richardson (London: Verso, 2002).

Székely, Michael, 'Text, trembling: Bataille, Breton and Surrealist eroticism' in *Textual Practice*, 19:1 (2005), pp. 113–129.

Szulakowska, Urszula, 'The Paracelsian Magus in German Art: Joseph Beuys and Rebecca Horn' in *Art & Alchemy*, ed. by Jacob Wamberg (Copenhagen: Museum Tusculanum Press, 2006), p. 173.

Tythacott, Louise, *Surrealism and the Exotic* (New York: Taylor & Francis, 2003), p. 61.

Wahl, Jean, *Entretiens sur le Surréalisme*, ed. by Ferdinand Alquié (Paris: Mouton, 1968), pp. 167–168.

Warlick, M. E., 'Max Ernst's Alchemical Novel: "Une Semaine de bonté"' in *Art Journal*, vol. 46, no. 1, *Mysticism and Occultism in Modern Art* (Spring, 1987).

Images (paintings, photos, sculptures, etc.)

Bellmer, Hans, 'Poupée: Variations sur le montage d'une mineure articulée' / 'Doll: Variations on the Montage of an Articulated Minor' in *Minotaure*, no. 6 (1935).

Ernst, Max, 'Chaque émeute sanglante la fera vivre pleine de grâce et de vérité' / 'Each bloody riot will help her to live in grace and truth' in *La Femme 100 Têtes* (1929).

Ernst, Max, 'Rome' in *La Femme 100 Têtes* (1929).
Ernst, Max, images (untitled) from 'Sunday – Mud' in *Une Semaine de Bonté* (1934).
Ernst, Max, image (untitled) from 'Saturday – Desire or the great one times one' in *Une Semaine de Bonté* (1934).
Ernst, Max, image (untitled) from 'Tuesday – Fire' in *Une Semaine de Bonté* (1934).
Ernst, Max, image (untitled) from 'Wednesday – Blood' in *Une Semaine de Bonté* (1934).
Ernst, Max, image (untitled) from 'Thurday – Blackness' in *Une Semaine de Bonté* (1934).
Ernst, Max, image 'Loplop et la Belle Jardinière' / 'Loplop and the Beautiful Gardener' from *La Femme 100 Têtes* (1929).
Ernst, Max, *Les Hommes N'en Sauront Rien / Men Shall Know Nothing of This* (1923).
Ernst, Max, *The Robing of the Bride* (1940).
Flamel, Nicolas, Two Illustrations from *Exposition of the Hieroglyphical Figures* in 'Le Mystère d'Abraham Juif' by Robert Desnos, *Documents* (1925).
Fludd, Robert, 'The Day and Night of the Microcosm' in *Le Musée des Sorciers, Mages et Alchimistes* by Grillot de Givry (1929).
Giacometti, Alberto, *Boule Suspendue / Suspended Ball* (1930–1931).
Gichtel, Johann Georg, image (untitled) from *Theosophia Practica* (1736) in *Documents*, no. 2 (1929).
Krafft-Ebing, Richard von, Taxonomy of "Perversions" or Sexual Paresthesias (diagram) from 'Note on the Psycho-Biological Classification of Sexual Paresthesias' / 'Note sur un Classement Psycho-Biologique des Paresthésies sexuelles' by Maurice Heine in *Minotaure*, nos. 3–4 (1933).
Masson, André, *La Métamorphose des Amants / The Metamorphosis of Lovers* (1938).
Matta, Roberto, *Octrui* (1947).
Matta, Roberto, *Science, conscience et patience du Vitreur / Science, Conscience and Patience of the Glacier* (1944).
Picasso, Pablo, 'Le Plumeau et la Corne' / 'The Feather Duster and the Bull's Horn' in *Minotaure*, no. 1 (1933).
Ray, Man, Photo of spoon in *Nadja* by André Breton (1928).
Valdés Leal, Juan de, *Finis Gloriae Mundi / End of the World's Glory* (1660).
Van Gogh, Vincent, *La Nuit Étoilée / The Starry Night* (1889).
Unknown Photographer, Photo of Mount Teide, Tenerife.
Unknown artist, Illustration of an anamorphoscope.
Unknown Photographer, Photo of cylindrical object purchased at flea-market in *Nadja* by André Breton (1928).
Unknown Photographer, Photo of glove in *Nadja* by André Breton (1928).

Index

Acéphale, 19, 61, 64–68
Adorno, Theodor, 81, 189
Aesthetic Dimension (*The*), 9, 123, 125, 142
agalma, 259
Âge d'Or (*L'*), 17, 135–38, 151
Agrippa, Heinrich Cornelius, 205
alchemical operation, 165, 173, 175, 210
alchemical symbolism, 156, 181, 183, 210
alchemists, 119, 155, 160–62, 166, 193, 198, 200, 203
alchemy, 14, 154–56, 158, 160, 162–63, 165–68, 171, 173, 175, 185–87, 193–94, 196–97, 199–200, 211, 213
  visual, 19, 185–86
  of the word, 19, 153, 167, 186
Alleau, René, 159
Allendy, René, 164, 194
altération, 83, 150
alterity, 44, 93, 208
Amour Fou (*L'*) (*Mad Love*), 11, 39, 70, 75, 80, 115, 130–31, 134–36, 143, 221–25, 227–28, 239–40, 246, 248, 271
anamorphoscope, 226
anamorphosis, 226, 229–30, 234
Anarchism, 120
Anniversary of Hysteria International Surrealist Exhibition, 105
Anthologie de l'Humour Noir (*Anthology of Black Humour*), 70, 73, 97–98, 100–101, 163, 257
antinomies, 35–36, 40, 44, 70, 73, 165, 173, 197, 213, 263
Arcane 17 (*Arcanum 17*), 8, 33, 113, 157–58, 176, 178
Art Magique (*L'*), 153, 164, 167, 172–73, 175, 177, 179–80, 196, 198–99, 203
Association of Revolutionary Writers and Artists, 56
Atheology, 102
automatism, 54, 88, 139–40

base materialism, 11, 44, 50, 74, 80, 95, 199
Bataille
  Acéphale, *see* Acéphale
  altération, see altération
  Atheology, *see* Atheology
  base materialism, *see* base materialism
  excrement philosopher, *see* excrement philosopher
  excrement, *see* excrement
  Georges Bataille, 11–12, 19, 41–45, 47, 49–53, 57–71, 74–76, 81, 83, 87–105, 150, 197–99, 235–36, 241–45, 264–67
  Le Gros Orteil, see Gros Orteil
  Histoire de l'Œil, see Histoire de l'Œil
  inner experience, *see* inner experience
  Solar Anus, see Solar Anus
  transgression, 239
Bataillean philosophy, 74, 77, 83, 101, 237, 241, 265
Baudelaire, Charles, 118, 127–28, 132
Baudry, Jean-Louis, 34
Bellmer
  dolls (*poupées*), 81, 83–85
  Hans Bellmer, 12, 50, 76, 81–84, 265

Benjamin, Walter, 120, 157, 166, 230
binaries, 154, 266
bird, 183, 192, 211, 218
black humour, 19, 50, 90, 98, 100–101, 105, 257
blasphemy, 162, 246, 256
Bois, Yve-Alain, 47, 54, 74–75, 87
Bosch, Hieronymus, 153–54, 173–74, 177, 180–82, 184–85
Boule Suspendue, 78–80
Bounoure, Vincent, 14, 159
bourgeois art, 127–28
Breton
  Amour Fou, see Amour Fou
  André Breton, 2–12, 21–27, 33–40, 43–47, 49–59, 83–89, 91–95, 100–121, 126–44, 157–70, 175–81, 194–203, 227–37, 239–48, 263–71
  Anthologie de l'Humour Noir, see Anthologie de l'Humour Noir
  Arcane 17, see Arcane 17
  Art Magique, see Art Magique
  capillary tissue, *see* capillary tissue
  Le Château Étoilé, see Château Étoilé
  Communicating Vessels, see Vases Communicants
  convulsive beauty, *see* convulsive beauty
  late Breton, 44, 159
  Mad Love, see Amour Fou
  Manifestoes of Surrealism, see Manifestoes of Surrealism
  Nadja, see Nadja
  para-erotic sensations, *see* para-erotic sensations
  Pour un art révolutionnaire indépendant, see Pour un art révolutionnaire indépendant
  Second Manifesto of Surrealism, see Second Manifesto of Surrealism
  sublime point, *see* sublime point
  Surrealism and Painting, see Surrealism and Painting
  Vases Communicants, see Vases Communicants
bricolage, 263–64, 269
Bull's Horn (Picasso), 85–86
Buñuel
  L'Âge d'Or, see Âge d'Or
  Luis Buñuel, 135, 137

Cadavre (*Un*), 43, 49
Cahun, Claude, 63
Caillois, Roger, 81, 148
capillary tissue, 37, 39, 271
capitalism, 28, 57–58, 123, 136, 269–70
caput mortuum, 155–58, 175, 197, 208–9, 211, 218
castration, 30–31, 34
chaos, 58, 226, 270
Château Étoilé (*Le*), 70–71, 75
chose en soi, la, see Ding an sich
Christianity, 35, 60, 64, 243, 247, 256
church, 35, 65, 123, 135, 161, 196, 220, 240, 242, 256–57
civilisation, 4, 6–7, 18, 28, 40, 53, 68, 90–91, 106, 115, 130, 215, 252
  non-repressive, 107
  unhappy, 5, 107
Civilisation and its Discontents, 4, 6, 90, 106, 111, 252
communism, 57, 61, 270
consciousness, 36, 92, 102, 116–17, 123–25, 127, 133–34, 137, 139, 142–43, 146–48, 269
Contre-Attaque, 54, 57, 59–61, 63–64, 69, 72, 94, 98, 105
convulsive beauty, 19, 42, 79–80, 104, 106, 108, 129–32, 143–44, 148, 151, 177, 269
corps morcelé, 259
Couilles Enragées (*Mad Balls*), 256, 258

counter-consciousness, 125, 151, 153, 202, 269
creation *ex nihilo*, 216, 218, 221, 223, 226, 230, 255
Crevel, René, 56

Dalí
  edible beauty, *see* edible beauty
  Modern Style, *see* Modern Style
  Salvador Dalí, 1, 12, 50, 76–78, 135, 148, 265
Daniel, Arnaud, 255
dead head, 155, 158, 197, 208
death, 30–31, 40, 43, 60–61, 65–67, 80–81, 83, 98, 101, 136, 138–41, 144, 146, 158–59, 238–39
death instinct, 136, 138–40, 142, *see also* Thanatos
debauchery, 101
Decadence, 120
decay, 173, 183, 194, 196, 209
derangement of the senses, 166, 187
Derrida, Jacques, 264
Descartes, René, 173
Desnos,
  Robert Desnos, 12, 154, 169–70, 172, 199–202
  Rrose Sélavy, see Rrose Sélavy
desublimation, 3–4, 9, 16–17, 43, 50, 81, 105, 125–26, 172, 189
  artistic, 17
  desublimatory art, 16, 68, 81
detours, 13, 193, 219–20, 227, 236
Détraquées (*Les*), 229
dialectical materialism, 28–29, 31, 37, 44, 56, 118, 264
dialectics, 36–38, 88, 146, 154, 213–14, 264
  Hegelian, 35
  master-slave, 38
  reinterpreted, 117
  and resolution, 36, 39–40, 73
Ding, das, 217–21, 223–24, 226, 229–30, 233–34, 236–38, 241, 243, 250, 255, 259
Ding an sich, das (the thing in itself), 217–18
divine, 42, 161, 194, 203–5, 207, 239, 242, 251, 270
Documents Group, 79, 197
Duché, Jean, 260
Ducornet, Guy, 14, 159, 161–62

edible beauty, 76
eggs, 53, 171, 175–76, 183, 255
ego, 2–3, 6, 12, 31, 100, 108–10, 217, 219
élan vital, 153, 178
Éluard, Paul, 12, 167, 216, 220, 233–36
energy, 3, 5, 41, 52, 116, 143–44, 149–50, 269
  libidinal, 5, 19, 112–14, 215, 219
engagement, 38, 50, 54, 101, 116, 118, 211, 214, 265
Engels, Friedrich, 11, 22, 31–32, 45, 115, 248
Eritis sicut Dii, 75
Ernst
  Hundred-Headless Woman, see Hundred-Headless Woman
  Max Ernst, 12, 76, 81, 127, 154, 158, 164, 185–93, 195–96, 209–11, 235, 265, 269
  visual alchemy, *see* alchemy, visual
Eros, 8–9, 11, 17–18, 106–7, 110–15, 125, 127, 129–30, 132, 135–37, 139–42, 144, 151, 169, 269
Eros and Civilization, 121
erotic instincts, 206, 215
eroticism, 13, 17, 50, 65–66, 68, 90–94, 104–5, 144, 239, 249
evil, 6, 52, 71, 97, 177, 180–81, 209, 238
excrement, 88, 99
excrement philosopher, 44, 89
Existentialism, 103

fascism, 28, 57, 60–61, 64, 118, 270
Femme 100 têtes (La), see Hundred-Headless Woman
ferula, 160–61
Flamel
    Hieroglyphical Figures, see Hieroglyphical Figures, Exposition of the
    Nicolas Flamel, 160, 200
flânerie, 13, 221
Flaubert, Gustave, 177–79, 181
Fludd, Robert, 200, 203–5
foreclosure, 24, 26–27
Formless, 43, 75, 85, 267
Foster, Hal, 42–43, 81, 267–68
Fourier, Charles, 45, 58, 113–14, 246
France, 57, 120, 159, 162, 164, 220
Freud
    Anna Freud, 3, 5–6, 31, 42, 215
    Civilisation and its Discontents, see Civilisation and its Discontents
    the *id, see id*
    Pleasure Principle, *see* Pleasure Principle
    Sigmund Freud, 3–6, 22–23, 25–26, 31, 38, 90, 106–7, 109–11, 115, 130–31, 133, 161, 164–65, 206–7, 214–19
    super ego, *see* super ego
    uncanny, *see* uncanny
Freudian theory, 15, 31, 77, 107–8, 163
Fulcanelli, 159

Germany, 32, 155–56
Giacometti
    Alberto Giacometti, 12, 44, 50, 76–80, 89, 224, 265
    Boule Suspendue, see Boule Suspendue
Givry, Grillot de, 200, 203–4
gnosis, 46, 197
God, 64–66, 101–2, 104, 161, 169, 176, 187, 195, 204–5, 207, 209, 240, 248, 259
Goethe, 12, 128
golems, 85
grace, 187–88, 193, 239–40, 248
Great Work (*magnum opus*), 167, 186, 189
Gros Orteil (Le), (*The Big Toe*), 74–75

happiness, 7, 121–22, 251
hasard objectif, see objective chance
Hegel, G.W.F., 21, 31–33, 35–39, 45–46, 101, 263
Hegelianism, 21, 39, 64, 264
Heidegger, Martin, 217
Heine
    Eritis sicut Dii, see Eritis sicut Dii
    Maurice Heine, 12, 58, 71–75, 98, 105
Heraclitus, 36, 45
Hermes Trismegistus, 154, 170
hermeticism, 146, 154, 162–63, 185–86, 197, 199, 213
Hieroglyphical Figures, Exposition of the, 200–201
Histoire de l'Œil, 53, 242, 255–56
Hollier, Denis, 2, 12, 41–42, 47
homosexuality, 44, 72, 93
Houdebine, Jean-Louis, 22–27, 44
humour, 98–102
    objective, 101
Hundred-Headless Woman, 209
Huysmans, Joris-Karl, 243

Icarus, 52
    Icarian downfall, 61
    flight, 52
    idealism, 19, 70
id, 3, 18, 31, 70, 108–10, 169, 183, 215, 258
idealisation of the female subject, 231
idealism, 13, 22, 25, 34, 37–39, 43, 64, 248, 265–66
    absolute, 21, 36, 46, 263
    Hegelian, 21, 28, 32, 155
    repressive, 19, 34

idealist, 2, 18–21, 43, 45, 47, 50, 53, 67, 84, 101, 248, 261
imagination, 7, 9, 14, 16, 28, 40, 54, 66, 75, 79, 117, 119, 121–22, 165–66, 168, 171
inner experience, 68–69, 92–94, 101, 244
instincts, 3, 5–6, 50, 70, 77, 83, 89–90, 104, 114, 129, 136, 139–41, 147, 151, 249
    aggressive, 108, 149–50
    destructive, 19, 144, 147
    sexual, 43, 52, 113, 136, 140, 143
interior revolution, *see* revolution, interior
Investigating Sex, see Recherches sur la sexualité

Jameson, Frederic, 267
Je Sublime, 170–71
jouissance, 134, 208, 238
Juif, Abraham, 200–201
Jung, Carl, 12, 14, 164–65, 193

Kant, 84, 209, 217, 238–39
    Ding an sich, see Ding an sich
Kojève, Alexandre, 39
Krafft-Ebing, Richard von, 73
Krauss, Rosalind E., 42–43, 79, 267

Lacan
    agalma, *see* agalma
    corps morcelé, see corps morcelé
    das Ding, see Ding, das
    jouissance, see jouissance
    petit objet a, see petit objet a
    Jacques Lacan, 12–13, 22, 214–23, 226, 229–32, 234, 237–39, 241–42, 244, 249–50, 255, 258–59, 270
Lacanian theory, 13, 214, 228, 240, 270
lack, 7, 13, 96–98, 100–101, 105, 130, 135, 139, 157, 214, 217, 250, 254, 257, 269–70
Lamba, Jacqueline, 222
language
    critical, 264
    desire-laden, 125
    freeing, 153, 171
    poetic, 160
    symbolic, 126, 153, 167
law, the, 237–39, 243
Leiris, Michel, 12, 49, 88, 199, 202, 208
lèse divinité, 209
Lévi-Strauss, Claude, 134, 264
liberation
    sexual, 10
    social, 8
libertinism, 44, 235, 258
    condemning, 72
    systemised, 235
    unquestioning, 93
libido, 11, 31, 113–14, 189, 195, 205, 214, 219, 271
Libido Theory, 215
love, 8, 27, 75, 136, 172, 186, 194, 225, 228, 232–33, 235–36, 240, 244, 246, 248
    carnal, 225, 245–46
    courtly, 20, 222, 251, 255
    elective, 105, 115, 235, 237, 258, 264, 270
    physical, 27, 75, 242, 258, 265
    spiritual, 246
    sublimated, 10, 16, 26, 245
    sublime (*amour sublime*), 246–55, 258, 260
    terrestrial, 194, 211, 220, 248
love object, 13, 20, 31, 216, 219–20, 222–23, 226–27, 230, 232, 234, 236–37, 240, 249–50, 258–60
    anonymous, 234

female, 244
lost, 80, 233, 237, 270
unique, 228
veiled, 218
love poetry, 20, 233, 244, 253, 255
love poets, 216, 255
Löwy, Michael, 14, 159, 166
Lucifer, 8, 34, 205, 240
Luciferianism, 155, 176, 240

macrocosm, 66, 170, 194, 198, 204, 269
Mad Love, see Amour Fou
madness, 117, 208, 221
magic, 164, 167, 172, 184, 186, 198
Magritte, René, 64
Manifestoes of Surrealism, 25, 28, 37, 40, 54–55, 84, 108, 123–24, 129, 132, 137–38, 163, 198, 200–201, 218, 220
Maoism, 22, 31, 41, 267
Marcuse
The Aesthetic Dimension, see Aesthetic Dimension
Eros and Civilization, see Eros and Civilization
Herbert Marcuse, 4, 8–9, 11–13, 19, 90, 104–7, 110–15, 121–28, 132–34, 142, 214, 269
model of aesthetic sublimation and desublimation, 125
model of sublimation and desublimation, 125
theory of non-repressive sublimation, 8
marvellous, the (*le merveilleux*), 39, 202–3
Marx, Karl, 22, 31–32, 36, 45, 121, 155–56
Marxism, 7, 17, 22, 28, 33, 46, 107, 118, 125, 127, 154–55, 264
Marxist
aesthetics, 9
principles, 155
revolution, 55, 118
terminology, 33
masking, 77
of body, 269
of characters, 192
facial, 269
masochism, 73, 81, 83
Masson, André, 12, 144, 146–47
materialism, 14, 37, 266
Matta, Roberto, 12, 139–43, 149, 265
Medievalism, 173
Meister Eckhardt, 36
metamorphosis, 144, 146–47, 157, 173, 176
metaphor, 17, 53, 78, 211, 218, 223, 228, 230, 239, 256
metonymy, 53, 228, 255, 259
microcosm, 170, 193, 197, 203–5
mimicry, 148
Minotaur (mythical), 70, 89
Minotaure (journal), 58, 68–71, 73–76, 79–82, 85–89, 148, 215, 265
Modern Style, 76
modernism, 267–68
montage, 81, 154
Moreau, Gustave, 243
Mount Teide, 224–25
Muzard, Suzanne, 222, 231–32
Myers, Frederic W. H., 13, 22–26
myth, 18, 49–50, 57, 60, 62–63, 97, 103–4, 158, 162, 230

Nadja, 103, 130–31, 222, 227, 229–32
Nazism, 60–61
Nerval, Gérard de, 202
Nietzsche, Friedrich, 12, 58, 60–61, 63, 184
nigredo, 173, 175, 197
Northern Renaissance, 185

objective chance (*hasard objectif*), 221–22, 237
objects
fetishised, 228
found (*trouvailles*), 222–23, 226, 237, 270
lost, 219
love, *see* love object
missing, 228
polysemic, 86
primitive, 223
symbolic, 13, 50, 77, 87, 265
occultism, 18, 36, 158–59, 166, 189, 202–3, 205, 207, 210
October group, 2, 4, 38, 45, 47, 74, 85, 156, 265–66
old mole, *see vieille taupe*
Oppenheim, Meret, 1
Orphic egg, 175
Osiris, 157

Paracelsus, 200, 205
para-erotic sensations, 134, 199
paresthesia, 72–73
Parinaud, André, 10, 35
PCF (*Parti Communiste Français*), 55–57, 129, 248
Association of Revolutionary Writers and Artists, *see* Association of Revolutionary Writers and Artists
Percé rock, 33
Péret
Benjamin Péret, 12, 63, 106, 163, 170–71, 216, 220, 246–53, 255–58, 260, 270
Couilles Enragées, see Couilles Enragées
Je Sublime, see Je Sublime
Mad Balls, see Couilles Enragées
sublime love (*amour sublime*), *see* love, sublime
perversion, 5, 41, 44, 58, 60, 71–73, 76–77, 79, 83, 87, 91, 94, 98, 242, 265
Petitjean, Armand, 101
petit objet a, 217, 259
Pfister, Oskar, 3
Phanes, 175–176
philosopher's stone, 119, 155, 160, 165–66, 168, 183, 198–202, 205
Picasso, Pablo, 12, 50, 76, 85–89, 127, 265
Bull's Horn, see Bull's Horn
Pierre, José, 14, 63, 65, 69, 92–93, 159
Platonic love, 249
Pleasure Principle, 215
poetic forms, 165, 167, 172, 202
poetry, 7–8, 10, 15, 19, 43, 45, 54, 58, 61, 126, 166–72, 202, 233–34, 253–56, 269–70
point sublime, see sublime point
Pollock, Jackson, 54
Pop Art, 22
pornography, 15, 255–56
porosity, 33
Postmodernism, 20, 35, 46, 259, 263–64, 267–68
Pour un art révolutionnaire indépendant, 28–29, 119–20, 123–24, 126
praying mantis, 148
prejudices, 92–93, 97
prima materia (primal matter), 14, 160, 165, 168, 186
primordial androgyne, 194, 211, 218
Prometheus, 52, 159–61, 169, 176
psyche, human, 7, 14, 129, 136, 153, 187
psychism, 14, 22
psychoanalysis, 2, 4, 12, 22, 41, 52, 98, 106, 108–9, 111, 121, 148, 164–65, 215–16, 218, 269–70
pudeur, 27, 243–45

putrefaction, 173

rebirth, 158, 175
Recherches sur la sexualité (*Investigating Sex*), 71, 92–93, 123, 199, 219, 228–29, 235–36, 239, 242–43, 245–46, 248
reconciliation of antinomies, 35–36, 44, 165, 263
refusal, 30, 122, 138, 237, 260, 270
  absolute, 155
  total, 268
regression, 11, 22, 68, 91, 114–15, 117, 258
religion, 39, 63–66, 90–91, 161, 164, 205, 207, 241, 246, 248, 250
Renaissance, 185, 226
repression, 6–7, 13, 18–19, 34–35, 41–43, 75, 104, 114, 119, 122, 130, 135, 139, 151, 153
resistance, 33, 121–22, 243, 245, 268
Rétif de la Bretonne, 74–75
retifism, 74
revolution, 16, 29–30, 39, 58–60, 74, 77, 97–98, 105, 121, 268
  interior, 165, 168, 189
  moral, 61
  political, 17
  social, 121, 151, 220, 237
Révolution Surréaliste (journal), 112
Rimbaud
  Arthur Rimbaud, 127, 166–67, 186–87, 202
  derangement of the senses, *see* derangement of the senses
Romanticism, 62–63
Rottenberg, Pierre, 31–35, 39, 155–56, 158, 211
Roudinesco, Élisabeth, 164
Rrose Sélavy, 169, 209
Sade, 58, 71–74, 89, 95–99, 101, 105, 243, 246, 252
sadism, 15, 73, 81, 83, 87, 155, 242, 265
Saint Anthony, 181–82, 184
Saint-Simon, 251
Salomé, 243
Scarpetta, Guy, 27–31
scatology, 242, 255–56
science, 23, 25, 73–74, 76, 92, 98, 116, 121–23, 128, 136, 139, 142–44, 202, 207, 257
Second Manifesto of Surrealism, 25, 27, 37, 40, 49, 54, 59, 119, 124, 132, 137, 163, 165, 167, 200–201
self-sublimation, 113
Semaine de Bonté (*Une*), *see Week of Kindness*
sexual
  behaviours, 87, 93, 105, 265
  instincts, 107, 151
  mores, 58, 236, 261
sexuality, 2, 5, 52, 87, 89–90, 94, 113–14, 133, 161, 172, 181, 185, 197, 205–7, 211
Shakti, 194–95
Shiva, 75, 194–95
signifier, 13, 24, 207, 214, 217, 222–23, 229–31, 233, 236–37
sodomy, 242
Solar Anus, 198
spirit, 32, 39, 41–42, 51, 93, 141, 147, 160, 179, 184, 192, 208, 240, 250
  absolute, 36, 39, 263
spiritualists, 23–25
subjectivity, 22, 116–17, 122, 125, 132
sublimatio, 164–65
sublimation, 2–6, 8–9, 11–13, 17–18, 20, 30–31, 34–35, 104–12, 137, 160–61, 163–65, 213–21, 237–38, 248–50, 255
  abortive, 184

aesthetic, 123, 125, 127, 132–33
alchemical, 14, 17, 19–20, 153, 159, 163
artistic, 110, 136, 269
Bretonian, 163
defining, 108, 164
Freudian, 22, 104, 131, 184, 223, 244
Lacanian, 20, 214, 217, 234, 255
of love, 27, 258
mechanisms of, 41, 112
non-repressive, 8–9, 13, 19, 76, 105–6, 111, 113, 214, 265, 270–71
process of, 109
repressive, 41, 90, 93, 106
term, 15, 165
theory of, 4, 215
sublimatory idealism, 65, 84
sublime point, the, 224–25
subliminal self, 25–26
super ego, 109, 183, 258
super-eagle, *see suraigle*
suraigle (super-eagle), 19, 51–52, 61, 267
surfascism, 63
Surrealism, 10–22, 35–38, 40–43, 45–47, 49–56, 62–66, 74–81, 83–85, 103, 123–27, 129–32, 136–40, 153–59, 161–66, 263–69
Bretonian, 9, 50, 68, 130, 163, 257, 264
critics of, 2, 266, 269
desublimatory strand of, 15–17, 58, 69, 81, 87
Surrealism and Painting, 151
Surréalisme au service de la Révolution (journal), 56, 78, 80, 248
Surrealist
art, 16–18, 42–43, 76, 79, 81, 106, 108, 118, 122, 135, 137, 139, 148, 156, 158
automatism, 140, 187
counter-consciousness, 197, 207
cult, 196, 213
eroticism, 102
imagery, 42, 70, 80, 200
movement, 20, 23, 50, 55, 79, 84, 86, 163, 168, 177
object, 16–17, 77–78, 158
philosophy, 45–46
poetry, 13, 53
practice, 3, 119
Surrealists, 2–4, 13–15, 17–21, 35–39, 64–65, 93–95, 117–18, 129–32, 138–40, 148–51, 162–64, 213–16, 260–61, 263–66, 268–71
Bretonian, 63, 68, 76, 81, 235, 246
dissident, 12, 43, 79, 197, 199

taboo, 90–91, 95, 97, 138, 219–20, 241, 245
Tabula Smaragdina, 170
Tel Quel, 2, 14, 20–24, 26–28, 30–36, 38, 41–45, 47, 155–56, 158, 200–201, 209, 263, 265
Tel Quelists, 22, 27, 31, 36, 38, 41, 43, 45, 47, 156, 158, 201, 209, 265
Baudry, Jean-Louis, *see* Baudry, Jean-Louis
Houdebine, Jean-Louis, *see* Houdebine, Jean-Louis
Rottenberg, Pierre, *see* Rottenberg, Pierre
Scarpetta, Guy, *see* Scarpetta, Guy
temptation, 52, 177, 181–84, 232–33, 238–40, 248, 266
Temptation of Saint Anthony (*La Tentation de Sainte Antoine*), 178, 181–82, 184
Thanatos, 66, 106, 125, 127, 129, 132, 137, 139–42, 151, 269
thing in itself, the (Kant), *see Ding an sich*
transcendence, 46, 64
transformation
inner, 19, 153, 158
personal, 107, 237
social, 107, 127

transgression, 15, 17, 19–20, 50, 83, 90–92, 95, 98, 104–5, 236–37, 239, 241, 253, 255, 257–58
transmutation, 148, 154, 160, 163, 167, 192
alchemical, 164, 211, 269
transposition, 3, 4, 38, 43, 58, 86, 96, 207
Trotsky
Leon Trotsky, 28–31, 119–20
Pour un art révolutionnaire indépendant, see Pour un art révolutionnaire indépendant
troubadours, 216, 218, 220
trouvailles, see objects, found

uncanny, 42, 81, 84, 130, 140, 209, 221, 227

Valdés Leal, Juan de, 195–96
Van Gogh
Nuit Étoilée, 149
Vincent Van Gogh, 149–50
Vases Communicants (*Communicating Vessels*), 38–39, 55, 107, 116–17, 232–33, 271
vieille taupe (old mole), 51–55, 57, 65, 265, 267
Vinci, Leonardo Da, 2–3, 207
Vitrac, Roger, 69
void, 13, 62, 64, 100–102, 115–16, 214, 216, 218, 221, 223–24, 226, 229, 236, 250, 266–67

Week of Kindness (*A*), (*Une Semaine de Bonté*), 189–93
Wölfflin, Heinrich, 265–66
woman, 26, 74, 135, 193, 209, 216, 229, 231, 234–35, 243–44, 250–51
woman-child, 243
woman-sorceress, 243
women, 72, 111, 218, 231, 233, 235, 243–44, 249, 254
idealisation of, *see* idealisation of the female subject

Zosimos, 165

Art and Thought: Histories of the Avant-Garde

If the past is continually retold in the present, as Walter Benjamin suggests, what can critical perspectives reveal and what do they obscure about the history of our modern time? *Art and Thought: Histories of the Avant-Garde* revisits and reconceptualises the histories of modernism, avant-gardism and postmodernism. Volumes in the series will each offer a critical perspective developed in response to specific cultural artefacts and their qualities. They will engage with literary, artistic and theoretical works, from the past as well as the present, and explore the interactions between literature, visual art, film and music, including the *livre d'artiste*. The series showcases work by new as well as established scholars, whether monographs, single- or multi-authored collections of essays, and new editions of salient or neglected primary texts in English or French, including original aesthetic works. Writing on translation as well as in translation is welcome. For further information, please contact oxford@peterlang.com.

Art et pensée : histoires des avant-gardes

Walter Benjamin nous rappelle que le passé se dit au présent. Dans quelle mesure la pensée critique permet-elle d'illuminer notre histoire ? La collection *Art et pensée : histoires des avant-gardes* se propose de penser à nouveaux frais les problématiques liant les esthétiques de la modernité, de l'avant-garde et du postmoderne. Chaque volume répondra aux qualités ponctuelles d'objets esthétiques et culturels considérés par une perspective critique propre. Des œuvres de littérature, d'art et de réflexion y seront abordées, qui souligneront les rapports intimes de l'écriture, du visuel, de la musique, du cinéma. Les livres d'artistes ne seront pas oubliés. La collection présentera, en langue française ou anglaise, le travail critique de chercheurs établis ou en début de carrière. Elle offrira à ses lecteurs des monographies, des collections d'essais, des volumes collectifs, et des éditions nouvelles d'œuvres marquantes ou jusqu'à présent négligées, y compris les œuvres littéraires et esthétiques. Les œuvres en traduction nouvelle tout comme les travaux sur la traduction même seront vivement accueillis. Pour tout renseignement supplémentaire, prière de s'adresser à oxford@peterlang.com.

DAWN ADES FBA CBE is Professor Emerita at the University of Essex, Professor of the History of Art at the Royal Academy and a former trustee of Tate. She has curated or co-curated numerous exhibitions including: *Dada and Surrealism Reviewed* (London, 1978); *Art in Latin America: The Modern Era, 1820–1980* (London, Stockholm and Madrid, 1989); *Salvador Dalí: The Centenary Retrospective* (Venice and Philadelphia, 2004); *Undercover Surrealism: Georges Bataille and Documents* (London, 2006); and *Hannah Höch* (London, 2014). Recent publications include *Surrealism in Latin America: Vivísimo muerto* (co-edited with Rita Eder and Gabriela Speranza, 2012) and *Writings on Art and Anti-Art* (Ridinghouse, 2015).

TIMOTHY MATHEWS is Emeritus Professor of French and Comparative Criticism at University College London. He is author of *Reading Apollinaire: Theories of Poetic Language* (1987 & 1990), *Literature, Art and the Pursuit of Decay in Twentieth-Century France* (2000 & 2006) and *Alberto Giacometti: The Art of Relation* (2013). He has co-edited the volumes *Violence, Théorie, Surréalisme* (with Jacqueline Chénieux-Gendron, 1994), *Tradition, Translation, Trauma: The Classic and the Modern* (with Jan Parker, 2011) and *Provocation and Negotiation: Essays in Comparative Criticism* (with Gesche Ipsen and Dragana Obradović, 2012). He has co-translated Michel Houellebecq's *The Art of Struggle* with Delphine Grass (2010), Luce Irigaray's *Everyday Prayers*, with Luce Irigaray (2004) and Gérard Macé's *Wood Asleep* with David Kelley (2003). He is Officier dans L'Ordre des Palmes Académiques and a member of the Academy of Europe.

Published volumes

1 Monique Yaari (dir.), « Infra-noir », un et multiple : un groupe surréaliste entre Bucarest et Paris, 1945–1947
2014. ISBN 978-3-0343-1762-7

2 Giovanna, Poèmes et Aphorismes (1989–2015)
2017. ISBN 978-1-78707-570-2

3 Klem James, Against Repression: Surrealism, Sublimation and the Recuperation of Desire
2019. ISBN 978-1-78707-769-0